Word
Workout

Word
Workout

BUILDING A
MUSCULAR VOCABULARY
IN 10 EASY STEPS

Charles Harrington Elster

ST. MARTIN'S GRIFFIN
NEW YORK

www.stmartins.com

Library of Congress Cataloging-in-Publication Data

Elster, Charles Harrington.
   Word workout : building a muscular vocabulary in 10 easy steps / Charles Harrington Elster.
      p. cm.
   ISBN 978-0-312-61299-3 (trade paperback)
   ISBN 978-1-250-02089-5 (e-book)
   1. Vocabulary—Problems, exercises, etc.   I. Title.
   PE1449.E458 2014
   428.1—dc23

                                                    2014030941

First Edition: December 2014

10 9 8 7 6 5 4 3 2 1

CONTENTS

INTRODUCTION

IN TODAY'S FAST-PACED WORLD, a large and precise vocabulary is a tremendous asset. It is the basis of knowledge and the foundation of eloquence. If you aspire to speak and write well—and think well—you owe it to yourself to build your knowledge of words.

The notion of building your vocabulary may call to mind the dull drills of grade school. But learning new words, and learning more about words, doesn't have to be tedious. Unlike with physical exercise, you can gain without pain. Unlike with dieting, the rewards are permanent. Best of all, you can start building your vocabulary at any age and, with a minimum of effort, keep it growing for the rest of your life.

In fact, like physical exercise, which can enhance your quality of life no matter what your age, vocabulary building can help keep your brain and memory vital—even into your nineties.* "Older adults can remember bigger vocabularies than younger people," says Christie Chung, associate professor of psychology at Mills College, in Oakland, California, and director of the Mills Cognition Laboratory. "Our semantic memory increases as we grow older."

Building a versatile vocabulary is a form of exercise—one essential to your professional, social, and even mental health. If you believe in the benefits of exercise for your body, why not do the same for your mind? Like your muscles, your brain needs regular

---

* See, for example, Kathleen Phalen Tomaselli, "Steps to a Nimble Mind: Physical and Mental Exercise Help Keep the Brain Fit," amednews.com, November 17, 2008.

stretching. And a workout with words is nowhere near as taxing as twenty minutes on a StairMaster. In fact, flexing your word muscles can be downright rejuvenating. (To *rejuvenate,* from *re-,* again, and the Latin *juvĕnis,* young, means to make young again.)

Of course, words won't just come to you; you must seek them out. And that's one reason I've written *Word Workout:* to make it easier for you to find, learn, and use new words. Consider me your personal trainer in all things verbal, and consider this book your personalized course in the ways and wonders of words.

Word Workout is not a set of flashcards masquerading as a book. Nor is it a monotonous march through a swamp of words. It doesn't rely on gimmicks or warmed-over pop psychology. It doesn't make you learn by rote or by hit-and-run memorization. And it doesn't take shortcuts, meaning that there aren't any superficial lessons with only a definition and a sample sentence. *Word Workout* is the real McCoy: a comprehensive, accessible vocabulary-building program, written by a nationally recognized expert on the English language, that will teach you hundreds of relevant, vigorous words used by our most eloquent writers and speakers.

If you've already completed my first vocabulary-building program for adults, *Verbal Advantage,* you know this well. You know that research has shown that we learn words in order of their difficulty, from easier words to harder ones, and that the best way to build your word power is to study words in ascending order of difficulty. That's why *Word Workout,* like *Verbal Advantage,* is a graduated program that begins with words known by most college graduates and ends with words known by only the most educated, intelligent, and well-read adults. And, even more than *Verbal Advantage, Word Workout* is chock-full of information about synonyms, antonyms, and word origins. You'll also get plenty of good advice on usage and pronunciation, and there are review tests all along the way to help reinforce what you've learned.

If you haven't yet read *Verbal Advantage,* don't worry. *Word Workout* is modeled on *Verbal Advantage,* but it's not a sequel or a prequel. It's a companion volume that teaches an entirely new set of words. In short, you'll learn a lot if you read this book, and a whole lot more if you read both.

Words are the key to knowledge, and knowledge is the key to success. Every word you add to your vocabulary broadens your understanding of the world, improves your comprehension of what you hear and read, and sharpens your ability to express your ideas. That is the premise, and the promise, of *Word Workout*—to help you become a more knowledgeable and confident user of the English language in the most effective and entertaining way possible.

So grab your verbal gym suit and a bottle of Evian (did you know that's *naive* spelled backward?) and let me pump you up with a professional word workout!

How Best to Use This Book

Like *Verbal Advantage, Word Workout* is arranged in ten increasingly challenging levels consisting of fifty keywords each, and each level is divided into five sets of ten keyword discussions. After each of these sets there is a review test. If you get eight answers or more right on the review test you may proceed to the next set of ten keyword discussions. But if you score fewer than eight correct you should review that set of keywords, or at least the ones you got wrong, before continuing with the program.

When it comes to building your vocabulary there is no substitute for discipline. Try to read *Word Workout* for a set amount of time each day, preferably thirty minutes. You will also benefit if you go over the material a second and even a third time before taking each review quiz and before beginning each new level.

Also, don't rush. You will make better progress if you take your time than if you try to ingest everything in a few big bites. And please resist the temptation to jump ahead. It's all right to follow my cross-references, but you will gain the most from *Word Workout* if you proceed through the lessons in order without skipping around.

KEY TO PRONUNCIATION

a—at
a̱—final, woman
ah—spa
ahr—car
air—fair
ay—hay
aw—saw
ch—chip
e—let
e̱—item, novel
ee—see
eer—deer
i—sit
i̱—charity, April, nation
kh—as in German *ach*,
   Scottish *loch* (a guttural
   sound)
'l—apple, cattle
'm—spasm
'n—hidden
(n)—as in French *bon, vin,*
   blanc (a nasalized sound)
ng—sing
o̱—carrot, summon

oh—go
oo—soon
or—for
oor—poor
ow—cow
oy—toy
sh—she
th—thin
tẖ—this
u̱—focus, column
uh—up, but
ur—turn
uu—pull, took
y or eye—by, I
zh—measure
(y)—indicates that some
   speakers employ the *y* sound
   of *you* and others do not: for
   example, N(Y)OO, *new*

Syllables printed in capitals are stressed. In words with primary and secondary stress, the syllable with primary stress is printed in boldface capitals and the syllable with secondary stress is printed in roman capitals: for example, pruh-NUHN-see-**AY**-shi̱n (*pronunciation*).

LIST OF KEYWORDS

LEVEL 1

Word 1: DEPRAVITY (di-PRAV-i-tee)
Wickedness, moral perversion, corrupt or evil character or behavior.

Synonyms of *depravity* include *deviancy, degeneracy, baseness, vileness, iniquity* (word 2 of Level 4), *debauchery* (di-BAWCH-uh-ree, see *debauch,* word 30 of Level 5), and *turpitude* (word 49 of Level 6). Antonyms include *virtue, integrity, uprightness, rectitude* (word 35 of Level 1), *scrupulousness, impeccability,* and *probity.*

Depravity began as the shorter word *pravity,* which came to English in the 16th century through Middle French *pravité* from the Latin *prāvitās,* crookedness, irregularity, deformity. The prefix *de-,* which has several meanings, was added by the mid-17th century and in this instance means completely, thoroughly, to the bottom or core, as in *denude* (di-N[Y]OOD), to strip completely, make bare; *despoil* (di-SPOYL), to take all the spoils, and thus to rob, plunder, pillage; and *deliquesce* (DEL-i-**KWES**), to melt away completely, dissolve.

In modern usage *depravity* always applies to morals and, because of that intensifying prefix *de-,* suggests thorough corruption or wickedness: *the sexual predator's depravity.* The adjective is *depraved,* corrupt, wicked, perverted, as *depraved fantasies, a depraved lifestyle, a depraved appetite for drugs.*

Word 2: PRESUMPTUOUS (pri-ZUHMP-choo-us)
Overly forward, taking undue liberties, acting or speaking too boldly, venturing beyond the limits of proper behavior or good sense.

Synonyms of *presumptuous* include *arrogant, impertinent* (word 20 of Level 1), *impudent, insolent* (word 5 of Level 2), *shameless, overweening* (word 46 of Level 6), and *brazen.*

One of the meanings of the verb to *presume* is to take undue liberties, or, to take upon oneself without permission or authority. For example, you can presume to know what's good for someone else, presume you can do something better than someone else, or presume to speak when you ought to be silent.

From this sense of *presume* comes the adjective *presumptuous,* overly forward, unduly confident or bold. When you are presumptuous you go beyond what is considered appropriate or proper, or you take it upon yourself to do or say something without permission or authority. A presumptuous person takes undue liberties with others, such as bossing them around or making unwanted amorous advances. Presumptuous speech is overly bold or arrogant. Presumptuous logic is overly confident in its rightness and arrogantly ignores the flaws in its reasoning.

In its more common sense, *presume* means to suppose, believe, take for granted, infer—as when Sir Henry Morton Stanley, upon finding the explorer David Livingstone in Ujiji, Tanzania, in 1871, famously asked, "Dr. Livingstone, I presume?" In this sense it is often interchangeable with *assume.* But sometimes a fine distinction can be drawn between these two words.

When you assume, you suppose something that is realistic or probable, that is likely to happen or be true: teachers assume that their students will do their homework; employees assume they will be paid. When you presume, you suppose more boldly and confidently, believing or asserting the likelihood or truth of something that may be doubtful or wrong: optimists presume things will always work out for the better; students often presume to know the answer to a teacher's question.

The distinction between the nouns *assumption* and *presumption,* however, is slightly different. An assumption can be anything supposed or taken for granted, often without any probable evidence: "Before Copernicus and Galileo, the common assumption was that the earth was flat." A presumption is anything supposed or believed that is based on probable, though not conclusive, evidence:

"The $3.8 trillion budget released by the White House on Monday includes $150 billion in deficit reduction over 10 years on the presumption that a health care bill will be adopted" (*The New York Times*).

In law, the notion that a defendant is innocent until proved guilty is called "presumption of innocence," which *Black's Law Dictionary* defines as "the fundamental principle that a person may not be convicted of a crime unless the government proves guilt beyond a reasonable doubt, without any burden placed on the accused to prove innocence."

Word 3: GRANDIOSE (GRAN-dee-ohs, rhymes with *handy dose*)
Showy and grand in an exaggerated, artificial way; affected, inflated, pompous.

Synonyms of *grandiose* include *pretentious, highflown, ostentatious* (AH-sten-**TAY**-sh<u>u</u>s), *bombastic* (bahm-BAS-tik), *grandiloquent* (gran-DIL-uh-kw<u>i</u>nt), and *turgid* (TUR-jid).

Although *grandiose* has been used of things that are impressive without being objectionable—as when Ralph Waldo Emerson, in 1843, wrote, "This grandiose character pervades his wit and his imagination"—the word is usually used in a disparaging way of something that tries so hard to impress or appear grand that it seems showy and pompous. A person's way of dressing, behaving, or speaking can be described as grandiose if it is so affected or exaggerated as to border on the absurd.

Grandiose may also mean unnecessarily complicated or elaborate, extravagant, overblown. In this sense we often hear or read of grandiose plans, ideas, or dreams, and grandiose architecture, music, or terminology.

The noun is *grandiosity* (GRAN-dee-**AH**-s<u>i</u>-tee).

Word 4: DISSEMINATE (di-SEM-i-nayt)
To spread widely, scatter as if sowing seed.

The verb to *disseminate* comes from the Latin *dissēmināre*, to sow, spread abroad, from *dis-*, apart, away, and *sēmen, sēminis*, seed, that which is sown or planted, the direct source of the English *semen* (SEE-m<u>i</u>n), which dictionaries typically define as "a viscid, whitish fluid produced in the male reproductive organs and carrying spermatozoa." *Viscid* (VIS–id), by the way, means thick and sticky.

The Latin *sēmen, sēminis,* seed, is also the source of the words *seminary* and *seminal.* A *seminary* may be a place where something originates and is nurtured and developed (*a seminary of provocative ideas for tackling social problems*), or a school where people study theology and are trained to become ministers, priests, or rabbis. The adjective *seminal* (word 39 of Level 5) literally means like a seed, and therefore so original and important as to influence later development or future events (*a seminal scientific study that charted the course of all subsequent research*).

Synonyms of *disseminate* include *broadcast, disperse,* and *promulgate.* Of these, to *broadcast,* to spread abroad, make widely known, is closest in meaning to *disseminate.* To *disperse* may mean to move or scatter in different directions, as *the crowd dispersed;* to send or drive off in different directions, as *the police dispersed the crowd;* or, like *disseminate,* to spread abroad or about, distribute, as *to disperse heat* or *a disease dispersed throughout the city.* To *promulgate* (pr<u>o</u>-MUHL-gayt or PRAHM-<u>u</u>l-gayt) means to make known formally or officially, publish, proclaim, as *to promulgate a new policy of amnesty,* or to teach publicly, advocate openly, as *to promulgate the doctrine of nonviolence.*

Word 5: ECLECTIC (i-KLEK-tik)
Varied or diverse in an interesting way; selecting, or consisting of selections, from a variety of sources, especially the best of those sources. "Not confined to any one model or system," says *The Century Dictionary,* "but selecting and appropriating whatever is considered best in all."

Although the adjectives *eclectic* and *diverse* are close in meaning, they are not synonymous. *Diverse* means having variety, consisting of different kinds. You can have *diverse opinions, a diverse society,* or *a diverse wardrobe.* In careful usage, *eclectic* does not mean merely varied but rather selected thoughtfully, with the goal of achieving an interesting variety. Thus, although an eclectic collection of music may include many kinds of music, and in this sense be diverse, *eclectic* also implies that this variety was achieved by careful selection rather than by chance.

Unfortunately, *eclectic* is often used as a showy substitute for *diverse* by writers who are not sensitive to the subtle distinction between these words. For example, the phrase *China's eclectic cuisine* is poor usage because the Chinese invented their own diverse cuisine; they did not select it with care from other great cuisines of the world. And the phrase *an eclectic mix of people milled in front of the building* is also poor usage because the mix is random, not intentionally arranged. Only if people have been chosen to create an especially interesting mix can a group be called eclectic.

Haphazard means selected or assembled at random or by chance, without any thought for arrangement. *Diverse* and *miscellaneous* both mean of mixed character, composed of different kinds of things, and usually do not imply judgment or taste in selection. *Eclectic* should always imply judgment and taste in selection, especially choosing the best from a variety of sources. An eclectic approach to philosophy or religion selects from them those ideas that seem best, while an eclectic diner will go to various restaurants, sampling a bit here and a bit there, looking for the best fare to be had.

Word 6: SERVILE (SUR-vil, rhymes with *chervil*)
Like a slave, slavish, submissive, obedient, subservient, yielding.

Servile is the adjective. The noun is *servility* (sur-VIL-i-tee), submissive behavior, unquestioning obedience, or the condition of being a slave or servant.

Synonyms of *servile* include *groveling, fawning, truckling, toadying, sycophantic* (SIK-uh-**FAN**-tik), and *obsequious* (uhb-SEE-kwee-us). All these words suggest submissive behavior, but in slightly different ways.

To *grovel* (GRAH-vul or GRUH-vul), from Middle English and Old Norse words meaning facedown, prone, is to lie or crawl with one's face down. Because, in days of yore, this position was assumed to show humility and obedience before a noble person or one's superiors, *grovel* came to be used figuratively to mean to humble oneself out of loyalty, remorse, or fear.

To *fawn,* which dates back to 1225, originally applied to animals, especially dogs, and meant to show delight, affection, or a desire for attention in the manner of a dog—in other words, to wag the tail, whine, crouch, roll submissively, and so on. By the early 14th century *fawn* had come to be used figuratively of submissive behavior intended to gain notice or favor, and today this word applies to anyone who curries favor by apple-polishing or kissing up: *the pop star's fawning admirers; she fawned on her boss in hopes of a promotion.*

What we now call a *trundle bed,* a kind of low bed that moves on casters and can slide under a larger bed when not in use, was originally called a *truckle bed.* The verb to *truckle* at first meant to sleep in a truckle bed, but because the person who slept in the truckle bed was invariably the servant or pupil of the master, who slept in the more comfortable high bed, *truckle* soon came to mean to act like a servant or a fawning pupil, to submit or yield meekly. You can *truckle to,* as in this 1789 quotation from Samuel Parr's *Tracts Warburton:* "He was . . . too proud to truckle to a Superior." Or you can *truckle for,* as in this quotation from 1885: "Doubtful people of all sorts and conditions begging and truckling for your notice."

In his *Dictionary of Word Origins,* Joseph T. Shipley tells how "medieval traveling medicine-men" used to have an assistant who would swallow a live toad, or seem to, "so that the master could display his healing powers." The assistant came to be called a *toad-eater,* which was eventually shortened to *toady* and used of any flattering follower, a person who truckles to the rich or powerful. To *toady* is to be like a toady, to be a yes-man or apple polisher.

A *sycophant* (SIK-uh-f<u>u</u>nt, with *-phant* as in *elephant*) is an especially self-serving kind of toady. The word goes back to ancient Greek and in English originally meant an informer or malicious accuser. Today the word refers to those who attempt to gain influence or advancement through fawning flattery and slavish subservience. And while the toady is merely a faithful follower or servant, underneath his guise of servility the sycophant is usually a scheming backstabber.

The adjective *obsequious* comes from the Latin *obsĕqui,* to comply with, yield to, obey. The obsequious person follows the wishes or bows to the will of another, and is always ready and willing to serve, please, or obey. "I see you are obsequious in your love," wrote Shakespeare in *The Merry Wives of Windsor.*

Our keyword, *servile,* comes from the Latin adjective *servīlis,* slavish, of a slave, from *servire,* to be a servant or slave. Because of this derivation, *servile* has always been used of those who accept an inferior position and whatever menial duties and undignified concessions come with it. A servile person is a bootlicker, a kowtower, one who behaves in the bowing, cringing manner of a servant or slave.

Antonyms of *servile* include *unruly, defiant, intractable* (in–TRAK-tuh–bul), *refractory* (ri–FRAK–tur–ee), *recalcitrant* (ri–KAL–si–trant), and *intransigent* (in–TRAN–si–jent).

Word 7: VORACIOUS (vor–AY–shus)

Extremely hungry, having a large appetite or cravings that are difficult to satisfy.

Voracious may be used either literally, of great physical hunger, or figuratively, either of a great appetite for intellectual or emotional nourishment or of an excessive eagerness or greed for something. A voracious reader is an extremely avid reader; a voracious lover is one whose appetite for erotic pleasure cannot be satisfied; a voracious look is a hungry, desirous, and perhaps predatory look.

Synonyms of *voracious* in its literal sense include *famished* and *gluttonous.* Synonyms of *voracious* in both its literal and figurative senses include *insatiable* (in–SAY–shuh–bul or in–SAY–shee-uh–bul), *ravenous, rapacious* (word 10 of Level 2), and *edacious* (ee–DAY–shus).

Word 8: CONVOLUTED (KAHN–vuh–LOO–tid)

Intricate, complicated, very involved, hard to unravel.

Convoluted comes from the Latin *convolūtus,* the past participle of the verb *convolvĕre,* to roll together, roll round, intertwine, the source also of the unusual verb to *convolve,* to roll up, coil, twist, and the more familiar noun *convolution,* a winding, coil, twist or fold, as of something rolled upon itself: "It hath many convolutions, as worms lying together have," says the earliest citation for this word, from 1545, in the *Oxford English Dictionary* (hereafter the *OED*).

The morning glory is a common plant known for its ability to support itself by twining around anything its vigorous tendrils can grasp. Like the morning glory, which twists and coils itself around things, that which is convoluted is so intricate and complex, so folded in upon itself, that it is difficult and sometimes impossible to unravel. A long, complex argument—or even a complicated sentence—is often described as convoluted. Mathematical equations and philosophical reasoning can be convoluted, and the regulations of the federal tax code are notoriously convoluted. The human body also has its well-known convolutions: the brain is a convoluted mass of gray and white matter, and if you were to unravel the convolutions of the small intestine it would stretch to more than twenty feet.

Word 9: RANT (rhymes with *slant* and *can't*)
To speak in an excited, vehement, or violent manner; speak fervently or furiously.

Synonyms of the verb to *rant* include to *storm, rage, rail, denounce, fulminate* (FUHL- or FUUL-mi-nayt), and *inveigh* (in-VAY).

To *rant* comes from an obsolete Dutch word meaning to talk foolishly, rave. In the early 1600s Shakespeare and Ben Jonson used *rant* to mean to speak or declaim in an extravagant or melodramatic manner, and the word has since often been applied to actors or orators who delivered grandiose speeches. Though this sense is still in good standing, by the mid-1600s the now-familiar expression *to rant and rave* had appeared in print, and *rant* by itself was more often used to mean to talk in a wild, furious, or delirious manner. By the early 20th century *rant* had also come to be used to mean to engage in a long, vehement, and often furious speech. The noun *rant* is a lengthy and intemperate expression of outrage, dissatisfaction, or disgust. (*Intemperate* is word 22 of Level 3.)

Word 10: STRATAGEM (STRAT-uh-jem)

A trick, deception, ruse, artifice; specifically, a clever scheme or artful maneuver used to deceive, outwit, or gain an advantage over an enemy, adversary, or rival.

Stratagem comes from the Greek *stratēgein,* to be in command, from *stratēgos,* a military commander, general, and is related to the more common word *strategy.* A *stratagem,* a deceptive and sometimes underhanded maneuver, is one element of a *strategy,* which is a more far-reaching plan to achieve a goal or attain victory. For example, the D-day invasion of Europe at Normandy was the stratagem the Allies employed in their final push to defeat Hitler. And a ruthless business strategy to outstrip the competition might involve various ethically questionable stratagems.

Although *stratagem* comes ultimately from ancient Greek, English acquired the word in the 15th century from the Old French *stratageme,* which is why we spell it with an *a* in the second syllable and not with an *e,* as in *strategy.* Take care to spell it *stratagem,* not *strategem.*

Review Quiz for Keywords 1–10

Let's review the ten keywords you've just learned. Consider the following questions and decide whether the correct answer is yes or no. **Answers appear on page 46.**

1. Would stealing a loaf of bread to feed your starving family be a sign of depravity?
2. Is it presumptuous to ask for directions when you're lost?
3. Can someone's speech be grandiose?
4. Does the sanitation department disseminate garbage?
5. Can a person's library be eclectic?
6. Is a disobedient child being servile?
7. If you can't get enough of something, are you voracious?

8. Can writing be convoluted?

9. Do radio talk show hosts sometimes rant about politics?

10. Would an unsuccessful stratagem help you gain an advantage?

Now let's turn to the first of the features that will appear throughout *Word Workout* after each set of ten keyword discussions.

Difficult Distinctions: May and Might

Some people think the words *may* and *might* are interchangeable, but they are not. There is a subtle difference in the degree of probability they express.

"*May* poses a possibility; *might* adds a greater degree of uncertainty to the possibility," writes Theodore M. Bernstein in *The Careful Writer*. "This shade of difference appears in the following sentence: 'Any broadcasting station that airs more commercials than the code allows may be fined, and in extreme cases its license might be taken away.'"

To put that another way, *may* indicates greater possibility than *might*. If a weather report says it *may* rain, you should take an umbrella. If it says it *might* rain, you can take the umbrella or take your chances.

Difficult Distinctions: A or An?

"In elementary school, I was taught to use *an* before vowels and *a* before consonants," writes a faithful reader named James. "But recently I've heard more and more people say *an* before words beginning with *h*, in phrases such as *an historic event*. Is this correct?"

Your teachers taught you right. If a word begins with a vowel or vowel sound, use *an* (*an idea*, *an egg*). If it begins with a consonant, use *a* (*a friend*, *a story*). The general rule, say nearly all the usage guides published since the 19th century, is that if the *h* is sounded, use *a*. If it is silent, use *an*. Thus, *a history, a happening, a humble man*, but *an hour, an honor, an herb*.

The problem with certain words beginning with *h*, such as

historic, is that the first syllable is not stressed and the *h* may seem to be suppressed, so the speaker is tempted to use *an.* The Brits, who have a history of dropping their *h*'s, tend to use *an*—except with *herb,* because they pronounce the *h.* But in American English the *h* is sounded in *historic, historical, hysterical, hypnosis, humble,* and *heroic,* and, as Mark Twain noted back in 1882, "Correct writers of the American language do not put *an* before those words."

Now let's move on to the next ten keywords in Level 1:

Word 11: EMACIATED (i-MAY-shee-ay-tid)

Of a person or animal, abnormally thin, wasted away from disease or starvation. The verb is to *emaciate* (i-MAY-shee-ayt), to waste away, become abnormally lean or thin.

Emaciated applies only to people and animals; it is not used of plants or inanimate objects. Thus, you could use *emaciated* of a starving person or an abnormally thin model, but you would say a *withered* or *shriveled* flower and a *deteriorated* or *dilapidated* house.

Synonyms of *emaciated* include *scrawny, gaunt, shrunken, skeletal, haggard, malnourished, rawboned,* and *wizened* (WIZ-und). Antonyms include *obese, portly, rotund, corpulent* (word 39 of Level 4), and *pursy* (PUR-see), which means short-winded from being overweight; hence, fat.

Word 12: MISGIVING (mis-GIV-ing)

A feeling of doubt, hesitation, uneasiness, suspicion, or dread.

The prefix *mis-* begins many English words and often means bad, badly, wrong, or wrongly. For example, a *misadventure* is a bad, unfortunate adventure; *misbegotten* means badly begotten, poorly or illegally conceived; to *misrepresent* is to represent wrongly or falsely; and to *misuse* is to use in the wrong way. A *misgiving* is by derivation the giving of a bad feeling.

The noun *misgiving* was formed in the late 16th century from the now unusual and literary verb to *misgive,* to arouse suspicion, doubt, or fear in the mind or heart, as when John Milton writes in *Paradise Lost* (1667), "Yet oft his heart, divine of something ill, misgave him." *Misgiving* is probably more often used in the plural, *misgivings,* of feelings that shake one's confidence, belief, or trust: "They began to have misgivings about the project after residents expressed their strong opposition at the town meeting"; "It was an amorous adventure, yet he did not enter into it without certain misgivings, for he did not know whether she was sincere or merely playing with his feelings."

The noun *qualm,* keyword 18 of this level, is a close synonym of *misgiving.*

Word 13: ADULATION (AJ-uh-**LAY**-shin)
Excessive admiration, praise, or flattery; overzealous devotion; hero worship.

Synonyms of *adulation* include *fawning, servility, blandishment, obsequiousness* (uhb-SEE-kwee-us-nis), and *sycophancy* (SIK-uh-fun-see). All these words—especially *servility, obsequiousness,* and *sycophancy*—imply submissive, deferential, or slavish behavior that is designed to gain favorable attention.

Adulation comes from the Latin verb *adūlāri,* to fawn upon like a dog, cringe before, and since the poet Geoffrey Chaucer used it, in 1380, the word has had the pejorative connotation of doglike servility. (Can you discern—to detect with the eyes or the mind—from the context what *pejorative* means? You'll meet *pejorative* again, as word 17 of Level 6.) While *adoration* is pure, denoting reverent homage (HAHM-ij), love, or worship, *adulation* is exaggerated and sometimes hypocritical, suggesting not respect or veneration but a servile devotion or false flattery that seeks to gain favor. "*Adulation* ever follows the ambitious, for such alone receive pleasure from flattery," wrote Oliver Goldsmith in 1766.

The words *compliment, flattery,* and *adulation* all suggest admiration, but in different ways. A *compliment* is courteous praise; it may be personal and heartfelt or dignified and formal, but it is never exaggerated or insincere. *Flattery* is artful and sometimes hypocritical praise designed to appeal to someone's vanity. *Adulation* is excessive praise, flattery taken to an undignified or shamelessly servile extreme.

Adulation is the noun. To *adulate* (AJ-uh-layt), to flatter, praise, or admire excessively, is the verb. A person who adulates is an *adulator* (**AJ**-uh-**LAY**-tur), and the adjective is *adulatory* (**AJ**-uh-luh-TOR-ee), marked by servile flattery or excessive praise. James Boswell was the *adulatory* biographer of the 18th-century English essayist and lexicographer Samuel Johnson. (A lexicographer [LEKS-i-**KAHG**-ruh-fur] is a maker or editor of dictionaries.)

Word 14: DEVOTEE (dev-uh-TEE)
A person devoted to something; an enthusiastic or ardent follower, admirer, or practitioner.

Synonyms of *devotee* include *fan, buff, enthusiast* (en-THOO-zee-ast, not -ist), and *aficionado* (uh-FISH-yuh-**NAH**-doh), which comes directly from the Spanish *aficionado,* from the verb *aficionar,* to become fond of. *Aficionado,* which first appeared in English in the 1840s, originally meant a devotee of the sport of bullfighting, but by the 1880s its meaning was extended to include any ardent fan, follower, or practitioner of something, as in this sentence from John Steinbeck's *Russian Journal,* published in 1949: "A little swing band was led by Ed Gilmore, who is a swing aficionado."

Devotee, as you might imagine, is related to the verb to *devote* and the noun *devotion.* All three words come from the Latin *dēvōtus,* devoted, attached, avowed. *Devotee* combines *devote* with the suffix -*ee,* which comes from French and denotes the object, beneficiary, or performer of whatever act or action the verb it is attached to specifies. For example, an *appointee* is a person you *appoint;* an *employee* is a person you *employ;* and an *escapee* is a person who *escapes.* *Devotees,* therefore, are people who *devote* themselves passionately to something. You can be a devotee of almost anything that can be followed or practiced enthusiastically, from sports, yoga, and cooking to music, history, and religion.

Word 15: VIVACIOUS (vi-VAY-shus *or, less often,* vy-VAY-shus)
Filled with lively spirit, vigorous, high-spirited, energetic.

The noun is *vivacity* (vi-VAS-i-tee), liveliness, vigorousness, high spirits.

Synonyms of *vivacious* include *frisky, sprightly, animated, vibrant, frolicsome,* and *effervescent* (EF-ur-**VES**-int). *Effervescent* comes from the Latin *effervescĕre,* to boil or foam up, and may mean either literally bubbling or full of bubbles, like soft drinks or champagne, or figuratively bubbling with energy or delight, as effervescent conversation or effervescent music.

Antonyms of *vivacious* include *lethargic, somnolent* (SAHM-nuh-lint, word 16 of Level 2), *listless* (word 39 of Level 2), *languid, enervated, apathetic, indolent* (word 48 of Level 4), *phlegmatic* (fleg-MAT-ik), and *torpid* (word 38 of Level 5).

Vivacious comes from the Latin adjective *vīvax, vīvācis,* which meant either long-lived or brisk, lively, vigorous. This Latin adjective comes in turn from the verb *vīvĕre,* to live, the source of various English words, among them to *revive,* to bring back to life; *vivid,* full of life, hence bright or intense; and *vital,* necessary to or pertaining to life, or having great energy or force. Since *vivacious* entered English in the mid-17th century, writers have used it to describe a person's appearance, mood, behavior, character, or intellect, as *a vivacious countenance, a vivacious temperament, a vivacious greeting, vivacious students,* and *a vivacious mind.* They have even used it of speech and writing, as in *loud, vivacious talk* and *a book filled with vivacious nonsense.*

The words *lively* and *vivacious* both mean vigorous, full of life, but *lively* suggests brisk energy, alertness, or quickness, while *vivacious* suggests high spirits, cheerfulness, or mirth.

Word 16: ANACHRONISTIC (uh-NAK-ruh-**NIS**-tik)
Misplaced in time, not in proper chronological place or order; hence, by extension, out-of-date, outmoded, obsolete.

An *anachronism* (uh-NAK-ruh-niz'm), the noun, is a person or thing out of its proper historical place, in the wrong time, or simply out-of-date.

Anachronism and *anachronistic* both go back to the Greek *anachronismós,* a wrong time reference. They are formed from the prefix *ana-,* which means against or back, and *chron(o)-,* a combining form from the Greek *chrónos,* time, that appears in many other English words, such as *chronic,* lasting over time; *chronological,* arranged in order of time; and *chronicle,* an account of events in order of time, a history. Thus, by derivation *anachronism* and *anachronistic* pertain to things that go *against* time, do not belong in their time, or that go *back* in time, that seem to belong to a previous time.

Something anachronistic may be out of keeping with the present time, as an anachronistic suit from the 1940s, or foreign to, not belonging to, any particular time—whether past, present, or future. In modern medicine, leeching is an anachronistic treatment, but a thousand years from now our most advanced treatments for cancer, such as radiation and chemotherapy, may be considered sadly anachronistic, belonging to a previous time, outmoded. And the author of a historical novel, set in the past, must take care to avoid words and expressions that are obviously anachronistic, out of keeping with the time period of the story because they were coined at some later date.

Word 17: GARISH (GAIR-ish)
Excessively showy or bright; harshly or crudely colorful; attracting attention in a loud and tasteless way.

Synonyms of *garish* include *flashy, gaudy, tawdry,* and *meretricious* (MER-uh-**TRISH**-u̲s). All these words are used of that which is showy and vulgar.

Flashy suggests sparkling or brilliant showiness that is momentary or superficial: *flashy piano playing; flashy travel destinations like Las Vegas.*

Gaudy suggests showiness that is especially tasteless: *gaudy costume jewelry; the bowlers' gaudy shirts.*

Tawdry means showy and cheap, of inferior quality, and may be used literally or figuratively: *the knockoff store's tawdry clothing; a tawdry reputation.*

Meretricious comes from a Latin word meaning pertaining to prostitutes, and is used of someone or something superficially or deceptively attractive: *meretricious eyes; meretricious decorations; a meretricious argument.*

Garish suggests excessive showiness or unpleasant brightness, and is used of that which tries to attract attention in a loud and tasteless way: *garish neon lights; New York City's garish Times Square; garish modern architecture that confuses ornamentation with style.*

Word 18: QUALM (KWAHM, rhymes with *bomb;* the *l* is silent)
A sudden uneasy, disturbing, or sickening feeling, especially when accompanied by a twinge of conscience or a pang of guilt.

Since the mid-1500s *qualm* has been applied either to a sudden, sickening emotional feeling or to a sudden, sickening physical feeling, and both these senses are standard today. You may have a qualm—a sudden uneasy or fearful feeling—about any important event or decision in life, such as having surgery, getting married, or changing careers. Or you may have a qualm—a sudden feeling of faintness or nausea—if you experience motion sickness or eat food that disagrees with you.

Since the early 17th century *qualm* has also been used specifically of a sudden, disturbing feeling of guilt or doubt concerning the rightness of one's behavior. To have a qualm about something is to feel a twinge of conscience or a pang of guilt about it. In this sense the word is now usually used in the plural, *to have qualms,* and often in negative constructions, as *to have no qualms about spending more money* or *she had no qualms about what she had said.*

The words *misgiving* (word 12 of this level), *compunction, scruple,* and *qualm* are closely related. All pertain to uneasy, disturbing, or doubtful feelings.

Misgiving refers to feelings that shake one's confidence, belief, or trust: *we had misgivings about hiring the new employee.*

A *compunction,* from the Latin verb *compungĕre,* to prick severely, is a pricking or stinging of conscience, either from anxiousness about the possibility of doing wrong or causing harm, or from remorse for having done wrong or caused harm: "In therapy she was finally able to admit her compunction about the mistakes she had made in her marriage. Her husband, on the other hand, felt no compunction for his offenses."

A *scruple* may be a moral or ethical principle that motivates one to do the right thing: "My scruples prevent me from supporting that ignoble cause." Or a *scruple* may be something that causes doubt or hesitation about the proper course of action, often something overrefined that others would disregard: *a vain scruple that springs from a flight of the imagination rather than from sound reason.*

A *qualm* is a sudden misgiving that often involves compunction, a disturbing or sickening feeling often accompanied by a pang of guilt or remorse: "The school board members expressed qualms about slashing the budget for the performing arts."

Word 19: CONSUMMATE (kun-SUHM-it or KAHN-suh-mit)
Of the highest or greatest degree, complete, utmost, utter.

Both the adjective *consummate* and the verb to *consummate* (KAHN-suh-mayt), to complete, fulfill, come from the Latin *consummāre,* to complete, form a whole, bring to perfection. You can consummate a business deal, complete it, or consummate a vision or goal, fulfill it. You can also consummate a marriage by having sexual intercourse, which symbolically completes or fulfills the union.

The adjective *consummate* is neutral and may imply perfect completion, as *consummate happiness,* or utter completion, to the utmost degree, as *consummate wisdom* or *consummate stupidity. Consummate* may be applied to those who are accomplished or skilled to the highest degree, as *a consummate actor* or *a consummate politician.* Or *consummate* may apply to those who possess a quality or characteristic in the greatest degree, as *a consummate fool* or *a consummate bore.* In like manner we can speak of *consummate virtue* or *consummate evil, consummate honesty* or *consummate hypocrisy.*

Word 20: IMPERTINENT (im-PUR-ti-nent)
Overly forward or bold; rude, meddlesome, or inappropriate in speech or behavior.

The noun is *impertinence* (im-PUR-ti-nints), unmannerly speech or behavior, rudeness, arrogance, incivility: *a teacher who would not tolerate impertinence.*

Synonyms of the adjective *impertinent* include *disrespectful, presumptuous* (word 2 of this level), *arrogant, uncivil, saucy, impudent, insolent* (word 5 of Level 2), *brazen, officious,* and *malapert* (MAL-uh-purt). Antonyms of *impertinent* include *respectful, courteous, civil, mannerly, gracious,* and *deferential.*

Impertinent combines the prefix *im-,* which here means not, and *pertinent,* relating directly, relevant. When *impertinent* entered English in the 14th century it meant not to the point, not pertinent, irrelevant, a meaning that survives today, but chiefly in legal usage. By the early 17th century *impertinent* had come to be applied to speech or behavior that was not pertinent or proper to the occasion, specifically "rude, unbecoming, or uncivil words or actions" (*Webster's New International Dictionary,* second edition, hereafter *Webster 2*). An impertinent remark is overly bold, rude, or intrusive. An impertinent person goes beyond what is considered proper or polite by being presumptuous, disrespectful, or meddlesome.

Review Quiz for Keywords 11–20

Let's review the ten keywords you've just learned. Consider the following statements and decide whether each one is true or false. **Answers appear on page 47.**

1. Some sumo wrestlers are emaciated.
2. "Buyer's remorse," regret for having bought something, is a misgiving.
3. Adulation can be subtle.
4. You can be a devotee of country music.
5. You can be vivacious when you're exhausted.

6. A manual typewriter is anachronistic today.
7. Something dull and ordinary is garish.
8. You are uncomfortable if you have qualms.
9. A consummate liar is a lousy liar.
10. A servile person is impertinent.

Synonym Discriminations: *Amiable, Affable; Blatant, Flagrant; Catastrophe, Calamity*

The adjectives *amiable* and *affable* both mean friendly and likable. *Amiable* suggests someone with a pleasant personality: "Everyone wanted to hang out with Ashanti because she was so amiable." *Affable* suggests someone who is easy to approach and talk to: "Carmen was relieved to find that her professors weren't high and mighty, but quite affable."

The adjectives *blatant* and *flagrant* both refer to what is extremely obvious, especially when it's offensive. With *blatant* there is no attempt to disguise or conceal the obvious; something blatant stands out in a glaring or repugnant (word 4 of Level 2) way: *blatant lies. Flagrant* implies serious wrongdoing. Something flagrant stands out in a shocking way; it is deplorable (di-PLOR-uh-bul), worthy of outrage: *a flagrant breach of trust.* Avoid the phrase *blatantly obvious,* which is redundant.

Finally, a *catastrophe* and a *calamity* are both disasters. *Catastrophe* puts the emphasis on the tragedy of the event: *the catastrophe of 9/11. Calamity* puts the emphasis on the toll of the event, on the grief, suffering, and misery it causes: "The calamity of Hurricane Sandy may linger for years."

Word 21: RAMIFICATION (RAM-i-fi-KAY-shin)

A far-reaching effect, related development, or consequence of something.

Implication, extension, outgrowth, and *offshoot* are synonyms of *ramification.*

The Latin *rāmus* means a branch, and the verb *rāmificāre* means to branch out. The unusual English word *ramiform* (RAM-i-form) means shaped like a branch, branchlike, and the verb to *ramify* (RAM-i-fy) means to spread out or extend like branches, divide into branchlike parts. *Ramify* may be used literally, as in "The railroad tracks ramify in all directions from the hub." Or it may be used figuratively, as in this 1861 quotation from Thomas Erskine May's *Constitutional History of England:* "Dissent had grown and spread and ramified throughout the land."

Ramification, from the same Latin *rāmus,* a branch, may also be used literally or figuratively. Literally, *ramification* means a branch or offshoot, or a branching out. For example, blood vessels and nerves have ramifications; they branch out in various directions. And scholars often try to master all the ramifications of their subject. Figuratively, *ramification,* as *Webster 2* puts it, is "that which springs from another in the manner of a branch or offshoot." It is an outgrowth, consequence, or far-reaching effect, often an unforseen or unwelcome one. An earthquake may have environmental ramifications; a decision by the Supreme Court can have long-lasting social ramifications; and seemingly every word that comes out of the mouth of the chair of the Federal Reserve has ramifications for the economy.

Word 22: ELUCIDATE (i-LOO-si-dayt)
To make clear, explain, cast light upon.

Synonyms of *elucidate* include *clarify, illuminate, interpret,* and *expound.* Antonyms of *elucidate* include *confuse, obscure, confound* (word 34 of Level 2), *muddle, mystify,* and *bewilder.*

The adjective *lucid* comes from the Latin *lūcidus,* clear, full of light. Something lucid is clear to the mind, easily understood, comprehensible, as *a lucid explanation* or *lucid conversation.* The verb to *elucidate* comes from the same Latin *lūcidus,* clear, and begins with the prefix *e-,* short for *ex-,* which in this instance means thoroughly, completely. Thus by derivation *elucidate* means to make completely clear.

The verbs to *explain,* to *expound,* and to *elucidate* all mean to make clear, but in different ways. *Explain* is the general word for making something clear that is not known or understood. To *expound* is to make something clear by giving a learned, detailed, and often elaborate explanation. To *elucidate* is to cast light upon something obscure or hard to understand by means of vivid explanation and illustration.

If you explain something you make it easier to understand. If you expound something, or expound *on* it, you explain it in great detail. And if you elucidate something, you shine a bright light on it so that its meaning is plain to all.

Word 23: ADAGE (AD-ij)
An expression of popular wisdom, an old saying, proverb.

English has many words for traditional, popular, and clever sayings.

A *saw*—often redundantly called an *old saw*—is a saying so old and shopworn that it has become tiresome and hackneyed (word 1 of Level 4).

An *axiom* (AKS-ee-um) is a generally accepted truth or principle, especially one that is self-evident and requires no proof, as the axioms of geometry. The fundamental axiom of democracy, enshrined in the Declaration of Independence, is "All men are created equal."

A *maxim* (MAKS-im) is a guiding principle or rule of conduct that expresses a general truth drawn from experience. The golden rule—"Do unto others as you would have them do unto you"—is a maxim. And Polonius's advice to his son Laertes (lay-UR-teez or lay-AIR-teez) in Shakespeare's *Hamlet* (Act I, scene iii) is full of maxims such as "Neither a borrower nor a lender be" and "Give every man thine ear, but few thy voice."

An *aphorism* (AF-ur-iz'm) is a general truth or shrewd observation expressed in a forceful, thought-provoking way. Aphorisms are terse—brief and to the point—and their tone is usually philosophical. A famous example comes from the 19th-century English historian Lord Acton: "Power tends to corrupt, and absolute power corrupts absolutely."

An *epigram* (EP-i-gram) is a brief and pointed saying that is notable for its wit or ingenuity. For example, in his play *Lady Windermere's Fan* (1892), the Irish poet and playwright Oscar Wilde wrote, "I can resist everything except temptation." (By the way, take care not to confuse *epigram* with *epigraph* [EP-i-graf], which means a quotation at the beginning of a literary work or an engraved inscription.)

Finally, we have the *proverb* and the *adage* (AD-ij), which are close in meaning. Both are well-known, oft-repeated sayings that express something universally accepted as wise or true. A proverb is a short, popular saying couched in simple, vivid, and often metaphorical language, as "A bird in the hand is worth two in the bush," "Good things come in small packages," and "You can lead a horse to water but you cannot make him drink." An *adage* is an expression of popular wisdom that has been passed down through the generations; it is usually so old that its origin has been forgotten. "Time waits for no man," "Where there's a will, there's a way," and "Nothing ventured, nothing gained" are adages.

Word 24: BESOTTED (bi-SAHT-id)
Very drunk, extremely intoxicated; also, infatuated, obsessed.

The prefix *be-* has several meanings. It may mean to deprive of, as in *behead*. It may mean all around, on all sides, as in *beset* and *besiege*. It may mean all over, as in *besmear, besprinkle,* and *beslobber*. And it may mean completely, thoroughly, as in *besotted,* completely drunk. Other words in which the prefix *be-* means completely, thoroughly, include *becalm,* to calm completely, and *benumb,* to numb thoroughly.

The noun *sot* was first used, more than a thousand years ago, to mean a stupid person, a fool. Later *sot* came to mean a person who habitually drinks to excess, a drunkard, which is how the word is used today. The adjective *besotted,* which entered English in the 16th century, means rendered stupid or foolish either from drinking or by infatuation. Drunken sailors are besotted sailors, and in Shakespeare's *Antony and Cleopatra,* Marc Antony becomes besotted with the exotic Egyptian queen.

Synonyms of *besotted* in the sense of very drunk include *befud-*

dled, groggy, addled (AD'ld), *inebriated,* and *stupefied.* (The verb to *stupefy* is word 30 of Level 3.) Antonyms of *besotted* in the sense of very drunk include *sober, temperate,* and *abstemious* (ab-STEE-mee-u̲s). Synonyms of *besotted* in the sense of infatuated, obsessed include *captivated, smitten, enamored, enraptured, enthralled,* and *beguiled.* Antonyms of *besotted* in the sense of infatuated, obsessed include *dispassionate* (word 20 of Level 2), *unruffled,* and *imperturbable* (IM-pur-**TUR**-buh-bu̲l).

Word 25: RUEFUL (ROO-fu̲l)
Sorrowful, mournful; showing or feeling sorrow, pity, or regret.

Synonyms of *rueful* include *melancholy, woeful, doleful, pitiable, lamentable* (traditionally LAM-i̲n-tuh-buul, but now usually luh-MEN-tuh-buul), and *lugubrious* (luu-GOO-bree-u̲s). Antonyms of *rueful*—and let's be glad that there are many—include *merry, cheerful, joyful, gleeful, blithe* (BLY**TH**, rhymes with *writhe*), *buoyant* (BOY-i̲nt), *mirthful, jovial, jubilant,* and *sanguine* (SANG-gwin).

The verb to *rue* is one of the oldest words in the English language, dating back to the 9th century. In its most common and enduring sense, to *rue* means to look upon with sorrow or regret, to wish that something had never been done or had never happened. You can *rue the day* you first laid eyes on someone, *rue the day* you were born, or *rue the time* that something terrible happened, as when Shakespeare writes in his play *King John,* "France, thou shalt rue this hour within this hour."

The noun *rue* is as old as the verb and means sorrow, regret, or deep distress, as in the famous 1896 poem by A. E. Housman: "With rue my heart is laden / For golden friends I had, / For many a rose-lipt maiden / And many a lightfoot lad. / By brooks too broad for leaping / The lightfoot boys are laid; / The rose-lipt girls are sleeping / In fields where roses fade."

Tack the suffix *-ful* onto the noun *rue* and you have the adjective *rueful,* filled with or expressive of sorrow, pity, or regret. A person can be rueful, and a person's eyes, face, heart, manner, or appearance can also be rueful. One's plight can be rueful, a cry can be rueful, and words are often rueful. The noun is *ruefulness.*

Word 26: SPASMODIC (spaz-MAH-dik)
Like a spasm: sudden, violent, and brief; also, happening in fits and starts, not regular or sustained, fitful, intermittent.

In *pathology* (puh-THAHL-uh-jee), which is the medical term for the study of diseases and abnormal conditions, a *spasm* (SPAZ'm) is a sudden, involuntary muscular contraction. *Spasm* is also used figuratively of anything that is like a spasm in its suddenness and violence. There are emotional spasms, as of anxiety, grief, or joy. There are political spasms, as of rebellion or war. And there are spasms of nature, such as hurricanes, earthquakes, and volcanoes.

The adjective *spasmodic* may mean sudden, violent, and brief like a spasm, and in this sense it is close in meaning to the adjective *convulsive*. Or *spasmodic* may mean occurring like a spasm, at irregular and unpredictable intervals, and in this sense it is close both in meaning and in sound to the word *sporadic* (spor-AD-ik). But that which is spasmodic happens at intervals, periodically, while that which is sporadic is scattered or dispersed, occurring only in isolated instances. The opposite of *spasmodic* is *constant* or *continuous,* while the opposite of *sporadic* is *widespread* or *epidemic.*

Word 27: DETRITUS (di-TRYT-is, rhymes with *arthritis*)
Debris, disintegrated material; specifically, rock fragments that have worn away from a mass, or sand, clay, or some other material that has been washed away.

Detritus comes from the Latin *dētrītus,* a rubbing away, and at first it was used in English to mean a wearing away, disintegration. But soon it came to be used of whatever material has been worn or washed away, and then it was used of any kind of disintegrated material or debris. These are the meanings of the word that have endured.

Some well-educated people mispronounce *detritus* with the accent on the first syllable: DE-tri-tus. Properly, *detritus* rhymes with *arthritis*.

Word 28: AWRY (uh-RY, rhymes with *the pie*)
Off course, amiss, in an unintended direction, in a wrong or unfortunate way.

Awry, which goes back to Middle English, is usually used with some form of the verb to *go:* a plan that *goes* awry; a mission that *went* awry; a relationship that *has gone* awry. The word always implies literal or figurative movement in an unexpected or improper direction: "In a grooming session that went awry, *Desperate Housewives* star Teri Hatcher accidentally sliced off her eyelashes" (DNAindia.com).

Headline writers are fond of using *awry,* perhaps because it's more vivid than *amiss* and shorter than *wrong.* Here are two shocking headlines that I gleaned from Google News: "Mom paralyzed after pole dance stunt goes awry," and "Plan to burn husband's genitals went awry, court told."

Word 29: ENCUMBER (en-KUHM-bur)
To burden, weigh down, place a heavy load upon; also, to frustrate or obstruct the action or motion of.

Synonyms of the verb to *encumber* include to *impede, hinder, hamper, handicap,* and *retard.* Antonyms of *encumber* include to *ease, alleviate, facilitate,* and *expedite* (EKS-puh-dyt), which means to speed up, hasten.

The noun is *encumbrance* (en-KUHM-brints), something that frustrates or obstructs action, a burden, hindrance, impediment (word 31 of this level).

Encumber comes from an Old French word meaning to obstruct, block up, which comes in turn from the Late Latin *combrus,* an obstacle, barricade. In modern usage *encumber* always implies weighing something down or placing an obstacle in the way. You can use it literally to mean to burden with something heavy, place a heavy load upon: "They were encumbered with bulky suitcases." You can use it figuratively to mean to burden with a heavy load of obligations or responsibilities: "They were encumbered by their young dependent children and by their elderly dependent parents." You can use *encumber* to mean to burden with a heavy load of debt, as *to financially encumber future generations*. And finally, you can use it to mean to load or fill with something useless or superfluous, to complicate unnecessarily: *a mind encumbered with trivia; an amendment that encumbers the legislation*.

Word 30: **BLEMISH** (BLEM-ish)
To damage or diminish the beauty or sound condition of something.

Synonyms of the verb to *blemish* include to *injure, impair, mar, deface, tarnish, taint, sully,* and *besmirch* (word 45 of Level 3).

    The noun *blemish* is used of anything that damages or detracts from the appearance of something, or of a flaw or defect that renders something imperfect. The word may be literal or figurative. A stain on a piece of clothing or a dent in a piece of furniture is a literal blemish. A black mark on someone's reputation is a figurative blemish.

    The verb to *blemish* suggests making something imperfect or less attractive. It is also used both literally and figuratively. Pimples blemish your complexion. Errors of grammar and usage blemish your writing. Drinking coffee and red wine can blemish your teeth. And if you don't pay your bills on time, you will blemish your credit rating.

    The adjective *blemished* means having a damaged or unattractive appearance: *a blemished piece of fruit, a blemished record in office*.

Review Quiz for Keywords 21–30
Let's review the ten keywords you've just learned. Decide if the pairs of words below are synonyms or antonyms. **Answers appear on page 48**.

    1. *Implication* and *ramification* are . . . synonyms or antonyms?
    2. *Elucidate* and *muddle* are . . .
    3. *Adage* and *proverb* are . . .

4. *Besotted* and *temperate* are . . .
5. *Rueful* and *buoyant* are . . .
6. *Intermittent* and *spasmodic* are . . .
7. *Debris* and *detritus* are . . .
8. *Awry* and *amiss* are . . .
9. To *expedite* and to *encumber* are . . .
10. To *blemish* and to *sully* are . . .

The Style File: The End Result Is Your Final Destination

Find the error in this sentence: "The end result has been runaway spending, tax increases, and reductions in core services." Now find the error in this sentence: "Board member Marci Cordaro predicted the final outcome of the growing debate." If you guessed that the trouble lies with the phrases *end result* and *final outcome,* you're right.

Redundancy is the use of more words than are necessary to express an idea, and if you want to be a more sensitive and careful user of the language, you must learn to root out redundancy from your writing and speech. *End result* is redundant because a result is what happens at the end. And *final outcome* is redundant because an outcome is how things come out in the end. In these phrases, the words *end* and *final* are unnecessary because *result* and *outcome* speak for themselves. And don't think you can get away with using the common variant *final result;* that's also redundant for the same reason.

As the game show *Who Wants to Be a Millionaire?* taught the world, it's all right to give your *final answer.* That's because in that game a contestant may give several answers before settling on a final one, and *answer* by itself doesn't imply finality. But it is redundant to make a *final decision* or reach a *final conclusion* because the words *decision* (from the Latin *dēcīdere,* to cut down or cut off) and *conclusion* (from the Latin *conclūsiōnis,* a shutting or closing) mean a judgment or determination that is final.

And while we're on the subject of finality and redundancy, have you noticed how flight attendants like using the phrase *final destination*? They say, "We'll be landing in Hartford in about five minutes. If this is your final destination, thank you for flying with us and have a nice day."

Yes, I know that flight attendants use this redundant phrase because an airplane often makes several stops before reaching that day's final stop. But a destination is not a stop along the way or a layover; it's where you wind up, where the traveling ends, the location at the end of the journey. So let's jettison *final destination* and proceed to the next stop on the way to the end of *Word Workout,* which is your proper destination.

Here are the next ten keywords in Level 1:

Word 31: IMPEDIMENT (im-PED-i-mint)
An obstacle, hindrance, something that slows down movement or stands in the way of progress.

An *impediment* may also be a speech disorder, or what the dictionaries call "an organic obstruction to distinct speech," such as a lisp or a stutter.

The verb to *impede* comes from the Latin *impedire,* which meant literally to snare or shackle the feet, and so to entangle. When you *impede* something, you slow down its movement or progress, stand in its way. Synonyms of *impede* include *hinder, retard, thwart,* and *encumber* (word 29 of this level).

The noun *impediment* comes from the Latin noun *impedimentum,* a hindrance; the plural is *impedimenta,* baggage, traveling equipment, especially the supplies carried by an army. For more than four hundred years this plural *impedimenta* has been used in English in precisely this way, of baggage, supplies, or equipment that encumber a traveling group, such as an army or caravan.

The more usual English plural, *impediments,* applies to things of any kind that get in the way or slow you down. A strained muscle is an impediment to an athlete. A thunderstorm is an impediment to a picnic. And to an architect, the red tape of the building department can be an annoying impediment.

Word 32: MODICUM (MAH-di-kum)
A small amount, modest portion, little bit.

Modicum comes directly from the Latin noun *modicum,* a small or modest amount, especially of money. This Latin *modicum* comes from the adjective *modicus,* moderate, limited, within bounds, which in turn comes from the noun *modus,* a measure or a standard of measurement. Other English words that come from this Latin *modus* include *modest, moderate,* and *modulate.*

The words *modicum, iota, minim, soupçon, smidgen,* and *skosh* all refer to small amounts.

Iota (eye-OH-tuh) and *minim* (MIN-im) denote the tiniest amounts. *Iota* is the ninth and smallest letter of the Greek alphabet, a diminutive vertical squiggle [ι], hence a minute or microscopic amount. (*Diminutive,* pronounced di-MIN-yuh-tiv, means exceedingly or strikingly small.) *Minim,* from the Latin *minimus,* smallest, least, may specify the smallest liquid measure, about one drop, or it may mean the smallest or least possible amount of anything, a jot or whit, as in this 1884 quotation from *Public Opinion:* "He has not the smallest intention of . . . yielding one minim of the rights and interests of Germany."

The word *soupçon* (soop-SAW[N], with a French nasalized *n*) means either a very small portion, tiny bit, as a *soupçon of brandy,* or the merest suggestion of something, such as a flavor, smell, or feeling: *a soupçon of resentment; a soupçon of nutmeg.*

A *smidgen* (SMIJ-in, rhymes with *pigeon*), a word of uncertain origin, is also a very small portion, but perhaps a bit larger than a soupçon. And a *skosh* (pronounced with the long *o* of *kosher*) is perhaps a bit larger than a smidgen. *Skosh* entered English in the 1950s, during the Korean War. It comes through Korean pidgin from the Japanese *sukoshi* (pronounced "skoshy") and means a small amount or portion, a little bit.

Of all these words, *modicum* suggests the most generous portion or amount, small but often adequate for one's needs or purpose. A modicum of money is neither a paltry* sum nor a fortune; it is a

---

* **paltry** (PAWL-tree): of an amount: extremely small, meager, measly, scanty; of a thing: insignificant, trivial, worthless, inferior.

modest amount that is usually sufficient. If you don't have an iota, a minim, or a smidgen of common sense, you're a blundering fool. But if you have a modicum of common sense, a modest portion of it, you have just enough to get by.

Word 33: DOSSIER (DAH-see-ay)
A comprehensive file; a bundle or collection of papers or documents containing detailed information about a particular person or topic.

The Latin *dorsum* means the back. From it come the English scientific words *dorsum,* the back (as of an animal), and *dorsal,* pertaining to or situated at or on the back. From this Latin *dorsum* also comes the French word *dos,* which means back, and from *dos* comes the French word *dossier,* which meant the back of a chair and also a bundle of papers or documents. In the late 19th century, English borrowed this French *dossier* in the latter sense. Here's an 1884 citation from *The Pall Mall Gazette:* "In neatly-docketed cabinets round his office stood the dossiers [DAH-see-ayz] of all the criminals with whom he has had anything to do for the past eight years."

What does a bundle of papers have to do with the back? Most dictionaries note that in French *dossier* referred to a bundle or file of papers with a label attached to the back or spine, and the *OED* suggests it was the bulging of the bundle that resembled a back.

A *file* and a *dossier* are both collections of papers about a person or a topic, but a file may be incomplete, lacking some important information, while the information in a dossier is always detailed and comprehensive.

Word 34: ALLITERATION (uh-LIT-uh-**RAY**-shun)
The repetition of the same letter or sound at the beginning of two or more neighboring words or stressed syllables: *And still the wind wailed and the incessant snow swirled and fell.* The adjective is *alliterative* (uh-LIT-ur-uh-tiv).

Alliteration is one of the writer's most powerful tools. The careful and considered use of alliteration (*careful and considered* is alliterative) can give your writing a graceful and pleasing musicality. But you must be careful and considered about it, for alliteration can grate on the ear and annoy the reader.

Shakespeare's plays and poems are full of alliteration; for example, he alliterates with the letter *f* in Ariel's song in *The Tempest:* "Full fathom five thy father lies." And listen to the hypnotic alliteration of these lines from Edgar Allan Poe's famous poem "The Raven": "The silken sad uncertain rustling of each purple curtain / Thrilled me—filled me with fantastic terrors never felt before." In the first line, the sibilant (word 9 of Level 4) sound of *s* creates the alliteration in four successive words—*silken, sad, uncertain, rustling*—while in the second line the alliteration comes from the repeated sound of *f*—*filled, fantastic, felt*.

The opening lines of Vladimir Nabokov's 1955 novel *Lolita* provide a striking example of sustained alliteration:

LOLITA, light of my life, fire of my loins. My sin, my soul. Lo-lee-ta: the tip of the tongue taking a trip of three steps down the palate to tap, at three, on the teeth. Lo. Lee. Ta.

  She was Lo, plain Lo, in the morning, standing four feet ten in one sock. She was Lola in slacks. She was Dolly at school. She was Dolores on the dotted line. But in my arms she was always Lolita.

Alliteration can be effective in titles. Among the many alliteratively titled books in my library are *Sin and Syntax* by Constance Hale; *The Treasure of Our Tongue* by Lincoln Barnett; *Devious Derivations* by Hugh Rawson; *The Glamour of Grammar* by Roy Peter Clark, and of course my own *What in the Word?* and *The Big Book of Beastly Mispronunciations*.

Alliteration is sometimes used to achieve a humorous or sarcastic effect. But when the writer's intention is serious and the alliteration occurs repeatedly, it can be disagreeable. In his usage manual *Right, Wrong, and Risky,* another alliteratively titled book,

Mark Davidson offers this advice: "Sometimes alliteration combines memory enhancement with poetic grace, as when . . . the Rev. Martin Luther King Jr. spoke of his dream of a world in which all people would be judged not 'by the color of their skin but by the content of their character.' But beware of the temptation to overdo it."

Word 35: RECTITUDE (REK-ti-t[y]ood)
Virtue, righteousness, moral integrity; correctness in principles or behavior, or conformity to accepted standards of proper conduct or thinking.

Synonyms of *rectitude* include *uprightness,* which implies straightforwardness and sincerity; *veracity* (vuh-RAS-i-tee), which implies truthfulness and trustworthiness; and *probity* (PROH-bi-tee), which implies honesty and integrity.

Antonyms of *rectitude* include *deceitfulness,* speech or behavior intended to mislead another or conceal the truth; *duplicity,* double-dealing, giving two impressions, one or both of which is false; and *perfidy* (PUR-fi-dee), a breach of faith, disloyalty, treachery. *Depravity,* the first word of this level, is also an antonym.

Rectitude comes through French from the Latin *rectitudo,* straightness, righteousness, ultimately from the Latin *rectus,* straight, upright, proper, correct. This Latin *rectus* has influenced a number of English words, including *correct, direct, rector,* a member of the clergy who directs; *rectify,* to make or set right; and, believe it or not, the anatomical term *rectum,* which denotes the relatively straight terminal part of the colon, or large intestine, ending in the anus.

Since the 15th century *rectitude* has also been used to mean straightness, as the rectitude of the spine. Though this use is still in good standing, *rectitude* more commonly means correctness or conformity in behavior or thinking, as *the rectitude of his judgment,* or moral integrity, righteousness, virtue, as *a woman of fidelity, rectitude, and courage.*

Word 36: VEXATIOUS (vek-SAY-sh<u>u</u>s)
Troubling, disturbing, annoying, irritating.

The verb to *vex* means to irritate, annoy, provoke, or to bother deeply, trouble, torment. The adjective *vexed* means annoyed, irritated, troubled: "His road rage vexed her." The noun *vexation* may mean the state of being vexed: "She dreaded when he drove because she had to put up with his constant vexation." Or *vexation* may mean something that vexes: "His angry outbursts while driving were her greatest vexation."

All these words come from the Latin *vexāre,* to shake, disturb, agitate, or by extension, to annoy, harass, disquiet. The adjective *vexatious,* formed from the noun *vexation,* may be used of people or things, as *a vexatious toddler* or *vexatious flies.* And for more than three hundred years it has also been used in law of malicious lawsuits, ones that are instituted, as the *OED* puts it, "without sufficient grounds for the purpose of causing trouble or annoyance to the defendant."

Word 37: EPITHET (EP-<u>i</u>-thet)
A word or phrase applied to a person or thing that describes some quality or characteristic of that person or thing.

Syonyms of *epithet* include *nickname, designation, appellation* (AP-uh-**LAY**-sh<u>i</u>n), and *sobriquet* (SOH-br<u>i</u>-kay, word 5 of Level 7).

Epithet comes from an ancient Greek word that meant added, attributed, placed upon. By derivation, an epithet is an attributed quality or characteristic, an especially descriptive word or phrase applied to a person or thing. An epithet may be an adjective that characterizes a noun, such as *green-eyed* in *green-eyed jealousy,* and *the terrible* in *Ivan the Terrible.* An epithet may also be a descriptive or meaningful word or phrase closely associated with a person or thing and used as a substitute for the actual name of the person or thing, such as *man's best friend* for a dog and *The Great Emancipator* for Abraham Lincoln.

Epithet is perhaps most often used today in a third sense, where it means a term of abuse, a slur, an insulting or contemptuous word or phrase, as *a racial epithet*. The word has been used in this way since at least 1712, when the Scottish physician and satirist John Arbuthnot (ahr-BUHTH-n<u>u</u>t *or* AHR-b<u>u</u>th-naht) penned this line: "Blockhead, Dunce, Ass, Coxcomb,* were the best Epithets he gave poor John." Students at Yale have long used the epithet *weenie* for a person who studies too much and never has fun, and they nicknamed the study cubicles in Yale's Cross Campus Library *weenie bins*.

Word 38: TRAVESTY (TRAV-<u>i</u>-stee)
An absurd or ludicrous imitation; a grotesque or grossly inferior likeness or resemblance.

In its original sense, which dates back to the 17th century, the noun *travesty* referred to an absurd or ludicrous literary or artistic imitation of a serious work, as in this 1846 citation from the essays of the English historian Thomas Wright: "Those romances were but barbarous travesties of the original stories." From this definition, which is still in good standing, the word broadened to refer to any grotesque or grossly inferior imitation, and today it often appears in phrases like *a travesty of democracy* or *a travesty of justice,* where it implies that something serious and dignified has been unfairly mocked or trivialized.

The words *caricature, burlesque, parody,* and *travesty* all refer to art or literature that makes use of exaggeration, imitation, and absurdity to achieve a comic or ludicrous effect. "A *caricature* . . . absurdly exaggerates that which is characteristic . . . by picture or by language," says *The Century Dictionary*. "A *burlesque* renders its subject ludicrous by an incongruous† manner of treating it, as by treating a grave subject lightly, or a light subject gravely. . . . A *parody* intentionally burlesques a literary composition, generally a poem, by imitating its form, style, or language."

---

*   *coxcomb* (KAHKS-kohm), a conceited, pretentious fool; a man whose vanity is so exaggerated that it's laughable. The word comes from "cock's comb," the cap worn by professional jesters in the Elizabethan era. Synonyms of *coxcomb* include *dandy, fop,* and *popinjay* (word 10 of Level 10).

†   *Incongruous* (in-KAHNG-groo-w<u>u</u>s) means out of place, inappropriate, inconsistent, unsuitable.

Travesty and *parody* should be carefully distinguished, says the *Century*. In a parody "the language and style of the original are humorously imitated," while in a travesty "the characters and the subject-matter remain substantially the same, the language becoming absurd or grotesque."

Travesty is frequently misused for *tragedy*. Here's an example of the rampant misuse: "It would be a travesty if the ethics and campaign finance reforms fizzle because of partisan wrangling." Remember: a *tragedy* is a disastrous event, terrible misfortune—or, in loose usage, an unfortunate occurrence or unhappy situation. A *travesty* is an absurd or ludicrous imitation, or a grotesque or grossly inferior likeness or resemblance.

The verb to *travesty* means to imitate in an absurd, grotesque, and ludicrous way, so as to ridicule.

Word 39: WANE (rhymes with *plane*)
To decrease or diminish gradually, fade away.

Synonyms of the verb to *wane* include to *dwindle, decline, ebb, abate* (uh-BAYT), *wither, shrivel,* and *subside.*

To *wane* and its antonym to *wax* come from Old English and are among the oldest words in the language. Both are commonly applied to the phases of the moon. When the moon waxes, the visible portion of it gradually increases until the whole orb is illuminated. Then the moon begins to wane, and the illuminated portion gradually shrinks until only a sickle-shaped sliver is visible.

The unusual words *falcate* (FAL-kayt) and *gibbous* (GIB-us) apply to opposite stages in this waxing and waning of the moon. They are roughly equivalent to the words *concave,* hollowed or rounded inward, and *convex,* curved or rounded outward. *Falcate* refers to the crescent shape of the moon when it is waning. The word comes from the Latin *falx,* a sickle, and means having a slender curve like a sickle or a scythe. *Gibbous* refers to the waxing moon, when the illuminated portion is more than half but not yet a full circle. The word comes from the Latin *gibbus,* a hump, and means shaped like or having a hump.

In addition to the moon, *wane* may be used of color or light: *the flush waned from her cheek*. It may be used of qualities, conditions, or feelings: *waning youth; waning enthusiasm*. And it may be used of people or things to mean to decrease gradually in power, intensity, or importance: *the waning of the Roman Empire*. Finally, to *wane* may mean to draw to a close, approach an end, as in this sentence from Edgar Allan Poe's classic horror story "The Tell-Tale Heart": "The night waned, and I worked hastily, but in silence." The expression *on the wane* means decreasing in frequency, importance, or power, diminishing, declining, as "One day a social networking site is a rising star and the next it's on the wane."

Word 40: HUBRIS (HYOO-bris)
Excessive pride or self-confidence.

Synonyms of *hubris* include *arrogance, insolence* (IN-suh-lints), *presumption,* and *hauteur* (hoh-TUR, word 7 of Level 7). *Modesty* and *humility* are antonyms of *hubris*.

The noun *hubris* and the adjective *hubristic* (hyoo-BRIS-tik), which means insolent, arrogant, contemptuous, come from the Greek *hybris,* insolence, arrogance. *The Oxford Companion to the English Language* notes that in ancient Greek tragic drama, hubris was "the overweening [word 46 of Level 6] self-confidence and ambition that leads . . . to the ruin of its possessor." Hubris is sometimes also called the *fatal flaw,* the weakness or defect in character that brings about the downfall of a tragic figure. In this technical, theatrical sense *hubris* is opposed to the word *nemesis* (NEM-uh-sis, word 2 of Level 5), divine punishment. In Greek tragedy, a character's hubris, arrogance, was depicted as an affront to the gods or to the divine order of nature, and would inevitably lead to an appropriate nemesis, divine punishment.

Hubris is also used generally to describe a person who exhibits excessive pride, self-confidence, or ambition, as in this sentence from a *Time* magazine review of the film *The Company Men*: "[Ben] Affleck always has trouble simulating high emotion . . . but he nails Bobby's plunge from hubris to humiliation." *Hubris* may also be used of an institution or a nation: *Wall Street's unchecked greed and hubris; the hubris of American foreign policy.*

Review Quiz for Keywords 31–40

Let's review the ten keywords you've just learned.

This time we're going to play a version of the old *Sesame Street* game One of These Things Is Not Like the Others. It's called One of These Definitions Doesn't Fit the Word. In each statement below, a keyword (in *italics*) is followed by three one-word or phrasal definitions. Two of the three are correct; one is unrelated in meaning. Decide which one doesn't fit the keyword. **Answers appear on page 48.**

1. An *impediment* is an obligation, hindrance, encumbrance.
2. A *modicum* is a modest portion, little bit, more than enough.
3. A *dossier* is a bundle of papers, secret document, comprehensive file.
4. *Alliteration* is similar sounds, repeated sounds, familiar sounds.
5. *Rectitude* means openness, integrity, virtue.
6. *Vexatious* means disturbing, annoying, frivolous.
7. An *epithet* is a nickname, designation, clever remark.
8. A *travesty* is an absurd imitation, grotesque likeness, grave misfortune.
9. To *wane* is to decrease, disappear, diminish.
10. *Hubris* means excessive greed, excessive self-confidence, excessive pride.

The Style File: Some Comments on the Serial Comma

"When preparing a PowerPoint slide show, our company often shows a direct quote from a Federal Manual," writes John in Denver, Colorado, where several times a year I am a guest language maven on the *Mike Rosen Show* on KOA-AM. "Sometimes the punctuation in the manual is incorrect. For example: 'workers, bicyclists, motorists, and pedestrians.' I know the preferred form is to not use a comma after the word *motorists*. If we show this sentence on a slide, should we eliminate the comma but still use quotation marks?"

Actually, the comma after *motorists* is the traditional way of punctuating a series, and it's called the serial comma (or sometimes the Oxford comma). It is endorsed by the *Chicago Manual of Style,* favored by many other authorities, and preferred by most book publishers. The practice of omitting the comma after the penultimate (word 15 of Level 7) item in a series, before the word *and,* comes from journalism; newspaper style calls for *red, white and blue* with one comma rather than *red, white, and blue* with two.

Both styles are acceptable and you may choose which one you prefer. But if you are quoting you may not change anything; you must reproduce what you are quoting precisely as it was printed. If you believe there's an error of grammar or style in the original, you may insert *sic* in brackets—[*sic*]—to show that it's not your mistake.

Incidentally, I favor the serial comma because, to me, it gives the series proper balance and avoids any potential ambiguities, as in this hilarious dedication: "To my parents, Ayn Rand and God."

Here are the last ten keywords in Level 1:

Word 41: VICARIOUS (vy-KAIR-ee-us)
Sharing the feelings or experience of others in one's own imagination.

Vicarious comes from the Latin *vīcārius,* taking the place of a person or thing, substituted, the source also of *vicar* (VIK-ur), a word that originally meant an earthly agent or representative of God or Christ and is now applied to various members of the Episcopal and Roman Catholic clergy.

The original meaning of *vicarious* was like the Latin *vīcārius,* taking the place of another, substituted for the proper person or thing. It later came to be used in law and theology to mean performed or endured by one person in place of another, as *vicarious liability* or *vicarious punishment.* And it has been used of a person or group that acts for or represents another, as *a vicarious ruler who wields vicarious power.*

You will find all these meanings of *vicarious* listed in modern dictionaries, but since the 1920s *vicarious* has also been used to mean sharing the feelings or experience of others in one's own imagination. This is the sense in which the word is best known and most often used today. A vicarious experience is one in which you imagine yourself going through what someone else is going through. A vicarious thrill or vicarious pain comes from participating sympathetically in another person's experience. And when you live vicariously, you derive satisfaction or pleasure from someone else's experiences or accomplishments. Parents are often said to live vicariously through their children.

Word 42: STIPULATE (STIP-yuh-layt)

In making an agreement: to require as an essential condition, demand as a requirement.

The noun is *stipulation,* an essential condition or demand in an agreement.

The verb to *stipulate* comes from the Latin *stipulari,* to demand a formal agreement, bargain. In Roman law the word *stipulatio* (STIP-yuh-**LAY**-shee-oh) designated an oral contract in which one party to the contract *stipulated,* made a formal requirement or demand of the other party in the form of a question. When *stipulate* entered English in the 17th century, it did not stray far from this legal usage. Since then we have used the word chiefly to mean to specify as a requirement in an agreement, require as an essential condition.

Laws, rules, standards, and regulations all typically stipulate, meaning that they establish requirements or specify certain conditions that must be met. A treaty between nations stipulates the terms of the treaty. A parole board can stipulate a record of good behavior as a condition for an inmate's release from prison. And a person's last will and testament can stipulate how the assets of an estate will be divided among inheritors.

Word 43: DESPOTIC (di-SPAHT-ik)

Ruling with absolute power, or pertaining to someone who has unlimited authority.

Synonyms of *despotic* include *dictatorial, tyrannical* (ti-RAN-i-kul), *authoritarian* (uh-THOR-i-**TAIR**-ee-in), and *autocratic* (AW-tuh-**KRAT**-ik).

A *despot* (DES-put) is a person who has absolute or unlimited power, a tyrant or oppressor. The absolute power that the despot exercises is called *despotism* (DES-puh-tiz'm). Like the word *tyrant,* the noun *despot* can be used of anyone who wields absolute power or authority, especially in a cruel and oppressive way. A country may be ruled by a despot, a cruel monarch or dictator. But other oppressive authority figures, such as hard-nosed military officers or insensitive employers, can also be despots, leaders who oppress those beneath them.

Both *despot* and the adjective *despotic* come from the Greek *despótēs,* master, lord, a word akin to the Greek *dómos,* house, and *pósis,* husband. So it could be said that by derivation a despot is the master of the house, a cruel husband who lords it over the rest of the family.

Despotic means ruling with absolute power, or pertaining to someone who has unlimited authority. In early 2011 the world watched, holding its breath, as the citizens of Egypt and Tunisia tried to peacefully overthrow their despotic governments and establish democracy.

Word 44: UNSAVORY (uhn-SAY-vuh-ree)

Literally, disagreeable or unpleasant to taste or smell; figuratively, undesirable, offensive.

The noun *savor* (rhymes with *flavor*) means a particular taste or smell, usually a pleasant one. As a verb *savor* means to enjoy the taste or smell of something, as *to savor every drop of soup,* or to give oneself over to enjoyment, as *to savor every moment.*

Unsavory combines the prefix *un-,* not, with the adjective *savory,* agreeable in taste or smell, as *a banquet of savory dishes.* Something unsavory is not agreeable either to the physical sense of taste or smell or to the moral sense of what is proper or good. Unsavory food is unpleasant or unwholesome to eat. An unsavory person is unpleasant or unwholesome to be around.

Synonyms of *unsavory* in its literal sense of disagreeable to taste or smell include *unappetizing, unpalatable* (uhn-PAL-uh-tuh-bul), and, when extremely disagreeable, *disgusting* and *nauseating*. The closest synonym of *unsavory* in its figurative sense of undesirable is *objectionable;* stronger synonyms include *beastly, repugnant* (word 4 of Level 2), *detestable, loathsome* (LOHTH-sum), *odious* (OH-dee-us), and *abhorrent* (ab-HOR-int).

Word 45: INTIMATE (IN-ti-mayt, rhymes with *motivate*)
To imply, hint, suggest or indicate indirectly, communicate obscurely or remotely.

The noun is *intimation* (IN-ti-MAY-shin), a hint, indirect suggestion: "She gave them only intimations of her true feelings."

The verb to *intimate* and the familiar adjective *intimate* (IN-ti-mit) both come through the Late Latin *intimāre,* to announce, make known, from the Latin *intimus,* innermost, deepest, most secret. The original but now archaic* meaning of the verb to *intimate* is to announce publicly, make known formally, as in this sentence from 1759: "This resolution she intimated to the leaders of both factions." Today, however, the verb to *intimate* pertains not to that which is announced publicly but to that which is made known in a carefully indirect or private way, as in this quotation from Sir Walter Scott's novel *Waverley,* published in 1814: "the open avowal [word 15 of Level 4] of what the others only ventured to intimate."

To *insinuate* (in-SIN-yoo-ayt) and to *intimate* both mean to hint, suggest, but they connote different ways of doing so. To *insinuate* is to suggest in a sly, subtle, and often devious manner; it may also mean to bring oneself into a situation by artful or stealthy means. Radio talk show hosts routinely insinuate derogatory (duh-

---

* **Archaic** (ahr-KAY-ik) means old-fashioned, no longer in ordinary use.

RAH-guh-tor-ee, insulting, offensive) things about their ideological opponents; undercover police officers insinuate themselves into criminal organizations to gather evidence. To *intimate* is also to suggest subtly and indirectly, but it does not imply devious or stealthy motives or behavior. When you don't want to say something outright, you can intimate. Politicians who don't yet want to announce their candidacy often intimate that they may run. And a good actor knows how to intimate unspoken thoughts and emotions through facial expressions and gestures.

Take care not to write *intimated* when you mean *intimidated,* a mistake that is surprisingly common even in the edited prose of reputable publications. To *intimidate*—pronounced in four syllables—is to frighten, make fearful. To *intimate*—pronounced in three syllables—is to suggest indirectly, hint, imply.

Word 46: PREDISPOSE (pree-di-SPOHZ)
To incline or tend toward beforehand, make susceptible or subject to.

Predisposition is the corresponding noun.

To *dispose* is to give a natural tendency to, incline. It may be used either of positive or negative inclinations, as *a man disposed to spontaneous acts of charity,* or *a dog disposed to bark wildly at strangers.* To *predispose* is to dispose beforehand, usually well in advance of any opportunity for the tendency or inclination to manifest itself. Your genetic makeup may predispose you to disease or to living a long, healthy life. People who grow up in New England are predisposed to become fans of the Boston Red Sox. And sociological studies have shown that men who grow up in families plagued by domestic violence often develop a predisposition for domestic violence themselves.

Word 47: APACE (uh-PAYS, rhymes with *a face*)
Swiftly, quickly, with speed.

Apace, which dates back to the 14th century, means at a quick pace. A well-known use of the word occurs in the opening lines of Shakespeare's *Midsummer Night's Dream,* when Theseus says to his wife-to-be, "Now, fair Hippolyta, our nuptial hour / Draws on apace. Four happy days bring in / Another moon; but, O, me-thinks, how slow / This old moon wanes!" (*Wane* is word 39 of this level. The adjective *nuptial,* properly pronounced NUHP-shul—*nup-* rhyming with *cup* and *-tial* as in *partial*—means pertaining to marriage or to the marriage ceremony.)

The *New Oxford American Dictionary* labels *apace* poetic or lit-erary, which it is, but that doesn't mean *apace* would be inappro-priate in an ordinary sentence today. In fact, the verbs to *continue, proceed,* and *grow* are often paired with *apace,* as in this sentence: "Iran says its nuclear program is proceeding apace" (*The Wall Street Journal*).

Although some dictionaries recognize *abreast* as a secondary meaning of *apace,* most do not, and the two words should not be used interchangeably. *Abreast,* which is chiefly used in the phrase *to keep (or stay) abreast,* means to keep up with, maintain a partic-ular level of understanding or rate of progress, as *to keep abreast of the latest news.* You may *keep abreast of* developments in technol-ogy, or *keep pace with* those developments, but you do not *keep apace with* them. That's simply not good English. Reserve *apace* for when you mean swiftly, quickly, with all due speed: "Efforts to rebuild the community after the earthquake continue apace."

Word 48: VERDANT (VUR-dint)
Green in color, or green with vegetation: *verdant hillsides.*

The adjective *verdant,* which entered English in the 16th century, comes from the Latin *viridis,* green. It has two older English cous-ins that hail from the same Latin source: the nouns *verdure* (VUR-jur) and *vert* (VURT). *Verdure,* which dates back to the 13th century, denotes the greenness of flourishing vegetation, or the vegetation itself. *Vert,* which dates from the 15th century, was used in English forest law to mean anything in a forest that bears a green leaf, especially vegetation that provides cover or food for deer.

A verdant lawn is green and fresh, and verdant fields are covered with growing plants or grass.

Word 49: CAJOLE (kuh-JOHL)
To persuade with repeated urging, flattery, or false promises.

The noun is *cajolery* (kuh-JOH-luh-ree), the act or an instance of cajoling.

Cajole, which entered English in the mid-17th century, comes from the French word *cajoler,* to chatter or sing like a jay or a magpie in a birdcage. Jays and magpies are notoriously noisy and garrulous★ birds, so it's easy to see the connection between the French verb and the English one. When you cajole, you figuratively chirp and chatter and sing insistently in an effort to persuade a reluctant or unresponsive person to do or give you what you want. In short, cajolery is a kind of artful nagging. Its object is usually human, as in this quotation from the English poet John Milton in 1649: "That the people might no longer be abused and cajoled . . . by falsities." But sometimes the object of cajolery is an entity: *a president who cajoled the nation into war.*

Synonyms of the verb to *cajole* include to *coax, wheedle, blandish, beguile,* and *inveigle* (in-VAY-gul). All these words mean to persuade, win over, or lure, but they imply the use of more flattery and enticement than *cajole,* which implies repeated urging.

Word 50: BANE (BAYN, rhymes with *sane* and *main*)
A cause or source of ruin, harm, or misery; a curse.

The noun *bane* is one of the oldest words in the language, dating back to the 9th century. It first meant a murderer or slayer of another, then that which causes death, then murder or destruction, and then poison—which is why a number of poisonous plants incorporate *bane* in their names: for example, dog's-bane, wolfsbane, ratsbane, and henbane.

★ *garrulous* (GAR-uh-lus), talkative, especially in a rambling, annoying, pointless, or long-winded way.

By the 16th century *bane* had come to be used figuratively of something that causes ruin, harm, or misery, or that is like a curse, and this is the word's ordinary sense today. *Bane* is often paired with *existence,* as in "He was the bane of her existence." This well-worn construction is best avoided. But *bane* can be artfully paired with many other words, as in "Corruption is not the bane of Nigeria's development" and "Snowed-in hydrants are the bane of firefighters." And *bane* is often juxtaposed (placed side by side) with the antonyms *blessing* and *boon,* as in "Time will tell if it's a bane or a boon for the economy." The adjective is *baneful,* ruinous, destructive, pernicious, malign (word 41 of Level 3).

The words *baneful* and *baleful* are close in spelling, and they share the notion of evil, but their connotations should be distinguished. *Baleful* means menacing, ominous, threatening evil: *a baleful stare; baleful clouds. Baneful* means causing harm or evil, ruinous: *a baneful influence; baneful consequences.*

Review Quiz for Keywords 41–50

Let's review the ten keywords you've just learned. This time the review word will be followed by three words or phrases, and you must decide which comes nearest the meaning of the review word. **Answers appear on page 49**.

1. Does *vicarious* mean silently understood, experienced sympathetically, or undertaken in secret?

2. When you *stipulate,* do you demand as a requirement, agree on specific terms, or refuse to negotiate?

3. Does a *despotic* person make unreasonable requests, act foolishly, or rule with absolute power?

4. Is something *unsavory* unpleasant, flavorless, or beyond redemption?

5. When you *intimate,* do you speak honestly, speak indirectly, or speak privately?

6. If something is *predisposed,* is it discarded first, inclined beforehand, or already committed?

7. If something happens *apace,* does it happen first, unexpectedly, or swiftly?

8. Is something *verdant* green, gold, or gleaming?

9. Does *cajole* mean to ridicule, to comfort, or to persuade?

10. Is a *bane* a curse, an herbal remedy, or an order to stop?

The Style File: *Theater* vs. *Theatre*

No doubt you have many times seen *theater* spelled *theatre,* with the final *-er* flipped around to *-re.* Many reputable theaters, in fact, use the variant spelling with *-re,* and, as Mark Davidson observes in his style guide *Right, Wrong, and Risky,* even the storied *New Yorker* magazine has always spelled it *theatre.*

So which is correct: *-er* or *-re*? Usage experts unanimously agree that *theater* is the preferred American spelling, while *theatre* is British. (The same distinction between American and British usage applies with *center/centre, caliber/calibre,* and *meter/metre.*) So why is American usage so divided? Davidson offers this explanation: "America's theatrical world was under considerable British influence when the Broadway stage was founded, and American theater owners today seem to think that the British *theatre* adds a touch of class." That's why, in the United States, you so often see malls with pretentious names like *Ye Olde Towne Centre* that have twelve-screen movie *theatres* instead of plain old movie *theaters.* Nevertheless, you should use the *-er* spelling unless you are citing the name of a theater that calls itself a *theatre* or quoting *The New Yorker.*

Finally, *theater* is often mispronounced thee-AY-tur or THEE-ay-tur. *The Random House Dictionary* calls these variants "characteristic chiefly of uneducated speech." The proper pronunciation of *theater* is THEE-uh-tur.

Answers to Review Quizzes for Level 1
KEYWORDS 1–10

1. No. Stealing bread because you are starving is a forgivable offense. *Depravity* means wickedness, moral perversion, corrupt or evil character or behavior.

2. No. Asking for directions when you're lost is normal. *Presumptuous* means overly forward, taking undue liberties, acting or speaking too boldly.

3. Yes. *Grandiose* means showy and grand in an exaggerated, artificial way; also, elaborate, extravagant, overblown.

4. No. That would be *un*sanitary. To *disseminate* is to spread widely, scatter as if sowing seed.

5. Yes. *Eclectic* means varied or diverse in an interesting way.

6. No. *Servile* means like a slave, submissive, obedient.

7. Yes. *Voracious* means extremely hungry, having a large appetite or intense cravings.

8. Yes. *Convoluted* means intricate, complicated, very involved, hard to unravel.

9. Yes, *often*. To *rant* is to speak in an excited manner, to speak fervently or furiously.

10. No. If it is unsuccessful you would be at a disadvantage because a *stratagem* is a clever scheme or artful maneuver used to deceive, outwit, or gain an advantage over an enemy, adversary, or rival.

KEYWORDS 11–20

1. False. Sumo wrestlers are abnormally fat. *Emaciated* means abnormally thin, wasted away from disease or starvation.

2. True. A *misgiving* is a feeling of doubt, hesitation, uneasiness, suspicion, or dread.

3. False. *Adulation* is never subtle. It means excessive admiration, praise, or flattery.

4. True. A *devotee* is a person devoted to something; an enthusiastic or ardent follower, admirer, or practitioner.

5. False. An exhausted person is enervated, worn-out. *Vivacious* means the opposite: vigorous, high-spirited, energetic.

6. True. *Anachronistic* means misplaced in time, not in proper chronological place or order; hence, by extension, out-of-date, outmoded, obsolete.

7. False. *Garish* means excessively showy or bright; attracting attention in a loud and tasteless way.

8. True. A *qualm* is a sudden uneasy, disturbing, or sickening feeling, especially when accompanied by a twinge of conscience or a pang of guilt.

9. False. *Consummate* means of the highest or greatest degree, complete, utmost, utter, and may apply to those who possess a quality to the greatest degree or who are skilled to the highest degree: *a consummate professional, a consummate liar.*

10. False. A servile person is submissive, subservient. *Impertinent* means overly forward or bold; rude, meddlesome, or inappropriate in speech or behavior.

KEYWORDS 21–30

1. Synonyms. A *ramification* is a far-reaching effect, related development, or consequence of something; hence, an implication.

2. Antonyms. To *muddle* is to confuse or make a mess of. To *elucidate* is to make clear, explain.

3. Synonyms. An *adage* and a *proverb* are both old sayings, expressions of popular wisdom.

4. Antonyms. *Temperate* means moderate, not excessive or indulgent. *Besotted* means either very drunk or infatuated, obsessed.

5. Antonyms. *Buoyant* (BOY-int) means cheerful. *Rueful* means sorrowful, mournful.

6. Synonyms. *Spasmodic* means sudden, violent, and brief, or happening in fits and starts. *Intermittent* means happening at intervals.

7. Synonyms. *Detritus* is *debris,* disintegrated material.

8. Synonyms. *Awry* means off course, *amiss,* in an unintended direction, in a wrong or unfortunate way.

9. Antonyms. To *encumber* is to burden, weigh down, place a heavy load upon; also, to frustrate or obstruct the action or motion of. To *expedite* is to speed up, hasten.

10. Synonyms. To *blemish* is to damage or diminish the beauty or sound condition of something. To *sully* is to stain or tarnish.

KEYWORDS 31–40

1. *Obligation* doesn't fit. An *impediment* is an obstacle, hindrance, something that slows down movement or stands in the way of progress.

2. *More than enough* doesn't fit. A *modicum* is the opposite: a little bit, modest portion.

3. *Secret document* doesn't fit. Although a *dossier*—a collection of papers containing detailed information, a comprehensive file—is sometimes kept secret because the information in it is confidential, there is nothing about the word that implies secrecy.

4. *Familiar sounds* doesn't fit. *Alliteration* is the repetition of the same letter or sound at the beginning of two or more neighboring words or stressed syllables.

5. *Openness* doesn't fit. *Rectitude* is virtue, righteousness, moral integrity.

6. *Frivolous* doesn't fit. *Frivolous* means lacking seriousness or importance. *Vexatious* means troubling, disturbing, annoying, irritating.

7. *Clever remark* doesn't fit. An *epithet* is a nickname or designation, a word or phrase that describes some quality or characteristic of a person or thing.

8. *Grave misfortune* doesn't fit. A *travesty* is an absurd imitation or grotesque likeness.

9. *Disappear* doesn't fit. To *wane* is not to pass out of view, notice, or existence, but to decrease or diminish.

10. *Excessive greed* doesn't fit. *Hubris* means excessive pride or self-confidence.

KEYWORDS 41–50

1. *Vicarious* means experienced sympathetically, sharing the feelings or experience of others in one's own imagination.

2. *Stipulate* means to require as an essential condition, demand as a requirement.

3. *Despotic* means ruling with absolute power, or pertaining to someone with unlimited authority.

4. It's unpleasant. Literally, *unsavory* means disagreeable or unpleasant to taste or smell; figuratively, it means undesirable, offensive.

5. You speak indirectly. To *intimate* means to hint, imply, communicate indirectly.

6. It's inclined beforehand. To *predispose* is to incline or tend toward beforehand, make susceptible or subject to.

7. It happens swiftly. *Apace* means swiftly, quickly, with speed.

8. It's green. *Verdant* means green in color, or green with vegetation.

9. *Cajole* means to persuade with repeated urging, flattery, or false promises.

10. A *bane* is a cause or source of ruin, harm, or misery; a curse.

LEVEL 2

Word 1: DIATRIBE (DY-uh-tryb, like *die a tribe*)
Bitter, abusive speech or writing; violent criticism or denunciation.

Diatribe comes from the Greek *diatribé,* which meant employment, study, or discourse, literally a wearing away of time. This Greek noun comes in turn from the verb *diatríbein,* to rub through or away. When *diatribe* entered English in the late 16th century it was used to mean a discourse, dissertation, critical treatise, as *a diatribe on the subject of descriptive poetry* or *a diatribe on the noises of insects.* Around 1800, people also began using *diatribe* in an unfavorable way of a bitter, abusive discourse or dissertation directed against a person or thing. By the early 20th century the original, neutral meaning had become archaic and the unfavorable sense became the modern meaning of the word. Today *diatribe,* when properly used, always implies rage or bitterness expressed in abusive, violently critical language.

Synonyms of *diatribe* include *invective* (in-VEK-tiv), *harangue* (huh-RANG), *tirade* (like *tie raid*), and *philippic* (fi-LIP-ik). Let's take a moment to discuss these interesting words.

Invective, from the Latin verb *invehere,* to attack with words, is vehement or abusive language involving bitter accusations or denunciations. An *invective* is an abusive and denunciatory attack in speech or writing.

Harangue, from an Old Italian word meaning to speak in public, may mean a pompous, tedious, sermonizing speech or lecture; a vehement and passionate speech, especially one delivered

51

in public; or, in its sense closest to *diatribe,* a scolding or ranting verbal attack. The verb to *harangue* means to deliver a harangue—to lecture tediously, to speak passionately at length, or to attack verbally.

A *tirade,* from the Italian *tirare,* to draw, pull, hurl, shoot, is a prolonged speech, especially a vehement and abusive one. A tirade is longer and more intense than a harangue. Generally speaking, *harangue* and *tirade* are used of vehement speeches, while *invective* and *diatribe* apply to denunciatory speech or writing.

Finally, a *philippic* is an especially scathing tirade, usually a vehement formal speech, for historically *philippic* refers to the speeches made by the ancient Greek orator Demosthenes (di-MAHS-thuh-neez) attacking Philip II of Macedon (MAS-i-dahn).

Antonyms of *diatribe* include *eulogy* (YOO-luh-jee), an oration honoring a deceased person or any offering of high praise, and *encomium* (word 25 of Level 9).

Word 2: EVOCATION (EV-uh-**KAY**-shin)
The act of summoning or calling forth.

The noun *evocation* and the verb to *evoke,* to call forth, elicit, come from the Latin *ēvocātiōnem,* a calling forth, which in turn comes from *ēvocāre,* to call or draw out. The English verb to *evoke* comes from this same Latin *ēvocāre* and means to call forth, draw out, elicit, as *online ads that evoke only frustration and annoyance.* The adjective is *evocative* (i-VAHK-uh-tiv), calling forth. In modern usage *evocative* is used of memories, emotions, images, sensations, and the like to mean tending to call forth or evoke, as *a book filled with lush and evocative description.*

In one of its earliest senses, *evocation* was used of the summoning or calling up of a spirit, and the rare verb to *evocate* (EV-uh-kayt) means to call up spirits from the dead. Today *evocation* still means a calling up, but it refers to the summoning of thoughts and feelings from the imagination. The historical novelist strives to create a convincing evocation of a time and place in the past. Pablo Picasso's famous painting *Guernica*—which depicts the bombing of the town of Guernica in northern Spain by German warplanes in 1937, during the Spanish Civil War—is a disturbing evocation of the horror and tragedy of war.

Word 3: IMBUE (im-BYOO)

To saturate or spread through, soak or penetrate deeply. Also, to influence or inspire deeply, as if by soaking.

Synonyms of *imbue* in the sense of saturate or spread through include *infuse, suffuse* (word 17 of Level 3), *pervade, permeate,* and *impregnate.* Synonyms of *imbue* in the sense of influence or inspire deeply include *instill, ingrain, endow, implant, indoctrinate* (word 28 of this level), *inculcate,* and *inoculate.*

Imbue comes from the Latin *imbuĕre,* to wet, steep, saturate, a verb akin to the Latin *bibere,* to drink, from which we inherit the English word *imbibe,* to drink, especially to drink alcoholic beverages. Figuratively *imbibe* means to drink in, absorb, soak up, as *to imbibe the culture of a foreign country.*

Imbue may be used literally of anything that is saturated with moisture, color, or perfume. But it is perhaps most often used figuratively of something that has been influenced or inspired deeply, as if by soaking. A person's mind can be imbued with almost anything it can soak up: literature, fine art, music, opinions, or cold hard facts. And a person's heart can be imbued, saturated, with emotion.

The words *imbue* and *imbrue* (im-BROO) differ in spelling by one letter and are close in meaning. *Imbrue,* which comes ultimately from the aforementioned Latin *bibere,* to drink, means to wet, stain, or drench, especially with blood: "These hands in murder are imbrued," wrote the English poet Matthew Prior in 1704. *Imbue* has no such gory implication, and is used of anything that soaks, penetrates, or influences deeply. You can be imbued with ambition, imbued with power and grace, or imbued with geekiness.

Although *imbue* and *instill* are synonyms, they are used in different ways. Something is instilled *in* or *into* something else, while something is imbued *with* something else.

Word 4: REPUGNANT (ri-PUHG-nint)
Disgusting, offensive.

Because there are so many things that can be described as disgusting or offensive, *repugnant* has no shortage of synonyms. Among the better-known are *objectionable, disagreeable, repulsive, detestable, loathsome, contemptible,* and *repellent.* Among the lesser-known are *odious, abhorrent, heinous* (HAY-nis), *opprobrious* (uh-PROH-bree-us), *flagitious* (fluh-JISH-us), and *execrable* (EK-si-kruh-buul), which comes from a Latin word meaning accursed and is used today of that which is so horrible or detestable as to be cursed or damned.

Repugnant comes from the Latin *repugnans,* opposed, contrary, and for several centuries opposed, contrary, hostile, antagonistic was the core meaning of the word, as in *repugnant laws* or *actions repugnant to God's word.* But this sense is now rare and today *repugnant* is used of anything that provokes distaste, aversion, or loathing.

Repugnant may be used with or without the preposition *to.* Something may be *repugnant to* you or someone else, or it may simply be *repugnant,* disgusting, offensive, disagreeable.

Word 5: INSOLENT (IN-suh-lint)
Boldly insulting and disrespectful; rudely presumptuous (word 2 of Level 1).

The words *impertinent, impudent,* and *insolent* are close in meaning. All refer to rude, disrespectful behavior.

Impertinent, whose literal meaning is not pertinent, inappropriate, is the least insulting of the three. *Impertinent* refers to behavior that is uncalled for because it is too forward or intrusive. People who say or do something that they know, or ought to know, is rude or out of place are impertinent. Someone who fails to show proper respect to a superior is impertinent, and an inappropriately personal question can be impertinent.

Impudent comes from the Latin *impudens,* shameless, and refers to behavior that is shamelessly bold or rude. An impudent reply is rude or insulting, and an impudent person is boldly disrespectful. Incidentally, *impudens,* the Latin source of *impudent,* comes in turn from the verb *pudēre,* to make ashamed or to be ashamed, the source of the unusual English words *pudency* (PYOO-din-see), modesty, bashfulness, and *pudendum* (pyoo-DEN-dum), which means literally "that of which one ought to be ashamed" and denotes the external genital organs, especially of a woman.

While *impertinent* is used of inappropriately forward behavior, and *impudent* is used of shamelessly bold behavior, our keyword, *insolent,* is stronger still. It comes from a Latin adjective that meant proud, haughty, arrogant, and it applies to behavior that is arrogantly and contemptuously disrespectful and insulting. An insolent soldier invites disciplinary action. Parents often punish an insolent child. And an insolent coworker or colleague is one who revels, takes pleasure, in insulting you or giving you grief.

The corresponding nouns are *impertinence, impudence,* and *insolence,* boldly insulting and disrespectful behavior.

Word 6: IMPUNITY (im-PYOO-ni-tee)
Freedom from penalty or punishment, exemption from harm or loss.

Impunity comes from the Latin *impūnitās,* exemption from punishment, which comes in turn from *poena,* a punishment, fine, the source of the English words *penal, penalty,* and *pain.*

The prefix *im-* is really the prefix *in-* in disguise. Why the alteration in spelling? It's difficult to articulate *in-* before words that begin with the letters *b, m,* or *p,* so we use *im-* instead for ease of pronunciation. Rather than saying *inbalance, inmoral,* and *inpossible,* we say *imbalance, immoral,* and *impossible.*

The Random House Dictionary explains that the words *exemption, immunity,* and *impunity* all "imply special privilege or freedom from imposed requirements." *Exemption* refers to freedom from a duty or burden: "Because of his disability he was granted exemption from military service." *Immunity* (in its legal sense) refers to freedom from liability or responsibility, especially for wrongdoing: we speak of diplomatic immunity or immunity from prosecution. Our keyword, *impunity,* implies freedom from penalty or punishment: "War and an atmosphere of impunity make Afghanistan one of the most dangerous places in the world to be a journalist" (Reuters). *Impunity* is often preceded by *with:* "When there is no authority to enforce the rules, those who break them will do so with impunity."

Word 7: STAGNATE (STAG-nayt)
To stop running or flowing; become stale or foul; cease to grow, develop, or advance.

The adjective is *stagnant* (STAG-nint), inactive, still, not flowing or running, as *stagnant water,* or not advancing, growing, or developing, as a *stagnant economy* or a *stagnant relationship.*

The verb to *stagnate,* the adjective *stagnant,* and the noun *stagnation*—a stagnant condition or state—all come through the Latin *stagnāre,* to form a pool, from the noun *stagnum,* a pool of standing water, marsh, swamp. And all these words imply the stillness and staleness of water that has pooled and does not flow. If you never stimulate your mind with interesting things to think and talk about, your brain will stagnate, become stale; your social life will become stagnant, cease to grow or develop; and eventually it will become harder to extricate yourself from your stagnation, an unhealthy absence of energy or activity. (To *extricate,* pronounced EKS-tri-kayt, means to release or free from an entanglement.)

Word 8: EMBLEMATIC (EM-bluh-**MAT**-ik)
Symbolic, serving as a symbol, representative, typical.

An *emblem* is a symbol or sign that represents or stands for something: "The dove is an emblem of peace." *Emblematic* is the adjective, and means serving as an emblem or symbol. Generally speaking, wherever you can use the words *symbolic, representative,* and *typical* you can also use *emblematic,* which is usually followed by the preposition *of: the rampant greed so emblematic of Wall Street; the emblematic chaos of New York City.*

Word 9: PLAINTIVE (PLAYN-tiv)
Mournful, melancholy, expressing sadness or sorrow.

The adjective *plaintive* and the noun *plaintiff* (PLAYN-tif) look and sound similar because they are closely related etymologically. Both entered English in the late 14th century from the Middle French *plaintif,* the feminine form of which was *plaintive.* This Middle French *plaintif* referred to the person or party that brings a civil suit to court, the complainant—the same meaning that *plaintiff* has today. But *plaintif* was also used to mean having the character of a lament, mournful, sad—the modern meaning of *plaintive.*

These same two coexisting senses can be seen in the related but unusual English noun *plaint,* which may mean a complaint; a grievance submitted to a court of law; a lament; or the sound of lamentation—a wailing or moaning, as in this sentence from T. C. Boyle's 1987 novel *World's End:* "The plaint of bass and guitar was amplified by the addition of a muddy quavering vocal track."

Although it is not uncommon in journalism, *plaintive* is what is often called a "literary word," one usually found in literature, poetry, and sophisticated nonfiction, such as criticism of the fine arts. Music, voices, and various sounds—the wind or an echo or the call of a bird—are often described as plaintive, expressing sadness or sorrow. The early 20th-century English novelist Virginia Woolf even used it of a facial expression: "The worry of nursing her husband had fixed a plaintive frown upon her forehead."

Word 10: RAPACIOUS (ruh-PAY-shus)
Excessively greedy or predatory; inclined to seize what one wants.

Synonyms of *rapacious* include *plundering, grasping, acquisitive, covetous, ravenous,* and *voracious* (word 7 of Level 1).

Rapacious comes through the Latin *rapāx,* greedy, predatory, from *rapere,* to seize. Also from this Latin verb *rapere,* to seize, come the English noun *rape;* the adjective *raptorial,* adapted for seizing prey, predatory; and the adjective *rapt,* which means either seized with powerful emotion, as *rapt with joy,* or deeply absorbed, en-grossed, as *rapt with attention.*

The words *ravenous, voracious,* and *rapacious* are close in meaning. *Ravenous* "implies excessive hunger and suggests violent or grasp-ing methods of dealing with food or with whatever satisfies an appetite," says *Merriam-Webster's Collegiate Dictionary.* You can be ravenous at the dinner table or ravenous for money. *Voracious* may also be used of great physical hunger, as *a voracious eater,* or it may be used figuratively to mean having a great appetite or greed for some-thing: *a voracious reader; a voracious, gas-guzzling engine.* Our keyword, *rapacious,* suggests greedy desire and a selfish, aggressive impulse to seize what one wants. We speak of rapacious pirates on the high seas, the rapacious destruction of the Amazon rain forest, or banks that offer credit cards with rapacious interest rates.

Review Quiz for Keywords 1–10
Consider the following questions and decide whether the correct answer is yes or no. **Answers appear on page 94.**

1. Is a diatribe ever complimentary?
2. Can a poem be an evocation of a poet's emotions?
3. If you are imbued with something, are you obsessed with it?
4. Is something repugnant ever pleasing?
5. Can an insolent remark be flattering?
6. If you do something with impunity, will you be punished?
7. When something stagnates, does it start to move?
8. Can something symbolic be emblematic?
9. Can the call of a bird be plaintive?
10. Is rapacious behavior aggressive?

Difficult Distinctions: *Recur or Reoccur?*
When something happens more than once, should we say that it *recurs* or that it *reoccurs?* Both words mean to happen again, but in slightly different ways.

To *reoccur* is to happen again only once; a *reoccurrence* is a one-time repetition. To *recur* is to happen more than once or repeatedly, often at fixed intervals or on a schedule; *recurrence* is regular repetition or a pattern of occurrence.

A traffic accident that reoccurs at a particular intersection might go ignored by city officials. But recurring accidents at that location would probably make the city install a stoplight. And a headache that reoccurs is not necessarily cause for alarm, but one that recurs may indicate a serious problem.

Difficult Distinctions: *Allude* and *Refer; Allusion* and *Reference*

In their literary senses, the verbs to *refer* and to *allude* are often confused—so much so that some dictionaries give *refer* as a synonym of *allude*. But the words should be carefully distinguished. Both imply directing the attention, but in different ways.

To *refer* is to mention or introduce specifically, to direct to a source that is named: "The professor referred the class to the bibliography for more information." To *allude* is to touch on something indirectly or by suggestion, without specifically mentioning the source: "When the professor said, 'We have miles to go before we sleep,' Marjorie knew it was an allusion to Robert Frost's poem 'Stopping by Woods on a Snowy Evening.'"

In short, to *refer* is to indicate or point to directly, while to *allude* is to hint, suggest indirectly.

Likewise with the nouns *reference* and *allusion*. Both imply directing the attention to a source, especially something literary or cultural. But in a reference the source is identified, mentioned specifically, while in an allusion the source is not stated directly. *As Mark Twain observed, "It is better to support schools than jails"* is a reference. *"Ay, there's the rub," she said* is an allusion to Shakespeare's *Hamlet*.

Now let's return to the *Word Workout* vocabulary for another ten keyword discussions.

Word 11: PEON (PEE-ahn)
An unskilled laborer; a person of low social status who does physically demanding and sometimes degrading work.

Synonyms of the noun *peon* include *menial, drudge,* and *lackey.*

The words *peon* and *pawn* are related etymologically, for both go back to the Medieval Latin *pedo,* a walker, pedestrian, hence a foot soldier, member of the infantry. *Peon* came into English in the early 1600s through Portuguese and French words meaning foot soldier. And in the game of chess a pawn is a foot soldier, the least valued and most expendable piece on the board.

Over the centuries *peon* has denoted various types of workers, all of them lowly. A peon was originally a foot soldier or low-ranking police officer in India, Sri Lanka, and Malaysia; later the word was applied to any servant, attendant, orderly, or messenger. In Latin America in the early 19th century a peon was a lowly member of society who was forced to do hard labor to pay off a debt to a creditor or satisfy other obligations to a master. *Peon* was then used of any unskilled laborer, such as a farmworker or a domestic worker, and by the early 20th century the word came to be applied as well to any lowly or unimportant person who serves others.

The noun *peonage* (PEE-uh-nij) means the state of being a peon or the use of peons for service. In the fairy tale "Cinderella," the title character lives in peonage to her malevolent* stepmother—until, of course, she marries the prince.

Word 12: INTUIT (in-T[Y]OO-it)
To know or understand instinctively, without deduction or reasoning.

Intuit is the verb corresponding to the familiar noun *intuition,* instinctive knowledge or insight, and the adjective *intuitive,* perceived by or involving intuition. All three words come from the past participle *intuitus* of the Latin verb *intuēri,* to gaze at, look at attentively, contemplate. To intuit is to know by intuition, instinc-

---

* *Malevolent* (muh-LEV-uh-lint) means full of ill will, wishing evil or harm to others.

tive knowledge, and to have an intuitive understanding of something is to know it immediately, "without the intervention of any reasoning process" (*OED*).

Anything that you know immediately or instinctively, without thinking logically about it, is intuited. For example, we often intuit through our senses, as when we know it's going to rain by smelling the air and looking at the sky, or when we make snap judgments about people based on our first impression of how they look or speak.

The antonym of *intuitive* is *counterintuitive,* a useful word that was invented in the 1950s. That which is counterintuitive is contrary to what intuition would lead you to expect, as in the expression *you have to spend money to make money.*

Word 13: OPINE (oh-PYN, like *oh pine*)
To have or express an opinion; especially, to express a formal opinion.

The verb to *opine* comes from the Latin *opīnāri,* to have an opinion, believe, suppose, the source also of the noun *opinion* and the adjective *opinionated,* having strong opinions, stubbornly believing in the superiority of one's point of view. A close synonym of *opinionated* is the word *dogmatic,* which means expressing an opinion, usually in an arrogant manner, as if it were fact. "When people are least sure," wrote the economist John Kenneth Galbraith (GAL-brayth) in 1955, "they are often most dogmatic."

Our keyword, *opine,* has been used since the 15th century to mean to have or express an opinion, as in this 1881 quotation from *The Academy:* "You may opine upon everything under the sun." But today, says *Garner's Modern American Usage,* the word "often connotes the forming of a judgment on insufficient grounds," and "it can suggest the giving of an idle or facetious (fuh-SEE-shus) opinion." (*Facetious* means not meant to be taken seriously, intended as a joke.) Nevertheless, the most common and enduring sense of *opine* in American English is to express a formal or authoritative opinion. It is used this way frequently in the law, where an expert witness opines in testimony and a judge or a court opines in a ruling.

You can opine *on* or *upon:* "In 1929, the readers of *The Manchester Guardian* were asked to opine on the 'novelists who may be read in 2029'" (*New Yorker*). You can opine *that:* "Legal scholars opine that Microsoft faces deep trouble" (CNN). You can opine *about:* "Pundits [word 10 of Level 4] and politicians who opine about the so-called war on women . . ." (*The Washington Post*). Or you can simply opine, without a preposition: "The pressroom has closed-circuit video footage of the proceedings, allowing the Twitter peanut gallery to opine in whatever fashion it desires" (*New York Daily News*).

Word 14: LANGUISH (LANG-gwish)
To be or become weak or feeble, lose strength or vitality.

Synonyms of *languish* include *decline, droop, wither,* and *flag.*

The adjectives *languid* (LANG-gwid), *languor* (LANG-gur, rhymes with *anger*), and *languish* all imply weakness or inactivity.

The adjective *languid* comes from the Latin *languidus,* faint, weak, feeble, and has a number of meanings: lacking energy, exhausted, listless (word 39 of this level), as *a recent illness had left him languid;* or slow, leisurely, unhurried, as *moving forward at a languid pace;* or lacking spirit or concern, indifferent, as *a languid look* or *a languid gesture;* or characterized by inactivity, idle, relaxed, as *a long, hot, languid summer;* or finally, lifeless, lacking force or interest, as *a disappointing thriller with a languid plot.*

The noun *languor* comes from the Latin *languor, languoris,* faintness, weariness, feebleness. It may mean a lack of energy, physical or mental fatigue, as in this quotation from Jack London's 1907 story "Love of Life": ". . . this deadly languor, that rose and rose and drowned his consciousness bit by bit"; or it may mean a pleasurable state of drowsiness or idleness, as *the delicious languor of lying on a tropical beach.* The corresponding adjective is *languorous* (LANG-gur-us), characterized by or producing languor: "The atmosphere was . . . languorous and heavy with the rich scent of flowers" (Anne Elliot, *An Old Man's Favour,* 1887).

Our keyword, the verb to *languish,* comes from the Latin

languēre, to be faint or weak, or to be inactive, sluggish, languid. The primary meaning of *languish* is to be or become weak or feeble, lose strength or vitality, weaken, wither, fade, as *to fall ill and languish in bed,* or *flowers languishing in the midday heat.* But *languish* also has several other useful meanings. It may mean to be ignored or neglected, as *for weeks his report languished unread on the boss's desk.* It may mean to suffer hardship or live in distressing conditions, as *to languish in prison* or *languishing in poverty.* And it may mean to yearn for, pine, suffer with longing. In his famous poem "The Raven," Edgar Allan Poe languishes for his "lost Lenore."

Word 15: VESTIGIAL (ve-STIJ-ee-<u>ul</u>)

Being, or pertaining to, a remnant or trace of something that has disappeared, been lost or destroyed, or that no longer survives.

The adjective *vestigial* and the noun *vestige* (VES-tij) both come from the Latin *vestīgium,* a footprint, trace, mark. A vestige is a mark or trace of something that has disappeared, that has been lost or destroyed, or that no longer exists. *Vestige* may be used of something actual, a remnant of something past and gone, as *vestiges of an ancient civilization.* Or it may refer figuratively to something lost or gone, as *a vestige of warmth,* or to the smallest trace or amount, a particle or scrap: *a vestige of an accent.*

Vestigial means of the nature of a vestige, being or pertaining to a trace or remnant of something that no longer exists. For example, in the age of science and reason, superstitions such as a belief in fairies or a fear of the number thirteen★ are vestigial, reminiscent of something that is past or that has disappeared. In biology, a vestigial body part, such as an organ or a tail, is one that is small and imperfectly developed but that, in an earlier stage of evolution, was once fully formed and useful.

★ The word for a fear of the number thirteen is *triskaidekaphobia* (TRIS-ky-DEK-uh-**FOH**-bee-uh).

Word 16: SOMNOLENT (SAHM-nuh-lint)
Tending to cause sleep or inclined to sleep. Also, drowsy, sleepy, heavy with sleep.

Somnolent comes from the Latin *somnus,* sleep, slumber, a word akin to the Latin *sopor,* deep sleep, the source of the English word *soporific* (SAH-puh-**RIF**-ik), an exact synonym of *somnolent.*

The Latin *somnus* is also the source of some interesting and unusual English words. *Somnambulate* (sahm-NAM-byuh-layt), a combination of *somnus* and *ambulate,* to walk, means to sleepwalk, and *somnambulism* (sahm-NAM-byuh-liz'm) is the act of walking in one's sleep. *Somniloquist* (sahm-NIL-uh-kwist) combines the Latin *somnus,* sleep, and *loqui,* to speak, and means a person who talks while asleep. The adjective *somniloquent* (sahm-NIL-uh-kwint) means talking in one's sleep.

Anything that is sleepy or that tends to cause sleep can be described as *somnolent.* A dull book or a boring lecture can be somnolent. Soft, relaxing music, or any sleep-inducing sound, can be somnolent. And a small town or village that is quiet, with little activity, may be called sleepy or somnolent.

Synonyms of *somnolent* include *weary, fatigued, lethargic* (le-THAHR-jik), *languid, torpid,* and *oscitant* (AHS-i-tint), a fancy word from the Latin *ōscitāre,* to yawn, gape, and *ōs,* mouth, that means drowsy, inattentive, yawning from sleepiness.

Antonyms of *somnolent* include *stimulating, invigorating, bracing, animating, exhilarating, revitalizing,* and *revivifying* (ree-VIV-i-fy-ing).

Word 17: SUPPLANT (suh-PLANT)
To take the place of, replace; especially, to take the place of another by dishonest means, such as by force, scheming, or treachery.

Synonyms of *supplant* include *overthrow, dispossess, undermine, subvert,* and *supersede,* which comes from the Latin *super,* above, and *sedēre,* to sit, the source also of *sedentary* (**SED**-in-TER-ee), given to sitting; *sediment* (SED-i-mint), that which sits on the bottom; and *sedate* (suh-DAYT, word 9 of Level 3), calm, composed, serious. That which *supersedes* by derivation sits, *sedēre,* above, *super,* and so takes the place of.

Supplant comes from the Latin verb *supplantāre,* to trip up, cause to stumble or fall, which comes in turn from *sub-,* under, beneath, and *planta,* the sole of the foot. *Supplant* once meant literally to trip up, cause to fall, and it also once meant to uproot, as when Shakespeare wrote in *The Tempest,* "Trinculo, if you trouble him anymore . . . I will supplant some of your teeth." But these senses are obsolete, and since the 14th century the chief meaning of *supplant* has been to supersede, take the place of, especially by dishonest or treacherous means—as when Shakespeare, also in *The Tempest,* wrote, "You three from Milan did supplant good Prospero."

Word 18: EUPHEMISM (YOO-fuh-miz'm)
The substitution of a milder, nicer, more agreeable word or expression for one considered unpleasant, blunt, or offensive; also, a more polite or pleasant word or phrase used in place of another felt to be impolite or unpleasant.

Euphemistic (YOO-fuh-MIS-tik) is the adjective. To *euphemize* (YOO-fuh-myz) is the verb.

Euphemisms are what we use when we want to avoid a word or phrase that seems impolite or too direct, or that is socially unacceptable. When we feel uncomfortable expressing something outright, in straightforward or earthy language, we resort to euphemism. In *How Not to Say What You Mean: A Dictionary of Euphemisms,* R. W. Holder observes that "we use euphemism when dealing with taboo or sensitive subjects."

Euphemisms have been with us for as long as we have been able to speak. When people say *darn* for *damn* and *by golly* or *by gosh* for *by God,* that's euphemism. When people say that someone has *passed away* or *gone the way of all flesh* instead of *died,* or that a woman is *with child* or *expecting* instead of *pregnant,* that's euphemism. And when we call the place where we urinate and defecate a *bathroom, restroom,* or *lavatory,* that's euphemism.

The Victorian era—Victoria was queen of Great Britain from

1837 to 1901—is remembered in large part for its prudery,★ and therefore also for its fondness for euphemisms. For example, proper Victorians never called the leg of a piece of furniture a *leg;* they called it a *limb.* And the word *underwear* was too indecent to be uttered in public, so those intimate articles of clothing were referred to as *nether garments.*†

My grandmother, who was born in 1883, was a fiercely progressive woman for her times, but her proper New England upbringing had taught her to use the euphemism *second joint* for a chicken thigh because *thigh* was an indelicate word. She passed this bit of daintiness along to my mother, who used it every time she served us roast chicken when I was growing up, so it came as a bit of a surprise to me when I eventually discovered that everyone else called them chicken thighs and no one outside my family, except Julia Child, had ever heard of a second joint.

Euphemism comes from the Greek *euphēmismós,* the use of words of good omen, from *eu-,* well, good, and *phémē,* speaking. In English, the same Greek *eu-,* good, well, is a combining form that appears in a number of interesting words. The noun *euphony* (YOO-fuh-nee), the quality of having a pleasant or sweet sound, and the adjective *euphonious* (yoo-FOH-nee-u̲s), having a pleasant or sweet sound, both combine *eu-* and the Greek *phōné,* voice, sound. *Euthanasia* (pronounced like *youth in Asia*) combines *eu-* with *thánatos,* death, to mean literally a good death; specifically it denotes the act of putting to death or allowing to die with as little pain as possible. And the *Eucharist* (YOO-kuh-rist), which combines *eu-,* well, good, and the Greek *charisma,* favor, gift—the direct source of the English word *charisma,* a special personal appeal or charm—is the sacrament of Holy Communion in the Christian church.

The antonym of *euphemism* is *dysphemism* (DIS-fuh-miz'm), "the substitution of a disagreeable word or phrase for a neutral or even positive one; or a word or phrase so substituted" (*Garner's Modern American Usage*). Examples of dysphemisms include *bean-counter* for

---

★ **Prudery** (PROO-dur-ee) is extreme modesty in relation to sexual matters.
† **Nether** (rhymes with *whether*) means lower, situated underneath or below, as the *nether regions,* the underworld or hell.

accountant; grease monkey for *mechanic; gumshoe* for *detective; sawbones* for *surgeon; egghead* for *intellectual;* and *shrink* for *psychiatrist.*

Word 19: VISCERAL (VIS-uh-r<u>u</u>l)
Of or pertaining to the gut or belly; hence, guided by instinct or intuition rather than by the mind or reason.

The English noun *viscera* (VIS-ur-uh) comes directly from Latin and, in anatomy and zoology, is used of the internal organs of the trunk of the body, especially those in the abdominal cavity, also known as the entrails (EN-traylz). The verb to *eviscerate* (i-VIS-ur-ayt) means to remove the entrails, disembowel, or figuratively, to empty of essential or vital parts: "Critics said the proposed cost-cutting plan would eviscerate funding for public education." In nontechnical usage *viscera* refers to the bowels or intestines, for which the simpler word is *guts*. The adjective *visceral* means affecting or pertaining to the viscera, the guts.

Because a person's gut or belly is considered the source of basic instinct and emotion, *visceral* came to mean instinctive or intuitive rather than intellectual or rational. Thus, a *gut feeling* and a *visceral feeling* are the same: a strong emotion that seems to come more from your bowels than your brain. A visceral reaction is a gut reaction, one that proceeds from instinct. And if you feel something on a visceral level, it touches you emotionally in a fundamental way.

An actor or singer can have visceral appeal. Lovers can feel a visceral connection with each other. And parents often have a visceral bond with their children.

Word 20: DISPASSIONATE (dis-PASH-uh-nit)
Not affected by passion, emotion, or prejudice; having no strong emotion or bias; not personally or emotionally involved.

Synonyms of *dispassionate* include *disinterested, unbiased, indifferent,* and *impartial.* The impartial person remains neutral and does not take sides: *an impartial review of the evidence; an impartial mediator of a dispute.* The indifferent person shows no interest or concern and often does not care to: *an indifferent shrug; indifferent to the opinions of others.* A bias is a preference or inclination—either a reasonable preference or an unfair one, a prejudice—so an unbiased opinion is free of bias, without prejudice, and an unbiased person does not have his mind already made up. The disinterested person is not selfishly motivated and has no personal interest or stake in the outcome of an event: *a disinterested observer.* The uninterested person, by contrast, simply has no interest and doesn't care.

To remember the distinction between *disinterested,* having no personal interest, and *uninterested,* lacking interest, just ask yourself whether, if you were on trial for your life, you'd rather have a disinterested jury or an uninterested one.

Our keyword, *dispassionate,* which combines the privative* prefix *dis-,* not, with *passionate,* may apply to people, actions, qualities, or opinions. A dispassionate mind is a calm, composed mind, unmoved by strong emotion. Dispassionate views are fair-minded, neutral, unbiased views. And a dispassionate judgment is one that has not been influenced in any way by emotion, personal interest, or prejudice.

Review Quiz for Keywords 11–20
Consider the following statements and decide whether each one is true or false. **Answers appear on page 95**.

1. A peon is a high-ranking, powerful person.
2. When you intuit something, you analyze it and figure out what it means.
3. To opine is to give a lengthy and often boring speech.
4. Something that languishes becomes weaker, is ignored, or suffers hardship.

---

* The adjective *privative* (PRIV-uh-tiv) means taking away, depriving. A privative prefix takes away or negates the meaning of the word that comes after. Other privative prefixes include *un-* (from Anglo-Saxon), as in *uncivil,* not civil, rude, impolite; *in-* and its variant *im-* (from Latin), as in *insuperable,* not capable of being overcome, and *immaterial,* not important or relevant, unrelated; *non-* (also from Latin), as in *nonpartisan,* not supporting a particular political party or special interest group; and *a-* or *an-* (from Greek), as in *amoral,* not moral, and *anarchy,* literally without a leader (from *an-,* lacking, and *archós,* a leader).

5. The rotary telephone is now a vestigial communication device.

6. Lying in a hammock on a warm day can make you somnolent.

7. When one thing supplants another, it supports it.

8. Euphemism is direct, blunt, and sometimes impolite.

9. A visceral reaction is the same as a gut reaction.

10. People who put their emotions on display are dispassionate.

Once Upon a Word: Decade Words

One of the pleasures of being a language lover and the author of various books about words is that people ask me lots of interesting questions. And the most interesting kind of question I get is from someone who is wondering, "Is there a word for this?"

One correspondent, who had heard me opine (word 13 of this level) on his local radio station, emailed me to say that he knew the word *octogenarian* (AHK-toh-juh-**NAIR**-ee-in), which begins with the combining form *octo-*, eight, meant a person eighty to eighty-nine years old, and he was wondering if there were other "decade words" for people's ages. There are indeed, but apparently not for folks in their twenties and thirties. It seems that's too young to warrant a highfalutin word.

All these decade words begin with a combining form that denotes a cardinal number and end with the suffix *-arian,* which designates a person who is or does something—such as a *librarian,* someone who works in a library.

The combining form *quadr(i)-* means four, so when you're forty or in your forties, you're a *quadragenarian* (KWAH-druh-juh-**NAIR**-ee-in). *Quinqu(e)* means five, so when you hit fifty you become a *quinquagenarian* (KWIN-kwuh-juh-**NAIR**-ee-in). When you hit sixty, you're a *sexagenarian* (SEK-suh-juh-**NAIR**-ee-in) because the combining form *sex-* means six. *Sept(i)-* means seven, so when you're in your seventies you're a *septuagenarian* (SEP-t[y]oo-uh-juh-**NAIR**-ee-in). You already know about about *octogenarian,* so let's talk about *nona-,* nine, which gives us *nonagenarian* (NAHN-uh-juh-**NAIR**-ee-in), a person who's made it to ninety. And if you make it to one hundred, congratulations. The combining form *cent(i)-* means hundred or hundredth, so you're a *centenarian* (SEN-tuh-**NAIR**-ee-i̲n).

Now let's return to the *Word Workout* vocabulary for Level 2.

Word 21: INDEFATIGABLE (IN-di̲-**FAT**-i̲-guh-buul, stress on *fat*)
Tireless, never lacking energy, not capable of being fatigued.

The familiar word *fatigue,* which as a noun means weariness and as a verb means to tire out, comes from the Latin *fatīgāre,* to tire, while *indefatigable* comes from a similar Latin verb, *dēfatīgāre,* with the same meaning, to weary, tire, wear out.

The unusual English word *defatigable* (di̲-**FAT**-i̲-guh-bu̲l), which you'll find only in a few unabridged dictionaries, means capable of being wearied, apt to get tired, as "The older I get, the more defatigable I become." Graft the privative prefix *in-,* not, onto *defatigable* and you have *indefatigable,* not apt to get tired, incapable of being wearied.

Indefatigable implies perseverance, strong commitment, or unwavering effort—what you might call, informally, *stick-to-it-iveness.* The word may be used of people, as *an indefatigable seeker of justice;* of qualities, as *her indefatigable passion for helping others;* or of actions, as *their indefatigable efforts to rescue the trapped miners.*

Word 22: ARCHETYPE (AHR-kuh-typ)
An original model, form, or pattern after which all things of the same kind are copied, or on which they are based.

Archetype comes through the Latin *archetypum,* an original, from the Greek *archetypon,* a model, pattern, from *arche-,* first, original, and *typos,* a stamp, mold, pattern. In modern usage, *archetype* usually implies not only an original model or pattern that can be copied but also a perfect example of something, an ideal form: "Although most critics agree that Edgar Allan Poe invented the detective story, Arthur Conan Doyle's Sherlock Holmes is generally considered the archetype of the private detective in fiction." *Archetypal* (AHR-kuh-**TYP**-u̲l *or* **AHR**-kuh-typ-u̲l) is the adjective:

"The movie stars Gary Cooper and John Wayne often played archetypal heroes of the American West."

The words *archetype* and *prototype* are close in meaning. Although both denote original types, *archetype* usually refers to qualities, characteristics, or concepts based on mythical examples or ideal forms, while *prototype* "most often refers to a physical model of a mechanical invention," says *Garner's Modern American Usage*. Michelangelo's statue of David is an archetype of male physical strength and beauty. Thomas Edison's prototypes for the lightbulb and the phonograph have been preserved in a museum.

In psychology, *archetype* has a specialized meaning popularized by the Swiss psychologist Carl Gustav Jung (1875–1961), whose last name is pronounced YUUNG, with the *u* of *put* or *full*. "For Jung, there were several layers to the unconscious mind, among which are the personal unconscious and the collective unconscious," explains Herbert Kohl in *From Archetype to Zeitgeist* (word 16 of Level 7). "The personal unconscious contains . . . material derived from one's experience," while the collective unconscious contains "archetypes of the unconscious" that "are part of an individual's inheritance from the history of the human race" and "express deep and often inaccessible levels of human experience."

Word 23: VERACITY (vuh-RAS-i-tee)
Truthfulness, correctness, accuracy, conformity with truth or fact.

The noun *veracity*, truthfulness, and the adjective *veracious* (vuh-RAY-shus) both come from the Latin *vērāx, vērācis*, speaking the truth, truthful. A veracious statement or story is true, accurate, or honest because it is characterized by veracity, truthfulness.

From this Latin *vērāx* and the related Latin words *vērus*, true, and *vēritās*, truth, come a number of useful English words.

The verb to *verify* combines *vērus*, true, with *facere*, to do, make, and means to establish or prove the truth of something, confirm, substantiate, as *to verify that the painting was genuine*. The unusual noun *verity* (VER-i-tee) is a fancy synonym of *truth*, as *historical verity*. It may also mean an established fact or fundamental truth, as *philosophy is the search for the verities of existence*. The adjective is *veritable* (VER-i-tuh-bul), genuine, actual, being truly or correctly so, as *a veritable whiz at math* or *this book is a veritable gold mine of words*.

The common word *very* is also from the Latin *vērāx*, truthful, as are its old-fashioned cousins, the words *verily*, truly, really, indeed, as in the biblical phrase *verily I say unto you*, and *veriest*, utmost, greatest, as in this line from Nathaniel Hawthorne's novel *The Scarlet Letter* (1850): "He had spoken the very truth, and transformed it into the veriest falsehood."

Finally, we have the noun *verisimilitude* (VER-i-suh-**MIL**-i-t[y]ood), which comes from the Latin *vērus*, true, and *similis*, like, resembling, and in English means the appearance of truth, as *a drama with ample verisimilitude* (appearance of truth) *but little verity* (actual truth).

Our keyword, *veracity*, traditionally means a habitual observance of or devotion to truth, as *a research scientist must have a passion for veracity*. And in its least common sense *veracity* may also mean a truth, something that is true, as in this 1867 quotation from the history lectures of William Stubbs, bishop of Oxford: "A world whose falsehoods and veracities are separated by so thin a barrier." But most commonly today *veracity* is used to mean truthfulness, correctness, accuracy, as *the prosecution questioned the veracity of her testimony*.

The antonym of *veracity* is *mendacity* (men-DAS-i-tee), lying, untruthfulness, deceit, from the Latin *mendāx, mendācis*, given to lying.

Word 24: MINION (MIN-yun)
A servile follower or assistant. (*Servile* is word 6 of Level 1.)

Synonyms of *minion* include *underling, subordinate, hanger-on,* and *henchman*.

Minion comes from the French and Middle French word *mignon*, delicate, dainty, familiar to English speakers in the name of the small and tender cut of beef *filet mignon*. But this French *mignon* is also an English adjective, pronounced min-YAHN, that means delicately formed, small and pretty; it is perhaps more often used in its feminine form, *mignonne* (also min-YAHN), as in *her graceful, mignonne figure.*

When the noun *minion* entered English in the 16th century it was used to mean a number of things: an effeminate man; a person kept for sexual favors; a specially favored person, a darling; and a person, usually male, who is favored by and dependent on someone powerful, usually another male. This last meaning evolved into the modern sense of the word—a slavish follower, subservient attendant—while the other senses, with their connotations of daintiness and sexual intimacy, became obsolete or rare.

Today *minion* is used chiefly of any subordinate person who unquestioningly follows, assists, or takes orders from someone more powerful, as *the movie star with her fawning minions.* The word is also sometimes used to denote a minor or low-ranking official, as in the idiom *minions of the law,* meaning police officers.

Word 25: INVETERATE (in-VET-ur-it)
Fixed in a habit or custom, firmly established by habit or practice.

Synonyms of *inveterate* include *confirmed, deep-rooted, long-standing, chronic, dyed-in-the-wool, ingrained, habituated* (huh-BICH-oo-ay-tid), *inured* (i-N[Y]UURD), and *incorrigible* (word 44 of this level).

Inveterate comes from the Latin *inveterātus,* of long standing, firmly rooted, established, the past participle of *inveterāre,* to age, become old, and is related to the noun *veteran.* In modern usage, *inveterate* applies chiefly to an unpleasant, offensive, or even evil habit, custom, attitude, or feeling that has been fixed or settled for so long that it cannot be changed, improved, or eradicated. We speak of inveterate drug use, an inveterate liar, inveterate child abuse, or inveterate hostility between families.

Word 26: EXTOL (ek-STOHL)
To praise highly.

Extol comes from the Latin *extollĕre,* to raise, lift up, and *extol* once had this literal meaning in English, as in this line from a book of psalms published in 1549: "Unto thee Lord I extoll, And lift my soule and minde." But since the early 16th century *extol* has also meant "to raise high with praise" (*OED*), and that is the only modern meaning of the word.

Synonyms of *extol,* to praise highly, include *glorify, magnify, exalt, laud* (rhymes with *Maude*), *eulogize* (YOO–luh–jyz), and *panegyrize* (PAN-i-juh-ryz). You may extol or laud a person or thing in private or in public, in writing or in speech, and in formal or informal language. But *eulogize* and *panegyrize* apply chiefly to formal, lofty, public expressions of praise, usually on some solemn occasion such as a funeral or inauguration.

Antonyms of *extol* include *discredit, disparage, denounce, denigrate,* and *stigmatize* (STIG-muh-tyz), to brand as shameful, set a mark of disgrace upon. In 1712, Joseph Addison wrote in *The Spectator,* "To find Virtue extolled, and Vice stigmatized."

Word 27: GAFFE (GAF, rhymes with *laugh*)
A conspicuous mistake, obvious blunder; "an instance of clumsy stupidity" (*OED*).

Gaffe is an early 20th-century borrowing of the modern French *gaffe,* a blunder, especially the kind of blunder where you put your foot in your mouth. Beyond that the origin of the word is uncertain. In English *gaffe* may apply to any kind of obvious mistake, but it is most often applied to a conspicuous social blunder, and in this sense it is virtually interchangeable with another borrowing from French, *faux pas* (foh-PAH), which means literally a false step. Both *gaffe* and *faux pas* may apply either to saying the wrong thing (such as being rude or tactless) or to doing the wrong thing (such as violating a custom or a rule of etiquette).

Word 28: INDOCTRINATE (in-DAHK-tri-nayt)
To instruct in a particular doctrine, set of principles, or belief.

A *doctrine,* from the Latin *doctrīna,* knowledge, learning, that which is imparted by teaching, is something that is taught, specifically a system of belief laid down as true or a set of principles to follow.

To *indoctrinate* is to instruct in a *doctrine,* teach a specific way of thinking or believing.

To *instill,* to *imbue* (word 3 of this level), to *implant,* to *inculcate* (in-KUHL-kayt), and to *indoctrinate* all mean to teach or introduce into the mind. To *instill* and to *imbue* suggest gradual and usually gentle instruction: *to instill good values; imbued with a love of reading.* To *implant* may be gradual or swift, and suggests firmly fixing something (such as a principle, opinion, or desire) in the mind: *the first play he ever saw implanted in him a deep ambition to become an actor.* To *inculcate,* from the Latin *calcāre,* to tread on, trample, and *calx,* the heel, is literally to stamp with the heel, and so figuratively to impress or urge on the mind with persistent and often emphatic instruction, as *a training program known for inculcating discipline in its graduates.*

Our keyword, to *indoctrinate,* may mean to teach the basics or fundamental principles of something, but more often today it is used to mean to instruct in a particular way of thinking, often a biased point of view. For example, a person can be indoctrinated with political ideology or religious dogma.★ In this sense *indoctrinate* is close in meaning to *brainwash,* except that brainwashing involves coercion and sometimes force, while indoctrination usually does not.

Word 29: NUANCE (N[Y]OO-ahnts)
A slight difference or subtle variation, as in meaning, expression, feeling, tone, etc.; a subtle shading or distinction.

In one of its many senses, the word *nicety* (NY-suh-tee), a fine point, subtle or minute distinction, is a close synonym of *nuance.*

The English noun *nuance* is a direct borrowing from French, in which *nuance* means a shade or gradation of color, a hue. This modern French *nuance* goes back through the Middle French *nuer,* to shade, cloud, to the Latin *nūbēs,* a cloud. From the same source comes the unusual English adjective *nubilous* (N[Y]OO-bi-lus),

---

★ **Dogma** (DAWG-muh) is an authoritative doctrine or system of principles, especially one laid down by a church concerning faith and morals.

cloudy, foggy, or vague, obscure, indefinite, as *a dense, elaborate, nubilous style of writing.*

A *nuance* can be literal, as in French, and denote a slight variation in color, a shade or hue: "The room was unhappily decorated with every possible nuance of brown." More often, though, *nuance* is used figuratively of any slight difference or fine distinction. If you can discern a subtle shade of meaning, tone, expression, or feeling, that's a nuance. We speak of the nuances, or slight differences in meaning, between words, or the nuances of expression in a poem, a painting, or a dramatic or musical performance. Facial expressions and gestures can also have nuances. In his 1956 novel *Anglo-Saxon Attitudes,* Angus Wilson aptly uses *nuance* of social interaction: "She knew that every relationship had a hundred overtones, a thousand nuances that made it unique and utterly fascinating."

The adjective is *nuanced,* having delicate and subtle gradations of expression, tone, or meaning, as *a nuanced interpretation* or *a nuanced approach.*

Word 30: PLACATE (PLAY-kayt)
To soothe the feelings of, make less upset or angry.

Synonyms of *placate* include *pacify, appease, mollify, assuage* (uh-SWAYJ), *propitiate* (pruh–PISH-ee-ayt), and *conciliate* (kun–SIL-ee-ayt). Antonyms of *placate* include *alienate, offend, antagonize, estrange* (word 8 of Level 4), and *disaffect.*

Placate comes from the Latin *plācātus,* soothed, appeased, pacified, the past participle of the verb *plācāre,* to soothe, calm, quiet. In Latin, *plācāre* was akin to another verb, *placēre,* to please, be agreeable to, which is the source of the English word *placid* (PLAS-id), calm, free of disturbance, peaceful, tranquil, serene, as in this sentence from Philip Larkin's 1947 novel *Girl in Winter:* "The sea was so placid that only an occasional heave . . . showed she was not on land."

The meanings of these Latin verbs *plācāre,* to soothe, and *placēre,* to please, combine in the English verb *placate,* which implies soothing hurt or angry feelings by attempting to please. When you placate, you calm someone down by being agreeable or making concessions. The ancients placated their angry gods by offering them a sacrifice. A mediator of a dispute tries to placate both sides so they will come to an agreement.

The preferred adjective is *placatory* (**PLAY**-kuh-TOR-ee), serving or intended to placate, soothe the feelings of, make less upset, as *a placatory smile.*

Review Quiz for Keywords 21–30

Decide if the pairs of words below are synonyms or antonyms. **Answers appear on page 96.**

1. *Indefatigable* and *debilitated* are . . . synonyms or antonyms?
2. *Archetype* and *prototype* are . . .
3. *Veracity* and *mendacity* are . . .
4. *Minion* and *underling* are . . .
5. *Inveterate* and *habituated* are . . .
6. *Extol* and *stigmatize* are . . .
7. *Gaffe* and *faux pas* are . . .
8. *Inculcate* and *indoctrinate* are . . .
9. *Gradation* and *nuance* are . . .
10. *Irritate* and *placate* are . . .

The Style File: *None Is or None Are?*

"What's proper with the word *none*?" asks a correspondent on my website. "Should I say 'None of my friends *is* going' or 'None of my friends *are* going'? I believe that *none* is an old contraction of *not one*. If that's true then *none is* seems correct. But *are* seems more idiomatic. I'm confused."

What's confusing here, I responded, is that we continue to delude ourselves that because *none* comes from an Old English contraction that meant *not one* it must take a singular verb in modern English. But it is pointless and misguided to insist that *none* always means *not one* and therefore takes a singular verb, as in "None of the seats *was* empty." In such a context, *none* more often means *not any,* and idiom and customary usage call for a plural verb: "None of the seats *were* empty"; "None of the weapons *have* been found"; "None of the pictures *were* subject to the architect's approval" (*The New York Times Magazine*); and "None of my friends *are* going." The only time *none* must take a singular verb is when it means *no part,* as in "None of the debt *has* been paid."

Here are the next ten keywords in *Word Workout:*

Word 31: DEIFY (properly DEE-i-fy, *not* DAY-)
To make a god of, or to adore or worship as a god.

The noun is *deity* (DEE-i-tee, *not* DAY-), a god or goddess, or supreme being.

The verb to *deify* comes from the Late Latin *deificāre,* to make a deity, which in turn comes from the Latin *deus,* god, and the suffix *-ficāre,* the source of the English suffix *-fy,* which means either to make (as in *simplify,* to make simple, or *beautify,* to make beautiful) or to become (as in *solidify,* to become solid).

To *deify* first meant to make a god of, render godlike or divine, but later came to mean to treat as a god, regard as godlike, and that is the more common meaning of the word today. We typically deify celebrities and superstars. Dictators often insist, with force to back it up if necessary, that their people deify them, treat them as if they were a god or divinely inspired. And when my younger daughter, Judith, was fourteen she deified the pop singer Justin Bieber by dubbing herself a "Belieber" and turning her bedroom into a poster-filled shrine.

Synonyms of *deify* include *exalt, immortalize, consecrate* (word 42 of this level), and *apotheosize* (uh-PAH-thee-uh-syz, discussed under *apotheosis,* word 50 of Level 9).

Word 32: RECAPITULATE (REE-kuh-**PICH**-uh-layt)
To repeat or restate briefly; summarize.

Recapitulate comes from the Late Latin *recapitulāre,* to sum up, from *re-,* again, and *capitulum,* a division of a book, chapter. The English *chapter* also comes from *capitulum,* which in classical Latin meant a little head, from the Latin *caput,* the head, the source also of the English words *capital,* a place that is the head of government; *decapitate,* to cut off the head; and *capitulate,* to list the terms of surrender under various headings in a document. The Latin phrase *per capita* (pur-KAP-i-tuh) means by or for each person, literally by heads, as *the state with the lowest per capita income.*

By derivation, to recapitulate is to go back again to the head or top; in modern usage it means to go over the theme or principal points in a concise manner. The noun *recapitulation* may be a brief restatement, concise summary, or specifically in music, the third section of a composition in sonata form, after the exposition and development, in which an earlier theme is repeated in somewhat different form.

To *reiterate* (ree-IT-ur-ayt) and to *recapitulate* both mean to repeat or restate. But *reiterate,* from the Latin *reiterāre,* to repeat, means to say or do something again or repeatedly, often insistently or in a tiresome manner. To *recapitulate* is never insistent or tiresome and always implies briefly repeating or reviewing so as to summarize. Poor speakers reiterate their message, say it again in an unoriginal way. Good speakers recapitulate their main points, summarize or briefly restate them, at the end of a speech.

The word *recap* (REE-kap) is an informal, shortened form of both the verb to *recapitulate* and the noun *recapitulation.* A TV news program can recap the day's events or provide a recap of the day's events.

Word 33: LUMINARY (LOO-mi-ner-ee)
An important person who is a source of light or inspiration to others.

Luminary comes from the Latin *lūmen, lūmĭnis,* light, the source also of the English words *luminous,* full of light, shining, brilliant; *luminosity,* the quality or state of being bright or luminous; and *lumen,* a unit of light or the rate of transmission of luminous energy. There is also a rare adjective *luminary,* pertaining to light.

The noun *luminary* began life in English meaning something that gives off light, especially a celestial body such as the sun or moon, and for centuries the phrase "the luminaries" has meant the sun and moon. But for just as long the word has been used in a figurative sense of an important or prominent person who for others is "a source of intellectual, moral, or spiritual light" (*OED*).

What's the difference between a leader and a luminary? A leader is a person who shows or tells others what to do or where to go. A leader may play a helping role, as a guide or conductor, or a leader may have power and control, as a manager or commander. By contrast, a luminary does not actively lead but sets an example for others through brilliant achievement. A luminary is a source of light in the world and an inspiration to others. Rosa Parks was a luminary of the civil rights movement; the Colombian writer and Nobel laureate Gabriel García Márquez is a luminary of Latin American literature; and James D. Watson and Francis Crick, who discovered the structure of DNA, are two of modern science's greatest luminaries.

Word 34: CONFOUND (kun-FOWND)
To confuse, perplex, bewilder, throw into confusion or disorder.

Synonyms of the verb to *confound* include to *astound, mystify, baffle, rattle, dumbfound, flabbergast, nonplus* (nahn-PLUHS, word 14 of Level 3), and *disconcert* (dis-kun-SURT).

Confound comes from the Latin *confundere*, to pour together, mix up, and so to confuse, throw into disorder. In modern usage *confound* still hews closely to this derivation, for the word is used chiefly to mean to mix up or confuse. For example, *confound* may mean to mix up in the mind so as to be unable to discern the difference between, as *to confound fantasy with reality*. It may mean to mix up or mingle so that the elements cannot be distinguished, as *a turbulent crowd of protesters confounded in all ways but in their collective outrage*. Perhaps most often, it may mean to throw the mind or feelings into confusion or disorder, render unable to speak or act, as *her reply caught him off guard and confounded him*.

Confound is also used as a mild curse or imprecation (IM-pruh-**KAY**-shin, word 50 of Level 6) in the old-fashioned and now chiefly British expression *confound it* (or *confound him, her, them,* etc.), in which *confound* means to damn or send to hell.

Word 35: SOJOURN (SOH-jurn)
To remain or live in a place for a while, stay temporarily.

You can see part of the word *journey* in *sojourn* because both words incorporate the French *jour,* a day, which comes from the Latin *diurnus,* belonging to or lasting for a day, the source of the English adjective *diurnal,* daily, happening each day, as *diurnal kitchen chores* or *the diurnal rotation of the earth.* By derivation a journey is a day's travel, while to sojourn is to spend a number of days—a few or many—in a place: "They sojourned in Italy for the summer."

A *sojourn* is a visit, temporary stay: *a sojourn in a strange land.* And a *sojourner* (SOH-jur-nur) is a person who stops or stays for a while in a place and then moves on.

Word 36: ASKEW (uh-SKYOO)
Crooked, slanted, distorted, out of line or proper position.

Straight, even, and *direct* are antonyms of *askew.*

The verb to *skew* means either to turn aside, swerve, or to distort, slant, represent unfairly so as to give a false impression, as *to skew the data in their favor. Askew* combines the verb to *skew* with the prefix *a-,* which was often used to form an adverb or adjective from a noun or verb, as in *asleep, ashore, aside, afoot, aglow,* and *ablaze.*

The three words *askew, awry* (like *a rye*), and *askance* (rhymes with *the pants*) all imply a lack of straightness, evenness, or directness. *Askance* may mean indirectly, obliquely, with a sideways glance, but more often it is used with verbs such as *look, view,* and *eye* to mean with disapproval, suspicion, or mistrust: "She looked askance at her son's dubious financial transactions." *Awry* suggests a twisting or turning to one side: "The wind had blown her hat awry"; figuratively, it suggests a turning away from the right course, position, or order: "When the dastardly Parlabane crashed the wedding, everything went awry." *Askew* suggests a lack of alignment and may be used of anything that is slanted, uneven, or distorted in some way, as in this line from Charles Dickens's 1856 novel *Little Dorrit:* "lattice-blinds all hanging askew."

Word 37: HISTRIONIC (HIS-tree-**AH**-nik)
Overly dramatic; excessively affected or emotional.

Histrionic comes from the Latin *histrionicus,* of or pertaining to the theater, from *histrio(n),* an actor, and the word has also long been used to mean of or relating to actors or acting, as *the histrionic art* or *the histrionic tradition.* But *histrionic* has come to be used more often of any behavior that is overly dramatic or emotional. A histrionic performance, whether onstage or not, is exaggerated, full of showy, feigned emotion. The same is true for the plural *histrionics,* which once meant simply acting but now is almost exclusively used of exaggerated emotional behavior designed to attract attention, as *a quarrelsome city council prone to histrionics and hissy fits.*

The words *dramatic, theatrical, melodramatic,* and *histrionic* all refer to acting or to behavior that resembles acting.

Dramatic is the most general and least negative word, and applies to "that which is emotionally striking and exciting," says *Crabb's English Synonymes,* "in which the normal effect of action and feeling is heightened and emphasized without transcending the bounds of reality." Unlike the other three words, *dramatic* does not suggest exaggeration or artificiality. Anything that stirs the emotions or the imagination can be dramatic: a movie, a novel, a daring rescue at sea, or even a family dinner can be dramatic, characterized by heightened or intense feeling and action.

Theatrical may be used neutrally to mean of or pertaining to the theater, but the word often "implies something falsely dramatic," says *Crabb's,* in which "the effect does not arise naturally, but is created simply by a method of presentation," usually one characterized by elements—such as manner of speaking, gestures, and facial expressions—that are suggestive of the stage and plainly artificial. In the 1939 film *The Wizard of Oz,* the actor Frank Morgan plays several characters—including the Wizard—with charming theatrical brio. (*Brio,* pronounced BREE-oh, comes from the Italian *brio,* fire, life, and means vigor, liveliness, enthusiasm.)

Melodramatic takes *theatrical* to the next level of exaggeration and pretense. Formed from the Greek *melós,* song, melody, and *dramatic, melodramatic* means like a *melodrama,* a dramatic form characterized by exaggerated emotions and an emphasis on plot and action rather than on character development. If a story is portrayed in an overly emotional way, with a sensational plot and characters who overstate their feelings, it's melodramatic.

Our keyword, *histrionic,* suggests excessive theatricality. It applies to any behavior that is deliberately affected so as to have an overly dramatic effect, and especially to an extravagant or flamboyant display of emotion: *the histrionic wailing of the widow at her husband's grave.*

Word 38: COALESCE (koh-uh-LES)

To grow or come together, unite, blend, merge, combine into one mass or body.

Synonyms of the verb to *coalesce* include *fuse, amalgamate* (uh-MAL-guh-mayt), and *commingle* (kuh-MING-gul, kuh- as in *commence* and *commit*).

The verb to *coalesce* comes from the Latin *coalescere,* to grow together, become one, the source also of the English word *coalition,* a union, alliance.

Coalesce may be used of people or groups of people to mean to unite, come together as one, form a whole, as *hostile tribes that put aside their differences and coalesced into a nation.* Or it may be used of things, either living, as *malignant cells can coalesce into a tumor,* or abstract, as *the writer's random thoughts eventually coalesced into a novel.*

Coalescence is the noun. The adjective is *coalescent.*

Word 39: LISTLESS (LIST-lis)

Showing no interest or effort, lacking energy or desire.

Listless comes from Middle English and combines the archaic word *list,* which meant pleasure, joy, or desire, appetite, with the suffix -*less,* without, devoid of. By derivation, that which is listless is without pleasure, devoid of desire, and so lacking energy or interest.

Since the 17th century—when the British physician Nathaniel Fairfax, in his *Philosophical Transactions,* wrote, "He was ever a listless, dull, and melancholy fellow"—*listless* has been used both of people and of things to mean lacking energy or desire. To do something in a listless manner is to do it with as little effort and as little concern as possible. We speak of listless students, listless readers, or a listless audience, meaning that they show no interest or effort. A person in a listless mood has no desire to act, a person with a listless handshake offers you a limp and lifeless hand, and a person with a listless mind has no intellectual energy or curiosity.

Synonyms of *listless* include *sluggish, spiritless, indolent* (word 48 of Level 4), *lethargic, languid, phlegmatic* (fleg-MAT-ik), *apathetic, impassive,* and *indifferent.* All of these words suggest a lack of energy or desire, or a lack of interest or concern, or both.

Word 40: ABATE (uh-BAYT)

To lessen, diminish, reduce in amount, force, degree, or intensity.

Synonyms of the verb to *abate* include to *decrease, weaken, subside, wane,* and *ebb.* Antonyms of *abate* include *increase, intensify, swell, amplify, magnify,* and *redouble,* as "They redoubled their efforts to find the lost child."

Abate comes from Middle English, Old French, and Latin words meaning to beat or knock down, and in the approximately eight hundred years since the word entered English, this forceful origin has gradually abated, been reduced or lessened, so that *abate* now means to diminish in various ways. You can abate a tax by lessening or suspending it. You can abate a nuisance, make it less troublesome, by reducing or removing it. You can abate the cost of something by reducing or subtracting from it. You can abate your appetite, curb or decrease it, or abate your pain, reduce its amount or intensity. And used intransitively (meaning that the verb does not perform its action directly on something), *abate* can mean to weaken, diminish, subside, lose force or intensity, as *eventually the storm abated* or *his drunken fury will not soon abate*.

Review Quiz for Keywords 31–40

In each statement below, a keyword (in *italics*) is followed by three definitions. Two of the three are correct; one is unrelated in meaning. Decide which one doesn't fit the keyword. **Answers appear on page 96**.

1. To *deify* is to exalt, exhume, glorify.
2. To *recapitulate* is to sum up, spell out, review briefly.
3. A *luminary* is a prominent person, respected person, unusual person.
4. To *confound* is to belittle, perplex, confuse.
5. To *sojourn* is to stay temporarily, vacation, live in exile.
6. Something *askew* is distorted, crooked, untrustworthy.
7. *Histrionic* means extremely sloppy, extremely emotional, extremely dramatic.
8. To *coalesce* is to come together, work together, unite.
9. *Listless* means sluggish, vivacious, languid.
10. To *abate* is to diminish, decrease, discontinue.

A Little Latin Is a Lovely Thing

And now for a few words about a dead language: Latin.

Good old *veni, vidi, vici* (WAY-nee, WEE-dee, WEE-kee). *I came, I saw, I conquered.* That famous Latin sentence was penned by Julius Caesar after his victory over Pharnaces (FAHR-nuh-seez), king of Pontus, in 47 B.C. It's the only sentence I can remember from my two years of high school Latin, during which I came, I saw, and I stumbled. How I struggled with that twisted syntax and rigid grammar toward a miserable C− and, the next year, a slightly less miserable C+. I never made it over the *pons asinorum* (PAHNZ AS-i-**NOR**-um), the asses' bridge, which *Webster 2* defines as "a critical test of ability imposed upon the inexperienced or ignorant."

But looking back, I don't regret a minute of it. Why? Because learning some Latin is one of the best ways to build your knowledge of English. Latin may be a dead language, but its soul lives on in thousands of English words—not a few of which you have already come across in *Word Workout.* In medicine, literature, philosophy, theology, science, and law, Latin words and phrases abound. But dozens of Latin phrases have also made their way into everyday English.

For example, *caveat emptor* (KAY-vee-at, KAV-ee-at, or KAV-ee-aht EMP-tor or EMP-tur) means let the buyer beware. In business, caveat emptor is the principle that the seller of a product cannot be held responsible for defects in quality or workmanship unless the product carries a warranty. *Pro bono,* short for *pro bono publico* (proh BOH-noh **POO**-bli-koh), means for the public good. *Quid pro quo* (KWID proh **KWOH**) means literally something for something; a *quid pro quo* is something given in return for something else, an equal exchange, a tit for tat.

Pro tempore (proh-TEM-puh-ree) means temporarily, for the time being; it is often abbreviated *pro tem,* as in an official title: chairman of the board pro tem. *Sine qua non* (SIN-ay kwah **NOHN**) means literally without which not; it refers to something necessary or indispensable: "Their cooperation was the sine qua non in the success of this project." And then there's the familiar *vice versa* (VY-suh-VUR-suh), which has nothing to do with *vice,* corruption, depravity (word 1 of Level 1). This *vice* comes from the Latin *vicis,* a change, turn, alternation, and the phrase means conversely, with the order flipped.

There are also many English abbreviations derived from Latin: *i.e.* stands for *id est,* which means that is or namely; *e.g.* stands for *exempli gratia,* which means for example; *q.v.* stands for *quod vide,* meaning which see; and *cf.* stands for *confer,* meaning *compare.* Then there's the common *etc.,* which stands for *et cetera* and should always be pronounced et-SET-uh-ruh, never ek-SET-uh-ruh. And don't say or write *and etc.,* which is redundant.

I could go on with these Latin phrases *ad infinitum* (ad-in-fi-NY-tum), forever, or *ad nauseam* (ad-NAW-zee-um), until it makes you nauseated, but instead I'll close by saying *verbum sat sapienti est* (WAIR-buum saht SAH-pee-**EN**-tee EST), which means a word to the wise is enough.

And now, because *tempus fugit* (TEM-p<u>u</u>s FYOO-jit), time flies, it's time to get back to the *Word Workout* vocabulary for another ten keyword discussions.

Word 41: PONDEROUS (PAHN-dur-<u>u</u>s)

Large and heavy, weighty, or hard to handle because of great size and weight.

Synonyms of *ponderous* include *massive, bulky, cumbersome,* and *unwieldy.*

Ponderous comes from the Latin *pondĕrōsus,* heavy, weighty, which comes in turn from the noun *pondus,* a weight, mass, burden, literally a weight used in a pair of scales. From *pondus* English has also inherited the verb to *ponder,* to weigh in the mind, contemplate, meditate, consider deeply, and the noun *pound,* a unit of weight, also a monetary unit used in the United Kingdom, so-called because before we used paper money people would weigh precious metals such as gold and silver to determine their monetary value. That's why we have expressions like *he is worth his weight in gold.*

Ponderous may be used in a number of ways, all of which suggest weight or heaviness. It may be used to mean heavy with meaning or importance, serious, profound, as *ponderous thoughts* or *ponderous words.* It may be used of movement to mean heavy and slow, deliberate, as *their ponderous trek up the mountain.* And it may be used of style or expression to mean heavy and dull, boring, labored, as *the ponderous lecture put her to sleep.* But perhaps most often *ponderous* is used to mean large and heavy, weighty, as *a ponderous giant of a man,* or hard to handle because of great size and weight, as *ponderous suitcases* or *a ponderous tome.* (A tome—rhymes with *home*—is a large and heavy book, especially a scholarly or learned one.)

Word 42: CONSECRATE (KAHN-suh-krayt)
To make or declare sacred, or to regard as worthy of great respect or reverence.

To *consecrate* comes from the Latin *consecrare,* to dedicate to the service of a god, which comes in turn from *sacrare,* to make holy, and *sacer,* holy, the source of the English words *sacred, sacrifice,* and *sacerdotal* (SAS-ur-**DOH**-tul), priestly or pertaining to the priesthood, as *sacerdotal functions* or *sacerdotal garments.*

The verb to *hallow,* to make holy or sacred, comes from Old English and is a close synonym of *consecrate.* Abraham Lincoln used both *consecrate* and *hallow* for rhetorical emphasis in the Gettysburg Address, delivered during the Civil War on November 19, 1863, at the dedication of the national cemetery at Gettysburg, Pennsylvania: "But, in a larger sense, we cannot dedicate—we cannot consecrate—we cannot hallow—this ground. The brave men, living and dead, who struggled here have consecrated it far above our poor power to add or detract."

Word 43: FLORID (FLOR-id or FLAH-rid)
Elaborately or overly decorated, flowery, showy.

Synonyms of *florid* include *flamboyant, ornate,* and *ostentatious* (AHS-ten-**TAY**-shus). Antonyms include *simple, plain, natural, homely,* and *unaffected.*

The adjective *florid* comes from the Latin *flōrĭdus,* flowery, blooming, which comes in turn from the verb *flōrēre,* to bloom, flower. The southeasternmost state in the United States, Florida, is literally the flowery state.

When *florid* entered English in the mid-1600s, it was used in several ways. It could mean consisting of flowers, floral, as *the florid glories of spring.* It could mean covered with or abounding in flowers: *a florid backyard.* It could mean flushed with red, rosy, ruddy, as *a florid complexion.* And it could mean elaborately decorated as if with flowers, full of flowery ornaments, as *a florid speech.* Of these four senses only the latter two have survived, and the last is the more common of the two.

Today you will often see *florid* used of style, composition, or expression to mean flowery, showy, overly adorned. Florid writing is excessively elaborate, overly rhetorical, "full of fine words and phrases" (*OED*). Florid architecture is highly embellished, full of showy decoration and elaborate details. And in music, *florid* is used of any highly decorated passage, especially one that elaborates a theme stated earlier in a simpler form.

Word 44: INCORRIGIBLE (in-KOR-ij-uh-bul or in-KAHR-)
Not capable of being corrected or improved; especially, of a person, bad beyond correction or reform.

Incorrigible combines the privative prefix *in-*, not, with the unusual English word *corrigible,* capable of being corrected or reformed, which comes from the Latin *corrigĕre,* to correct, reform, make straight. That which is incorrigible is either so bad that it cannot be made better or so firmly fixed that it cannot be changed or controlled. We speak of incorrigible children whose behavior is so unruly that it is beyond correction or control, incorrigible criminals who are so depraved that they are beyond hope of reform, and incorrigible habits that are so ingrained they cannot be altered or broken.

Synonyms of *incorrigible* include *irreformable, unmanageable, inveterate* (word 25 of this level), *willful, delinquent,* and *depraved.*

Word 45: ASSAIL (uh-SAYL)
To attack violently, either physically or verbally.

The verb to *assail* comes from the Late Latin *adsalīre,* which combines *ad,* to, and *salīre,* to leap, spring, jump. Since the 13th century, when it entered English, *assail* has meant to leap or jump on, "especially with hostile intent" (*OED*). A person may be assailed either physically, as *they assailed him with vicious blows,* or verbally, as *the critics mercilessly assailed her new novel.* Whether physical or verbal, *assail* always implies a vigorous or vehement attack with a forceful effect: *thunderous music assailed their ears; the prosecutor assailed the defendant with pointed questions.*

The words *attack, assault, accost,* and *assail* are close in meaning.

Attack is the most general and implies initiating hostilities or conflict of any kind. You can attack physically or verbally, with weapons or with words. To *assault* is to attack physically and suddenly in an attempt to overpower, and it almost always implies unlawful, hand-to-hand violence. Thus, an army attacks but a robber or a rapist assaults.

To *accost* means to approach and speak to, often in an aggressive manner: *accosted by a stranger.* The word is sometimes used to imply force or violence, but this is merely a confusion with *assault;* a panhandler or a police officer can accost you on the street without laying a hand on you. So take care to use *accost* only to mean to approach abruptly and challenge in some way.

Our keyword, *assail,* implies wearing down an opponent's resistance by attacking repeatedly, either with physical violence or with vehement words. A boxer can assail an opponent with repeated jarring blows, and the reputations of celebrities are often slanderously assailed in the tabloid press. The noun is *assailant* (uh-SAYL-int), an attacker, a person who assails.

Word 46: ELIXIR (i-LIK-sur)

A medicinal drink or potion; specifically, a sweetened liquid containing alcohol that is used as a vehicle to administer a medicinal substance, such as a tincture of herbs.

Elixir is a very old word, dating back to the 14th century and the poetry of Geoffrey Chaucer, who wrote *The Canterbury Tales.* At the time it entered English—coming through medieval Latin and Arabic ultimately from a Greek word meaning a drying preparation for wounds—*elixir* was used in the pseudoscience of alchemy of a substance or preparation capable of turning base metals into gold. The word was soon applied to any drug, preparation, or liquid supposed to be able to indefinitely prolong life.

In the 17th century *elixir* came to mean a cure-all, a remedy for all diseases and difficulties, a synonym of *panacea* (PAN-uh-**SEE**-uh), from the Greek *pan-,* all, and *akos,* cure. In this sense *elixir* became associated with the quack medicines or nostrums commonly sold by the proverbial snake oil salesman or mounte-bank. (A *nostrum* [NAHS-trum] is a remedy of dubious effective-ness, and a *mountebank* [MOWN-tuh-bangk] is a person who mounts a bench or platform and delivers a flamboyant sales pitch to attract customers and hawk wares of dubious value.)

Today you may use *elixir* to mean any medicinal drink or con-coction, especially one supposed to do wondrous things—such as change ordinary metal into gold, prolong life or youth, or mi-raculously cure ailments and diseases.

Word 47: IMPRESARIO (IM-pruh-**SAHR**-ee-oh)
A producer or sponsor of public entertainment, especially the organizer or manager of an opera, ballet, or concert.

Impresario comes directly from the Italian *impresario,* one who un-dertakes a business, a contractor. The word originally referred to someone who manages an opera, ballet, or symphony orchestra, and this meaning is still current. But increasingly *impresario* is being used of a producer, organizer, or sponsor of any kind of public en-tertainment, as *a literary impresario, a Broadway impresario, a pop music impresario,* or *a TV impresario.*

Word 48: SENTIENT (SEN-shint, *not* SEN-tee-int)
Aware, conscious, capable of feeling or perceiving with the senses.

The noun is *sentience* (SEN-shints), feeling, sensation, awareness.

Sentient and *sentience* come from the present participle of the Latin verb *sentire,* to feel, perceive, experience. The antonym of *sentient* is *insentient* (in-SEN-shint), lacking perception, incapable of feeling, unconscious. Two related words from the same Latin source are *sensate* (SEN-sayt), having physical sensation or per-ceived by the senses, and *insensate* (in-SEN-sayt), lacking sensation, feeling, or consciousness: *insensate stone.*

Sentient often appears in the phrase *sentient being,* as "We must learn to live in harmony with all sentient beings." A sentient be-ing is a conscious being, a creature capable of feeling through the senses, whether human or animal.

Word 49: LACKLUSTER (LAK-lus-tur)
Lacking brilliance or energy, dull, boring, lifeless.

Synonyms of the adjective *lackluster* include *mediocre, uninspired, colorless, drab,* and *monotonous.*

The noun *luster* comes from the Latin *lustrāre,* to make bright, and has three common senses. It may mean sheen, gloss, polish, a shine from reflected light, as *the luster of precious stones* or *the luster of polished wood.* It may mean radiance, brilliance, brightness, as in this line from Charles Dickens's novel *Barnaby Rudge* (1841): "The sun was shining with uncommon luster." And it may be used figuratively to mean brilliant distinction or merit, glory, excellence, as *an award that added luster to her reputation.*

Lackluster combines the verb to *lack,* to be without, be in need of, and the noun *luster,* polish, excellence, brilliance. That which is *lackluster* is without excellence, in need of polish, lacking brilliance or energy, and therefore mediocre, uninspiring, lifeless. You can use *lackluster* of anything that fails to shine or stand out, either literally, as *lackluster eyes* or *her lackluster evening gown,* or figuratively, as *a lackluster performance* or *a lackluster essay.*

Word 50: BENEFICENT (buh-NEF-i-sint, *not* buh-NIF-)
Marked by goodwill and charity, serving a kind and worthy purpose.

The familiar adjective *beneficial,* the less familiar noun *beneficence* (buh-NEF-i-sints), and the adjective *beneficent* all come from the Latin *bene,* well, and *facere,* to do. *Beneficial* means helpful, having a good purpose, conferring benefits: *beneficial insects; beneficial advice. Beneficence* is the act or practice of doing good, kindness, charity, and *beneficent* means doing good, charitable, serving a kind and worthy purpose, as *a beneficent influence* or *the nonprofit organization's beneficent goals.*

The combining forms *bene-* and *male-* (MAL-uh-) are antonyms, and both come from Latin—*bene-* from the aforementioned *bene,* well, which is akin to *bonus,* good; and *male-* from *male,* badly, ill, which is akin to *malus,* evil, bad. Whenever you see a word beginning with *bene-* or *male-* you can safely assume it denotes some quality or thing that is good or evil. Thus, a bene-diction, from *bene-*, well, and *dicere,* to speak, is a speaking well of, an expression of good wishes, a blessing, while a malediction, from *male-*, badly, and *dicere,* to speak, is a speaking evil of, a curse. Like-wise, a benefactor, from *bene-*, well, and *facere,* to do, is a person who does good, especially through charitable giving, while a malefactor, from *male-*, badly, and *facere,* to do, is a person who does harm or evil, a criminal. And that which is beneficent, marked by goodwill and charity, is the opposite of that which is maleficent (muh-LEF-i-sint, *not* muh-LIF-), harmful, evil, malicious.

Review Quiz for Keywords 41–50

In this quiz the review word is followed by three words or phrases, and you must decide which comes nearest the meaning of the review word. **Answers appear on page 97**.

1. If something is *ponderous,* is it large and heavy, hard to explain, or lively?
2. When you *consecrate* something, do you make it permanent, make it sacred, or make an exception for it?
3. Is something *florid* colorful, warm, or overly decorated?
4. If you are *incorrigible,* are you unhappy, unmotivated, or unmanageable?
5. When you *assail,* do you attack, plead, or question?
6. Is an *elixir* a prophecy, a potion, or a mystery?
7. Is an *impresario* a producer, a salesperson, or a performer?
8. Are *sentient* beings harmless, unresponsive, or conscious?
9. Is something *lackluster* old, imperfect, or mediocre?
10. Is something *beneficent* beautiful, kind, or perfect?

Difficult Distinctions: *Famous* and *Infamous*

In a book by a well-known writer I once saw the phrase "Mom's infamous recipe for pumpkin soup," in which one mischosen word turned the meaning of the phrase around. Something *famous* is well known for its good or desirable qualities; a famous person is

WORD WORKOUT 94

outstanding or distinguished in some way, and therefore admired. But something *infamous* (IN-fuh-m<u>u</u>s) is remarkable for its bad qualities and bad reputation; it is notorious, scandalous, disgraceful, or evil. Thus, a family with a famous recipe for soup would cherish that recipe for generations, while a family with an infamous recipe for soup would have a hard time filling the chairs at the dinner table.

Difficult Distinctions: *Shined* and *Shone*

Consider this sentence from a contemporary novel: "When the sun shined directly on the bricks, they seemed to jump from the building and hang together in the air, like a red sheet, hovering." What's wrong with it?

The verb to *shine,* meaning to polish or to aim a beam of light, is transitive, which means it acts on something. You shine your shoes or shine a flashlight. But the verb to *shine,* meaning to emit light, be radiant, or to stand out, excel, is intransitive, which means it performs its action on its own, without an object: the sun shines, a diamond necklace shines, and a virtuoso musician can give a performance that shines.

But what do you do when you want to say that something was shining in the past? Do you write *the sun shined* or *the sun shone*? The past tense and past participle of the transitive *shine* is *shined,* so you *shined* your shoes yesterday. But the past tense and past participle of the intransitive *shine* is *shone,* so the sun, that necklace, and that virtuoso musician shone. This sentence, from Mark Davidson's *Right, Wrong, and Risky,* illustrates the proper use of *shined* and *shone:* "While Jonathan *shined* his shoes in preparation for proposing to Rosie, he noticed that the moon *shone* brightly."

Answers to Review Quizzes for Level 2
KEYWORDS 1–10

1. No. A *diatribe* is speech or writing that is bitter and abusive.
2. Yes. An *evocation* is the act of summoning or calling forth, and poems are often evocations of a poet's emotions.

3. No. To be obsessed is to be excessively preoccupied with something. *Imbue* means to saturate, soak deeply, or to influence or inspire deeply, as if by soaking.

4. No. Something *repugnant* is disgusting, offensive, and never pleasing.

5. No. Flattery may be insincere, but it is always complimentary. *Insolent* means boldly insulting and disrespectful.

6. No. *Impunity* means freedom from penalty or punishment.

7. No. When something *stagnates,* it stops moving and either becomes stale or foul or ceases to grow or develop.

8. Yes. *Emblematic* means symbolic, representative.

9. Yes. To human ears many birdcalls sound *plaintive,* mournful, melancholy, expressive of sadness or sorrow.

10. Yes. *Rapacious* means greedy, predatory, aggressively seizing what one wants.

KEYWORDS 11–20

1. False. A *peon* is an unskilled laborer, a person of low social status.

2. False. To *intuit* is to know or understand instinctively, without deduction or reasoning.

3. False. To *opine* is to have or express an opinion, especially a formal opinion.

4. True. To *languish* means to be or become weak or feeble, to be neglected or ignored, to suffer hardship or live in oppressive conditions, or to long for.

5. True. *Vestigial* means being, or pertaining to, a remnant or trace of something that has disappeared, been lost or destroyed, or that no longer survives.

6. True. *Somnolent* means tending to cause sleep or inclined to sleep, or drowsy, sleepy, heavy with sleep.

7. False. To *supplant* is to take the place of, replace, overthrow.

8. False. *Euphemism* is the substitution of a milder, more agreeable word or expression for one considered unpleasant, blunt, or offensive.

9. True. *Visceral* means of or pertaining to the gut or belly; hence, guided by instinct or intuition rather than by the mind or reason.

10. False. *Dispassionate* means having no strong emotion or bias; not personally or emotionally involved.

KEYWORDS 21–30

1. Antonyms. *Debilitated* means weak, exhausted, worn out. *Indefatigable* means tireless, never lacking energy, not capable of being fatigued.

2. Synonyms. An *archetype* is an original model, form, or pattern after which all things of the same kind are copied, or on which they are based. A *prototype* is usually an original model of a mechanical invention.

3. Antonyms. *Mendacity* is untruthfulness, lying. *Veracity* is truthfulness, accuracy.

4. Synonyms. A *minion* is a servile follower or assistant, an underling.

5. Synonyms. *Inveterate* means fixed or firmly established in a habit or custom.

6. Antonyms. To *stigmatize* is to set a mark of disgrace upon. To *extol* is to praise highly.

7. Synonyms. A *gaffe* is a conspicuous mistake, obvious blunder, faux pas.

8. Synonyms. To *indoctrinate* means to instruct in a particular doctrine, set of principles, or belief; to inculcate.

9. Synonyms. A *nuance* is a slight difference, a subtle variation, gradation, or distinction.

10. Antonyms. To *placate* is to soothe the feelings of, make less upset or angry.

KEYWORDS 31–40

1. *Exhume,* to dig up, doesn't fit. To *deify* is to make into or treat as a god, exalt, glorify.

2. *Spell out,* to explain in detail, doesn't fit. To *recapitulate* is to review or restate briefly, sum up.

3. *Unusual person* doesn't fit because it's too vague. A *luminary* is an important, prominent, respected person who is a source of light or inspiration to others.

4. *Belittle,* to make less of, doesn't fit. To *confound* is to confuse, perplex, bewilder.

5. *Live in exile* doesn't fit. To *sojourn* is to remain or live in a place for a while.

6. *Untrustworthy* doesn't fit. *Askew* means crooked, slanted, distorted.

7. *Extremely sloppy* doesn't fit. *Histrionic* means overly dramatic or emotional.

8. To *work together* doesn't fit. To *coalesce* is to unite, blend, merge, come together.

9. *Vivacious,* high-spirited, energetic, doesn't fit. *Listless* means showing no interest or effort, lacking energy or desire.

10. *Discontinue* doesn't fit. To *abate* is to lessen, diminish, decrease.

KEYWORDS 41–50

1. Something *ponderous* is large and heavy, or hard to handle because of its size and weight.

2. To *consecrate* is to make or declare sacred, or to regard as worthy of great respect or reverence.

3. Something *florid* is flowery, showy, overly decorated or elaborate.

4. *Incorrigible* means irreformable or unmanageable.

5. To *assail* is to attack violently, either physically or verbally.

6. An *elixir* is a medicinal drink or potion.

7. An *impresario* is a producer or sponsor of some public entertainment.

8. *Sentient* means aware, conscious, capable of sensation or feeling.

9. Something *lackluster* has no energy or brilliance, and is therefore mediocre and dull.

10. *Beneficent* means serving a kind and worthy purpose, charitable.

LEVEL 3

Word 1: TRIBULATION (TRIB-yuh-**LAY**-sh<u>i</u>n)
Great distress, trouble, or suffering, or a cause of great distress or trouble, a trial.

Synonyms of *tribulation* include *misery, anguish, adversity, affliction, oppression, persecution, calamity,* and *woe.*

Tribulation comes from the Latin *trībulāre,* to press, squeeze, also to oppress, afflict. This Latin verb comes in turn from the noun *trībulum,* a sledge—a strong, heavy sled—used for threshing grain. The *trībulum,* says *The Century Dictionary,* consisted of "a wooden block studded with sharp pieces of flint or with iron teeth." Imagine what it would be like to be threshed by a *trībulum* and you probably won't forget that *tribulation* means great distress or trouble or a cause of great distress or trouble.

Incidentally, English has some homegrown expressions that evoke the tribulation of being threshed by a *trībulum. To put through the mill,* or *to go through the mill,* comes from the days when grain was ground by millstones. Today we use this expression to mean to subject or be subjected to severe hardship or distress, as if we ourselves could be ground up in a mill. We use the expression *to put* (or *go*) *through the wringer* in the same way—the wringer in this case being a machine with rollers used to squeeze liquid out of wet clothing.

Tribulation dates back to the 14th century and the poet Geoffrey Chaucer, who wrote in *Troilus and Criseyde,* a love poem, "Myn herte is now in tribulacion." Life certainly has its pleasures and its moments of joy, but it also has plenty of tribulation, and the Bible,

not surprisingly, is filled with it: "In the world ye shall have tribulation, but be of good cheer" (John 16:33); "Rejoicing in hope,
patient in tribulation" (Romans 12:12); "Who comforteth us in all
our tribulation, that we may be able to comfort them which are in
any trouble" (2 Corinthians 1:4).

Tribulation may mean great distress or trouble, or it may mean
a cause or instance of great distress or trouble, a painful trial, as *he
endured the humiliating tribulation of a fraternity hazing.* The word also
often appears in the expression *trials and tribulations,* as *the trials and
tribulations of motherhood.* This common pairing is both a cliché and
redundant, and careful writers avoid it. Other common and redundant pairings that careful writers avoid include *if and when, unless and
until, compare and contrast, first and foremost, various and sundry,* and *each
and every.*

Word 2: DERIDE (di-RYD)
To ridicule, make fun of, laugh at scornfully or contemptuously.

Synonyms of the verb to *deride* include *mock, jeer, flout, scoff, taunt,
gibe, heckle,* and *lampoon* (lam-POON). A person who derides, ridicules, makes fun of, is a *derider;* the noun *derision* (duh-RIZH-in)
is the act of deriding, ridicule, mockery; and the adjective *derisive*
(di-RY-siv, *not* di-RIS-iv) means expressing derision, mocking,
scornful, contemptuous.

Deride comes from the Latin verb *dērīdēre,* to laugh at, mock,
scorn, make fun of. *Dērīdēre* combines the Latin prefix *de-,* which
in this case serves to intensify the meaning, and *rīdēre,* to laugh,
the source of the English words *ridicule, ridiculous,* and, from the
Latin past participle *rīsus,* the word *risible* (RIZ-i-buul), provoking
or capable of provoking laughter, as *a risible face* or *risible remarks.*

The verb to *ridicule* "implies a deliberate [and] often malicious
belittling," says *Merriam-Webster's Collegiate Dictionary.* In other
words, someone who ridicules you not only wants a laugh at your
expense but also wants to put you down, make you look bad in
front of others. The verb to *deride* "suggests contemptuous and
often bitter ridicule," says the *Collegiate.* Thus, when you ridicule
you make fun of in a deliberately mean way, but when you deride

you take ridicule to a nastier level, making fun of someone or something in a sneering, condescending way.

Word 3: NEFARIOUS (ne-FAIR-ee-us)
Extremely wicked, infamously evil.

Nefarious comes from the Latin *nefārius,* wicked, vile, abominable, which comes in turn from the noun *nĕfas,* a sin, crime, abomination, offense against divine law. By derivation, that which is nefarious is horrible or evil because it violates our moral code.

Nefarious has been used in English for more than four hundred years to describe people, things, or deeds that are extremely or unspeakably wicked. We speak of a nefarious plot, a nefarious crime, nefarious activities, a nefarious cult, or a nefarious tyrant. The word may also be used without modifying a following noun, as in *something nefarious is afoot.*

Synonyms of *nefarious*—and there are many because human beings have such a long and regrettable history of being wicked—include *villainous, sinful, vicious, heinous* (HAY-nis), *abominable, atrocious, diabolical, depraved, egregious* (i-GREE-jus), *flagitious* (fluh-JISH-us), *odious, execrable,* and *iniquitous* (i-NIK-wi-tus; *iniquity* is word 2 of Level 4).

Word 4: IDEOLOGUE (EYE-dee-uh-lahg *or* -lawg)
A zealous, uncompromising advocate or follower of an ideology.

Ideologue is built from two combining forms, or word-forming elements: *ideo-,* idea, and *-logue,* which comes from the Greek *lógos,* word, and designates either a type of speaking—as in *dialogue* (a speaking, *dia-,* across) and *prologue* (a speaking, *pro-,* before)—or, much less often and in this case, a person. By derivation, then, an *ideologue* is an "idea person," but specifically a person who is passionately or even fanatically devoted to an ideology.

While the word *ideology* can be neutral, denoting "a set of beliefs governing conduct" (*OED*), the word *ideologue* usually has a pejorative, or negative, connotation, suggesting an overly opinionated person who adheres to and promotes a set of beliefs in a fervent, uncompromising way. If you are older than about ten, no doubt you have encountered ideologues of all stripes: political, social, economic, religious, racial, artistic, scientific, and so on. And because the world is full of people who hold passionately and rigidly to a set of beliefs, or to a theory or doctrine, we will probably forever look upon those who do not agree with us, or who refuse to compromise with us, as ideologues, never realizing that we may be ideologues ourselves.

Word 5: DALLIANCE (DAL-ee-ints)
Frivolous play, especially amorous toying or flirtation.

In modern English, to *dally* may mean to delay, waste time, dawdle, or it may mean to act playfully in a flirtatious or frivolous way. A dalliance is an act of dallying in this latter sense, a flirtation or playful, trifling involvement. The word is traditionally applied to love affairs, especially brief affairs in which one or both participants have no interest in a serious relationship. For example, the tabloid press takes great interest in the dalliances of celebrities, and the dalliance between President Bill Clinton and Monica Lewinsky was perhaps the most scandalous in American history. But *dalliance* may also be used of any frivolous involvement with or trifling interest in something. For example, a person can have a dalliance with fame or politics or drugs, or a foreign language; the world of fashion often has dalliances with styles from bygone eras; and a brutal dictator, under pressure from the free world, may have a dalliance with democratic reform.

Word 6: FATUOUS (FACH-oo-us)
Silly, foolish, idiotic.

Fatuous entered English in the mid–1600s directly from the Latin *fatŭus,* which had the same meaning—silly, foolish, idiotic. Like its Latin source, *fatuous* may be used either of people or of things. Someone can have a fatuous smile or simply be fatuous. An idea, an argument, or a question can be fatuous. And there is no shortage of fatuous television shows these days. But perhaps the arena in which *fatuity* (fuh-T[Y]OO-i-tee, the noun) flourishes the most is the online world, where fatuous comments and posts and tweets abound.

The words *witless, inane, asinine, sophomoric,* and *fatuous* all suggest foolishness, silliness, and stupidity.

Wit is often used to mean a sense of humor, and a person who is a clever talker with a quick sense of humor is often called a wit. But in its most basic sense, *wit* denotes intelligence, understanding, mental capability. Thus to be a *halfwit* or *dim-witted* is to be foolish, stupid, an imbecile. And to be *witless* is to be without wit altogether, completely lacking intelligence or understanding, as *a witless bore* or *witless small talk*.

Inane (i-NAYN, rhymes with *insane*) comes from the Latin *inānis,* empty, void, and is most often used in English to mean empty of sense or substance, devoid of meaning or intelligence, and therefore silly, frivolous, pointless: *an inane conversation*.

Asinine (AS-i-nyn) comes from the Latin word for an ass, *asĭnus,* and means "having the qualities by which the ass is characterized: obstinate, stupid, doltish" (*OED*). Asinine behavior or speech is not only stupid but stubbornly, idiotically stupid; *The Random House Dictionary* says the word also suggests "a lack of social grace or perception."

Sophomoric (SAHF-uh-**MOR**-ik) may mean of or pertaining to a sophomore, a student in the second year of high school or college, but more often it is used disparagingly to mean characteristic of the traditional sophomore: intellectually pretentious, conceited, and immature: "John was nauseated every time Marty opened his mouth in class to offer yet another sophomoric comment."

Our keyword, *fatuous,* is distinguished from the more general words *silly, foolish,* and *stupid* by suggesting not only dim-witted pointlessness but also smug self-satisfaction. The fatuous person is unconsciously silly, foolishly conceited, or self-importantly stupid. "Here's something that did end today," writes Richard Valeriani in *The Huffington Post.* "Donald Trump's fatuous, laughable flirtation with running for president."

Word 7: MEANDER (mee-AN-dur)
To proceed by winding and turning, take an indirect or intricate course.
Also, to wander aimlessly or idly, ramble.

The verb to *meander* comes from the ancient name of a river in
Asia Minor (now called Büyük Menderes) that follows a winding
and wandering course as it flows west through one of the world's
most fertile valleys and empties into the Aegean Sea.

Meander can be used of people or things that wind, turn, or take
an indirect or intricate course. For instance, a train can meander
through mountains, and a crack can meander across a ceiling. Visitors to a museum can meander through its galleries, and travelers
with time on their hands can meander along the streets of an unfamiliar city. *Meander* can also be used figuratively of any sort of
idle wandering or rambling. Your thoughts can meander, a speaker
can meander from one topic to another, and young people often
meander for a while before discovering what they want to do
in life.

When you *wander* you go from place to place often without a
plan or purpose: "She was alarmed by all the creepy people wandering the streets at night." When you *roam* you travel or wander
freely, often out of restlessness or curiosity: "The bird-watchers
roamed the countryside, on the lookout for rare specimens."
When you *ramble* you wander for pleasure without caring where
you go: "As children, they loved to ramble through the fields on
summer days." When you *rove* you go from place to place usually
for a specific reason: "The frigate roved the seas in search of enemy warships." When you *range* you wander over a large area,
like cattle on the prairie, or you cover a lot of ground: "A fascinating discussion that ranged over many topics." When you
traipse (rhymes with *drapes*) you go from place to place without
finding what you seek or reaching your goal: "They traipsed all
over America looking for a bagel like the ones they loved back in
New York." And finally, when you *meander* you wander idly,
taking a winding, indirect course: "Footpaths that meander
through verdant woods and beside bubbling brooks." (*Verdant* is
word 48 of Level 1.)

Word 8: CULPABLE (KUHL-puh-bul)
Guilty, blameworthy, responsible; deserving blame, reprimand, or punishment.

Synonyms of *culpable* include *reprehensible, censurable* (SEN-shur-uh-bul), and *peccable* (PEK-uh-bul), liable to sin or do wrong, the opposite of the more common *impeccable,* incapable of sin, unable to do wrong.

   Culpable comes from the Latin *culpābilis,* guilty, blameworthy, from *culpāre,* to blame, accuse, and *culpa,* fault, blame. The Latin phrase *mea culpa* (MAY-uh KUHL-puh or -KUUL-puh), which means literally "my fault, I am to blame," has been used in English for centuries to acknowledge guilt or responsibility for an error. *Mea culpa* may also be an acknowledgment of guilt: "His speech was a public mea culpa."

   Any act for which you can be blamed, punished, or found responsible is something for which you can be culpable. Have you ever made an illegal left turn because you didn't see the road sign prohibiting it? That kind of mistake, a blameworthy act that could have been avoided had you known something that you didn't know, is called "culpable ignorance." Although *guilty* and *culpable* are in general interchangeable, *guilty* is the stronger word and usually applies to serious crimes, while *culpable* usually applies to lesser offenses involving misconduct or negligence.

Word 9: SEDATE (si-DAYT)
Calm, quiet, composed, unexcited, undisturbed by passion.

Synonyms of *sedate* include *unruffled, placid, serene, sober, unperturbed,* and *staid* (pronounced like *stayed*). Antonyms of *sedate* include *excited, frantic, high-strung, frenzied, disconcerted, perturbed* (to *perturb* is word 25 of Level 6), *ruffled,* and *overwrought.*

   The adjective *sedate,* calm, quiet, comes from the Latin *sēdāre,* to calm, soothe, settle, a verb akin to the Latin *sedēre,* to sit, the source of the English words *sedentary, sediment, supersede,* and *sedulous* (word 28 of Level 7). *Sedate* is also a verb used in medicine to mean to calm or quiet by administering a *sedative,* a drug designed to soothe nervousness or excitement, a tranquilizer. *Sedation* is the state of being calmed or settled down by a sedative. All these words also come from the same Latin *sēdāre,* to calm, soothe, settle.

The adjective *sedate* may refer to something that is untroubled or undisturbed, as *a safe, sedate neighborhood.* The word is also often applied to that which is solemn or dignified by nature or design, as *sedate architecture, sedate music,* or *a sedate, soft-spoken old lady.*

Word 10: IMPROPRIETY (IM-pruh-**PRY**-i-tee)
The state or quality of being improper, incorrectness or inappropriateness.

Impropriety, which comes from the Latin *improprius,* unsuitable, combines the privative prefix *im-,* not, and *propriety,* appropriateness, suitability, conformity with a rule or custom: "Elsie questioned the propriety of the gruff and sometimes hostile way in which her husband, Max, spoke to the solicitors who knocked on their door." Thus, impropriety is a lack of propriety, and refers to something improper, incorrect, or inappropriate.

Impropriety may be used of something unsuitable, as the impropriety of wearing informal clothing to a funeral. It may also be used of unsuitable or incorrect behavior: "Harold tried to teach his two young sons, to no avail, that licking their soup bowls was an inexcusable impropriety." But *impropriety* is perhaps most often used of unseemly, indecent, or illegal behavior: "After a lengthy investigation, the company was sued for financial impropriety"; "We must at all costs avoid the appearance of impropriety."

Impropriety is also often used of an improper or unacceptable use of language. For example, it is an impropriety to pronounce *mischievous* in four syllables (mis-CHEE-vee-us) instead of the proper three (MIS-chi-vus), or to say "I feel *badly*"—which means you don't do a good job of feeling—instead of the correct "I feel *bad.*"

Review Quiz for Keywords 1–10
Consider the following questions and decide whether the correct answer is yes or no. **Answers appear on page 145.**

1. Would a tribulation be hard to endure?
2. When you deride someone, do you make fun of that person?
3. Would a nefarious person be inclined to help others?
4. Would an ideologue be willing to compromise?
5. If two people have a long, unhappy affair, is that a dalliance?
6. Is a fatuous speaker likely to be boring?
7. Does a meandering speaker stick to the main point?
8. If you are culpable, are you blameless?
9. Is an ideologue likely to be sedate?
10. Would the appearance of impropriety be a good thing for your reputation?

The Style File: Me, Myself, and I

Consider the following phrases and decide which ones use *myself* correctly and which do not: "someone like myself"; "for my wife and myself"; "neither Joshua nor myself"; "myself and a few other folks"; "Mr. Smith, Ms. Jones, and myself."

If you guessed that all of them are wrong, you're right. *Myself* is continually misused for *me* and *I*. Some attribute this mistake to a desire to sound sophisticated; others claim the misuser is affecting modesty. Whatever the motivation, the source of the problem is British English.

In *The New Fowler's Modern English Usage*, a style guide geared toward British English, R. W. Burchfield says using *myself* to mean *I* is "beyond reproach," as long as *myself* is placed after the other elements in the sentence. He even offers one of his own published sentences to illustrate the point: "This booklet . . . [was] undertaken by Professor Denis Donoghue, Mr Andrew Timothy and myself." To Burchfield, "the rift between myself and Lord Hailsham" is bad British English, but "his nervousness communicated itself to Isaac and myself" is good British English. He fails to note, however, that both are objectionable in American English. For years American usage experts have railed against using *myself* for *I* and *me*, and 88 percent of the *American Heritage Dictionary's* usage panel finds it unacceptable in the sentence "The boss asked John and myself to give a brief presentation."

In American English there are only two proper ways to use *myself*: intensively, for emphasis, as in *I did it myself* or *I myself have been there;* or reflexively, to turn the action back on the grammatical subject, as in *I dressed myself* or *I will exclude myself.*

So when the actor Harrison Ford, of Indiana Jones fame, says that "Steven Spielberg, George Lucas, and *myself* are agreed on what the fifth adventure will concern," he's wrong; it should be "Spielberg, Lucas, and *I* are agreed . . ." And when a trustee of the University of California writes, in a letter to the editor, "I assure you that no one, including . . . *myself,* was anything other than candid and frank," he's also wrong; it should be "no one, including . . . *me.*"

Are you ready for another ten keyword discussions? Here they are:

Word 11: MEGALOMANIA (MEG-uh-loh-**MAY**-nee-uh)

A mental disorder characterized by exaggerated feelings of greatness or power; in a general sense, an obsession with doing grand, extravagant things.

Megalomania is the medical term for what in lay terms* is often called *delusions of grandeur* (GRAN-jur). A *megalomaniac* is a person afflicted with megalomania, an exaggerated and often delusional belief in one's own importance, or an obsession with grandiose ideas or plans. Adolf Hitler was a megalomaniac who thought he could rule the world, and in literature, Captain Ahab, in Herman Melville's 1851 novel *Moby-Dick,* was a megalomaniac obsessed with hunting down the white whale.

Megalomania is a combination of two Greek-derived combining forms: *megalo-,* large, great, grand; and *-mania,* unreasonable or excessive enthusiasm. *Megalo-* appears in the English *megalopolis* (MEG-uh-**LAHP**-uh-lis), a large, densely populated area consisting of several adjoining cities and suburbs; in *megalocardia* (MEG-uh-luh-**KAHR**-dee-uh), enlargement of the heart; and in the rare word *megalopod* (MEG-uh-luh-pahd), which incorporates the

---

* **Lay** in the sense used here is an adjective that means pertaining to the laity (LAY-i-tee), the people who do not belong to a given profession or specialized field, nonprofessionals.

combining form -*pod,* foot, and means a person with very large feet. The combining form -*mania* appears in many words for delusions and obsessions, including *bibliomania,* a passion for books (the combining form *biblio-* means book); *Anglomania,* a passion for England and all things English; *trichotillomania* (TRIK-uh-TIL-uh-**MAY**-nee-uh), a compulsion to pull out one's hair; and *bruxomania* (BRUHKS-uh-**MAY**-nee-uh), compulsive grinding of the teeth.

Word 12: VOCIFEROUS (voh-SIF-ur-<u>us</u>)
Crying out noisily; making a loud and vehement outcry; uproarious.

Vociferous comes from the Latin *vōcǐférāri,* to cry aloud, shout, the source also of the English verb to *vociferate* (voh-SIF-ur-ayt), to cry out loudly, shout, clamor, utter in a loud voice, as in this sentence from Emily Brontë's 1847 novel *Wuthering Heights:* "He entered, vociferating oaths dreadful to hear." The Latin *vōcǐférāri* comes in turn from *vocāre,* to call, and *vox, vōcis,* a voice, cry, call, the source of the English words *vocal,* pertaining to or produced with the voice, and *vocation,* a calling, an occupation that one feels called upon to pursue. The phrase *vox populi* (vahks PAHP-yuh-ly), borrowed directly from Latin, means the voice of the people, popular opinion.

   Boisterous, clamorous, strident, obstreperous (uhb-STREP-ur-<u>us</u>), *raucous* (RAW-k<u>us</u>), and *vociferous* all mean strikingly, insistently, or unpleasantly loud.

   Boisterous suggests the noise that comes from being rowdy or having fun: *a boisterous party. Clamorous* suggests noise that is loud and continuous: *clamorous music coming from next door. Strident* applies to noise that is disagreeably loud, harsh, and shrill; a piercing scream, screeching brakes, and the whining of a power tool are all strident. *Obstreperous* suggests noisiness accompanied by unruly behavior: *an obstreperous child; the obstreperous mob. Raucous* may suggest the noisy unruliness of *obstreperous* (*raucous laughter, a raucous crowd*) or the harshness and roughness of *strident* (*a raucous voice*). *Vociferous* applies to any noisy outcry, especially a prolonged and vehement one: "Republican Congressman Todd Akin's ill-advised comments about 'legitimate rape' sparked an immediate and vociferous response from liberals and conservatives alike."

Word 13: CONTRIVE (kun-TRYV)

To invent or devise with ingenuity; to design, plan; also, to manage, bring about by a plan, especially by some scheme or stratagem (word 10 of Level 1).

The verb to *contrive* suggests inventing, designing, planning, or managing in an ingenious or clever way. The word may be neutral, implying ingenuity of design or management, as *to contrive solutions for a difficult problem; the generals contrived a strategy for war;* or *a campaign contrived to win over people's hearts.* Or *contrive* may have a negative connotation, implying trickiness or deviousness in inventing something or making something happen, as *they contrived to defraud innocent people; the lovers contrived to meet secretly once a week;* or *a campaign contrived to strike terror in citizens' hearts.*

The participial adjective* *contrived* always has a negative connotation and means devised or planned in an obvious, artificial, forced way. A contrived answer is a bogus, insincere answer; a contrived plot is labored or strained; contrived interest is forced or fake interest; contrived outrage is sham outrage; and a contrived relationship is artificial and unconvincing.

The adjective *ill-contrived* means badly designed or planned, as *ill-contrived approaches to social reform* or *an ill-contrived project that was soon abandoned.*

Word 14: NONPLUS (nahn-PLUHS)

To puzzle or perplex completely; bring to a standstill; render utterly confused so as to be at a loss for what to say or do.

The verb to *nonplus* comes from the Latin phrase *nōn plūs,* not more, no further. This Latin phrase was first used in English in the late 16th century as a noun, stressed on the first syllable, to mean "a state in which no more can be said or done . . . a standstill" (*OED*). In modern usage, to be *in* or *at* a nonplus, or to *bring* or *reduce to* a nonplus, means to render utterly confused so as to be

---

* A partipical adjective is an adjective created from a verbal form, such as the present participle (which ends in -*ing*) or the past participle (which usually ends in -*ed*). Thus, in *his loving, devoted friend,* both *loving* and *devoted* are participial adjectives.

at a loss for what to say or do, as in this quotation from J. M. Dillard's 1989 novel *The Lost Years:* "Reduced to a perfect non-plus, McCoy half-rose from his chair."

The participial adjective *nonplussed*—which is the preferred spelling over *nonplused,* with one *s,* because the stress falls on the second syllable—has in recent years been used to mean unimpressed, undisturbed, undaunted, as in "[Bill] Gates seemed nonplussed by the Net until late 1995." This usage, which is perhaps a confusion of *nonplussed* with *unfazed,* is a slipshod extension of the word that should be avoided. *Nonplussed* is properly used, as *The New York Times Manual of Style and Usage* tells us, to mean "bewildered to the point of speechlessness," as in this citation from the *San Francisco Chronicle:* "At first, [Clint] Eastwood seemed to suck most of the excitement out of the convention center, leaving the crowd a bit nonplussed."

You may use *nonplus* whenever you mean to puzzle or perplex completely, confound (word 34 of Level 2), render speechless, bring to a standstill, as in this sentence from Louisa May Alcott's 1875 novel *Eight Cousins:* "Rose was one of the children who observe and meditate much, and now and then nonplus their friends by a wise or curious remark."

The rare word *nonplussation* means the state of being nonplussed, at a loss for what to say or do.

Word 15: IMPERIOUS (im-PEER-ee-us)
Domineering, overbearing, dictatorial, commanding.

Synonyms of *imperious* include *tyrannical, despotic* (word 43 of Level 1), *high-handed, supercilious, magisterial* (word 28 of this level), and *overweening* (word 46 of Level 6). Antonyms include *submissive, meek, passive, deferential, tractable* (TRAK-tuh-bul), which means willing to be led, and *acquiescent* (AK-wee-**ES-**int), which means willing to agree.

The adjective *imperious* comes from the Latin *imperiōsus,* commanding, possessing power, which in turn comes from *impĕrium,* command, power, mastery, the direct source of the unusual English word *imperium* (im-PEER-ee-um), which means either absolute power or an area of dominion, an empire. The better-known adjective *imperial,* pertaining to an empire or befitting the commanding aspect of an emperor or empress, and the familiar noun *empire* also come from the Latin *impĕrium.*

Imperious is most commonly used today to mean commanding in an arrogant, arbitrary, overbearing way, as in this sentence from *The New York Times:* "About a dozen members of WikiLeaks left that month, accusing Mr. Assange of imperious behavior and of jeopardizing the project . . ." A tyrant who rules with an iron fist, a domineering boss who rides roughshod over the employees, a dictatorial teacher who is condescending and overly demanding, a despotic parent who imposes unreasonable rules and metes out unfair punishment—all are imperious.

Imperiousness is the corresponding noun.

Word 16: PRIVATION (pry-VAY-shin)

A state of extreme hardship; specifically, a lack of food or other necessities for survival.

Privation comes from the classical Latin *prīvātĭo, prīvātiōnis,* a freeing from, taking away. Through the Latin verb *prīvāre,* which in a good sense means to free from and in a bad sense means to take away, strip of, *privation* is related to the English words *deprive,* to take away, remove; *private,* which by derivation means set apart from the state, and therefore individual; and *privative,* which means taking away, depriving.*

The words *privation* and *deprivation* (DEP-ri-VAY-shun) have often been used interchangeably to mean the act of depriving or the state of being deprived. But in modern usage *deprivation* is the ordinary word either for the taking away of something enjoyed (such as a possession, a position, or a privilege) or for a deprived condition (such as sleep deprivation or oxygen deprivation), while *privation,* the literary word, applies specifically to the state of being deprived of what is necessary for survival.

---

* For more on *privative* see the footnote under **dispassionate,** word 20 of Level 2.

To suffer privation is to live in a state of extreme hardship, where it is continually difficult to procure adequate food, clothing, and shelter. Privation is a heartrending consequence of poverty and political oppression, and it is often a tragic by-product of war. The science fiction writer Ray Bradbury (1920–2012) once wrote, "While our art cannot, as we wish it could, save us from wars, privation, envy, greed, old age, or death, it can revitalize us amidst it all."

Word 17: SUFFUSE (suh-FYOOZ)
To overspread; to fill or cover as with light, a liquid, or color.

Synonyms of *suffuse* include *imbue* (word 3 of Level 2), *infuse, permeate,* and *pervade.*

Suffuse comes from the Latin *suffūsus,* the past participle of *suffundere,* to spread through, steep, stain, cover, from *sub-,* under, and *fundere,* to pour.

Suffuse may apply to anything that is overspread or imbued with, or as if with, color, liquid, or light. For example, faces are often described as being suffused. A face suffused with rage is an angry, red face, and a face suffused with beauty is a lovely face. Elements in the natural world are also often described as being suffused. *The Century Dictionary* quotes the English poet Alexander Pope (1688–1744), who wrote, "When purple light shall next suffuse the skies"; and the English poet Matthew Arnold (1822–1888), who wrote of "Alpine meadows soft-suffused / With rain."

Word 18: DISCONSOLATE (dis-KAHN-suh-lit)
Extremely sad or unhappy, completely miserable, utterly discouraged or distressed.

Because unhappiness, misery, and distress are regrettably common emotional states, synonyms for *disconsolate* abound. If it is your heart that is disconsolate, deeply unhappy, you can be *downhearted, heartbroken, brokenhearted,* or *heavyhearted.* And if it's your mind that's disconsolate, utterly miserable or discouraged, you can be *sorrowful, melancholy, downcast, dejected, desolate, dispirited, despondent, inconsolable* (IN-kun-**SOH**-luh-bul), *forlorn, doleful,* or *lachrymose* (LAK-ri-mohs), a literary word that means tearful, mournful.

The verb to *console* (kun-SOHL) means to comfort, lessen someone's sorrow or trouble. It comes from the Latin *consōlāri,* to comfort, alleviate, the source also of the English noun *consolation,* something that comforts or the act of comforting: "The fruit-cakes and casseroles the neighbors left for Nancy after her husband's funeral were little consolation for her grief." *Disconsolate* combines the privative prefix *dis-,* which takes away or negates the meaning of the word that follows, with *consolation* to mean literally without comfort, and therefore miserable.

Whatever makes you feel extremely sad or hopeless makes you disconsolate. Losing a poker game or a tennis match may make you feel discouraged or distressed, but losing something important that you depend on, such as a job or a place to live, or losing a loved one, can make you disconsolate. Not surprisingly, unrequited lovers (because their love is *un-,* not, *requited,* returned in kind, reciprocated) are often disconsolate.

Word 19: CONUNDRUM (kuh-NUHN-drum)
A riddle or puzzle, the answer to which involves a pun or a play on words; also, any perplexing question or problem.

The origin of *conundrum* has been lost. Most authorities agree that it is pseudo-Latin, like the word *hocus-pocus,* which was originally used by jugglers and magicians. *Conundrum* may have been a slang term used in the 16th century by students at the great English universities, Oxford and Cambridge, and the *OED* suggests that it may have originated in a joke or a parody of Latin.

Funk & Wagnalls *Standard Dictionary of the English Language* defines *conundrum* as "a riddle founded on some odd resemblance between unlike things or their names, or some odd difference of like things or their names, often depending on a pun; as 'What kind of fruit does the electric plant bear?' 'Currents.'" One of my favorite books as a child was *Bennett Cerf's Book of Riddles,* a collection of conundrums presented in language suitable for young readers. The answer to each riddle, or conundrum, always involves an amusing and—at least for a child—unpredictable play on words. For example: "What goes up when the rain comes down?" "An umbrella." "What dog keeps the best time?" "A watchdog." "What gets lost every time you stand up?" "Your lap."

Although *conundrum* is still used to mean a riddle whose answer involves wordplay, current usage favors the more general sense of the word: any question or problem that puzzles or perplexes. There are all sorts of conundrums, from mathematical, technological, and metaphysical conundrums to ethical, financial, and legal conundrums. Sometimes just figuring out the right thing to do or say can be a conundrum, a perplexing question or problem.

You may come across *conundrum* used in the phrase *in a conundrum,* as in this sentence from the *Oshkosh Northwestern:* "With a No-Tipping law, customers would never again feel embarrassed or in a conundrum about tipping." Strictly speaking, this is a misuse, a confusion of *conundrum* with the words *dilemma, predicament,* and *quandary* (KWAHN-duh-ree). Those three words all refer to a complicated, perplexing situation from which it is hard to disentangle oneself, while *conundrum* properly refers to a complicated, perplexing question or problem. "One corpse. Nine names, but no identity," begins a story in the *Independent Online.* "This is the conundrum North West police are dealing with when they tried to identify a dead man by running his fingerprints through the system—and came up with nine different names and ages for him."

In addition to *riddle, puzzle,* and *mystery,* the noun *enigma* (i-NIG-muh)—something or someone hard to understand or explain—is a close synonym of *conundrum.*

Word 20: DOTAGE (DOH-tij)
Senility; the mental decline associated with old age, sometimes called *second childhood.*

Dotage comes from the Middle English *doten,* to behave foolishly, become feebleminded, and is related to the verb to *dote* (rhymes with *coat*), which may mean to exhibit the feeblemindedness of old age or to be foolishly fond of, bestow excessive attention on, as *a mother who dotes on her only child.*

Dotage can also mean excessive fondness or foolish affection, the act of doting on someone, but more often today it is used of the decline in mental ability associated with old age, or sometimes, loosely, of old age itself: "It seems a handsome male lead can be a handsome male lead well into his dotage, but there are fewer chances for beautiful female lead actresses to follow suit" (bbcamerica.com).

The expression *in one's dotage* means in old age, especially in the time of old age when the mental faculties decline, and the noun *dotard* (DOH-turd) is a person in his or her dotage, a feebleminded or foolish old person.

Review Quiz for Keywords 11–20

Consider the following statements and decide whether each one is true or false. **Answers appear on page 146.**

1. In Herman Melville's novel *Moby-Dick,* Captain Ahab suffers from megalomania; he is obsessed with hunting down the white whale.
2. The soft hum of a dishwasher or washing machine is vociferous.
3. When you contrive to do something, you try but don't succeed.
4. A person who has been nonplussed is likely to object vociferously.
5. It wouldn't be unusual for a megalomaniac to make an imperious remark.
6. Privation is the act of saving for a rainy day, frugality.
7. To suffuse is to use up completely, consume or devour.
8. Being unemployed for a long time could make a person disconsolate.
9. A conundrum is a complicated, perplexing situation.
10. People in their dotage often have exceptional mental powers.

Synonym Discrimination

The words *predicament, dilemma,* and *quandary*—mentioned in the discussion of *conundrum,* word 19 of this level—all apply to situations or conditions that are difficult and perplexing. A *predicament* is a difficult situation that is especially unpleasant or unfortunate: "Losing his job left Pete in a predicament." *Dilemma* is often used loosely of any difficult problem or troublesome situation, but in the best usage it is used only of situations in which one faces a choice between equally undesirable alternatives. When you're "damned if you do and damned if you don't," that's a dilemma. A *quandary* is a state of uncertainty or confusion that renders one unable to act. To be *in a quandary* means to be puzzled, full of doubts, and not sure what to do.

Let's return again to the *Word Workout* vocabulary.

Word 21: VACUOUS (VAK-yoo-u̲s)
Empty, without content or substance; hence figuratively, empty of ideas or intelligence.

Synonyms of *vacuous* meaning without content or substance include *blank, void, vacant, hollow, insubstantial,* and *depleted.* Synonyms of *vacuous* meaning lacking ideas or intelligence include *thoughtless, pointless, purposeless, expressionless, inane,* and *fatuous* (word 6 of this level).

The noun is *vacuity* (va-KYOO-i̲-tee), emptiness, absence, vacancy of matter or of mind, as in this quotation from Marion Harland's 1854 novel *Alone:* "She heard and saw all that passed; but in place of heart and sense was a dead vacuity."

The adjective *vacuous* comes from the Latin *vacuus,* empty, void, vacant, the source also of the English noun *vacuum,* a space devoid of matter, and the verb *evacuate,* to vacate, leave empty or void. Although *vacuous* may be used literally of something that is empty, as *he stood in the vacuous, echoing corridor of the vacant stadium,* today the word is far more often used figuratively to mean empty of ideas or intelligence, devoid of substance, sense, or interest. We speak of vacuous fools, a vacuous speech, a vacuous look or stare, vacuous reality TV shows, vacuous celebrities, vacuous novels, and—perhaps the most vacuous thing on earth—that horrible, ubiquitous, vacuous Muzak. (*Ubiquitous,* pronounced yoo-BIK-wi-tus, means existing or seeming to exist everywhere at the same time.)

When you think of the adjective *vacuous,* think of a vacuum cleaner sucking all the substance or intelligence out of something.

Word 22: INTEMPERATE (in-TEM-pur-it)
Without moderation, extreme or excessive, going beyond reasonable bounds.

The adjective *temperate* comes from the Latin *temperāre,* to exercise restraint, and means moderate, not excessive, keeping within reasonable limits, as *a temperate climate,* one with moderate temperatures, or *temperate criticism,* meaning criticism that is mild or moderate rather than extreme or violent. Tack the privative prefix *in-* onto *temperate* and you get its antonym, *intemperate,* lacking moderation, immoderate, excessive: "He was cautious in his writing but intemperate in his speech."

Intemperate may be used of anything that is extreme or goes beyond reasonable bounds, as *intemperate remarks* or *intemperate lust.* But it is also often used to mean excessively indulgent, going beyond reasonable limits to satisfy an appetite or desire, especially a desire for alcohol or drugs, as in this 1793 quotation from James Beattie's *Elements of Moral Science:* "Men habitually intemperate justly forfeit the esteem of their fellow-citizens."

The noun *temperance* may mean moderation, restraint, or abstinence from alcohol and drugs, while its antonym, the noun *intemperance,* may mean a lack of moderation or habitual indulgence in alcohol or drugs.

Synonyms of *intemperate* meaning without moderation, excessive, include *extravagant, uncontrolled, unbridled,* and *inordinate* (in-OR-di-nit). Synonyms of *intemperate* meaning overly indulgent include *besotted* (word 24 of Level 1), *dissolute* (word 7 of Level 6), *dissipated, wanton, profligate* (PRAHF-li-git), and *debauched* (the verb to *debauch* is word 30 of Level 5).

Word 23: STYMIE (STY-mee, rhymes with *try me*)
To obstruct, block, thwart, stand in the way of, present an obstacle to.

The precise etymology of the verb to *stymie* is uncertain, but we do know that its origin is probably Scottish and it is probably related to the ancient Scottish game of golf. Consult any dictionary and you will see that in golf the noun *stymie* denotes a situation in which a ball on the putting green obstructs the line of play of another ball on the green. From this notion of one player's golf ball blocking another player's putt it is easy to see how, since about 1900, we came to use *stymie* as a verb to mean to block or obstruct.

You can use *stymie* of almost anything that gets in the way, blocks progress, or thwarts success. In politics, a faction may try to stymie discussion of an issue so as to prevent a vote. In business, a company can try to stymie the competition, stand in its way, and a deep dip in the stock market can stymie, present an obstacle to, economic growth. Bureaucracy, informally called red tape, can stymie an attempt to gain approval for a construction project, and if the project is approved, a month of heavy rain can stymie work on it. Sportswriters commonly use *stymie* to mean to defeat, thwart the efforts of: "The Beavers used a suffocating defense to stymie Wisconsin 10–7."

Synonyms of *stymie* include *frustrate, hinder, hobble, impede, inhibit,* and *encumber* (word 29 of Level 1). Antonyms of *stymie* include *aid, promote, encourage, accelerate, facilitate, disencumber,* and *expedite* (EKS-puh-dyt), from the Latin *expedire,* to free from a snare, disentangle, hence to speed up or perform promptly.

Word 24: AMBROSIA (am-BROH-zhuh)
In ancient Greek and Roman mythology, the food of the gods, which made them immortal. Hence, something divinely sweet and pleasing to taste or smell.

Ambrosia comes directly from an ancient Greek word that meant both immortality and the food of the gods. It was "a celestial substance, capable of imparting immortality," says *The Century Dictionary,* "commonly represented as the food of the gods, but sometimes as their drink, and also as a richly perfumed unguent [an ointment or oil]." Because it was unclear whether ambrosia was only a food or also a drink, ambrosia is sometimes also called nectar, or the nectar of the gods.

When it is not used historically of the food of the gods, *ambrosia* is commonly used of something sweet and delicious to taste or smell. This use may be literal—there is a sweet dessert called ambrosia that is made with oranges, shredded coconut, and sometimes pineapple, nuts, and whipped cream or yogurt for dressing—or figurative, as *she inhaled the bouquet's intoxicating ambrosia* or *he tasted the ambrosia of her lips.*

The adjective is *ambrosial* (am-BROH-zhee-ul), which may mean either immortal, divine, worthy of the gods, or exceptionally sweet, delicious, or fragrant.

Word 25: VIVIFY (VIV-i-fy)

To give life or renewed life to, animate, stimulate. Also, to make more vivid or striking.

Synonyms of *vivify* include *energize, quicken, enliven,* and *vitalize.* Antonyms of *vivify* include *weaken, exhaust, debilitate, enfeeble,* and *enervate.*

Vivify comes from the Latin *vīvus,* alive, living, and *facere,* to make, and by derivation means to make more alive. From the same Latin *vīvus,* alive, and the verb *vīvĕre,* to live, be alive, come the English words *revive; vivid; vivacious* (word 15 of Level 1); and the legal term *inter vivos* (IN-tur VEE-vohs or VY-vohs), which means literally "between the living" and is used of gifts or trusts that take effect during the lifetimes of the parties involved.

Vivify can be used wherever the intended meaning is to give life to, stimulate, or to make more vivid, striking, or bright. Painters vivify with brilliant colors and bold brushstrokes. Biographers try to vivify the people whose lives they chronicle, making their words and experiences come alive again. The economy can be vivified, stimulated, given renewed life, by an increase in production and consumer spending. And bright sunlight can vivify a landscape, making it more clear and striking.

Word 26: PURLOIN (pur-LOYN)
To steal, make away with, take dishonestly, often by a breach of trust.

The verbs to *steal, rob, plunder,* and *loot* are usually used of serious crimes in which something valuable is seized or taken unlawfully, often with force or violence. By contrast, the verbs to *swipe, filch, pilfer, poach,* and *purloin* usually apply to petty theft in which something is taken secretly and often in a cunning or deceptive way.

To *swipe* and to *filch* both imply snatching something quickly while no one is looking: "She swiped some makeup from the drugstore"; "Every day the boy filched an extra cookie from the jar." To *pilfer* implies taking something repeatedly, usually in small amounts: "A clever fox was pilfering chickens from the henhouse." To *poach* is to trespass for the purpose of stealing game or fish: "They poached elephants for their ivory tusks." Our keyword, to *purloin,* often suggests breaching another's trust by taking something dishonestly for one's own purposes. In his *History of the English-Speaking Peoples* (1956), Winston Churchill wrote, "This son, by an act of bad faith which after many stormy years was to cost him his life, purloined a note which his father had preserved."

To *purloin* may also mean to plagiarize, to steal someone else's words or ideas and try to pass them off as your own. In *Roughing It* (1872), Mark Twain wrote, "It has been purloined by fifty different scribblers who were too poor to invent a fancy but not ashamed to steal one."

Word 27: BULWARK (BUUL-wurk, like *bull work*)
A powerful defense or protection, strong support or safeguard.

When *bulwark* came into Middle English in the first half of the 15th century it was used to mean a wall or mound of earth, stones, or other material used for defense, a rampart, fortification. "With bulwarks strong their city he enclosed," wrote the English poet William Cowper (KOO-pur) in his 1791 translation of Homer's *Odyssey.*

In the 16th century *bulwark* took on another meaning: a breakwater or seawall, as in this 1865 quotation from Sir Archibald Geikie's *Scenery of Scotland:* "To check the further ravages of the waves a stone bulwark was erected." And in the 19th century *bulwark* also came to be used of the low wooden wall running along the sides of a ship above the level of the deck. In his classic naval memoir *Two Years Before the Mast* (1840), Richard Henry Dana wrote, "Our ship had uncommonly high bulwarks and rail."

The figurative sense of *bulwark,* a powerful defense, strong support, came along in the late 16th century. It is in this sense that the word is commonly used today—to denote any important safeguard: a thing, idea, or person that protects or gives support in time of need. Here are some examples of this figurative use from news reports: "The Bombay High Court . . . has been a spectacular bulwark of freedom in independent India"; "The U.S. Fifth Fleet is based in Bahrain as a bulwark against Iran"; "The Amazon Basin, traditionally considered a bulwark against global warming, may be becoming a net contributor of carbon dioxide."

Bulwark may also be used as a verb to mean to safeguard, fortify, provide strong support or protection: "We offer strategies that can bulwark investments against uncertainty and increase chances of making a profit."

Word 28: MAGISTERIAL (MAJ-i-**STEER**-ee-ul)
Like or befitting a master or someone who speaks with authority; hence, authoritative, masterly, weighty, commanding.

The noun *magister* (MAJ-i-stur) is an old and formal word for a master; it comes directly from the Latin *magister,* a master. The adjective *magisterial* comes from the Latin *magisterialis,* of a magister or master.

Magisterial may be used in a neutral way to mean having or exhibiting the authority of a master, or displaying the skill of a master: *a magisterial work of scholarship; a magisterial speech; her magisterial debut on the concert stage.* Or, like *imperious,* word 15 of this level, *magisterial* may be used disparagingly of a person to mean domineering or dogmatic, forcing others to accept your opinions or follow your orders. The English philosopher John Locke used *magisterial* this way in 1690: "It would become us to be . . . less magisterial . . . and imperious, in imposing our own sense and interpretations."

Magisterial has one other meaning that should be noted. A *magistrate* (MAJ-i-strayt) is a justice of the peace, a minor judicial officer with limited jurisdiction. *Magisterial* is sometimes used to mean pertaining to or befitting a magistrate, as *a magisterial inquiry* or *a magisterial court.*

Word 29: TALISMAN (TAL-is-mun *or* TAL-iz-mun)
A charm, amulet; an object believed to have the magical power to ward off evil, bring good fortune, or influence how people act or feel.

Talisman, which came into English first through French, Spanish, and Italian, and before that Arabic, hails ultimately from the Greek *télesma,* a religious rite, consecration, which in turn comes from *telein,* to complete, fulfill, or perform a religious rite.

Historically a talisman is a stone, a ring, or some other small object that has been cut or engraved with supposedly magical letters, figures, or celestial images. "The talisman is supposed to exercise extraordinary influences over the bearer, especially in averting evils, as disease or sudden death," says *The Century Dictionary.* Since the 18th century *talisman* has also been used figuratively of anything believed capable of producing magical or miraculous results, or that exercises an extraordinary influence on human actions or emotions—in short, a good-luck charm.

Webster's New International Dictionary, second edition, says that the words *talisman, amulet,* and *charm* are often interchangeable, but *amulet* "applies especially to an object worn to avert evil," while *charm* can also be used of "a magical combination of words." *Talisman,* by contrast, "denotes wider and more positive powers," as suggested by this quotation from the 19th-century novelist and short story writer Nathaniel Hawthorne: "The little circlet of the schoolboy's copper coin . . . had proved a talisman, fragrant with good, and deserving to be set in gold and worn next [to] her heart."

Would you like to learn an unusual synonym of *talisman, amulet,* and *charm*? A *periapt* (PER-ee-apt), from *peri-,* around, about, and the Greek *haptein,* to fasten, is something worn to prevent or cure illness, to avoid bad luck, or to ward off spells.

Word 30: STUPEFY (STOO-puh-fy *or* STYOO-puh-fy)
To dull the senses of, make stupid or groggy, put into a daze, deaden.

The noun is *stupefaction* (ST(Y)OO-puh-**FAK**-shin), the state of being stupefied, groggy or dazed, or the act of stupefying, rendering insensible.

Synonyms of the verb to *stupefy* include *daze, bemuse, benumb,* and *stun,* all of which, says the *American Heritage Dictionary,* "mean to dull or paralyze the mental capacities with or as if with a shock." An unusual synonym of *stupefy* is *hebetate* (HEB-i-tayt), to make or become dull or stupid, from the Latin *hebes,* blunt, dull.

Stupefy comes from the Latin *stupefacĕre,* to render senseless, stun, a combination of two verbs: *stupēre,* to be struck senseless, astounded, stunned, and *facĕre,* to make. *Facĕre* is also the source of the common English suffix *-fy,* which is used in creating verbs that mean either to make or render, as in *clarify,* to make clear, and *simplify,* to render simple, or to become, as in *liquefy,* to become liquid. The Latin *stupēre* is also the source of the English words *stupid, stupendous,* and *stupor,* a severely dulled or senseless mental state, a daze.

To *stupefy* is to put into a stupor or daze, either with or as if with a narcotic, as *political rhetoric designed to stupefy the nation* or *stupefied with liquor.* The word is also often used to mean to shock, stun, astonish, as *stupefied by this sudden twist of fate.*

Stupefy is occasionally misspelled *stupify,* with an *i* instead of an *e* in the middle, no doubt through confusion with *stupid.* Take care not to make this mistake.

Review Quiz for Keywords 21–30

Decide if the pairs of words below are synonyms or antonyms.
Answers appear on page 146.

1. *Void* and *vacuous* are . . . synonyms or antonyms?
2. *Besotted* and *intemperate* are . . .
3. *Stymie* and *expedite* are . . .
4. *Ambrosia* and *nectar* are . . .
5. *Vivify* and *enervate* are . . .
6. *Purloin* and *pilfer* are . . .
7. *Menace* and *bulwark* are . . .
8. *Magisterial* and *imperious* are . . .
9. *Amulet* and *talisman* are . . .
10. *Stupefy* and *invigorate* are . . .

Difficult Distinctions: *Farther* and *Further*

"*Further. Farther,*" began the query on my website comments page. "Shall we just call the whole thing off, or can you specify their meanings?

No need to call the whole thing off, I responded. The distinction isn't hard to master. *Farther* is literal and refers to physical distances, while *further* is figurative and refers to every other kind of distance. Thus, you walk farther toward your destination, take physical steps toward it, but you figuratively take a step further toward your goal. You go farther down the road, not further. And while physical things can drift farther away from each other, people in bad relationships drift further apart.

Unfortunately, the British insist on confusing things by using *further* for both physical and figurative distance. And the Ford Motor Company isn't helping, either. During the 2013 Major League Baseball playoffs, Ford promoted its wares with the slogan *Go further.* Apparently the copywriters thought it would be a slick sales gimmick to merge the notions of physical and figurative distance. All I can say is, *Go figure.*

Here are the next ten keyword discussions in Level 3:

Word 31: RANCOROUS (RANG-kur-<u>us</u>)
Feeling or exhibiting deeply rooted hostility, bitterness, or resentment.

The adjective *rancorous* and the noun *rancor* (RANG-kur) come from the Latin *rancēre,* to be rotten or putrid (PYOO-trid), the source also of the English adjective *rancid* (RAN-sid), rotting, stinking, having a disgusting smell because of decomposition, as *rancid meat* or *rancid butter.* The noun *rancor* means bitter and long-lasting hostility or ill will, as in this 1767 quotation from a letter written by the Anglican clergyman John Wesley, who founded Methodism: "Such hatred, malevolence, rancor, bitterness, as you show to all who do not exactly fall in with your opinion was scarce ever seen." The adjective *rancorous* means full of or showing rancor, bitter ill will, malice.

Unlike *fury,* which builds to a fever pitch and explodes, and unlike *spite,* which suggests petty resentment or envy, *rancor* implies a deep-seated, long-lasting hatred or resentment that festers, causes bitterness and irritation, over time. Someone can feel rancorous anger for a wrong done years ago, or feel rancorous envy of someone who always gets the breaks but doesn't deserve them. Rancorous parents headed toward divorce often use their children as pawns in their ongoing rancorous drama. And many societies throughout the world have suffered for generations, even centuries, from rancorous divisions based on race, class, and religion.

Word 32: ENNUI (ahn-WEE)
Boredom, tedium; a feeling of weariness and discontent brought on by a lack of interest in what one is doing or a lack of something interesting to do.

Synonyms of *ennui* include *listlessness* (*listless* is word 39 of Level 2), *languor* (LANG-gur, discussed in *languish,* word 14 of Level 2), and *lassitude,* weariness, fatigue, a sluggish relaxation of body or mind.

Ennui comes from the French *ennui,* boredom, annoyance, tediousness. In modern usage *ennui* usually implies something deeper, more pervasive, and longer-lasting than *boredom* and *tedium,* which are often temporary. *Ennui* suggests a persistent state of mind, an enveloping world-weariness, a chronic fatigue with existence or boredom with the world and its material pleasures. Too much of the same thing—or of anything, good or bad—can get boring, and when the boredom and what causes it show no signs of going away, we lapse into ennui.

Wealthy people, who think they can afford everything, and fashionable people, who think they have seen everything, are often described as experiencing ennui, a world-weary dissatisfaction with all the privileges and creature comforts they enjoy. And these days many voters suffer from ennui, an overwhelming fatigue brought on by the constant sniping and divisiveness of political discourse.

Word 33: CENSORIOUS (sen-SOR-ee-<u>us</u>)
Severely critical, blaming or condemning harshly, expressing stern disapproval of.

The adjective *censorious* comes from the Latin *censōrĭus,* which meant relating to the *censor,* a Roman magistrate who administered the census, a tally of the population and an assessment of property. This ancient Roman *censor* was also charged with "the supervision of public morals" (*OED*), so the Latin *censōrĭus* also came to mean stern, rigid, severe, and the Latin *censor* also came to mean a severe judge or rigid moralist.

From this implication of severity and judgment we inherit the English word *censor* (SEN-sur). As a noun *censor* means a person who suppresses any material (in books, movies, radio and television programs, etc.) deemed objectionable, immoral, or offensive to the government. As a verb to *censor* means to suppress or delete something objectionable, as to censor a book by removing words or passages considered offensive.

From the related Latin word *censūra,* the office of a censor, comes the English *censure* (SEN-shur), which as a noun means strong disapproval or an official reprimand, and as a verb means to criticize harshly, find fault with, often through a formal proceeding, as to censure a member of Congress for unethical conduct.

Censorious suggests behaving like a censor, a rigid and severe judge, and the act of censuring—criticizing or condemning harshly. A censorious eye is an eye always on the lookout for something or someone to censure, to disapprove of sternly. A censorious society or censorious government suppresses any action or expression that it deems offensive or dangerous. And the censorious Hays Code—named for William Harrison Hays, president of the Motion Picture Producers and Distributors of America from 1922 to 1945—imposed strict moral guidelines for Hollywood movies.

Synonyms of *censorious* include *faultfinding, denunciatory, captious, carping,* and *vituperative* (vy-T[Y]OO-pur-uh-tiv).

Word 34: MARGINALIZE (MAHR-ji-nuh-lyz)

To remove from the mainstream, send to the border or outer edge; specifically, to force a person or group into an inferior, unimportant, or powerless role or condition.

A *margin,* in one of its many senses, is a border or edge, and specifically the space around what is printed or written on a page. The adjective *marginal* means pertaining to or placed at the margin, the border, edge, or outer limit. Thus, when you marginalize something, you place it in a marginal position, on the edges or outer limits, so as to ignore it or minimize its importance or influence. Usually it is unpopular, powerless, or controversial individuals or groups that are marginalized by the mainstream, which is always bent on maintaining stability and control. Artists and dissidents that challenge the status quo are often marginalized, and for much of American history the powers that be took pains to consolidate their power by marginalizing women and minorities.

The past participle *marginalized* may also be used as a noun to mean removed from the mainstream and placed in an inferior or powerless role or condition: "We all have work to do to put the marginalized, the hungry, and the homeless on the election agenda" (*Times* of London).

Word 35: REPROVE (ri-PROOV)

To criticize, scold, or correct gently; also, to express strong disapproval of, condemn.

The nouns *reproof* and *reproval* both mean the act of reproving, a criticism, correction, or expression of disapproval, as in this sentence from Sherwood Anderson's 1911 novel *Winesburg, Ohio:* "She . . . wrote down a series of sharp, stinging reproofs she intended to pour out upon him."

The verb to *reprove* comes from the Latin *reprobāre,* to condemn, reject, disapprove of strongly, the source also of the English word *reprobate* (**REP**-ruh-BAYT), which may be a noun, an adjective, or a verb. As a noun *reprobate* means a corrupt, unprincipled person, a scoundrel. As an adjective *reprobate* means morally abandoned, lacking all sense of decency and duty. And as a verb to *reprobate* is a strong synonym of *reprove* and means to condemn, disapprove of.

When you reprove, it may be relatively mild, a gentle and well-meaning scolding or correction, a figurative rap on the knuckles: "She was a gifted teacher who knew precisely when to reprove and when to console her students." Or *reprove* may imply harsher disapproval or condemnation: "The letter would reprove Moore for allegedly using his office for personal gain, dispensing favors, and bringing discredit against the House" (thehill.com).

Synonyms of *reprove* in the milder sense, to criticize or correct gently, include to *lecture, chide, admonish, caution, chasten* (rhymes with *hasten*), and *remonstrate* (ri-MAHN-strayt). Synonyms of *reprove* in the harsher sense, to express strong disapproval, include to *rebuke, reprimand, denounce, reproach, berate* (word 37 of Level 4), *upbraid, reprehend, revile* (word 43 of Level 4), *castigate,* and *censure* (discussed in *censorious,* word 33 of this level).

Word 36: RELEGATE (REL-uh-gayt)

To assign to an inferior or insignificant position, role, or condition: *outcasts relegated to the fringes of society.*

The verb to *relegate* comes from the Latin *relēgāre,* to banish, send away, and this was the meaning of the word when it entered English in the 16th century. Although this sense survives in historical contexts pertaining to banishment, the common meaning of *relegate* since the 18th century has been to remove to an inferior position or place, assign to an insignificant or obscure role: "Her noteworthy scientific contributions have sadly been relegated to the dust-heap of history"; "The teacher relegated her impertinent (word 20 of Level 1) pupil to a seat in the back of the room."

The verbs to *delegate* and to *relegate* have often been used interchangeably, but a useful distinction between them can and should be made. To *delegate* implies an assignment of equal responsibility, and means to entrust or deliver to another's care or management. You delegate your duties to someone you trust. To *delegate* may also be to appoint as an agent or representative to act in your stead: "Henry delegated Robert to speak for him at the council meeting." To *relegate* implies giving an inferior or insignificant assignment, placing in an obscure or unimportant position so as to put out of sight or mind: "The Balkans are dominated by patriarchal societies, in which men dictate morality and women are relegated to the home" (*The New York Times*).

Word 37: BEHEMOTH (bi-HEE-muth)
Anything of montrous size and power; a massive and mighty creature or thing.

Behemoth comes from a Hebrew word meaning a beast, but the *OED* notes that it may come ultimately from an Egyptian word that meant a water-ox and that was "assimilated in Hebrew mouths to a Hebrew form." That is perhaps why some dictionaries speculate that the original behemoth—mentioned in the Bible in the book of Job—was probably a hippopotamus.

"Behold now behemoth," begins Job 40:15; ". . . he eateth grass as an ox." His "bones are like bars of iron," "the mountains bring him forth food," he "drinketh up a river," and "none is so fierce that dare stir him up." I live in San Diego, California, and at our city's famous zoo they have a big pool that some very big hippopotamuses frolic in. I've seen these monstrous creatures up close and personal, and I can assure you they are behemoths—massive, powerful, practically toothless, and more than a little daunting when they sidle up to the glass and snort at you.

Chapter 41 of the book of Job introduces us to another formidable (FOR-mi-duh-buul, not for-MID-uh-buul) creature, leviathan (li-VY-uh-thin), a massive and menacing sea monster: "Canst thou draw out leviathan with a hook? . . . When he raiseth himself up, the mighty are afraid. The arrow cannot make him flee. . . . He laugheth at the shaking of a spear. . . . He maketh the deep to boil like a pot." From this language you can see how this biblical leviathan became the inspiration for the enormous white whale that Captain Ahab hunts obsessively in Herman Melville's 1851 novel *Moby-Dick*. Even the hefty novel itself is sometimes referred to as a leviathan: "Moby-Dick is the leviathan of American literature—a great white whale of a book that everyone has heard of but few have actually read" (*The Guardian*).

In modern usage the words *leviathan* and *behemoth* may be used of huge animals—*leviathan* of any huge sea creature, such as a whale, and *behemoth* of any huge land creature. But probably more often today these words are used figuratively of things that are immense, powerful, and intimidating. Massive buildings and giant corporations are often referred to as behemoths or leviathans. Enormous athletes, such as football players and weight lifters, are sometimes playfully called behemoths. And the *Titanic* was called a leviathan, until it sank.

Word 38: INCENDIARY (in-SEN-dee-er-ee)
Exciting passion; tending to inflame the emotions; stirring up violence or rebellion.

The adjective *inflammatory* (in-FLAM-uh-tor-ee), exciting anger, hostility, or disorder, is a close synonym of *incendiary*—which is not surprising because both words come from Latin verbs that meant to kindle, set fire to, inflame. Inflammatory comments ignite anger or resentment, while an incendiary speech kindles the sort of passionate emotion that can lead to bloodshed.

Incendiary may be used literally to mean pertaining to or involving arson, the intentional and malicious setting on fire of property or land. Or it may be used of anything designed to set property on fire, as *an incendiary device* or *incendiary bomb*. But more often *incendiary* is used figuratively to mean igniting or inflaming the passions, stirring up strife or controversy, especially in regard to social or political issues.

Incendiary ideas stir up people's emotions and disrupt the status quo. Incendiary publications disseminate incendiary ideas to ignite debate and shake up society. And incendiary radio shows and incendiary rallies feature incendiary rhetoric that is designed to inflame people's emotions and excite them to action. But, all too often, incendiary speech can be so strong and inflammatory that it leads to violence.

Incendiary may also be used as a noun to mean either an arsonist, a person who maliciously sets fires, or a person who sets people at odds with each other, an agitator, troublemaker, rabble-rouser, firebrand.

Word 39: STALWART   (STAWL-wurt, rhymes with *fall hurt*)
Stalwart has three senses in common use: (1) strongly built, sturdy, stout; (2) strong and brave, bold, valiant; and (3) strong in one's position or belief, firm, steadfast, resolute.

Perhaps you noticed that all three senses of the adjective *stalwart* involve strength. A stalwart person may be strong physically, or have a strong, brave heart, or have a strong, unwavering opinion or position.

A stalwart oak tree is solid and strong, and a stalwart football player is big and strong. A stalwart ally is one who will stick by you, who is strongly on your side. A stalwart dog is strong, brave, and loyal. A stalwart commitment is a strong, solid commitment. And the stalwart pioneers of the American West had to be both physically strong and strong in their resolve to survive.

Stalwart is frequently used to describe people who either strongly favor or strongly oppose something: "Conservatives were stalwart supporters of the measure, while liberals were stalwart opponents of it." *Stalwart* may also be used as a noun to mean a stalwart person, either one who is strong and brave or one who is a loyal, unwavering supporter or member: "Jim Johnson, who . . . had been a stalwart of the Valley's choral music scene for decades, died Friday" (Canada.com).

Now let's talk for a moment about how *not* to use *stalwart.* Writers fond of sprinkling their prose with interesting words that they haven't bothered to learn sometimes misuse the noun *stalwart* for the noun *staple,* which means either a basic or necessary item of food or a basic or principal element or feature. Here's a sentence where the writer mistakenly thought *stalwart* could denote a basic item of food: "Traditionally seen as a stalwart [*staple*] of thrifty cookery, bacon . . . is increasingly seen as a way to add a little zest to burgers and lunchtime dishes" (*The Guardian*). And here's a sentence where the writer mistakenly thought *stalwart* meant a basic element or feature: "The badger, a stalwart [*staple*] of BBC nature programs, is one of Britain's most beloved animals and is a protected species" (npr.com).

Word 40: ENMITY (EN-mi-tee)
Active hatred or hostility, deep-seated ill will.

Hatred and dislike are such common human emotions that the English language is replete (ri-PLEET, well-stocked, abundantly supplied) with synonyms for *enmity.* Many begin with the letter *a: animosity, aversion, antipathy, acrimony,* and *animus* (word 20 of Level 4). Several others begin with *m: malice, malevolence,* and *malignity.* And in word 31 of this level, *rancorous,* we discussed another synonym of *enmity:* the noun *rancor,* which means bitter and long-lasting hostility or ill will.

Antonyms of *enmity* include *friendliness, warmheartedness, sociability, cordiality, harmony,* and *concord,* and there are no fewer than four antonyms beginning with *a: amiability, affability, amicability,* and *amity.*

Not surprisingly, the words *enmity* and *enemy* are related. Both come ultimately from the Latin *inimīcus,* unfriendly, hostile, which combines the privative prefix *in-,* not, and *amīcus,* a friend. Thus, you harbor enmity, hatred, hostility, for an enemy because an enemy by derivation is *in-,* not, *amīcus,* a friend. Incidentally, the

Latin *inimīcus,* unfriendly, hostile, is also the source of the English adjective *inimical* (i-NIM-i-kul), which means like an enemy, hence unfriendly, hostile, or unfavorable, harmful: "Singapore's censorship laws . . . are inimical to the liberal arts spirit" (*Yale Daily News*).

Because having an enemy is usually reciprocal—meaning that the hostility goes both ways, and your enemy also considers you an enemy—the word *enmity* often implies a shared or mutual hatred. For example, there can be long-standing enmity between two nations, or an entrenched enmity among rival religious sects.

Review Quiz for Keywords 31–40

In each statement below, a keyword (in *italics*) is followed by three definitions. Two of the three are correct; one is unrelated in meaning. Decide which one doesn't fit the keyword. **Answers appear on page 147**.

1. *Rancorous* means bitter, reluctant, resentful.
2. *Ennui* is ignorance, boredom, tedium.
3. *Censorious* means criticizing, condemning, dismissive.
4. To *marginalize* is to force into a powerless position, give little or no credit to, remove from the mainstream.
5. To *reprove* is to condemn, get back at, criticize gently.
6. To *relegate* is to assign an inferior role, to entrust to another's care, to give an insignificant position.
7. A *behemoth* is something massive, something monstrous, something miraculous.
8. *Incendiary* means stirring up interest, exciting passion, inflaming the emotions.
9. *Stalwart* means sturdy, steadfast, straightforward.
10. *Enmity* is hatred, haughtiness, hostility.

The Style File: *A Lot* or *Alot?* *All Right* or *Alright?*

"I would like to know if *a lot* should be spelled as one word or two," asks a correspondent at my website. I love getting questions like this because they take only a few words to answer, never a lot. So you see: *a lot* is always two words, never one.

The same goes for the expression *all right*. Despite the usage note in *Merriam-Webster's Collegiate Dictionary*, which claims that the one-word form *alright* "has its defenders and its users"—as if that alone makes it legitimate—no usage expert with a reputation to lose would tell you it's *all right* to write *alright*, and copyeditors routinely change the one-word form to two. The one-word form strikes me as an affectation, a bit of stylistic cutesiness, like writing *thru* for *through*. *Garner's Modern American Usage* says *alright* "has never been accepted as standard" in American English, and it "cannot yet be considered good usage—or even colloquially all right."

Now let's return to the *Word Workout* vocabulary.

Word 41: MALIGN (muh-LYN, rhymes with *align*)
To speak evil or ill of, utter untruths about, say harmful or misleading things about.

Synonyms of the verb to *malign* include to *slander, defame, disparage, denigrate, stigmatize, revile* (word 43 of Level 4), *traduce* (truh-D[Y]OOS), *vilify, calumniate* (kuh-**LUHM**-nee-AYT), and *vituperate* (vy-**T[Y]OO**-pur-AYT).

Malign comes from the Latin *malignus,* wicked, malicious, disposed to do evil. From the same source comes the adjective *malignant* (muh-LIG-nint), which may mean showing ill will, malicious, as *her spiteful, malignant schoolmates;* or having an evil or harmful nature or influence, injurious, as *there's something malignant lurking in the house;* or, perhaps most commonly today, tending to produce deterioration and death, as *a malignant tumor.*

Malign is also an adjective that may mean evil in effect, injurious, as *no one was aware of the teacher's malign influence on the students.* Synonyms of *malign* in this sense include *deleterious* (DEL-i-**TEER**-ee-<u>us</u>), *noxious, baneful,* and *pernicious.* The adjective *malign* may also mean characterized by ill will, having an evil disposition, malicious, spiteful, as *malign remarks* or *a malign stare.* The antonym of the adjective *malign* is *benign* (buh-NYN), kindly, gracious, mild, having or showing a gentle disposition, as *a benign smile* or *benign intent.*

Since the 15th century the verb to *malign* has been used to mean to speak ill or evil of, and the word implies doing so by saying subtly misleading things intended to insult or belittle. An author can be maligned by a malicious book reviewer. The tabloid press specializes in maligning celebrities and politicians. And politicians commonly air attack ads designed to malign an opponent.

Word 42: LIBATION (ly-BAY-shin)

A drink-offering; the pouring out of wine or some other liquid in honor of a god; hence, the liquid poured out, a drink, beverage, potation (poh-TAY-shun).

Libation comes ultimately from the Latin verb *lībāre,* to give a taste of, pour out as an offering to the gods. As practiced by the ancient Greeks and Romans, *libation* was "the act of pouring a liquid, usually wine, either on the ground or on a victim in sacrifice, in honor of some deity," says *The Century Dictionary.* In 1697, the English poet and dramatist John Dryden wrote, "The goblet then she took, with nectar crown'd, / Sprinkling the first libations on the ground."

Because pouring out a liquid in honor of a deity has long been an obsolete practice, *libation* gradually came to be used of the liquid itself, especially when it's an alcoholic beverage, as in this 1797 quotation from Horace Walpole's *Memoirs of the Reign of King George the Third:* "Some jovial dinners and libations of champagne cemented their friendship." Some modern dictionaries label this use of the word facetious (fuh-SEE-shus) or jocular (JAHK-yuh-lur)—meaning intentionally silly or humorous. But in fact *libation* is chiefly used today when a writer wants a fancier-sounding way to say *drink* or *beverage.* As the citations on Google News show, *libation* meaning a drink, especially an achoholic drink, is a staple of journalistic prose, as in this sentence from a television news report: "Participants will taste twelve unique martinis and vote on which libation should take the crown."

Word 43: **GESTICULATE** (je-STIK-yuh-layt)
To gesture with the hands or body, usually energetically or excitedly.

Gesticulation, the act of gesturing or gesticulating, is the noun.

The verb to *gesticulate* comes from the Latin *gesticulāri,* to make gestures, pantomime, which comes in turn from *gestus,* action, gesture, especially the studied gestures of an actor or orator.

Usually people gesticulate while they are speaking, as a way of physically emphasizing or elaborating on what they are saying, as when a person points an index finger in the air or pounds a fist on a table while making an important point. But you can also gesticulate without speaking, as a way of physically communicating something unsaid, as when someone waves for a taxi, gives a thumbs-up sign to signal approval or encouragement, or at a doorway or entrance politely extends an arm with an open hand as if to say, "After you. You go first."

Gesticulation includes a range of gestures and is not limited to motion of the arms and hands. You can also gesticulate, make lively gestures, by shrugging, winking, shaking your head, or moving any part of your body in a way that sends a message.

Word 44: **CIRCUMLOCUTION** (SUR- kum-loh-**KYOO**-shin)
A roundabout or indirect way of speaking or writing; evasive speech or writing.

Circumlocution blends the combining form *circum-,* around, with the Latin *loqui,* to speak, and means literally a speaking or talking around a subject.

Three other useful English words that incorporate *circum-,* around, are *circumscribe, circumspect,* and *circumvent.* The verb to *circumscribe* (sur-kum-SKRYB), from the Latin *scrībĕre,* to write, draw lines, means literally to draw a line around, encircle, and figuratively to enclose within narrow limits, restrict, confine, as *a law that circumscribes certain rights.* The adjective *circumspect* (SUR-kum-spekt), from the Latin *specĕre,* to look at carefully, observe, means cautious, watchful, wary, carefully considering things before acting or making a decision: "After the big downturn in

the economy, they became more circumspect about their investments." And the verb to *circumvent* (sur-k*u*m-VENT), from the
Latin *venīre,* to come, means literally to come or go around, and
so to bypass, especially in a clever or resourceful way: "She had to
circumvent a lot of red tape to get the job done."

Our keyword, *circumlocution,* implies the use of many more
words than are necessary to express an idea, and it often suggests a deliberate attempt to avoid being clear and direct so as to
cover something up or evade scrutiny: "Reporters repeatedly
pressed the senator for straight answers, but all they got was circumlocution."

Periphrasis (puh–RIF–ruh–sis), a term used in rhetoric, is a fancy
synonym of *circumlocution.* But *periphrasis* does not imply deliberate evasion and refers only to roundabout expression, the use of
more words where fewer would suffice. Candid, straightforward
expression is the opposite of circumlocution, while concise, plain
English is the opposite of periphrasis.

The adjective is *circumlocutory* (SUR-k*u*m-**LAHK**-yuh-tor-ee),
speaking indirectly or in a roundabout way, talking around a
subject.

Word 45: BESMIRCH (bi-SMURCH)

To soil or stain, as if with mud or soot; also, to dishonor, tarnish, bring
disgrace on.

Synonyms of the verb to *besmirch* in its literal sense include to
smear, begrime, beslime, and *bedaub;* synonyms of *besmirch* in its figurative sense include to *discredit, debase, defile,* and *denigrate.* The verb
to *sully* is a close synonym of *besmirch* in both its literal and figurative senses.

The verb to *smirch* means literally to make dirty or discolored,
stain, smear; it is also used figuratively of actions or people to mean
to taint, tarnish, discredit, cast disgrace upon. As you learned in the
discussion of *besotted* (word 24 of Level 1), the prefix *be-* has various
meanings. In *besmirch* it is an intensifier meaning completely, thoroughly. Thus, to *besmirch* is to *smirch* thoroughly, soil or stain completely.

If something can be soiled or tarnished, if it can be disgraced or dishonored, it can be besmirched: "For years now, shocking revelations of widespread child sexual abuse have besmirched the Catholic priesthood"; "If you want to be famous, be prepared to have your reputation besmirched in the tabloid press."

Emily Post, the original expert on good manners, wrote in her book *Etiquette,* which was published in 1922 and is still in print, "No matter who he may be, whether rich or poor, in high life or low, the man who publicly besmirches his wife's name, besmirches still more his own, and proves that he is not, was not, and never will be, a gentleman."

Word 46: IMMUTABLE (i-MYOO-ti̱-buul)
Not changeable, fixed, unalterable.

The adjective *mutable,* changeable, not constant or fixed, comes from the Latin *mūtābĭlis,* changeable, variable, inconstant, which comes in turn from the verb *mūtāre,* to change, the source of the English verb *mutate,* to change, alter; the noun *mutation,* "a change or alteration, as in form or nature" (*Random House*); and *mutant,* which as an adjective means undergoing or caused by mutation, and as a noun denotes either something produced by mutation, such as a new organism, or, as commonly used in science fiction, something abnormal or freakish produced by mutation.

Immutable adds to *mutable* the privative prefix *im-,* which negates the meaning of what follows so that *immutable* means not subject to change, and therefore unalterable, fixed, permanent. Truth, justice, and the laws of nature are considered immutable. Certain standards—such as the golden rule, which says "Do unto others as you would have them do unto you"—are considered immutable. And facts, being by definition both actual and true, are thought of as immutable, at least until they are shown to be false.

The noun is *immutability,* insusceptibility to change, fixedness, changelessness.

Word 47: DECLAIM (di-KLAYM)
To make a formal speech, speak forcefully for rhetorical effect.

The Latin *dēclāmāre* meant either to speak loudly and violently or simply to practice speaking in public. Both these meanings survive in this Latin verb's offspring, the English verb to *declaim*.

Declaim has been used to mean to speak in an impassioned or ranting way, appealing to the emotions rather than to the reason, as in this 1884 quotation from *Christian World:* "To declaim is more easy than to convince." In this sense *declaim* is a synonym of *harangue*. And like the word *inveigh* (in-VAY), which comes from the Latin *invĕhĕre,* to attack with words, *declaim* is sometimes followed by *against*. When you inveigh or declaim against something, you express angry disapproval or impassioned condemnation of it, as *to declaim against injustice*.

Declaim has also been used to mean to speak or recite publicly in a studied way, as an exercise in elocution. You can declaim poetry, declaim Bible verses, or declaim famous speeches from the plays of Shakespeare.

But *declaim* has probably most often been used to mean to make a formal speech, to speak in an oratorical manner. A preacher declaims from the pulpit; the self-styled orators in London's Hyde Park declaim in Speakers' Corner; and every January the president of the United States declaims to the country about the state of the union.

Word 48: THRALL (THRAWL, rhymes with *tall*)
Slavery, bondage, servitude, captivity.

The noun *thrall* may denote a person in bondage, a slave to or servant of some power or influence, as when Shakespeare, in *Macbeth,* writes, "The slaves of drink and thralls of sleep." Or it may denote the condition of a thrall, enslavement, bondage, servitude, as when the 19th-century English Romantic poet John Keats writes, "I saw pale kings and princes too, / Pale warriors, death-pale were they all; / They cried—'La Belle Dame sans Merci / Hath thee in thrall!'"

Whatever enslaves you, or controls all your energy and attention, has you in thrall. A person seduced by a cult is in its thrall. Lovers can be in each other's thrall. A beautiful piece of music or a captivating book can hold you in thrall. Parents can be in thrall to their demanding children. Politicians can be in thrall to special interests. And many ambitious people are in thrall to their careers.

You can see the word *thrall,* slavery, bondage, captivity, inside the verb to *enthrall,* which means to completely absorb, steal the attention of, hold spellbound, engross, as *a magical performance that enthralled the audience.*

Word 49: SATE (rhymes with *late*)

To fill or satisfy completely, supply to satisfaction, gratify; also, to fill or supply beyond what is necessary or desired, to glut. Synonyms of *sate* in this latter sense include *stuff, cram, gorge, choke, inundate* (word 26 of Level 4), and *cloy.*

To *surfeit,* to *satiate,* and to *sate* all imply satisfying some appetite or desire, either completely or too much. To *surfeit* (pronounced like *surf it*) is always to fill or supply to excess, often to the point of discomfort or disgust: "She spent a miserable weekend lying on the couch watching TV and surfeiting herself with potato chips and ice cream." To *satiate* (**SAY**-shee-AYT) and to *sate* may imply supplying more than is necessary or desired, so as to make weary: "They were soon satiated by the nonstop media coverage of the story"; "Showing too little affection can stimulate a lover's desire, just as showing too much can sate it." Or *satiate* and *sate* may imply satisfying completely, gratifying to the full without any discomfort. You can satiate hunger, sate your curiosity, satiate your longing, or sate your lust.

The noun corresponding to the verb to *sate* is *satiety* (suh-TY-i-tee), weariness brought on by being sated, filled or satisfied either completely or beyond what is necessary or desired.

Word 50: GADFLY (rhymes with *bad guy*)

A person who continually pesters, criticizes, or provokes others.

A gadfly, literally, is any of several stinging flies that pester and bite livestock. Since the 16th century *gadfly* has also been used figuratively of a person who persistently annoys others in the manner of a stinging fly.

The most celebrated gadfly in history is the ancient Greek philosopher Socrates, a citizen of Athens, who believed he had been put on earth for the intellectual and moral improvement of his fellow Athenians. To this end, he would accost★ people in public places and pester and provoke them with questions about virtue, justice, and truth. When brought to trial in 399 B.C. for allegedly corrupting youth and committing religious heresies, Socrates, in his famous *Apology* (his self-defense before the tribunal that eventually condemned him to death), argued that his proper and necessary role as a philosopher was to nettle the people of Athens into greater self-awareness:

> For if you put me to death, you will not easily find another, who, to use a rather absurd figure, attaches himself to the city as a gadfly to a horse, which, though large and well bred, is sluggish on account of his size and needs to be aroused by stinging. I think God fastened me upon the city in some such capacity, and I go about arousing, and urging and reproaching each one of you, constantly alighting upon you everywhere the whole day long.[†]

In modern usage, *gadfly* refers to people who, like Socrates, appoint themselves guardians of civic life or watchdogs of public institutions or programs. Gadflies sometimes have recognized roles in which they are expected to criticize—such as community leaders, columnists, television and radio commentators, and public intellectuals. But more often gadflies are argumentative eccentrics who take it upon themselves to speak their version of truth to power, persistently and sometimes annoyingly, without compensation or reward.

★ For more on *accost*, review *assail*, word 45 of Level 2.
† From Harold North Fowler's translation of Plato's *Apology* (Cambridge, MA: Harvard University Press, 1966).

Review Quiz for Keywords 41–50

In this quiz the review word is followed by three words or phrases, and you must decide which comes nearest the meaning of the review word. **Answers appear on page 148**.

1. Is to *malign* to do evil to, to say harmful or misleading things about, or to construct something badly?

2. Is a *libation* something you give away, something you believe, or something you drink?

3. When you *gesticulate,* do you complain, gesture, or object?

4. Is *circumlocution* an indirect path, a long ordeal, or roundabout speech?

5. If you *besmirch* something, do you dishonor it, praise it, or wipe it?

6. Would something *immutable* be unalterable, unquenchable, or unknowable?

7. When you *declaim,* do you speak angrily, speak formally, or speak at length?

8. When you are in *thrall,* are you in trouble, in a rage, or in captivity?

9. If you are *sated,* are you gratified, groggy, or at rest?

10. Is a *gadfly* someone who travels around, who investigates crimes, or who is a persistent critic?

Good Writers Are Good Readers

One of my high school teachers once said, "When you're all grown up, you're going to remember only ten minutes of what you learned in high school."

I think that assertion holds true for most of us. You may re-member well the tribulations (word 1 of this level) of your life in high school, but how much of what you were supposed to learn from your classes do you recall? I can't remember a single thing I wrote in my term paper on E. M. Forster's novel *A Passage to India,* but to this day I carry with me a few precious words of ad-vice from my English teacher that junior year.

It was an off-the-cuff remark, part of an informal exchange before or after class, I can't remember now. I'm not sure what led up to it. All I know is that this wise teacher, aware of my juvenile literary aspirations, said to me, "Listen, Charlie. If you want to be a writer, then you must *read, read, read.*"

Reading lays the groundwork for writing in every way. Reading good fiction teaches you about plot, character, narration, imagery, and detail. Reading good nonfiction teaches you about theme, argument, description, proportion, and substantiation. Reading both will teach you about voice, tone, idiom, syntax, diction, and rhetorical devices such as alliteration (word 34 of Level 1) and anaphora (word 12 of Level 7). And if you extend your reading to include some of the English language's great poetry, you will also learn about rhythm, imagery, and metaphor.

Reading teaches us how words work. From reading we learn what makes sense and what sounds insincere or foolish. From reading we learn what kind of writing commands attention and what kind makes the eyelids droop. From reading we see how words can be used to confuse or stifle us, or to stir our hearts and stimulate our minds.

People sometimes ask me what I learned in college, and when they do I tell them that I learned three things: how to read, how to write, and how to think critically—but not necessarily in that order.

First, I learned how to open my mind to the infinite possibilities of language. I learned how to lurk in a line of poetry or a page of prose until it undressed itself for me and I saw its beauty bare.* By doing this I learned how to think like a writer, how to ask pertinent questions and discern a writer's intentions. I learned that knowledge is in the eye of the interpreter, and that, contrary to popular belief, the writer is at the mercy of the reader. Finally I learned that you can read for pleasure, for profit, or for enlightenment—and the greatest of these is enlightenment.†

All this insight, gained from reading, helped me learn to write, but not all that well. Although college gave me opportunities to exercise a raw talent for writing, it didn't do much to refine it.

---

* This is an allusion to Edna St. Vincent Millay's sonnet "Euclid Alone Has Looked on Beauty Bare."
† This an allusion to the Bible, 1 Corinthians 13:13: "And now abideth faith, hope, charity, these three; but the greatest of these is charity."

With the exception of the first essay I submitted, a two-page paper that came back with thirty-seven red question marks on it, I didn't receive any rigorous writing instruction in college. I was expected to write often and write thoughtfully about what I had read, but I don't remember getting much advice on how to do that effectively. The essays I wrote in college were good practice in putting my thoughts into words, but it was the thoughts that came under scrutiny, rarely the words.

Only later, after much autodidactic (word 32 of Level 7) effort plying my trade, did I come to understand a thing or two about writing, and the revelation that struck me most was that everything I knew about writing I had learned from reading.

There is a maxim I am fond of, which I often use as an inscription when signing copies of my two vocabulary-building novels for high school students, *Tooth and Nail* and *Test of Time*. This is what I write: "Read, read, read, and you will succeed." I think my high school junior English teacher would be pleased.

Answers to Review Quizzes for Level 3

KEYWORDS 1–10

1. Yes. *Tribulation* means great distress, trouble, or suffering, or a cause of great distress or trouble, a trial.

2. Yes. To *deride* is to ridicule, make fun of, laugh at scornfully or contemptuously.

3. No. *Nefarious* means extremely wicked, infamously evil.

4. No. An *ideologue* is a zealous, uncompromising advocate or follower of an ideology.

5. No. A *dalliance* is never a long involvement, and it's usually not unhappy. It's a brief, playful, trifling involvement, a flirtation.

6. Yes. A *fatuous* speaker is silly, foolish, idiotic, and therefore probably boring.

7. No. To *meander* is to proceed by winding and turning, or to wander idly.

8. No, just the opposite. *Culpable* means blameworthy, guilty.

9. No. An ideologue is passionate, even fanatic. A *sedate* person is calm and composed.

10. No. You want to avoid the appearance of impropriety because *impropriety* refers to incorrect, inappropriate, unseemly, indecent, or even illegal behavior.

KEYWORDS 11–20

1. True. *Megalomania* is a mental disorder characterized by exaggerated feelings of greatness or power; or generally, an obsession with doing grand, extravagant things.

2. False. *Vociferous* means crying out noisily; making a loud outcry; uproarious.

3. False. *Contrive* means to invent or devise with ingenuity, design, plan; also, to manage, bring about by a plan, especially by some scheme or stratagem.

4. False. A person who's been nonplussed is not likely to say anything, much less object vociferously. To *nonplus* means to puzzle or perplex completely, render utterly confused so as to be at a loss for what to say or do.

5. True. A megalomaniac, a person obsessed with greatness and doing grand things, can often be *imperious,* domineering, overbearing, dictatorial, commanding.

6. False. *Privation* is a state of extreme hardship; specifically, a lack of food or other necessities for survival.

7. False. To *suffuse* is to overspread; to fill or cover as with light, a liquid, or color.

8. True. *Disconsolate* means extremely sad or unhappy, completely miserable, utterly discouraged or distressed.

9. False. A *dilemma,* a *predicament,* and a *quandary* are all complicated, perplexing situations from which it is hard to disentangle oneself. A *conundrum* is a complicated, perplexing question or problem, a riddle or puzzle.

10. False. People in their dotage are senile. *Dotage* is the mental decline associated with old age, sometimes called *second childhood.*

KEYWORDS 21–30

1. Synonyms. *Vacuous* means empty, without content or substance; hence figuratively, empty of ideas or intelligence.

2. Synonyms. *Intemperate* means without moderation, extreme or excessive.

3. Antonyms. *Stymie* means to obstruct, block, thwart, stand in the way of.

4. Synonyms. *Ambrosia* is the food of the gods, also called nectar, which made them immortal. It may also denote something divinely sweet and pleasing to taste or smell.

5. Antonyms. *Vivify* means to give life or renewed life to or make more vivid or striking. *Enervate* means to deprive of energy, wear out.

6. Synonyms. *Purloin* means to steal, take dishonestly, often by a breach of trust.

7. Antonyms. A *bulwark* is a powerful defense or protection, strong support or safeguard.

8. Synonyms. *Magisterial* means authoritative, masterly, weighty, commanding.

9. Synonyms. A *talisman* is an amulet, good-luck charm.

10. Antonyms. *Stupefy* means to dull the senses of, put into a daze, deaden.

KEYWORDS 31–40

1. *Reluctant* doesn't fit. *Rancorous* means feeling or exhibiting deeply rooted hostility, bitterness, or resentment.

2. *Ignorance* doesn't fit. *Ennui* is boredom, tedium, a feeling of weariness and discontent.

3. *Dismissive* doesn't fit. *Censorious* means criticizing, blaming, or condemning harshly.

4. *Give little or no credit to* doesn't fit. To *marginalize* means to remove from the mainstream or force into an inferior, unimportant, or powerless role or condition.

5. To *get back at* doesn't fit. To *reprove* is to criticize or scold gently, or to condemn, express strong disapproval of.

6. *To entrust to another's care* doesn't fit. To *delegate* is to entrust to another, give equal responsibility for. To *relegate* is to give an inferior position or insignificant role to.

7. *Something miraculous* doesn't fit. A *behemoth* is anything of monstrous size and power; a massive and mighty creature or thing.

8. *Stirring up interest* doesn't fit. *Incendiary* means exciting passion, inflaming the emotions, stirring up violence or rebellion.

9. *Straightforward* doesn't fit. *Stalwart* means strongly built, sturdy; or strong and brave; or strong in one's position or belief, steadfast.

10. *Haughtiness* doesn't fit. *Haughtiness* is arrogance, condescension. *Enmity* is active hatred or hostility, deep-seated ill will.

KEYWORDS 41–50

1. To *malign* is to say harmful or misleading things about someone or something.

2. A *libation* is a drink, beverage; originally, a drink-offering to a god or gods.

3. When you *gesticulate* you gesture with your hands or body, usually energetically.

4. *Circumlocution* is roundabout or indirect speech or writing.

5. When you *besmirch* something, you literally soil or stain it or you figuratively dishonor or bring disgrace on it.

6. Something *immutable* is unchangeable, unalterable.

7. Someone who *declaims* may be angry and may speak at length. But *declaim* means to speak formally and forcefully for rhetorical effect.

8. When you are in *thrall* you may be in big trouble and furious about it too, but that's because *thrall* means captivity, servitude, bondage.

9. A *sated* person may be both groggy from indulgence and at rest, but to *sate* means either to gratify, fill or satisfy completely, or to glut, fill or supply beyond what is necessary or desired.

10. A *gadfly* is a person (often a cranky, eccentric one) who continually pesters, criticizes, or provokes others.

LEVEL 4

Word 1: HACKNEYED (HAK-need, like *hack need*)
Made ordinary and dull by overuse, lacking freshness and interest: *a hackneyed plot.*

Synonyms of *hackneyed* include s*tale, trite, commonplace, shopworn, insipid, banal* (BAY-n<u>u</u>l or buh-NAL), *humdrum, threadbare, pedestrian, jejune* (j<u>i</u>-JOON), and *platitudinous* (PLAT-<u>i</u>-**T[Y]OO**-d<u>i</u>-n<u>u</u>s).

The noun *hackney,* which dates back to the 14th century, once meant a horse hired out for transportation, and a *hackney coach* was a four-wheeled coach drawn by two horses and available for hire—the predecessor of the modern taxicab.

The noun *hack,* a shortened form of *hackney,* has numerous meanings. It may denote a hackney coach—which is why taxicabs, and sometimes their drivers, are today often called *hacks.* It may denote a horse kept for common hire or an old, worn-out horse, a jade. It may denote a sellout: a creative person, such as a writer or artist, who produces dull, unimaginative work in the hope of gaining commercial success. It may denote a hireling: someone who sacrifices independence and integrity in return for money. And it may denote a drudge: a person who does boring, routine work, especially a second-rate writer who takes on any kind of literary work that will make money.

The adjective *hackneyed* means literally like a hack or done by a hack, and therefore dull, lacking imagination or freshness, overdone, worn-out, stale. We speak of hackneyed words and expressions; hackneyed stories, characters, or dialogue; and

149

hackeneyed subjects, slogans, and songs—all made ordinary and dull by overuse.

Word 2: INIQUITY (i-NIK-wi-tee)
Wickedness, evildoing, gross injustice; also, a wicked or grossly unjust act.

The plural, *iniquities,* refers to wicked or harmful actions, injuries, sins. The adjective is *iniquitous,* wicked, sinful, characterized by wickedness or injustice, as *iniquitous deeds* or *iniquitous lies.*

Iniquity comes from the Latin *inīquĭtās,* unevenness or unfairness, which in turn comes from *inīquus,* uneven, unequal, a combination of *in-,* not, and *aequus,* equal, even, fair. From *in-* and *aequus* also comes the English word *inequity* (in-EK-wi-tee), injustice, unfairness, especially as displayed through favoritism or bias.

Iniquity is a literary word, one suited more for serious writing than for conversation, and nowhere in English literature does iniquity get as much attention as in the Bible, where good and evil clash on every page. The Bible teems (abounds, overflows) with citations for both *iniquity* and *iniquities,* from "the iniquity of the Amorites" in Genesis (15:16), the first book of the Old Testament, to "God hath remembered [Babylon's] iniquities" in Revelation (18:5), the last book of the New Testament. The world-weary preacher of Ecclesiastes sees iniquity everywhere: "And moreover I saw under the sun the place of judgment, that wickedness was there; and the place of righteousness, that iniquity was there" (3:16). In the Sermon on the Mount, Jesus issues a commandment against the forces of evil: "Depart from me, ye that work iniquity" (Matthew 7:23). And the hackneyed phrase *den of iniquity,* a place inhabited by wicked people or where evil things happen, may have been inspired by the phrase *den of thieves,* found in Matthew 21:13 and Mark 11:17.

Synonyms of *iniquity* include *villainy, infamy, depravity* (word 1 of Level 1), *atrocity, abomination,* and *enormity*—which in careful usage refers to something monstrously wicked or evil, such as the Holocaust or the genocide in Rwanda in the 1990s, and not, as many miscontrue it, to something very large.

Word 3: **WHIMSICAL** (HWIM-zi-k<u>u</u>l *or* WIM-)
Oddly fanciful or comical; exhibiting odd, playful, fickle humor.

Whimsicality, the quality of being whimsical, is the noun.

A *whim* is an odd, unpredictable, and often sudden notion, fancy, or desire, an urge that seems to come not from the brain but from the gut: "They took off for Europe on a whim, without a care or a dollar in their pocket." The related noun *whimsy* (WHIM-zee) has often been used interchangeably with *whim,* but in modern usage *whimsy* more often denotes either fanciful, playful, extravagant humor, as *a novel filled with more whimsy than wisdom,* or something humorously odd, playful, or fanciful, as *a Venetian palace full of architectural whimsies.* Our keyword, *whimsical,* means given to or arising from a whim or from whimsy, exhibiting odd, playful, unpredictable humor: "On every episode of the TV show *The Office,* Michael Scott, the nutty, whimsical manager played by Steve Carrell, finds some playfully bizarre way to make a fool of himself."

A *caprice* (kuh-PREES) is a sudden change of mind or change in the emotions, and the adjective *capricious* (kuh-PRISH-<u>u</u>s) means subject to caprice, hence unpredictable, changing abruptly for no apparent reason: "The stock market is notoriously capricious." A caprice often gives rise to a whim, an oddly fanciful notion or desire, and that which is capricious, unpredictable, flighty, fickle, is also often whimsical, playful or comical in an odd, unpredictable way: "The whimsical drawings by . . . Jimmy Liao burst with colour, and tell of dreamy fantasy worlds" (asiaone.com).

Word 4: **ENSCONCE** (en-SKAHNTS)
To shelter, cover, or hide securely; also, to settle or fix comfortably and securely.

In its best-known sense, a sconce is a wall-mounted bracket candlestick with screens to shield the candle flames, or a wall-mounted electric light fixture resembling a bracket candlestick. This sense of *sconce* comes from the Old French *esconse,* a screened candle or lantern, or a hiding-place. In another, less familiar sense a sconce is a small detached defensive work, a protective screen or shelter. This sense hails from the Dutch *schans,* a bundle of wood or sticks, or a screen for soldiers made from brushwood. Both these senses of the noun *sconce* have influenced the meaning of the verb to *ensconce,* to shelter securely or settle comfortably.

The verb-forming prefix *en-,* explains *The Random House Dictionary,* may mean to confine in or place on, as in *enshrine, enthrone,* and *entomb,* or it may mean to restrict on all sides, as in *encircle* and *enclose.* Combine this prefix *en-* with the noun *sconce* and you have *ensconce,* literally to confine or restrict behind a protective screen or shelter.

Ensconce may be used to describe something sheltered or hidden securely or something snugly and securely settled. When Falstaff, in Shakespeare's *Merry Wives of Windsor,* says, "She shall not see me: I will ensconce me behind the arras," he means he will hide himself behind a screen.* When, in my vocabulary-building novel *Test of Time,* I described an ATM as "a shiny metal machine ensconced in the wall of a brownstone building," I meant that the machine was securely fixed in the wall.

You can be ensconced in an armchair, settled comfortably in it. You can ensconce your valuables in a secret wall safe, hide them securely in it. And if you're a dairy farmer you can ensconce your livestock in a warm, dry barn during a thunderstorm.

Word 5: PLUTOCRAT (PLOO-tuh-krat)

A wealthy and powerful person; someone whose power comes from wealth.

A *plutocracy* (ploo-TAHK-ruh-see) is rule or government by the wealthy; the word comes from the Greek *ploutos,* wealth, and *kratein,* to rule, govern. *Plutocracy* has a rare synonym: *chrysocracy* (kri-SAHK-ruh-see), from the Greek *chrysos,* gold, the source also of *chrysanthemum,* literally a golden flower; and one of my favorite

---

* An *arras* (AR-is) is a tapestry used as a wall hanging, curtain, or screen. It is a toponym (TAHP-uh-nim), a word formed from the name of a place, in this case the city of Arras in northern France. For more on toponyms, see the chapter "Putting Words in Their Places" in *Crazy English,* Richard Lederer's classic and charming joyride through the English language.

words, *chryselephantine* (KRIS-el-uh-**FAN**-tin), made of gold and ivory.

From the same Greek *ploutos,* wealth, come the unusual words *plutolatry,* worship of money, which incorporates the combining form *-(o)latry,* worship or excessive admiration of something; and *plutomania,* an obsession with money or wealth, which incorporates the combining form *-mania,* which comes from a Greek word meaning madness and denotes excessive enthusiasm or obsessive desire.

A plutocrat, a person whose power comes from great wealth, is a member of the plutocracy, a ruling class composed of wealthy people. The so-called robber barons of the 19th century—men like Cornelius Vanderbilt, John D. Rockefeller, and Andrew Carnegie, who amassed enormous wealth and power by building railroads, refining oil, manufacturing steel, manipulating the financial markets, and manipulating elected officials—were plutocrats. And in the 21st century, when we refer to "the one percent," meaning the one percent of Americans who control nearly half the nation's wealth, we are talking about the American plutocracy, the wealthy and powerful elite.

Word 6: BEATIFIC (BEE-uh-**TIF**-ik)

Having, showing, or imparting supreme happiness or bliss: *a beatific smile.*

Synonyms of the adjective *beatific* include *blissful, glorious, angelic, saintly, divine, rapturous,* and *ecstatic* (pronounce the *c:* ek-STAT-ik). The noun is *beatitude* (like *be attitude*), a state of great bliss or happiness, as *to seek peace and beatitude in solitary meditation.* The plural, *beatitudes,* refers specifically to the declarations Jesus makes in the Sermon on the Mount that begin with "Blessed are"; for example, "Blessed are the meek: for they shall inherit the earth" is one of the beatitudes. The verb to *beatify* (bee-AT-i-fy) means either to make supremely and blissfully happy or, in the Roman Catholic Church, to declare that a dead person is now among the blessed in heaven and is entitled to special honor from the living.

Beatific comes from the past participle of the Latin verb *beāre,* to bless or make happy. You can use *beatific* to describe practically anything that possesses or exhibits not just ordinary happiness but happiness of an exalted nature, supreme bliss. Cherubs (CHER-ubz)—the beautiful and usually chubby young children typically seen in Renaissance painting and sculpture—often have beatific expressions on their faces. A spiritual leader may have a beatific presence or a beatific aura. And two people who are deeply in love may enjoy a beatific moment watching a sunset together.

Word 7: UNFETTERED (uhn–FET-urd)
Free, unrestrained, unrestricted, without restraint or control.

The noun *fetter,* which is usually used in the plural, *fetters,* is a shackle, a chain fastened around the ankles. Figuratively, *fetters* may be anything that restrains or confines: "Her boring day job put fetters on her creativity." The verb to *fetter* may mean either to put fetters on, shackle the feet of, or figuratively to restrain, impede, or confine: "Too many rules will fetter spontaneity"; "Those long fettered by superstition will dismiss the lessons of science and shun the light of reason."

Add the privative prefix *un-* to the verb to *fetter* and you have the verb to *unfetter,* to free from fetters or restraint. For example, you can unfetter captives, unchain them, or you can unfetter your heart from someone you no longer love. From this verb to *unfetter* comes the participial adjective *unfettered,* without restraint or control, free.

Unfettered movement is unrestricted movement. Unfettered access is free access. And one of the core principles of democratic societies is the right to unfettered speech, meaning the right to express opinions freely without fear of restraint or retaliation.

Word 8: ESTRANGE (e-STRAYNJ, rhymes with *the range*)
To make unfriendly or hostile, alienate the affections of; to distance or push away.

The verb to *estrange* goes back through Middle English and Old French to the Latin *extrāneāre,* to treat as a stranger, which comes in turn from *extrānĕus,* foreign, strange, external, literally "that is outside." This Latin *extrānĕus* is also the direct source of the useful English adjective *extraneous* (ek-STRAY-nee-u̱s), which may mean coming from the outside, not belonging to a thing, as *extraneous ingredients,* or not vital or essential, unrelated, irrelevant, as *extraneous comments.*

Antonyms of *estrange,* to make unfriendly or hostile, include to *reconcile, conciliate, pacify, mollify, placate, assuage* (uh-SWAYJ), and *propitiate* (pro̱-PISH-ee-ayt). Synonyms of *estrange* include *alienate, offend, isolate, antagonize,* and *disaffect.*

To *alienate,* to *disaffect,* and to *estrange* all "refer to disruption of a bond of love, friendship, or loyalty" (*American Heritage*). *Alienate* "always implies loss of affection or interest" (*Merriam-Webster's Collegiate*) and "often calls attention to the cause of antagonism or separation" (*Random House*): "Robert continually alienated his dates by flirting with other women." *Disaffect* "usually refers to relationships involving allegiance or loyalty rather than love or affection" (*Random House*), and often implies discontent, resentment, or rebellion. An imperious (word 15 of Level 3) ruler can disaffect the people, make them discontented and no longer loyal. Our keyword, to *estrange,* "often implies replacement of love or belonging by apathy or hostility" (*Random House*). When you estrange someone you distance yourself, push that person away. Friends, lovers, and family members can sometimes become estranged, emotionally distant, unfriendly, or hostile.

Word 9: SIBILANT (SIB-uh-li̱nt)
Hissing; having or producing the hissing or whistling sound of *s.*

The adjective *sibilant* comes from the present participle of the Latin verb *sībilāre,* to hiss, whistle. In phonetics, the study of speech sounds, *sibilant* means having any of the soft, hissing sounds associated with the letter *s,* such as the hard *s* of *this* and *miss,* the soft *s* of *rose* and *laser,* the *sh* sound of *fashion* and *pressure,* or the *zh* sound of *measure* and *vision.*

The verb to *sibilate* means to utter with a hissing sound, like certain snakes. People with spaces or gaps between their teeth—for which the word is *diastemata* (DY-uh-**STEE**-muh-tuh), the plural of *diastema* (DY-uh-**STEE**-muh)—are also prone to sibilate. The noun is *sibilance,* which may mean a hissing sound or "an undue prominence of sibilants" (*OED*), as in the tongue twisters "She sells seashells by the seashore" and "Six silly sisters sell silk to six sickly seniors."

When you whisper to a friend, when you hiss in disfavor at a baseball game, when you say *shush* to tell someone to be quiet, or when you say *pssst* to attract someone's attention, you are being sibilant or making sibilant sounds.

Word 10: PUNDIT (PUHN-dit, rhymes with *fund it*)
An expert, critic, commentator; specifically, a person with special knowledge of a subject who is frequently called on to express opinions about it to the public.

Punditry (PUHN-di-tree) is the occupation or pronouncements of a pundit.

Synonyms of *pundit* include *connoisseur* (properly pronounced kahn-uh-SUR, with *sir* at the end, not *sewer*); *past master; maven* (rhymes with *raven*), from the Yiddish *meyvn,* literally one who understands;* *adept* (AD-ept), the noun corresponding to the adjective *adept* (uh-DEPT), highly skilled; and *sage* (SAYJ) and *savant* (suh-VAHNT), both of which come ultimately from the Latin *sapĕre,* to be wise or sensible—the source also of *sapience* (SAY-pee-ints), profound knowledge; *sapient* (SAY-pee-int), deeply wise and discerning; and *Homo sapiens* (HOH-moh SAY-pee-inz), the modern species of human beings, literally "wise man."

Pundit comes from the Sanskrit *pandita,* a learned man, and dates back to the mid-1600s. The word was originally spelled *pandit* and used as a title of respect for a learned man in India. Since the early 19th century *pundit* has been used of anyone with special knowledge of a subject, and in the 20th century the word acquired the additional implication of an expert who is called on

---

* The late journalist William Safire, who wrote the column On Language for *The New York Times Magazine* for thirty years, liked to call himself a language maven, and I have adopted that habit from him.

to offer an opinion to the public. Although there are pundits for practically every subject—from medicine and economics to food and fashion—the most common type of pundit one encounters in the media today is the political pundit. Perhaps there are so many political pundits because politics allows for both the broadest range of opinion and the broadest definition of an expert.

Pundit is often mispronounced with an intrusive *n* in the second syllable, as if it were spelled *pundint*. This mistake is especially common with the plural *pundits*. Remember, there is no *dint* in *pundit*. Put a *dit* in it.

Review Quiz for Keywords 1–10

Consider the following questions and decide whether the correct answer is yes or no. **Answers appear on page 198**.

1. Can something hackneyed be fresh and interesting?
2. Is petty theft considered an act of iniquity?
3. Can a person be whimsical?
4. When you ensconce something, do you expose it to view?
5. Is a plutocrat poor and powerless?
6. Is a beatific mood a whimsical mood?
7. Is a person who is unfettered by debt likely to go bankrupt?
8. Would an estranged relative be likely to call you often?
9. Is a sibilant noise like the hissing of a snake?
10. Would a pundit be likely to express an opinion publicly?

The Style File: Avoid *Between* with *To*

Blanche Woolford writes, "It seems that many media writers now use *to* following *between* in a phrase having to do with a time span, as in 'Road crews are scheduled to work between 7:30 p.m. to 5:30 a.m.' I was taught that the phrase should be *between . . . and*. Could you clarify this for me, please?"

The construction *between . . . to* is flat-out wrong, I wrote back; one commentator calls it "a subliterate idiom." You're correct in saying that *between* should be followed by *and*, but in the example you cite there's a hitch. With numbers, and especially time spans, *between* can be problematic.

Even when corrected, the sentence "Road crews are scheduled to work between 7:30 p.m. and 5:30 a.m." is just ambiguous enough to cause concern. Are those crews going to work the entire time specified or for some shorter period or periods between those hours? If you mean the entire time (which is usually the case), then the precise way to word it would be "from 7:30 p.m. to 5:30 a.m." Thus, "They plan to visit their cousins between July 27 and July 31" is better rendered as "from July 27 to July 31" because they will arrive there on July 27 and stay till July 31.

When you're talking about a range of numbers, with a high point and low point, there are three ways you can properly phrase it: *from . . . to; between . . . and;* or just *to* by itself. For example: "winds out of the northwest *from* 10 *to* 20 mph"; "spending somewhere *between* six *and* seven million a year."; and "a boat forty *to* fifty feet long."

The Style File: How to Use *Myriad*

The word *myriad* (MIR-ee-id) comes in two flavors: adjective and noun. The adjective means consisting of a very great but indefinite number, innumerable, as *myriad stars.* The noun *myriad* originally meant ten thousand, as *a myriad of soldiers,* because in ancient Greece a myriad was a military division composed of ten thousand soldiers. Although that sense is still in good standing, today the noun *myriad* is most often used to mean a great or indefinite number, as *a myriad of problems* or *a myriad of details.*

Some people assert that the noun *myriad* should be avoided, but there is no reasonable basis for the objection. In fact, the noun is more than two hundred years older than the adjective and has been used by many reputable writers. The choice between adjective and noun, says *Garner's Modern American Usage,* "is a question of style, not correctness." If you want to economize verbally, use the adjective. If *a myriad of* suits your context better, don't be ashamed to use it.

Word 11: REDOLENT (RED-uh-l<u>i</u>nt)

Strong-smelling, exuding either a pleasant or a strong odor; hence, in extended use, strongly suggestive or reminiscent of something.

When *redolent* entered English in the 14th century it was used to mean having a sweet or pleasant smell, fragrant, aromatic. Although this meaning is still in good standing, and you will see writers refer to such sweet-smelling things as "redolent flowers," "redolent incense," and "the redolent scent of spring," over time *redolent* came to be used more often of strong odors that may or may not be pleasant, such as motor oil, fish stew, and the damp scent of the jungle, and of strong odors that are decidedly unpleasant, such as cigar smoke, sewage, and the stench of the abbatoir (AB-uh-twahr), a loanword from French that is the equivalent of the English *slaughterhouse*.

My ninety-nine-year-old father—whose mind is as keen as someone half his age—used *redolent* in this way with me recently. When I complimented him on his excellent personal hygiene, he said, "Well, as I'm sure you know, old people can sometimes be quite redolent, and I'd rather avoid that."

From the notion of giving off a strong aroma, or being permeated with a strong aroma, as *a kitchen redolent with sauteed onions, redolent* then also came to mean strongly suggestive or reminiscent of something, evoking some particular thing. That particular thing could be something with a pleasant or strong smell, such as a wine redolent of dried herbs, plums, and chocolate; or cool, crisp air redolent of autumn. Or the particular thing being suggested or evoked could have nothing to do with aromas, such as a pop tune redolent of the music of the 1980s or an old hotel redolent with the grandeur of a bygone era.

Synonyms of *redolent* include *scented, fragrant, aromatic, pungent* (PUHN-j<u>i</u>nt), *piquant* (PEE-k<u>i</u>nt), *odorous,* and *odoriferous.* The last four of these words should be carefully distinguished. Something *pungent* is sharp or penetrating to the taste or smell, and may be pleasant or unpleasant: *a pungent garlic-chili sauce.* Something *piquant* is mildly pungent—perhaps tart, tangy, or spicy—and pleasant to the taste or smell: *a piquant lemon-herb vinaigrette.* In modern usage something *odorous* is strong-smelling usually in a distinctly unpleasant way, as *an odorous ashtray* or *an odorous skunk,* while in careful usage something *odoriferous* (OH-duh-**RIF**-ur-<u>us</u>) is always sweet-smelling, fragrant, as *odoriferous cookies* or *an odoriferous garden.*

Word 12: DEMAGOGUE (DEM-uh-gahg)

A dishonest person who gains popularity and power by distorting the truth, arousing people's passions, and appealing to their prejudices; a rabble-rouser.

The noun is *demagoguery* (**DEM**-uh-GAHG-ur-ee).

The Century Dictionary defines *demagogue* as "an unprincipled popular orator or leader; one who endeavors to curry favor with the people or some particular portion of them by pandering to their prejudices or wishes, or by playing on their ignorance or passions; specifically, an unprincipled political agitator; one who seeks to obtain political power or the furtherance of some sinister purpose by pandering to the ignorance or prejudice of the populace." (The verb to *pander* is word 30 of this level.)

How many demagogues can you think of? Adolf Hitler, of course. And perhaps a few that you've heard ranting about politics on radio and TV? But let's not forget Mark Antony in Shakespeare's *Julius Caesar,* whose subtle demagoguery at Caesar's funeral arouses the fury and passion of his fellow Romans.

Demagogue comes from the Greek *dēmagōgós,* a leader of the people, which comes in turn from *dēmos,* the people, and *agōgós,* leading, guiding, from the verb *agein,* to lead. From this Greek *dēmos,* the people, we get the common English noun *democracy,* government by the people, as well as the more unusual words *demography* (di-MAHG-ruh-fee), the study of the vital statistics of human populations—their births, deaths, marriages, migrations, diseases, and so on—and *demotic* (di-MAHT-ik), which may mean either pertaining to the common people, popular, or pertaining to the common, ordinary form of a language, also called the colloquial (kuh-LOH-kwee-<u>ul</u>) or vernacular (vur-NAK-yuh-lur), as *the demotic diction of William Carlos Williams's poetry.*

Word 13: MAUDLIN (MAWD-lin)

Tearfully sentimental, weakly or foolishly emotional, especially from drunkenness.

The adjective *maudlin* dates back to the early 1600s and is an alteration, both in spelling and pronunciation, of the name *Mary Magdalene,* the repentant woman Jesus forgives in Luke 7:37–50. In art, Mary Magdalene is often depicted as a weeping penitent, and *maudlin* originally meant given to tears, lachrymose (LAK-ri-mohs, tearful, mournful, from the Latin *lacrima,* a tear). That sense, which is now obsolete, quickly gave way to the meaning foolishly tearful or sentimental, displaying excessive emotion, especially because of drunkenness. As far back as 1699 a dictionary defined "mawdlin" as "weepingly drunk," and that is how the word is still used today; someone who is besotted (word 24 of Level 1), extremely intoxicated, may become maudlin. Often, though, *maudlin* doesn't imply actual drunkenness but the excessive and sometimes silly sentimentality typical of an inebriated person. Maudlin humor and maudlin affection are foolishly emotional, and a maudlin story is tearfully sentimental.

Word 14: BEGRUDGE (bi-GRUHJ)

To envy or resent someone else's good fortune, pleasure, or possession of something; also, to be unwilling to give or allow, especially because of envy or resentment.

The familiar noun *grudge* is a closely held feeling of resentment or ill will: "Duels were often fought to settle a grudge." Combine the noun *grudge* with the prefix *be-* and you have the verb to *begrudge,* "to grumble, especially from envy" (*Webster 2*). Incidentally, yet another of the various functions of the prefix *be-* is to make transitive verbs out of nouns, adjectives, or other verbs, as in *bewitch,* to cast a spell over, enchant (from the noun *witch*); *bedim,* to make dim (from the adjective *dim*); and *bemoan,* to moan over, feel grief or distress about (from the verb *moan*).

The verb to *begrudge* always implies some combination of envy, ill will, resentment, dissatisfaction, and reluctance. Someone who begrudges others' success feels envy and resentment at their good fortune. Many of us, quite understandably, begrudge the wealthiest members of society their disproportionate share of money, resources, and power. And if your indolent (word 48 of this level) nephew asks you for a loan, or your spendthrift (wasteful, extravagant, foolishly spending) daughter wants money for a shopping spree, you may fork over the dough but still *begrudge every penny,* an old expression that means to give or allow with reluctance and displeasure.

Word 15: AVOWAL (uh-VOW-ul, like *a vowel*)
An open declaration; a frank acknowledgment, admission, or affirmation.

The noun *avowal* and the verb to *avow,* to declare openly, acknowledge frankly, come from the Latin *advocāre,* to summon, call to one's aid, the source also of the verb to *advocate* (AD-vuh-kayt), to plead the cause of another, and the noun an *advocate* (AD-vuh-kit), a person who pleads the cause of another in court, or a person who champions a cause, as *an advocate of social reform.*

A *vow* is a solemn promise or pledge, as *a marriage vow,* and the verb to *vow* means to make a solemn promise. Even more solemn and formal than a vow is an *oath* (rhymes with *both*), which may involve an appeal to a deity, as when an elected official takes the *oath of office* or a person about to testify in court swears to tell "the truth, the whole truth, and nothing but the truth, so help me God." An *avowal* is less formal and solemn but still serious: a public statement or assertion of something one is not ashamed of, an affirmation or admission of the truth. An avowal of one's principles is an open declaration of one's beliefs. An avowal of one's misdeeds is a frank acknowledgment of one's mistakes.

To *disavow* (dis-uh-VOW) is the opposite of to *avow* and means to openly refuse to acknowledge, accept, or take responsibility for: "Sheila disavowed having any involvement in the incident." A *disavowal* (DIS-uh-**VOW**-ul), a refusal to accept or acknowledge something or someone, is the opposite of an avowal.

Word 16: PROSELYTIZE (PRAHS-uh-luh-tyz)

To convert or attempt to convert from one religion, party, cause, or opinion to another; to recruit.

The verb to *proselytize* and the noun *proselyte* (PRAHS-uh-lyt) come from an ancient Greek word that meant a newcomer. *Proselyte* was first used in the 14th century in the Wycliffe Bible to mean a gentile who has converted to Judaism. The word is still used in this sense today, but now more often a *proselyte* is someone who has switched from one religion, party, or opinion to another, a convert or recruit.

Since the late 1600s *proselytize* has been used to mean "to make, or seek to make, proselytes or converts" (*OED*). Some religious groups, such as the Mormons and Jehovah's Witnesses, make proselytizing obligatory, and political parties and movements often try to proselytize, convert or recruit others to their beliefs or cause.

Evangelize and *proselytize* are similar in meaning. To *evangelize* (i-VAN-juh-lyz) is to convert or try to convert to Christianity, or to preach the gospel to. To *proselytize* is to convert or try to convert from one religion, party, cause, or belief to another.

Proselytize is sometimes misused as a snazzy-sounding substitute for *publicize* or *promote,* as in *to proselytize this message globally* or *to proselytize her political views.* This is poor usage. You can't proselytize an opinion or a message. You proselytize people or groups, converting them to your opinion or belief or persuading them to endorse your message.

Word 17: GUILELESS (GYL-lis, rhymes with *file this*)

Honest and innocent, open and sincere.

Guileless combines the noun *guile,* deceitful or treacherous cunning, crafty or hypocritical deception, with the suffix *-less,* which means without, as in *hopeless,* without hope, and *shameless,* without shame. A guileless person or a guileless smile is without guile, and is therefore honest and innocent, as in *the golden days of guileless* *youth.* Sadly, guileless youth is also easily *beguiled,* led astray by guile, deception, deceit.

Synonyms of *guileless* include *frank, candid, straightforward, artless, unaffected, naive,* and *ingenuous* (in-JEN-yoo-u̱s). The direct antonym of *guileless* is *guileful,* full of guile. Other antonyms include *insincere, wily, slippery, crafty, cunning, hypocritical, insidious, deceptive, fraudulent,* and *disingenuous.*

Word 18: UNCONSCIONABLE (uhn-KAHN-shuh-nuh-bu̱l)
Not guided or restrained by conscience, lacking conscience; also, unfair, unreasonable, or excessive.

The adjective *conscionable* may mean reasonable, just, fair-minded, as *a conscionable supervisor who treats us with respect,* or governed by one's conscience, as *a supervisor conscionable in her dealings with employees. Unconscionable,* beginning with the privative prefix *un-,* which negates the meaning of what follows, denotes the opposite: unreasonable, unjust, not governed by one's conscience.

All sorts of behavior can be described as unconscionable, lacking conscience—aggressive and selfish driving, the deceptive lending practices of banks, and child abuse are all unconscionable. And anything unreasonable, unfair, or excessive can also be described as unconscionable, as *an unconscionable delay, an unconscionable assault on civil rights,* or *unconscionable budget cuts.*

Scrupulous, honest, upright, having moral integrity, is a close synonym of *conscionable. Unscrupulous,* dishonest, corrupt, lacking moral integrity, is a close synonym of *unconscionable.*

Word 19: CONFLATE (ku̱n-FLAYT)
To merge, bring together, fuse into one.

Conflate comes from the Latin *conflātus,* the past participle of the verb *conflāre,* to blow together, melt, fuse, a combination of *com-,* together, and *flāre,* to blow, the source of the English word *flatus* (FLAY-tu̱s), intestinal gas. The noun is *conflation,* a merging or combining into one, fusion, amalgamation, as *a conflation of musical styles, a conflation of government agencies,* or *a conflation of words.*

When you conflate you bring together two or more separate or different things to form one unified thing. For example, the United States of America is a nation formed by the conflation of fifty states. A bottleneck in a roadway is a conflation of two or more streams of traffic into one. Conflated issues are different issues brought together into one, and conflated ideas are different ideas fused into a single idea, as when the Unitarians and the Universalists conflated their religious doctrines into a unified doctrine. And words are often carelessly conflated, their separate meanings merged into one, as when people pompously use the adjective *reticent,* which means reluctant to speak, when they mean reluctant, unwilling, hesitant. Thus, someone may be reticent, but not *reticent to talk.*

Writers often incorrectly use *conflate* when they mean to *equate,* to regard as the same or equivalent, as in the following examples found on Google News: "Turkish authorities conflate [*equate*] support for the Kurdish cause with terrorism itself"; "People should not conflate [*equate*] a work of art's aesthetic or historical importance with its price tag." *Conflate* is also sometimes misused for *confuse:* "We conflate [*confuse*] freedom from responsibility with true freedom." Take care to use *conflate* only when you mean to merge, bring together, fuse into one: "When two other storm systems conflated with Hurricane Sandy in the northeastern U.S. in November 2012, a fearsome storm was transformed into a 'Frankenstorm.'"

Word 20: ANIMUS (AN-i-mus)
A deep-seated dislike or feeling of ill will; spiteful hostility or animosity.

Animus is borrowed directly from the Latin *animus,* which meant the mind or the soul. It was originally used in English, beginning in the 14th century, to mean the mind or will, a person's animating spirit. But by the end of the 18th century the spirit of the word had turned decidedly negative, and *animus* was used in its more common modern sense: intense and often spiteful dislike or ill will.

Enmity (word 40 of Level 3) is a close synonym of *animus.* Other synonyms include *hostility, animosity, antagonism, antipathy,* and *rancor* (discussed in *rancorous,* word 31 of Level 3). Of these, hostility and animosity are most likely to be expressed openly, often by aggressive actions. Antipathy is strong repugnance or aversion: *her strange antipathy toward classical music.* Antagonism is strong and active dislike between conflicting people or groups: *the antagonism between Democrats and Republicans.* Rancor is a bitter, brooding, and resentful hatred nurtured over time; it is more often felt than expressed. Both enmity and animus are entrenched feelings of ill will and may be openly expressed, like hostility and animosity, or held in private, like rancor.

The *American Heritage Dictionary* notes that *animus* is "personal, often based on one's prejudices or temperament." Because it is personal, animus is also often irrational or malicious, as the following citations illustrate: "For Obama, governing at a time of such extreme partisan animus and still coping with a torpid economy, a second term was hardly assured" (*Newsweek*); "Al Qaida . . . feels a particular animus toward France because France was the former colonial power in most of north Africa" (NPR).

Review Quiz for Keywords 11–20

Consider the following statements and decide whether each one is true or false. **Answers appear on page 198.**

1. If something gives off a strong odor, it is redolent.
2. A plutocrat can be a demagogue.
3. A maudlin person is cheerful and witty.
4. An employee who is passed over for a raise might begrudge a fellow employee who is earning more money.
5. An avowal of one's mistakes is a refusal to acknowledge them.
6. When you proselytize, you attempt to persuade others to adopt your cause or belief.
7. You cannot trust a guileless person.
8. Cheating on a test is unconscionable behavior.
9. When you conflate things, you regard them as equal.
10. An animus is a feeling of excitement or enthusiasm for something.

Difficult Distinctions: *Jealousy* and *Envy*

In loose usage *jealousy* is often used interchangeably with *envy*, but there is a subtle distinction between these two words that careful writers observe.

Envy is a feeling of discontent born of a desire for something, such as a possession, advantage, or achievement, that another person has: "Every time Joe saw John's huge house, red convertible, and trophy wife, he was consumed with envy."

Jealousy is resentment and suspicion of a rival, especially one who may take something you value away from you or who has gotten something that you or someone else deserves: "Joe burned with jealousy every time he saw his back-stabbing rival sitting in the corner office that by all rights should've been given to him."

Morally and philosophically, envy is worse than jealousy, for even in its worst manifestations jealousy is a venial sin, while envy is one of the seven deadlies—right up there with wrath, avarice, sloth, pride, lust, and gluttony.

Now let's return to the *Word Workout* vocabulary.

Word 21: SWATH (SWAHTH *or* SWAWTH, with *th* as in *path*)
The space covered by the stroke of a scythe or the pass of a mowing machine, or a row of a crop cut down by a scythe or mower; hence, any long strip, belt, or area.

Swath dates back to before 900, when it was used in Old English to mean a track, trace, footprint. By the 15th century it had come to be used to mean either the space covered by the sweep of a scythe or a row of a crop that has been mowed. These senses are still current today. For example, you could say that a mower cut a deep swath around the edge of a field, or you could say that the mower left long swaths of hay in the field.

By the 17th century the word had come to be used of any long strip or belt, as *a swath of fabric, a swath of mist,* or *a swath of undeveloped land.* In 1849 the American philosopher and naturalist Henry David Thoreau wrote, "The great mower Time, who cuts so broad a swath." Today this extended use is common, and we speak of *a large swath of undecided voters* or *a broad swath of middle-class America.* Here's an example from *The Wall Street Journal:* "The Landmarks Preservation Commission voted Tuesday to create a historic district encompassing a large swath of the East Village and Lower East Side."

Take care to distinguish the similarly spelled words *swath, swatch,* and *swathe.* The verb to *swathe* (rhymes with *bathe*) means to wrap or bind with a bandage, or as if with a bandage, as *a baby swathed in a blanket. Swathe* may also mean to envelop or enfold, as *the house was swathed in fog.* The noun *swatch* (rhymes with *watch*) is a sample, a representative piece of something, often cloth, as *a swatch of unbleached cotton,* but it may also refer to any small portion, as *a swatch of silvery hair* or *they read a swatch of 19th-century British literature.* Our keyword, *swath,* is a long broad strip, belt, or area, as *a swath of low pressure that will bring rain to the valley.* A *swatch* of linen is a sample piece. A *swath* of linen is a long, broad strip.

Word 22: CONFLAGRATION (KAHN-fluh-**GRAY**-shin)
A great, destructive fire; an extensive, disastrous blaze.

The adjective is *conflagrant* (kun-FLAY-grint), burning, blazing, on fire, as *a conflagrant building* or, figuratively, *a heart conflagrant with love.*

The noun *conflagration* comes from the Latin *conflagrāre,* to burn up, a combination of *con-,* completely, and *flagrāre,* to burn, blaze, the source of *flagrant,* which means shockingly and shamelessly bad, offensive, or immoral, as *a flagrant breach of trust.*

The words *inferno* and *holocaust* are synonyms of *conflagration.*

Inferno comes through the Italian *inferno,* hell, from the Late Latin *infernus,* hell, the source also of the English adjective *infernal,* which means either hellish, fiendish, damnable (as in *Stop that infernal racket!*), or pertaining to or resembling hell. In the 20th century *inferno* also came to be used to mean a place resembling hell, a furnace, oven, conflagration: "The explosions turned the building into a raging inferno."

When the word *holocaust** entered English in the 14th century from the ancient Greek *holócaustos,* burnt whole, it denoted a burnt offering, a sacrifice consumed by fire. By the 17th century it had come to mean horrendous destruction or devastation involving great loss of life, especially by fire. That is what we mean when we speak of a nuclear holocaust. *Holocaust* may still be used in this way, but in the 20th century the word, spelled with a capital *H,* took on another, specific sense—the systematic slaughter of millions of Jews and other Europeans by the Nazis during World War II—and this is the most familiar sense of the word in current usage.

In recent years our keyword, *conflagration,* has been pressed into service as a fancy-sounding, polysyllabic alternative for *conflict* or *war,* as "an international military conflagration" (forbes.com). *Conflagration* may suggest the destructive fires of war, but using the word to mean a widespread conflict is pretentious. The careful writer, mindful of the perils of verbal inflation, will confine *conflagration* to its traditional meaning: a great, destructive fire.

Word 23: RAREFIED (RAIR-i-fyd)

Of a highly refined or sublime nature, elevated or lofty in character or style; hence, belonging or of interest to a small, exclusive group, esoteric.†

Exalted is a close synonym of *rarefied.*

The adjective *rarefied* comes from the Latin *rārēfacěre,* to make thin or less dense, from *rārus,* thin, loose, and *facěre,* to make or do. The verb to *rarefy* (RAIR-i-fy) means either to make thin or less dense, as *a gas rarefied by heat,* or to refine, purify, make more spiritual or exalted, as in this sentence by the English essayist William Hazlitt (HAYZ-lit) from 1817: "Love is a gentle flame that rarefies and expands her whole being." The noun *rarefaction* (RAIR-i-**FAK**-shin) means the process or state of being rarefied, refined, purified, exalted.

---

* Properly pronounced **HAHL**-uh-KAWST, with the first syllable as in *hollow,* not like *hole* or *haul.*
† *Esoteric* (ES-uh-**TER**-ik) means intended for or designed to be understood only by a select group; hence, secret, confidential.

Rarefied may be used to mean thinner or less dense, as *rarefied air,* but today it is most often used figuratively to mean highly refined, elevated, lofty, as *a rarefied literary style* or *the rarefied world of philosophy.* By extension, *rarefied* is also applied to something so elevated or refined that it belongs only to a small, select group, as *a rarefied taste in wine* or *a rarefied social circle.*

And now a note on spelling. *Rarefy* and *rarefied* are often misspelled *rarify* and *rarified,* with an *i* in the middle instead of an *e.* In fact, this misspelling is so common that some dictionaries list *rarified* as a standard alternative. Don't be misled by this; dictionaries record whatever a lot of people do, even if a lot of other people think it's wrong. Remember that the word *rare* resides within *rarefy* and *rarefied* and you'll always spell them right.

Word 24: MENDICANT (MEN-di-kunt)
A beggar; a person who survives by asking for food or money.

Mendicant comes from the Latin *mendīcāre,* to beg, and *mendīcus,* which as a noun meant a beggar and as an adjective meant beggarly, impoverished, destitute (DES-ti-t[y]oot), indigent (IN-di-jint), impecunious (IM-pe-**KYOO**-nee-us).

Originally, a mendicant was a member of one of the Christian religious orders—such as the Franciscans, Dominicans, and Carmelites—that relied on alms (AHMZ), or charity, to survive. By the end of the 15th century *mendicant* had come to be used as a more dignified synonym for *beggar,* and this is its primary sense as a noun today: "Her heart went out to the ragged mendicants that occupied nearly every corner of downtown."

Mendicant may also be an adjective meaning either belonging or pertaining to one of the religious orders of mendicants, as *a mendicant monk,* or, more often, begging or suggestive of a beggar: "Greece and Spain have become mendicant nations, relying on the charity of the European Union to keep their economies afloat."

The noun *mendicancy* (MEN-di-kun-see) means the state of being a beggar or the act of begging.

Word 25: RECOMPENSE (REK-um-pents)

To reward or repay for something done or given; also, to repay or compensate for a loss, damage, or injury.

Recompense comes from the Late Latin *recompensāre,* to give in return, give in compensation. It may be a verb meaning to repay for something done or to compensate for a loss, as "The migrant farmworkers were not recompensed for their labor," or "The court ordered the defendant to recompense the plaintiff for damages." The word may also be a noun meaning repayment or reward, as *recompense for services rendered,* or compensation for a loss or injury, as *to make recompense for a hurtful comment* or *a lawsuit seeking recompense for fraud.*

The verbs to *remunerate* (ri-MYOO-nuh-rayt) and to *recompense* both mean to repay, but they differ in their connotation. To *remunerate,* from the Latin *remūnerārī,* to repay, and *mūnus,* a gift, is to pay or compensate—often generously—for services rendered, trouble taken, or goods provided. For example, it is customary to remunerate with a holiday tip those who provide special services for you, such as a housekeeper, massage therapist, mail carrier, or hair stylist. *Recompense* suggests making a fair or just payment or reward, either for something done or given—as "She recompensed the staff for their hard work by taking them to lunch"—or for some loss, damage, or injury sustained, as "Nothing could recompense them for what they suffered in the war."

Word 26: INUNDATE (IN-un-dayt, *occasionally* in-UHN-dayt)

To overflow, overwhelm, flood; to fill or cover with or as if with a flood.

The verb to *inundate* comes from the Latin *inundāre,* to overflow, stream over like a torrent, which comes in turn from the noun *unda,* a wave, the source also of the English verb to *undulate* (UHN-juh-layt), to move in a sinuous (SIN-yoo-us) and flowing manner, like a wave, as *a flag undulating in the wind* or *bodies undulating to music.* (*Sinuous* means winding, bending, turning, moving in a graceful, curving manner, as *a sinuous road* or *a sinuous dancer.*)

Inundate may mean literally to flood, overflow: a beach can be inundated at high tide and heavy rain can inundate a valley. But *inundate* is also often used figuratively to mean to overwhelm, fill or cover with or as if with a flood: an employer can be inundated with job applications, weeds can inundate a garden, and tweeters can inundate their "followers" with tweets.

Synonyms of *inundate* include to *drown, swamp, submerge, overspread, engulf,* and *deluge* (DEL-yooj), to inundate destructively or oppressively, as "Hurricane Sandy deluged the Northeast," or "The students were deluged with homework."

Inundation (IN-uhn-**DAY**-sh<u>i</u>n), a flood or overwhelming flow, is the noun, as *the inundation of the coastline* or *an inundation of TV ads the week before the election.*

Word 27: AGGRANDIZE (uh-GRAN-dyz)

To increase, enlarge, magnify, augment; especially, to increase or enlarge the power, influence, wealth, rank, or status of.

The verb to *aggrandize* comes from the French *agrandir,* to increase, enlarge, augment, which comes in turn from the Latin *grandire,* to make great, increase. By derivation, that which aggrandizes makes someone or something greater by increasing its power or enlarging its influence. The noun *aggrandizement* (uh-GRAN-diz-m<u>e</u>nt) means the increase or enlargement of power and influence. In the 18th and 19th centuries, England sought to aggrandize its power in the world by conquering various foreign countries, colonizing them, and creating an empire. This territorial aggrandizement of a country into an empire is called *imperialism.*

In modern usage *aggrandize* is often used reflexively, meaning it is either preceded by the combining form *self-* or followed by a reflexive pronoun (one incorporating *-self* or *-selves*). We speak of the self-aggrandizing rhetoric of political campaigns, of dictators who aggrandize themselves at the expense of their people, and of the greedy self-aggrandizers on Wall Street.

Word 28: OUTRÉ (oo-TRAY, rhymes with *you pay*)

Beyond the bounds of what is considered usual, normal, or proper; unusual, peculiar.

Synonyms of *outré* include *bizarre, extravagant, eccentric, unconventional, outlandish,* and *unorthodox.* Antonyms of *outré* include *normal, ordinary, customary, traditional,* and *orthodox.*

As you may have already guessed from the acute accent over its final letter, *outré* is French. It comes directly from *outré,* the past participle of the verb *outrer,* to go beyond, go to excess, push the limits of. By derivation, that which is *outré* goes beyond the boundaries of convention, pushing the limits of what is considered normal or proper.

Outré may be used of anything that flies in the face of convention or that challenges notions of what is normal and proper. Someone's clothing may be *outré,* outlandish, bizarre. Certain words may be *outré,* unsuitable for polite conversation. And a movie may be *outré* because it goes beyond what is considered acceptable and proper.

You can use the adjective *outré* by itself, as "The new fashions for fall are outré." Or you may pair it with a noun, as *The New York Times* did when it called JCPenney "a department store not known for outré fashion." Outré politics are radical politics. Outré behavior is unconventional, eccentric behavior. And an outré subject is one that pushes the limits of propriety.

You can also pair *outré* with the definite article *the* to refer to that which goes beyond what is considered usual or normal, something extravagant or bizarre: "Foodies who embrace the new, the outré, the different, may hail an unusual item on the menu . . . horsemeat tartare" (horsetalk.co.nz).

Word 29: QUINTESSENTIAL

Being the perfect, most refined, or most typical example or instance of something.

Quintessential is the adjective corresponding to the noun *quintessence* (kwin-TES-ints). Both words come ultimately from the Medieval Latin *quinta essentia,* fifth essence. In ancient and medieval philosophy, *quintessence* was "the fifth or last and highest essence or power in a natural body," explains *Webster 2.* "The ancient Greeks recognized four elements, fire, air, water, and earth. The Pythagoreans and Aristotle added a fifth, the ether, out of which they said the heavenly bodies are composed." In modern usage *quintessence* is "the pure and concentrated essence; the best and purest part of a thing" (*The Century Dictionary*); figuratively, the perfect embodiment or most typical example of something, as *the quintessence of beauty, the quintessence of virtue,* or *the quintessence of stupidity.*

Quintessential retains from the ancient fifth essence the idea of concentration and purity, and in modern usage the word is used to describe the perfect or most typical example of something: "Naomi aspired to write a novel about the struggles of her immigrant grandparents that she hoped would portray the quintessential American experience"; "Paella is the quintessential dish of Spanish cuisine"; "The ancient Greek warrior Achilles was a quintessential tragic hero"; "With its white picket fence, bright red barn, and tall maple trees, the bed-and-breakfast had quintessential New England charm."

Quintessential may also be used to mean of utmost importance or significance, indispensable, as *a quintessential history of feminism,* or "Law and order is quintessential to the well-being of society."

Word 30: PANDER (PAN-dur)

To cater to or indulge the vulgar tastes and desires of others or exploit their passions, prejudices, or weaknesses.

Pander is an eponymous (i-PAHN-uh-mus) word, one formed from a name, in this case a name from literature. In classical mythology and in Homer's epic poem *The Iliad,* which tells the story of the Trojan War, Pandarus [PAN-duh-rus] was a Trojan who violated the truce between the Trojans and the Greeks by trying to assassinate Menelaus (MEN-uh-**LAY**-us), the king of Sparta, a treacherous act that prolonged the war. *Merriam-Webster's Encyclopedia of Literature* explains that the name resurfaced "in the medieval tale of Troilus and Cressida [TROY-lus and KRES-i-duh], as well as in William Shakespeare's play by the same name," where "Pandarus acted as the lovers' go-between; hence the word 'pander.'"

The noun *pander,* which entered English in the 15th century, denotes either a go-between in amorous intrigues—namely, a procurer or pimp—or a person "who ministers to the gratification of any of the baser passions of others" (*The Century Dictionary*). The verb to *pander,* which came along in the early 17th century, originally meant to act as a pander or go-between, but today to *pander* is commonly used to mean "to minister to others' passions or prejudices for selfish ends" (*Century*).

An employee, to gain favor, panders to the whims and desires of his boss. An ambitious writer panders to the vulgar tastes of the reading public—or to its snobbery. Special-interest groups pander to venal (VEE-nul) politicians. (*Venal* means corruptible, capable of being bribed or bought off.) Demagogues (word 12 of this level) gain influence by pandering to people's prejudices, ignorance, and passions. And retailers, eager to exploit the public for profit, pander to consumers who are eager to own the trendiest clothing and commodities.

Review Quiz for Keywords 21–30

Decide if the pairs of words below are synonyms or antonyms. **Answers appear on page 199**.

1. *Swath* and *belt* are . . . synonyms or antonyms?
2. *Conflagration* and *blaze* are . . .
3. *Rarefied* and *mundane* are . . .
4. *Mendicant* and *plutocrat* are . . .
5. *Recompense* and *reward* are . . .
6. *Inundate* and *submerge* are . . .
7. *Aggrandize* and *minimize* are . . .
8. *Outré* and *traditional* are . . .
9. *Quintessential* and *ordinary* are . . .
10. *Pander* and *cater* are . . .

Once Upon a Word: The Name Game

An *eponym* is a word derived from a name, or a name that becomes a word. The English language has many eponymous words, both common and obscure. Science, medicine, and the natural world are sources of many familiar eponyms.

Every educated person knows that the verb to *pasteurize* comes from the name of the French chemist and bacteriologist Louis Pasteur (1822–1895), who developed the process of sterilizing by heating and rapid cooling. But did you know that the lovely climbing shrub *wisteria* (wi-STEER-ee-uh) takes its name from the American anatomist Caspar Wistar (1761–1818)?★ And did you know that the hardy, colorful plant called *poinsettia* is named after an American diplomat, J. R. Poinsett (1779–1851), who brought it from Mexico to the United States in 1828? Incidentally, there is no *point* in *poinsettia,* and the word is properly pronounced in four syllables, not three: poyn-SET-ee-uh.

Another eponymous scientific word that is often mispronounced is *salmonella* (SAL-muh-**NEL**-uh), which has nothing to do with salmon (SAM-<u>u</u>n) and everything to do with Daniel E. Salmon (1850–1914), an American veterinarian and pathologist who identified this genus of bacteria and whose last name is pronounced SAL-m<u>u</u>n.

Many flowers and plants take their names from names. One of my favorites is the beautiful woody vine called *bougainvillea* (BOO-g<u>u</u>n-**VIL**-ee-uh), with its delicate and brilliant flowers, which is named after the French navigator and explorer Louis Antoine de Bougainville (1729–1811), who fought for the United States during the Revolutionary War and discovered the Solomon Islands.

Our two methods of measuring temperature, *Celsius* and *Fahrenheit,* are both eponyms. The former comes from Anders Celsius (1701–1744), a Swedish astronomer, and the latter from Gabriel Daniel Fahrenheit (1686–1736), the German physicist who introduced the use of mercury in thermometers. The Bunsen burner, familiar to all high school chemistry students, is named after Robert Wilhelm Bunsen (1811–1899), a German chemist. And the

---

★ Are you wondering why the man's name is spelled *Wistar* but the genus is spelled *Wisteria?* A Harvard naturalist named Thomas Nuttall (1786–1859) accidentally printed *Wisteria* instead of *Wistaria,* and the mistake has since become the norm.

word *guillotine* (GIL-uh-teen, not GEE-yuh-teen) is named after Joseph Guillotin (1738–1814), a French physician who did not invent this gruesome decapitation device but who advocated for its use as more humane than hanging.

Now let's return to the *Word Workout* vocabulary.

Word 31: SACROSANCT (SAK-roh-SANGT)
Extremely sacred or holy; hence, not to be violated or altered.

Synonyms of *sacrosanct* include *hallowed, divine, sanctified,* and *inviolable* (in-VY-uh-luh-bul).

Sacrosanct comes from the Latin phrase *sacro sanctus,* which means made holy, sacred, or inviolable by a religious rite. This phrase comes in turn from the Latin *sacer,* sacred, holy, the source of the English words *sacred* and *sacrifice,* and the Latin verb *sancire,* to consecrate (word 42 of Level 2), the source of the English words *saint, sanctity,* and *sanctify,* to set apart as sacred.

In modern usage *sacrosanct* is often used of anything that cannot or should not be violated or trespassed upon. If you hold something sacrosanct, you treat it as if were holy and therefore immune from criticism or interference. A sacrosanct belief or tradition is one that must not be violated or changed. A sacrosanct room is a room that is secret or private and not to be entered. A sacrosanct text is one whose words are so revered that they are beyond criticism and must never be altered.

Word 32: INDOMITABLE (in-DAHM-i-tuh-bul)
Unconquerable, unyielding, invincible, not capable of being overcome or subdued.

Indomitable comes from the Latin *indomitus,* untamed, wild, which comes in turn from the privative prefix *in-,* not, and *domitāre,* to tame, subdue. By derivation, that which is indomitable is wild and strong and cannot be tamed or subdued.

An indomitable army, an indomitable enemy or foe, and an

indomitable sports team are all incapable of being defeated. Someone with an indomitable spirit is unyielding in the face of opposition and stubbornly persistent in overcoming obstacles. An indomitable force is so wild and powerful that it cannot be resisted or subdued: Hurricanes Katrina and Sandy were indomitable forces of nature. And an indomitable hero is invincible: "Indiana Jones is the ultimate action-hero academic: played by Harrison Ford, the indomitable professor outwits Nazis and other villains in search of religious relics, lost temples, and alien artifacts" (*The Economist*). *Indomitable* may also be used figuratively, as in this sentence from *D'Aulaire's Book of Greek Myths:* "Zeus pounded his indomitable fist and Hera sat silent."

Synonyms of *indomitable* include *insuperable* (in-SOO-pur-uh-bul), *masterful*, *indefatigable* (word 21 of Level 2), *omnipotent* (ahm-NIP-uh-tint), *redoubtable* (ri-DOW-tuh-bul), and *puissant* (PYOO-i-sint *or* pyoo-IS-int). Antonyms of *indomitable* include *weak, helpless, feeble, vulnerable, decrepit* (di-KREP-it), *debilitated, impotent* (IM-puh-tint), and *effete* (i-FEET).

Word 33: METTLE (MET'l, like *metal*)

A person's disposition or temperament; "the 'stuff' of which one is made, regarded as an indication of one's character" (*OED*). Also, courage, vigor, strength of spirit or character, or stamina, endurance, staying power.

Mettle is a variant spelling of *metal* and is probably a figurative use of *metal*—the idea being that if the stuff of which you are made, your temperament, is strong and durable, like *metal*, then you have *mettle*, strength of spirit or character. A man or woman of mettle is a person who displays exceptional vigor, courage, or stamina.

Mettle is commonly used in a number of set phrases. *To test one's mettle*, or sometimes *to try one's mettle*, is to put one's character, spirit, or skill to the test. *To be on one's mettle* is to be inspired to do one's best. *To put on one's mettle* is to test someone's endurance or resourcefulness. And *to show one's mettle* or *to prove one's mettle* is to show or prove one's admirable character by displaying courage, spirit, or resilience.

Word 34: ELLIPSIS (i-LIP-sis)

An omission; specifically, the omission of one or more words that are understood in context but that would otherwise be required for a clear or grammatically complete construction.

Ellipsis comes from the Greek *élleipsis,* an omission. *Ellipsis* is the singular, *ellipses* (i-LIP-seez) the plural.

An ellipsis is a grammatical construction—a phrase or sentence—that leaves out one or more words. Usually what is left out is implied by the context and is often not necessary, as in *She has written several novels I admire,* which without the ellipsis would be *She has written several novels **that** I admire;* or *He's interested, but I'm not,* which without the ellipsis would be *He's interested, but I'm not **interested**.*

Sometimes *ellipsis* refers to the omission of a word or words that would clarify the context, as in *You don't want to,* which leaves out a verb at the end that would specify what you don't want to do. In such instances it's assumed that the reader or listener can mentally supply what has been omitted.

"All writers and speakers of English . . . omit words which never will be missed," write Bergen and Cornelia Evans in their *Dictionary of Contemporary American Usage.* "This is never objectionable unless the sentence becomes misleading, that is, unless the omitted words actually are missed." For example, the sentence *I like to interview people sitting down* is misleading because the ellipsis is unclear; we're not sure whether it means *I like to interview people **who are** sitting down, I like to interview people **while I am** sitting down,* or *I like to interview people **while we are** sitting down.**

In writing and publishing, *ellipsis* is used to mean "the omission of a word, phrase, line, paragraph, or more from a quoted passage" (*Chicago Manual of Style,* 15th edition). To indicate an ellipsis, an omission from a quoted passage, writers and editors use *ellipsis points,* three or sometimes four dots or periods.

Elliptical, the adjective corresponding to the noun *ellipsis,* has several meanings. It may mean pertaining to or marked by a

---

* I have adapted this example from *The Random House Dictionary.*

grammatical ellipsis, an omission of a word or words, as *an elliptical construction.* It may be used of speech or writing to mean characterized by extreme verbal economy, expressed in the fewest words possible, as *an elliptical message scrawled on the back of an envelope.* Or it may be used of any manner of expression that is disjointed, incomplete, ambiguous, or obscure, as *a story told in a fractured, elliptical style* or *a poet known for her elliptical verse.*

Word 35: PETULANT (PECH-uh-lint)
Showing sudden impatience, irritation, or anger, especially over something trivial.

Petulant comes from the Latin *petulans, petulantis,* impudent, and when the word entered English in the late 16th century it was used of impudence or forwardness in speech or behavior. In modern usage, however, *petulant* connotes impatience and irritability rather than impudence.

The words *peevish* and *petulant* are close synonyms. Both suggest ill-humored annoyance. But while peevish people are irritable and full of complaints because they are fussy and difficult to please, petulant people are prone to self-centered outbursts and apt to express childish irritation or impatience over insignificant things. Someone in a peevish mood has a reason to be irritable and complaining, though it may not be a legitimate reason. Someone in a petulant mood quickly gets irritable and impatient over unimportant things.

Word 36: DEIGN (DAYN, rhymes with *rain*)
To do something one considers beneath one's dignity; to condescend reluctantly.

The verb to *deign* comes from the Latin *dignāre,* to consider worthy, which comes in turn from the adjective *dignus,* worthy, deserving, suitable, fitting. *Dignus* is also the source of the English words *dignity; dignify; dignitary,* a person who holds a position of dignity or honor; *indignation,* righteous anger at something thought to be unworthy, unjust, or undignified; and *indignant,* filled with indignation: "The gadfly pointed an indignant finger at the object of his contempt, the city council."

When you deign, you decide that it is worthy or fitting for you to do something you would normally consider beneath your dignity. In other words, you never deign willingly, hoping to be of help. You always deign reluctantly, condescending to do something that you wouldn't otherwise do: "After much complaining, their food-snob friend deigned to eat at their favorite greasy spoon"; "In 1972, when Nixon was the incumbent and far ahead in the polls, he barely deigned to say McGovern's name during the fall campaign" (CNN).

In modern usage, *deign* always has an infinitive as its object. The infinitive is the *to* form of a verb, so we deign *to do* something: "He deigned to answer"; "The virtuoso deigned to give an encore." You can also deign *not* to do something: "She wouldn't deign to notice him"; "My kids won't deign to eat vegetables."

Word 37: BERATE (bi-RAYT)
To scold harshly, criticize sharply.

The verbs to *chide, admonish, reproach, upbraid, reprimand, reprove* (word 35 of Level 3), *rebuke,* and *berate* all mean to scold, criticize, or express disapproval.

To *chide* and to *admonish* imply gentle scolding with the intention of correcting improper behavior, while to *reproach* is to express disapproval or disappointment less mildly. You chide your dog for chewing the furniture, you admonish your children to spend less time on Facebook and more on their homework, and you reproach an employee for being late to work three days in a row.

To *upbraid* implies a more formal, usually justifiable, and often public criticism or scolding: "Political columnists upbraid public officials who have abused the public's trust." To *reprimand* is more formal still, to scold or criticize publicly, officially, and often severely, as *the officer reprimanded the impertinent* (word 20 of Level 1) *soldier.*

To *reprove* may be relatively mild, suggesting a well-meaning

scolding like *chide, admonish,* and *reproach,* or it may be more severe, suggesting harsher and more vehement disapproval like *rebuke.* A judge might reprove offenders for a first offense but
rebuke them for a second.

Finally, our keyword, to *berate,* is a close synonym of *rebuke.* Both
words mean to scold sharply or criticize harshly, but *rebuke* usually
refers to a single expression of stern disapproval—"Janice rebuked
Jim for neglecting to load the dishwasher"—while *berate* often implies prolonged or repeated scolding: "Jim was sick of hearing Janice
berate him for neglecting to do his share of the housework."

Word 38: HARBINGER (HAHR-bin-jur)
A sign of something to come, indication of a future event, forerunner,
herald.

Harbinger, which is related to the word *harbor,* comes from a Ger-
manic word that meant shelter for an army, and later lodging in
general, a place of shelter and entertainment.

Harbinger is one of the oldest words in English, dating back to
the 12th century. Like many old words, it has shed its earliest meaning and taken on new ones. In English, *harbinger* was first used to
mean a keeper of a lodging house, a host, entertainer, a sense now
obsolete. The word next came to mean a person or company sent
ahead to provide for lodging, especially for an army or traveling
royalty. Over time this sense broadened and *harbinger* was used of
anyone who goes before, especially to announce the coming of
another. Finally, the word came to be used figuratively to mean a
sign of something to come. In 1630, the English poet John Milton
used *harbinger* this way, describing the sun as "the bright morning
star, day's harbinger," which "comes dancing from the east."

Today *harbinger* means anything that indicates the arrival of
something or that foreshadows some future event. A harbinger of
spring indicates that spring will soon be here. A harbinger of recession tells us that tough economic times lie ahead.

Forerunner, precursor, herald, and *harbinger* all denote people or
things that come before. *Forerunner* and *precursor* (pree-KUR-sur),
from the Latin *prae-,* before, and *currere,* to run, both mean literally

one who runs before, and both are often used figuratively of that which has a logical connection to what follows: "The Boston Massacre was the precursor of the American Revolution"; "Infantile fears are often the forerunners of adult anxieties." *Herald* and *harbinger* are used chiefly of that which precedes in order to announce or draw attention to the coming of something else: Shakespeare called the lark "the herald of the morn," and Washington Irving called "the boding cry of the tree-toad" a "harbinger of storm."

An *omen,* a *portent,* and a *harbinger* are all signs of things to come. Both an omen and a portent are prophetic signs, supposedly indicating the nature or outcome of some uncertain future event. Though by definition an omen may be either good or bad, perhaps because of the adjective *ominous,* which is almost always used of something evil or menacing, an omen is often unfavorable. A portent may be a sign that something momentous, of great consequence, is about to happen, or a warning of impending disaster, as *a portent of the subprime mortgage crisis that sent the global economy into a tailspin.* Like *omen* and *portent, harbinger* may be used of calamitous signs, as *a harbinger of doom,* but the word more often has a positive or neutral connotation, as *a harbinger of peace* or *a harbinger of change.*

And now for a word about usage. Here's a faulty sentence from the *Los Angeles Times* that typifies a common misuse of *harbinger:* "It is too early to tell whether the upticks are a harbinger of things to come." What's wrong with that?

If you guessed that it's redundant, you're right. Writers often tack the phrase "of things to come" not only after *harbinger* but sometimes also after *portent* and *omen.* All three words denote a sign of some future event, of something to come, so adding *of the future* or *of things to come* after them is repetitive and superfluous.

Word 39: CORPULENT (KORP-yuh-lint)
Having a large, bulky body; fat, fleshy.

Corpulence, the state of being corpulent, fatness, is the noun.

Synonyms of *corpulent* include *obese, stout, stocky, portly, pursy* (PUR-see), short of breath because of fatness, and *rotund* (roh-TUHND), round and plump.

Antonyms of *corpulent* include *thin, lean, slender, slim, svelte* (SVELT, rhymes with *felt*), and *lithe* (rhymes with *writhe*), which are usually complimentary, and the always uncomplimentary words *scrawny, spindly, gaunt, haggard* (HAG-urd), *emaciated* (i-**MAY**-shee-AY-tid), and *cadaverous* (kuh–DAV-ur-<u>us</u>), which means pertaining to or resembling a *cadaver* (kuh–DAV-ur), a dead body.

Corpulent comes from the Latin *corpulentus,* fat, stout, which in turn comes from *corpus,* body, substance. This Latin *corpus* is also an English word meaning either the dead body of a human being or an animal, or a large collection of writings, the whole body of literature on a subject or by a particular author. From the Latin *corpus,* body, substance, also come the English words *corpse,* a dead body; *corpuscle* (KOR-puh-s<u>u</u>l), a free-floating cell, such as a red or white blood cell; *corporeal* (kor–POR-ee-<u>u</u>l), of or pertaining to the body; its antonym, *incorporeal,* lacking material substance or physical existence, spiritual; the verb to *incorporate,* literally to combine into one body; and the phrase *corporal* (KOR-pur-<u>u</u>l) *punishment,* punishment inflicted on the body.

When our keyword, *corpulent,* came into English in about 1400 it meant solid, dense, like a physical or material body, but it soon came to be used to mean fat, having a large, bulky, fleshy body— its only meaning today. *Corpulent* usually applies to people who are not only fat but also ponderous (word 41 of Level 2), large and slow-moving, as *he was far too corpulent to dance.* William Howard Taft, the 27th president of the United States, was corpulent in the extreme, at one point weighing about 340 pounds.

Word 40: AGGRIEVED (uh–GREEVD, rhymes with *relieved*)
Wronged, offended, injured, having a grievance.

A *grievance* is a wrong, an offense, something that causes injury or distress and that is grounds for resentment or complaint: "They submitted a long list of grievances regarding safety violations in the workplace." To be aggrieved is to have a grievance, to feel wronged or injured, to have a complaint about an alleged offense.

The verb to *aggrieve,* to bring grief, pain, or trouble to, to distress, and the participial adjective *aggrieved* both entered English in the 14th century from the Latin *aggravāre,* to make heavier, make worse, the source also of the verb to *aggravate,* to worsen, make more serious or severe, as *to aggravate an injury.*

At first *aggrieved* meant troubled, worried, distressed, as *the aggrieved unemployed who have lost hope of finding work.* But by the mid-15th century *aggrieved* had taken on its more common modern meaning: "upset or resentful at having been unfairly treated" (*OED*). The word may apply to anyone who feels wronged, offended, or injured in some way, as *the aggrieved wife of an adulterous husband* or *an aggrieved former employee who went on a rampage.* In a civil lawsuit, both parties—the plaintiff, the person who brings the lawsuit, and the defendant, the person being sued—will insist that they are aggrieved, wronged, injuriously affected.

In a less common sense, *aggrieved* may also mean expressing grief, offense, or resentment, as *an aggrieved tone of voice* or *an aggrieved outpouring of angry letters.*

Review Quiz for Keywords 31–40

In each statement below, a keyword (in *italics*) is followed by three definitions. Two of the three are correct; one is unrelated in meaning. Decide which one doesn't fit the keyword. **Answers appear on page 199.**

1. *Sacrosanct* means very secret, very sacred, very holy.

2. *Indomitable* means unmanageable, unconquerable, unyielding.

3. *Mettle* is a person's temperament, a person's disposition, a person's circumstances.

4. An *ellipsis* is an omission, a mistake, something left out.

5. *Petulant* means showing sudden irritation or anger, impatient over trivial things, desperate for love and attention.

6. To *deign* is to do something beneath one's dignity, do something unthinkingly, grant reluctantly.

7. To *berate* is to judge unfairly, scold harshly, criticize sharply.

8. A *harbinger* is an indication, sign, answer.

9. *Corpulent* means fleshy, frumpy, fat.

10. *Aggrieved* means offended, wronged, unsatisfied.

The Style File: Seven Deadly Sins of Usage

"Hey, Mr. Language Dude, so you think you're so great?" some dude once asked me. "Don't you ever make a mistake?"

When you've been a language maven as long as I have, you get all kinds of questions, and I mean *all*. With my tongue firmly in my cheek, I sent him this reply: "Irregardless of what some think, when it comes to usage, nobody's perfect. But some people make more mistakes and some make less. And I'm one of those people who rarely makes mistakes. I see no reason to feel badly about it. I can write pretty good. You won't catch me laying down on the job. And don't ask me to repeat that again."

Perhaps you noticed that in those seven sentences I commited seven deadly sins of usage (intentionally, of course). Did you catch them all? You can find these seven errors in print and hear people utter them every day, but anyone who aspires to be a careful writer and speaker should scrupulously avoid them.

First, the word *irregardless,* which is probably a dialectal blend of *irrespective* and *regardless,* has long been ridiculed by usage commentators, and even the most permissive dictionaries label it "nonstandard," which is a namby-pamby way of saying that many people will think less of you for using it. *Irregardless* is a double negative, like *don't never,* and if you don't never want to be criticized for your diction, use *regardless,* the proper word, instead.

In the second sentence I used *less* when I should have used *fewer. Less* applies to quantities: *less time, less sugar, less money. Fewer* applies to things that can be counted or itemized: *fewer minutes, fewer dollars, fewer mistakes.* The classic boo-boo is the sign for the express lane at the supermarket: *15 Items or Less.* Make that *fewer* because items can be itemized. It's *less* food but *fewer* groceries.

In the third sentence the error is more subtle. When *one of the* is followed by a plural noun and *who* or *that,* you should follow with a plural, not a singular, verb. Thus, *one of the people* (plural noun) *who rarely **makes*** (singular verb) *mistakes* should be *one of the people who rarely **make*** (plural verb) *mistakes.* Turn the sentence around and you'll see the logic of its grammar: *Of the people who rarely make mistakes, I am one.*

In the fourth sentence *feel badly* should have been *feel bad*. Here we are not talking about how you perform the act of feeling but about how you feel; that's why Maria in *West Side Story* sings *I feel pretty* and not *I feel prettily*. Linking verbs such as *feel, look, smell, taste, seem,* and *be* properly connect a subject with an adjective, not an adverb. That's why *you* (the subject) *feel* (the linking verb) *bad* (the adjective), and why *something* (the subject) *looks, smells, tastes, seems,* or *is* (the linking verbs) *bad* (the adjective), not *badly* (the adverb).

The fifth sentence, *I can write pretty good,* should be *I can write pretty well*. Here *good* is the adjective (as in *I feel good*) while *well* is the adverb, which tells us how we perform the action of the verb: *I write well*.

The problem in the sixth sentence is the misuse of *laying* for *lying*. No doubt you've heard educated people say *I'm going to lay down* instead of *lie down,* and tell their dogs to *lay down* instead of *lie down*. Perhaps you even say it that way yourself. But despite the frequency of this usage it is not standard, and authorities continually admonish us to distinguish properly between the verbs to *lay,* which means to put or place, and to *lie,* which means to recline or come to rest. Thus, you *lay* something down, put it down, but when you take a nap you *lie* down, recline.

Finally, in the seventh sentence I used the common redundancy *repeat that again*. Why is that phrase redundant? Because *repeat* already means to say again. This bit of wordiness also often occurs with other verbs beginning with *re-* such as *rewrite, replay,* and *remarry,* in which *re-* means again. Thus, you don't *remarry again;* you either *remarry* or *marry again*.

Now let's return to the *Word Workout* vocabulary for the last ten keywords in Level 4:

Word 41: POLYGLOT (PAHL-ee-glaht)
Able to speak and write various languages, multilingual.

Less often, *polyglot* means spoken or written in multiple languages, as *a polyglot Bible* or *an impressive display of polyglot swearing*. Polyglot is also a noun meaning a multilingual person, one who speaks and writes several languages.

Polyglot comes from Latin and Greek words that meant many-tongued. It is a blend of two combining forms: poly-, much, many, several, and -glot, language. The combining form poly- appears in dozens of English words both common and obscure. For example, polygamy (puh-LIG-uh-mee) is marriage to more than one person at one time, and the unusual verb to polylogize (puh-LIL-uh-jyz) means to talk too much: "She came to resent her polylogizing coworkers, whose constant chirping and cackling distracted her." Later in Word Workout you will also meet polymath (word 24 of Level 9), a person who knows a great deal about many subjects.

Our keyword, polyglot, means able to speak and write several languages. A person can be polyglot, multilingual, and sometimes a thing can be described as polyglot. For example, the celebrated 20th-century novelist Vladimir Nabokov,* who was born in Russia, grew up in a polyglot home speaking Russian, French, and English. And New York City is a polyglot city, where on any given day you can hear many different languages from all over the world.

Word 42: COMPORT (kum-PORT)
To bear or conduct oneself, behave, act in a certain way.

The verb to comport comes from the Latin comportāre, to carry together, from com-, with, and portāre, to carry, the source also of the English words import; export; deport; report, literally to carry back, bring back; portable, literally able to be carried; and portfolio, a portable case for carrying loose papers, drawings, and the like.

To comport is always followed by a reflexive pronoun, meaning one with -self or -selves at the end, such as herself, myself, or themselves, and it suggests behavior that conforms to what is expected, required, or considered proper. In other words, you would comport yourself differently at a fancy restaurant or in church than at a bar or a ball game. Experienced trial lawyers know how to

---

* Properly pronounced vluh-DEE-mur nuh-BAW-kuf (the author's pronunciation).

comport themselves in front of a judge and jury. Professional chefs know how to comport themselves in a busy kitchen. And if you want to be an actor you must learn how to comport yourself onstage.

Comportment, one's behavior, conduct, or bearing, is the corresponding noun. *Demeanor* (di-MEE-nur) is a close synonym of *comportment,* but *comportment* is used of conduct that is appropriate and expected, while *demeanor* is used of conduct that expresses one's feeling or attitude toward others: "Nancy was articulate and composed during the interview, and the search committee was impressed with her comportment. They were not impressed with Betsy, her chief rival for the job, whose demeanor they thought was smug."

To *comport* may also mean to be in agreement or accord, conform, and in this sense it is followed by *with,* as *a state law that comports with federal law* or *statements that do not comport with the truth.*

Word 43: REVILE (ri-VYL)

To subject to verbal abuse; to attack with angry, contemptuous, insulting words.

The verb to *revile* combines the prefix *re-,* which in this case means again and again, and the Latin *vīlis,* of little worth, cheap, base, the source of the verb to *vilify,* to speak ill of, belittle, defame, slander, a synonym of *revile.* Other synonyms of *revile* include *disparage, denigrate, reprove* (word 35 of Level 3), *malign* (word 41 of Level 3), *berate* (word 37 of Level 4), *reproach, upbraid, traduce* (truh-D[Y]OOS), *vituperate* (vy-**T[Y]OO**-pur-AYT), *castigate,* and *execrate* (**EKS**-uh-KRAYT).

To *traduce, castigate, execrate, vituperate,* and *revile* are the harshest of this family of words. All imply verbal abuse. To *traduce* is to slander or defame viciously and falsely: "Political campaigns tend to focus on traducing the opposition." To *castigate,* which comes from the Latin *castigāre,* to punish with words or blows, means to beat up verbally, criticize severely, especially to subject to harsh public criticism: "Talk radio show hosts like Rush Limbaugh make their living castigating those with whom they disagree." To *execrate,* which by derivation means to put a curse upon, suggests vehement denunciation prompted by intense loathing: "There will always be a loud faction devoted to execrating the president, regardless of who occupies the White House." To *vituperate,* from the Latin *vitium,* a fault, defect, blemish—the source also of the English verb to *vitiate* (VISH-ee-ayt), to corrupt, contaminate—means to find fault with in violent, abusive language, to rant (word 9 of Level 1) or rail at: "When Republicans and Democrats spend all their time vituperating each other, cooperation and compromise are impossible."

Our keyword, to *revile,* suggests verbal abuse prompted by hatred or contempt. When you revile, you attack someone or something you dislike with angry, insulting words: "The Syrian tyrant Bashar al-Assad was reviled for his crimes against his people."

Word 44: PERSPICACIOUS   (PUR-spi-**KAY**-sh<u>u</u>s)
Having a powerful and penetrating mind, quick to see and understand.

Synonyms of the adjective *perspicacious* include *keen, insightful, discerning, astute, perceptive, shrewd,* and *sagacious* (suh-GAY-sh<u>u</u>s). The noun is *perspicacity* (PUR-spi-**KAS**-i-tee), powerful mental perception, penetrating insight, keen understanding: "Great leaders must have not only a vision for the future but also the perspicacity to realize it."

Perspicacious comes through the Latin *perspĭcax,* sharp-sighted, from *perspĭcere,* to see through, investigate, perceive, discern. When the word entered English in the early 1600s it was used literally of the eyes and the faculty of sight to mean keen, sharp. But it was soon used of people to mean highly perceptive or discerning, having acute or penetrating mental vision. This is the meaning of *perspicacious* in modern usage, and the literal sense, keen-eyed, is now archaic. Today we speak of the perspicacious teacher who can discern each child's needs, the perspicacious reporter who asks penetrating questions, the perspicacious coach who knows just what to say to motivate the team, and the perspicacious humorist who acutely sees the flaws and follies of human nature.

The words *perspicuous* (pur-SPIK-yoo-<u>us</u>) and *perspicacious* look and sound similar, and both come ultimately from the Latin *perspĭcere,* to see through. But despite this kinship they are sharply distinguished in meaning. *Perspicuous* refers to that which is lucid or clearly expressed: a perspicuous prose style is plain and clear; a perspicuous poem is easily understood. *Perspicacious,* on the other hand, refers to exceptional clarity of mind, keen mental perception, the ability to see and understand things clearly: "The report showed a perspicacious grasp of the facts and the complexities of the problem."

Word 45: TRIUMVIRATE (try-UHM-vur-it, *not* TRY-<u>um</u>-**VY**-rit)
A group or set of three, a trio.

The word *triumvir* (try-UHM-vur) comes from the Latin *trium virōrum,* of three men, from *trēs,* three, and *vir,* a man. In ancient Rome a *triumvir* was one of three officers or magistrates who, acting as a commission, fulfilled various public duties, from basic things such as guarding against fires at night to serious matters such as overseeing the execution of the condemned.

Triumvirate has traditionally applied to a group of three people wielding power, as when Henry Adams, in 1879, wrote that "Jefferson, Madison, and Gallatin were a triumvirate which governed the country during eight years," or to any three people of distinction or influence, as "Byron, Shelley, and Keats are the triumvirate of Romantic poetry." But the word has increasingly been applied to a set of three things related in some way, a trio. For instance, the Axis—the alliance of Germany, Italy, and Japan in World War II—was a triumvirate. And when Yahoo, AOL, and YouTube worked together in 2012 to encourage social media interaction during the presidential debates, Steve Friess of politico.com called it "an unlikely triumvirate."

Word 46: AUGURY (AWG-yur-ee)
An omen, indication, portent; a sign of something in the future.

In ancient Rome, an *augur* (AW-gur) was a kind of soothsayer or prophet, specifically a religious official charged with interpreting omens and making predictions. (Take care not to confuse this augur with an *auger,* a tool for boring.) The Roman augur would observe various natural signs—for example, the movements or cries of birds, the entrails of a sacrificed animal, or the position of the stars—and tell whether they indicated a favorable or unfavorable future event.

The noun *augury* comes from the Latin *augurium,* which meant either the work of an augur or the observation and interpretation of omens. When it entered English in the 14th century, *augury* meant skill in making prophecies or the practice of foretelling events, also called divination. This sense is still in good standing today. By the early 17th century *augury* had also come to mean that from which a prediction is drawn, an omen, sign, indication, harbinger (word 38 of Level 4). An augury may be unfavorable, as "When interest rates climb it is often an augury of inflation." Or it may be favorable, as "The dove is an augury of peace," or "The film's awards at the festival may be an augury of success at the Oscars."

Writers sometimes use *augury* in phrases like *an augury of things to come* or *an augury of the future.* These are redundant constructions that should be avoided because *augury* already means a sign of something to come, an indication of the future.

Word 47: PALLID (PAL-id, rhymes with *valid*)
Lacking color or liveliness.

Pallid comes from the Latin *pallidus,* pale, colorless, which comes in turn from the verb *pallēre,* to be pale, especially with fear or anxiety. Because of this etymology, since its first documented use in 1590 *pallid* has often implied paleness from illness or strong emotion. Skin, faces, cheeks, and lips are often described as pallid, pale, ashy white, especially when they belong to a person who is sick, in shock, or dead. But *pallid* may also apply to anything with faint coloring, as *a pallid bookworm whose complexion had never seen the sun.* In "The Eve of St. Agnes," John Keats used *pallid* of the light of the moon: "Out went the taper as she hurried in; / Its little smoke, in pallid moonshine, died." And in "The Raven," Edgar Allan Poe used *pallid* to describe the milky white color of a marble statue: "the pallid bust of Pallas just above my chamber door."

In its extended figurative use, which also dates back to the late 1500s, *pallid* means lacking liveliness or vitality. Something may be pallid, lacking in liveliness, because it is weak or feeble, as *a pallid response* or *a pallid economic recovery.* Or something may be pallid because it lacks energy or interest, and is therefore dull, uninteresting, as *a novel with a pallid plot* or *a pallid remake of a classic film.*

Synonyms of the adjective *pallid* meaning lacking color, pale, include *wan* (WAHN), *sallow* (SAL-oh), *ashen,* and *haggard* (HAG-urd). Synonyms of *pallid* meaning lacking liveliness include *lifeless, cheerless, drab, tedious, tiresome, humdrum,* and *vapid* (VAP-id). The corresponding noun is *pallor* (PAL-ur), extreme paleness, as from illness or death, as *the pallor of contemporary fashion models.*

Take care not to confuse *pallor,* paleness, with the word *pall* (pronounced like the name *Paul*). A *pall* is something that covers or overspreads with darkness or gloom, as *the thick pall of smoke from the chimneys,* or a feeling of gloom, as *his ominous presence cast a pall over the room.*

Word 48: INDOLENT (IN-duh-lint)
Lazy, idle, inactive; avoiding work, activity, or effort.

The noun is *indolence,* a state of lazy inactivity or an inclination to be lazy: "Nights of wild indulgence and days of sleepy indolence— that was Dustin's life until the money ran out."

The adjective *indolent* and the noun *indolence* come from the Latin privative prefix *in-*, not, and *dolēre,* to suffer pain, grieve. By derivation *indolent* means not suffering pain, and when the word entered English in the late 17th century it was a medical term that meant causing little or no pain, inactive or benign, as *an indolent tumor* or *an indolent ulcer.* This medical use is still in good standing, but by the early 18th century *indolent* was already being used of people to mean lazy, idle, inclined to avoid work or activity, as in this 1774 citation from the letters of Horace Walpole, fourth Earl of Orford: "I am naturally indolent, and without application to any kind of business." More than two and a half centuries later *indolent* is still used in this way. We speak of indolent adolescents who sleep till noon, or indolent slackers who shirk their duties at work. *Indolent* may also be used as a noun: "You don't become a billionaire, the plutocrat Malcolm Prendergast liked to say, by dispensing charity to the indolent." (*Plutocrat* is word 5 of this level.)

Synonyms of *indolent* include *sluggish, slothful, apathetic, spiritless, shiftless, listless* (word 39 of Level 2), *lethargic, languid, phlegmatic* (fleg-MAT-ik), *otiose* (OH-shee-ohs), *faineant* (FAY-nee-int), which comes from French and means literally "he does nothing," and *hebetudinous* (HEB-uh-T(Y)OO-di-nus), which comes from the Latin *hebēre,* to be blunt, dull, heavy, or inactive.

Antonyms of *indolent* include *busy, industrious, diligent, assiduous* (uh-SIJ-oo-us), and *sedulous* (SEJ-uh-lus, word 28 of Level 7).

Word 49: UTILITARIAN (yoo-TIL-uh-TAIR-ee-in)
Practical, useful, functional; concerned with or intended for ordinary, practical use.

The noun *utility* means practical usefulness, fitness for some practical purpose, as *a prehistoric tool whose utility has long puzzled archaeologists.* A public utility provides a practical service to the community, such as distributing water, electricity, or natural gas. A utility knife is a knife used for a number of practical purposes. And a utility room is a room for appliances, such as a washing machine or water heater, that perform everyday, practical functions.

Utility, which entered English in the 14th century, and *utilitarian,* which entered English in the late 18th century, both come from the Latin *ūtĭlis,* useful, fit, serviceable, beneficial, the source also of the English verb to *utilize,* to make practical or profitable

use of, and the unusual adjective *utile* (YOO-t̲i̲l), a fancy synonym of *useful.*

Utilitarianism is the ethical doctrine, promulgated★ in the late
18th century chiefly by the English philosopher Jeremy Bentham
(BEN-th̲u̲m, 1748–1832), that the greatest happiness of the greatest number should be the prime consideration of society and the
aim of all public action. This doctrine naturally led to the idea
that the virtue or value of something must be judged by its utility, its ability to promote the public good or its practical usefulness to all.

The adjective *utilitarian* may mean pertaining or adhering to the
doctrine of utilitarianism, as *a utilitarian law,* one intended to promote the welfare of all citizens. But more often *utilitarian* means
having utility, practical usefulness, fitness for a useful purpose.
That which is utilitarian values function over form and usefulness
over beauty. A utilitarian car offers no frills or amenities and simply gets you where you need to go. A utilitarian building is a functional building, with no ornamentation. A utilitarian dress is
practical, not attractive. And while many would use the word *wild-
life* for wild animals, hunters tend to take a more utilitarian view
and call them *game.*

Word 50: SALACIOUS (suh-LAY-sh̲u̲s, rhymes with *flirtatious*)
Lustful, expressing sexual desire; also, appealing to sexual desire, indecent
or obscene.

Synonyms of *salacious* include *sensual, lewd, lecherous, wanton, pruri-
ent* (PRUUR-ee-i̲nt), *lascivious, libidinous* (li-BID'n-u̲s), *debauched*
(the verb to *debauch* is word 30 of Level 5), *dissolute* (DIS-uh-loot,
word 7 of Level 6), and *concupiscent* (kahn-KYOO-pi-si̲nt), which
comes ultimately from the Latin *cupĕre,* to desire, long for, the
source also of the name *Cupid,* the ancient Roman god of love,
typically depicted as an infant boy with wings carrying a bow

---

★ **Promulgate** (pruh-MUHL-gayt or PRAHM-u̲l-gayt) means to make known, publish, proclaim,
make public in an official manner.

and arrows, and the English word *cupidity,* excessive desire or lust to possess something, especially wealth; hence greed, avarice.

Antonyms of *salacious* include *modest, prim, prudish, puritanical, straitlaced,* and *sanctimonious,* which means characterized by hypocritical self-righteousness, virtuousness, or religious piety: "Viewers were outraged when the popular televangelist was exposed as a sanctimonious humbug who had committed fraud."

Salacious comes from the Latin *salax,* lustful or exciting lust, which comes in turn from the verb *salīre,* to leap, spring. A salacious look or gesture is lustful; it expresses sexual desire. Salacious images or salacious details excite lust and are therefore indecent or obscene. In the news these days we often hear about a politician exchanging salacious email or text messages with a paramour (PAR-uh-moor), an illicit lover.

Review Quiz for Keywords 41–50
In this quiz the review word is followed by three words or phrases, and you must decide which comes nearest the meaning of the review word. **Answers appear on page 200.**

1. Does *polyglot* mean extremely hungry, able to speak various languages, or proficient in many subjects?

2. When you *comport* yourself, do you behave in a certain way, calm down, or move from one place to another?

3. If you *revile* something, do you find it disgusting, abuse it verbally, or adore it?

4. Are *perspicacious* people extremely cautious, very curious, or very insightful?

5. Is a *triumvirate* a group of three, a group of four, or a group of five?

6. Is an *augury* a favorable opportunity, an indication, or an initiation ceremony?

7. Is *pallid* writing uninteresting, uncultured, or unreadable?

8. Are *indolent* people lazy, stupid, or uncooperative?

9. Is something *utilitarian* old-fashioned, ideal, or practical?

10. Is a *salacious* look hopeful, furious, or lustful?

The Style File: Proper Placement of *Only*

In *Sin and Syntax,* her lively guide to effective style, Constance Hale reminds us that adverbs are modifiers: "They need to cozy up to the word they modify." Take the adverb *only,* for example. Most writers toss the word into a sentence with little regard for how it can subtly affect meaning. But careful writers know that *only* should be placed as close as possible to the word or phrase it's meant to modify.

Look at how moving around the adverb *only* in the sentence *She told me that she thought about me* changes the meaning:

Only she told me that she thought about me. (No one else has mentioned it.)

She **only** told me that she thought about me. (She didn't write me or say anything else.)

She told **only** me that she thought about me. (She doesn't want anyone else to know.)

She told me **only** that she thought about me. (She didn't say anything else about me.)

She told me that **only** she thought about me. (Nobody else thinks about me.)

She told me that she **only** thought about me. (She didn't take any other action.)

She told me that she thought **only** about me. (I am the sole object of her thoughts.)★

"In general, *only* ought to be attached to the word or phrase it is modifying and not set adrift," says *Bryson's Dictionary of Troublesome Words.* The *New York Times* reporter who wrote that "insurgencies can *only* be defeated when . . . communities and military forces work together" needed a thoughtful copyeditor to reposition *only* so that it would be next to what it's supposed to modify: "insurgencies that can be defeated *only* when . . . communities and military forces work together."

★   I have adapted this exercise from page 96 of *Sin and Syntax.*

The next time you're about to type the word *only,* consider how its position in your sentence affects the meaning, and whether it's next to what it's supposed to modify.

Answers to Review Quizzes for Level 4

KEYWORDS 1–10

1. No. Something *hackneyed* lacks freshness and interest or is ordinary and dull from overuse.
2. No. *Iniquity* means wickedness, gross injustice, or a wicked or grossly unjust act—and petty theft is not wicked or grossly unjust.
3. Yes. *Whimsical* means oddly fanciful or comical, exhibiting odd, playful, fickle humor. The word may apply to things or people.
4. No. *Ensconce* means the opposite of exposing to view: to shelter, cover, or hide securely; also, to settle or fix comfortably and securely.
5. No. A *plutocrat* is a wealthy and powerful person.
6. No. *Whimsical* implies playfulness and odd humor. *Beatific* means having, showing, or imparting supreme happiness or bliss.
7. No. If you are unfettered by debt you are free of it. *Unfettered* means unrestrained, unrestricted, without restraint or control.
8. No. *Estrange* means to make unfriendly or hostile, to distance or push away.
9. Yes. *Sibilant* means hissing or making the whistling sound of *s.*
10. Yes. A *pundit* is an expert, critic, or commentator who is frequently called on to express opinions to the public.

KEYWORDS 11–20

1. True. Something redolent is strong-smelling or reminiscent of something else.
2. True. A plutocrat is a wealthy and powerful person, and there's nothing to stop someone like that from being a demagogue, a rabble-rouser.
3. False. A maudlin person is tearfully sentimental or foolishly emotional, especially from drunkenness.
4. True. When you begrudge, you envy or resent someone else's good fortune, pleasure, or possession of something, or you are unwilling to give or allow something because of envy or resentment.

5. False. A disavowal is a refusal to accept or acknowledge. An avowal is an open declaration; a frank acknowledgment, admission, or affirmation.

6. True. When you proselytize you attempt to convert others from one religion, party, cause, or opinion to another.

7. False. A guileless person is honest and innocent, open and sincere.

8. True. Unconscionable behavior is not guided or restrained by conscience.

9. False. When you conflate you bring together two or more separate or different things to form one unified thing.

10. False. Animus is a deep-seated dislike or feeling of ill will.

KEYWORDS 21–30

1. Synonyms. A *swath* is a long strip, belt, or area.

2. Synonyms. A *conflagration* is a great, destructive fire; a disastrous blaze.

3. Antonyms. *Mundane,* from the Latin *mundus,* world, means of the world, earthly, material as distinguished from spiritual. *Rarefied* means highly refined, elevated, lofty, or belonging only to a small, select group, esoteric.

4. Antonyms. A *plutocrat* is a person of great wealth and power. A *mendicant* is a beggar.

5. Synonyms. To *recompense* is to reward or repay for something done or given; also, to repay or compensate for a loss, damage, or injury.

6. Synonyms. To *inundate* is to overflow, overwhelm, flood.

7. Antonyms. To *aggrandize* is to increase the power, influence, wealth, or status of.

8. Antonyms. *Outré* means beyond the bounds of what is considered usual, normal, or proper; hence, untraditional.

9. Antonyms. *Quintessential* means being the perfect, most refined, or most typical example or instance of something.

10. Synonyms. To *pander* is to cater to or indulge the vulgar tastes and desires of others or to exploit their passions, prejudices, or weaknesses.

KEYWORDS 31–40

1. *Very secret* doesn't fit. *Sacrosanct* means very sacred or holy.

2. *Unmanageable* doesn't fit. *Indomitable* means unconquerable, unyielding.

3. *A person's circumstances* doesn't fit. *Mettle* is a person's disposition or temperament, or strength of spirit or character.

4. *A mistake* doesn't fit. An *ellipsis* is an omission, something left out.

5. *Desperate for love and attention* doesn't fit. *Petulant* means showing sudden irritation or anger, impatient over trivial things.

6. *Do something unthinkingly* doesn't fit. To *deign* is to do something beneath one's dignity or to grant reluctantly.

7. *Judge unfairly* doesn't fit. To *berate* is to scold or criticize harshly.

8. *Answer* doesn't fit. A *harbinger* is a sign or indication of something to come.

9. *Frumpy,* drab and unattractive, doesn't fit. *Corpulent* means fleshy, fat.

10. *Unsatisfied* doesn't fit. *Aggrieved* means wronged, offended, injured.

KEYWORDS 41–50

1. *Polyglot* means able to speak various languages, multilingual.

2. When you *comport* yourself, you behave in a certain way, especially in a way that is appropriate, expected, or required.

3. When you *revile* something you abuse it verbally, attack it with angry words.

4. *Perspicacious* people are very insightful, quick to see and understand.

5. A *triumvirate* is a group of three, a trio.

6. An *augury* is an indication, omen, sign of something in the future.

7. *Pallid* writing is uninteresting, dull. *Pallid* means either pale, lacking color, or lacking liveliness or vitality.

8. *Indolent* people are lazy and tend to avoid work, activity, or effort.

9. Something *utilitarian* is practical, useful, functional.

10. A *salacious* look is lustful. *Salacious* means expressing or appealing to sexual desire.

LEVEL 5

Word 1: BEREFT (bi-REFT)
Forcibly deprived, dispossessed, or robbed; deprived of something needed, wanted, or expected. Also, grieving, bereaved, deprived of a loved one.

The verb to *bereave* (bi-REEV) may mean to rob, dispossess, deprive of something, or to be deprived of a loved one by death. *Bereaved* and *bereft* are both past tenses and past participles of *bereave,* and the two forms are distinguished in careful usage. *Bereaved* means deprived of a loved one by death: "The bereaved family occupied the front pew at the memorial service." *Bereft* means deprived, often forcibly, of something immaterial, such as a possession, a quality, or an emotion, as *a house bereft of joy, a woman bereft of her youthful beauty,* or *spending cuts that left the program bereft of financial support.*

"To be bereft of something is not to lack it but to be dispossessed of it," notes *Bryson's Dictionary of Troublesome Words,* which cites the following sentence as an example of the common but careless use of *bereft* to mean *lacking:* "Many children leave school altogether bereft of mathematical skills." Were those children stripped of their math skills before graduation? Unless their teachers somehow managed to unteach them, they merely *lack* math skills; they cannot be deprived of skills they never possessed.

The phrase *bereft of ideas* is also commonly misused to mean lacking ideas or barren of ideas rather than deprived of ideas.

When you're bereft you have lost or been deprived of something you want, need, or expect. "Madam, you have bereft me of all words," writes Shakespeare in *The Merchant of Venice*. If you are in a hopeless situation, you're bereft of hope. If you're a smoker who's just smoked the last cigarette in the pack, you're bereft of cigarettes. And when people lose their composure and do crazy things, we say they're bereft of their senses.

Word 2: NEMESIS (NEM-i-sis)
A person or thing that metes out vengeance or punishment, that brings about someone's downfall, or that cannot be overcome; an unconquerable avenger.

Nemesis comes from the name *Nemesis,* the ancient Greek goddess of *retribution* (RE-tri-**BYOO**-shin), repayment in return for a wrong, vengeance. In Greek mythology, explains *The Century Dictionary,* Nemesis was "a goddess personifying allotment, or the divine distribution to every man of his precise share of fortune, good and bad. It was her especial function to see that the proper proportion of individual prosperity was preserved, and that any one who became too prosperous or was too much uplifted by his prosperity should be reduced or punished; she thus came to be regarded as the goddess of divine retribution."

Traditionally, a nemesis is an agent of retribution, an unconquerable avenger, as in this sentence from 1870: "Scientific skepticism . . . is the Nemesis which will crush institutionalized religion into nothingness." In his usage guide *Right, Wrong, and Risky,* Mark Davidson cites a 1997 *New York Times* headline that "identified Mississippi Attorney General Michael C. Moore as a 'Tobacco Industry Nemesis' for filing 'the first lawsuit by a state against the nation's cigarette manufacturers . . . [and leading] a cross-country crusade that has rallied 21 other states to the cause.'"

In contemporary usage this traditional meaning has been watered down, and the word is now frequently used as a fancier-sounding synonym of *rival, opponent,* or *enemy,* often in the hackneyed (word 1 of Level 4) phrase *old nemesis* or combined with *arch-* to form a pretentious substitute for *archenemy* or *archrival.* Here are two examples of this diluted usage: "The Mets rose up to batter their old nemesis, the Braves, 9–4" (*Star-Ledger*, New Jersey); "His arch-nemesis is the evil Lex Luthor, who diminishes Superman's power with Kryptonite" (David Mansour, *From Abba to Zoom*, 2005).

Citations like these perturb (word 25 of Level 6) many usage experts. "A nemesis," cautions *Bryson's Dictionary of Troublesome Words*, "is not merely a rival or traditional adversary . . . but one who exacts retributive justice or is utterly unvanquishable." Careful writers and speakers avoid using *nemesis* for any old rival or enemy and reserve the word for a person or thing that metes out retributive justice or that is impossible to overcome.

Word 3: EQUIVOCATE (i-KWIV-uh-kayt)

To use evasive or ambiguous language so as to avoid commitment or to willfully mislead.

The verb to *equivocate* entered English in 1590, formed from the past participle of the Middle Latin *aequivocāre*, to call by the same name, from *aequus*, equal, and *vocāre*, to call, the source also of the English *evoke*, to call forth, and *vocation*, a calling to some occupation or course of action.

In his landmark dictionary of 1755, Samuel Johnson defined *equivocate* as "to use words of double meaning; to use ambiguous expressions; to mean one thing and express another." This is still the core sense of the word today. When you equivocate you express yourself in a subtle and evasive manner, using ambiguous words and double meanings so as to mislead. In short, you say one thing but mean another. "The witness shuffled, equivocated, [and] pretended to misunderstand the questions," wrote Thomas Babington Macaulay in his celebrated *History of England* (1849–61).

Synonyms of the verb to *equivocate* include to *dodge, shuffle, quibble, dissemble* (di-SEM-bul), *prevaricate* (pri-VAR-i-kayt), *palter* (PAWL-tur), and *tergiversate* (TUR-ji-vur-sayt). Of these words, to *dissemble* means specifically to disguise or cover up the facts, or to conceal one's true feelings or motives; to *prevaricate* is to evade the truth, sometimes with an outright lie; to *palter* is to trifle with the truth by expressing oneself insincerely or deceitfully; and to *tergiversate* is to use evasive language so as to avoid taking a firm stand. The well-worn expressions *to mince words* and *to beat around the bush* are also close in meaning to our keyword, to *equivocate*.

The noun is *equivocation,* an evasive or ambiguous statement. The adjective is *equivocal,* deliberately vague, evasive, or ambiguous, as *an equivocal answer.* Its antonym, *unequivocal* (un–i–KWIV-uh-kul), means straightforward, clear and direct: "They voiced their unequivocal support."

Word 4: PHILISTINE (FIL-i-steen)

A narrow-minded person with ordinary tastes who has no interest in the arts or learning; an uneducated and uncultured person.

In the ancient world of the 12th and 11th centuries B.C., Philistia (fi-LIS-tee-uh) was a country on the east coast of the Mediterranean Sea between Egypt and Syria whose inhabitants, the Philistines, were continually engaged in territorial warfare with the ancient Israelites. "In the Bible the great Hebrew antagonists of the Philistines are Samson, Saul, and David," says the *Columbia Encyclopedia.* Saul was the "first king of the ancient Hebrews," whose "proximity to the Philistines brought him into constant conflict with them"; Samson was delivered into the hands of the Philistines by the treacherous Delilah, who cut off the hair that gave Samson his great strength; and young David slew the formidable (FOR-mi-duh-buul) Philistine giant Goliath with a slingshot.

From this wartorn ancient history *philistine* came to be used, often humorously, of any enemy or persecutor, or of a debauched or drunken person. (The verb to *debauch* is word 30 of this level.) But by the early 1800s the word had acquired its modern and dominant meaning: an uneducated, materialistic person who is smugly indifferent to art and culture.

In modern usage, a philistine is the opposite of a *connoisseur* (KAHN-uh-**SUR**, like *con a sir,* not *con a sewer*). While the connoisseur has expert knowledge and subtle appreciation of some art form or aesthetic pursuit, the philistine is uneducated and uncultured and doesn't care a whit. Fine art, literature, classical music, and gourmet cooking—often called haute cuisine (OHTkwi-**ZEEN**)—are all lost on the philistine, whose tastes are ordinary and whose sensibility is unrefined.

Word 5: BACCHANALIAN (BAK-uh-**NAY**-lee-<u>i</u>n)
Characterized by, or given to, drunken revelry; frenzied, riotous, or orgiastic.

Bacchanalian is an eponymous word—one derived from a name—because nestled within it is the name Bacchus (BAK-<u>us</u>, not BAH-k<u>us</u>), the ancient Roman god of wine and ecstasy, called Dionysus (DY-uh-**NY**-sis) by the ancient Greeks. Because Bacchus, or Dionysus, "apparently represented the sap, juice, or lifeblood element in nature, lavish festal orgies in his honor were widely instituted," says *Merriam-Webster's Encyclopedia of Literature.* (*Festal,* pronounced FES-t<u>ul</u>, means pertaining to or befitting a feast or festival.) A riotous, drunken celebration of Bacchus was called a *bacchanal* (BAK-uh-**NAL**, like *back canal*), a word often used today of any wild, drunken party. These *bacchanalia* (BAK-uh-**NAY**-lee-uh), drunken celebrations, were attended by carousers known as *bacchants* (BAK-<u>i</u>nts), a word still used today of drunken revelers.*

    Bacchanalian originally referred to the orgiastic Roman festival of Bacchus, but the word was soon applied to any riotous, drunken revelry or wild carousing. The peculiar American ritual known as spring break, in which cartloads of college students travel to the beach for a week of unrestrained revelry involving copious amounts of booze and bare skin, is decidedly bacchanalian.

Word 6: SCHISM (SIZ'm; commonly but improperly, SKIZ'm)†
A division, split, or break; specifically, disunion, a division or separation into opposing factions of a group that previously acted together as one.

Schism comes through Middle English, French, and Late Latin from the Greek *schisma,* a rent, cleft, division. This Greek *schisma*

---

* A male drunken carouser is a *bacchant,* while a female carouser is a *bacchante* (buh-KAN-tee). The plural for both men and women is *bacchants.*
† For a history of the pronunciation of *schism,* see my *Big Book of Beastly Mispronunciations.*

comes in turn from the verb *schizein,* to split or rend, which is related to the English verb to *shed.*

Originally a *schism* was a formal division or breach of unity in a church or religious body. This sense of the word is still in good use today. Later *schism* was applied to any sect, party, or group formed by a schism, a division or split, as in this 1647 quotation from the English historian James Howell: "Hence comes it that the earth is rent into so many religions, and those religions torn into so many schismes, and various formes of devotion." Finally, since the 15th century *schism* has also been used generally of any split or division resulting from discord and disunity within a group, as *a schism in the city council,* or any severance of unity between people or things, as *the schism in the American electorate between blue states and red states* or *a schism of the mind and heart.*

The adjective is *schismatic* (siz–MAT–ik), of or pertaining to a schism, and the verb is *schismatize* (SIZ–muh–tyz), to cause a schism in.

Word 7: LINGUA FRANCA (LING-gwuh FRANK-uh)
A common language; a medium of communication between people who speak different languages.

The plural is preferably *lingua francas* (FRANK-uhz).

Lingua franca comes to English directly from Italian, where it means literally "Frankish tongue." (*Frankish,* a synonym of *French,* in this case means pertaining to the nations of Europe or the West.) Originally, *lingua franca* was a mixture of languages—consisting mostly of Italian with bits of French, Spanish, Greek, Arabic, and Turkish—used by sailors and merchants in Mediterranean ports. The term soon broadened to designate any language, mixed or not, that serves as a means of communication for people who speak different languages. For example, for a long time Latin was the lingua franca of the Roman Catholic Church, and although Hindi is not the native language of most Indians, it is the lingua franca of India.

Today *lingua franca* is most often used either to denote a common language used by people who speak different languages or, figuratively, to denote something that functions like a common language: "Discontent with high prices is the lingua franca of shoppers everywhere" (*Sydney Morning Herald*).

In the 20th century English displaced French as the lingua franca of diplomacy. It is also the lingua franca of international aviation. And because English is now spoken, with at least some degree of fluency, by perhaps more than two billion people around the world, it has become the lingua franca of the global marketplace, of the Internet, and of popular culture worldwide—partly because of its insatiable appetite for foreign words and phrases like *lingua franca*.

Word 8: WINSOME (WIN-sum)
Charming, agreeable, and pleasant in appearance or manner.

Synonyms of *winsome* include *winning, captivating, engaging, enchanting, prepossessing*—which means creating a favorable impression, as *a well-spoken, prepossessing job candidate*—and *beguiling,* which may mean deceptive, misleading, as *beguiling words,* or charming, alluring, delightful, as *a beguiling melody.*

Winsome, which comes from an Old English word that meant joy, always implies sweet and sincere charm as opposed to the stiff, insincere charm people manufacture to be polite or make a good impression. Pleasant and friendly young people, or pleasant and friendly older folks who seem young at heart, are often called winsome, for a certain childlike innocence and lightheartedness are qualities often implied by *winsome.*

Almost anything sweetly charming and agreeable in appearance or manner can be called winsome. A face, a laugh, a voice, a smile, a piece of music, a painting, a novel, a poem, a ballerina, or an attractive and agreeable person (usually a young woman) can all be winsome.

Word 9: PATRICIAN (puh-TRISH-in)
Aristocratic; of high birth or social standing; upper-class.

Synonyms of *patrician* include *noble, royal, blue-blooded,* and *silk-stocking*—as *a silk-stocking district,* an area where you will find wealthy people engaged in fashionable pursuits. Antonyms of *patrician* include *plebeian* (ple-BEE-in, word 20 of this level); *proletarian* (PROH-luh-**TAIR**-ee-in), of or pertaining to the *proletariat* (PROH-luh-**TAIR**-ee-it), the working class; and *bourgeois* (boor-ZHWAH), pertaining to or characteristic of the middle class, especially the mediocrity and materialistic aspirations of the middle class. (Be sure to pronounce the *r* in the middle of **bourgeois** and rhyme the first syllable with *poor*. Don't say boozh-WAH, buuzh-WAH, or buush-WAH.

Patrician comes from the Latin *patrĭcĭus,* which meant either a member of the *patres,* the ancient Roman nobility, or belonging to that upper class. In ancient Roman history, a patrician was someone who belonged to one of the original citizen families of the city, and specifically a member of the senatorial aristocracy appointed by Romulus, the legendary founder of the city. By the 17th century *patrician* had come to denote a person from an established and wealthy family, a member of the upper class, and as an adjective it was used to mean pertaining to well-educated, privileged people of refined tastes. Today the adjective is used of almost anything that smacks of upper-class membership or manners, as *a patrician air, a patrician style, patrician courtesy, a patrician accent,* and even *a patrician nose.*

Word 10: REDACT (ri-DAKT)

To edit, revise, prepare a piece of writing for publication; especially, to adapt or remove text from a document to make it suitable for publication.

The verb to *redact* comes from the Latin *redactus,* the past participle of the verb *redĭgĕre,* to drive, lead, or send back, which comes in turn from *re-,* back, and *agĕre,* to drive or set in motion, the source of the English noun *agent,* a person or thing that acts, and *agitate,* to shake, disturb, excite.

To *revise* and to *edit* are the general words for preparing a text for publication. To *redact* is to edit or revise with greater scrutiny, particularly with an eye toward deleting or masking any objectionable or sensitive material. This implication sometimes makes *redact* a synonym of *censor, purge, expurgate* (**EKS**-pur-GAYT), and *bowdlerize* (BOWD-luh-ryz): "The judge denied defense counsel's request to redact the names of the alleged conspirators from the transcript of the trial."

The noun *redaction* is the act of editing text for publication, particularly by removing inappropriate material, or any text that has been redacted, revised and adapted so as to make suitable for publication.

Review Quiz for Keywords 1–10

Consider the following questions and decide whether the correct answer is yes or no. **Answers appear on page 247**.

1. Is a family whose house has just burned down bereft of a place to live?
2. In careful usage, is your nemesis your enemy or rival?
3. Does someone who equivocates speak honestly and straightforwardly?
4. Is a philistine likely to enjoy going to the opera?
5. Would a bacchanalian event be calm and quiet?
6. Is a schism a coming together of groups that were formerly divided?
7. Is English the lingua franca of international aviation?
8. Can something sweetly charming and agreeable be winsome?
9. Does *patrician* mean belonging to the middle class?
10. Are newspaper stories usually redacted before publication?

Difficult Distinctions: *Practical* and *Practicable*

Have you ever wondered whether there's a difference between the adjectives *practical* and *practicable*? There is, not only in meaning but also in pronunciation—*practical* has three syllables but *practicable* has four: PRAK-ti-kuh-bul.

Practical means having a useful purpose or capable of being put to good use. *Practicable* means workable, feasible, doable, capable of being put into practice. A useful tool is practical, of good use; a well-designed plan is practicable, workable.

Here are the next ten keyword discussions:

Word 11: PRÉCIS (pray-SEE)
A brief summary, especially of a book, article, or other text; a concise outline of essential points or facts.

Synonyms of *précis* include *digest, synopsis, condensation, abstract, abridgment, conspectus,* and *aperçu* (ap-air-SOO). The word *résumé* (REZ-uh-may), familiar to millions of job-seekers who prepare one to outline their professional experience and accomplishments, may also be used to mean a summary, condensed statement, and in this sense it is also a synonym of *précis*.

Précis comes directly from the French noun *précis,* a summary, and in English *précis* is most often used to mean a concise summary of something written, such as a speech, novel, or academic treatise. But a précis may also be a summary of a topic, as *a précis of the scientific consensus on climate change.* Précis-writing is the art of composing précis, brief summaries or abstracts, and a précis-writer is a person who writes précis. (The plural is pronounced pray-SEEZ.)

Although *précis* has been used in English since about 1750, it is still always printed with an acute accent over the *e,* as in French.

Word 12: TAXONOMY (tak-SAHN-uh-mee)
The branch of biology that deals with classification, or an orderly system of naming and classifying organisms.

Taxonomy, which English borrowed in the early 19th century from French, is a blend of two combining forms from Greek: *taxo-,* arrangement, order, and *-nomy,* which designates "a system of laws governing a (specified) field or the sum of knowledge regarding them" (*Webster 2*), as in *astronomy,* the study of the laws of the universe, and *agronomy* (uh-GRAH-nuh-mee), the science of soil management and crop production.

In biology, taxonomy is a system of identifying, naming, and classifying living things, such as plants and animals. The related word *nomenclature* (**NOH**-men-KLAY-chur) refers to the system of names used in a science, art, or branch of knowledge. In the 18th century, the Swedish botanist Carolus Linnaeus (KAR-uh-lus li-NEE-us) invented the binomial (by-NOH-mee-ul) system of nomenclature, in which two Latin names are assigned to each species (properly SPEE-sheez, not SPEE-seez), the first identifying the genus (JEE-nus), or general kind, and the second identifying the species itself.

Traditionally *taxonomy* denotes the classification of organisms, but in modern usage it may also refer to the orderly classification of anything, as in *the taxonomy of time travel in movies, the social taxonomy of high school,* and *a taxonomy of sports coaches.*

Word 13: SUBLIMINAL (suhb-LIM-i-nul)
Below one's level of awareness; existing in, coming from, or subtly affecting the subconscious mind.

The adjective *subliminal* combines the Latin *sub,* under, and *līmen,* the threshold, border, and by derivation means below the threshold or border of consciousness. Something subliminal functions below the level of your awareness, as *a subliminal desire* or *a subliminal impulse.*

Subliminal messages may either originate in your subconscious or influence your subconscious mind. For example, advertising often sends the subliminal message that you will be happier, healthier, wealthier, or smarter if you buy or consume a certain product. Post-hypnotic suggestion operates on a subliminal, or subconscious, level, as do self-improvement programs that promise to teach you while you sleep. (Whether they can fulfill that promise is another matter.) Propaganda also works subliminally because it can evoke a response without awareness of that response; in other words, it can persuade people or call them to action by stirring up strong emotions—fear or hatred or self-interest—that lie below their threshold of consciousness.

The verb to *sublimate* (SUHB-li-mayt) and the noun *sublimation* have specific meanings in psychology. To *sublimate* is to suppress one's primitive, instinctive, or socially unacceptable impulses—to keep them beneath one's level of consciousness—and to modify or divert the antisocial energy of those impulses into something socially acceptable. *Sublimation* refers to the act of sublimating, of keeping distasteful impulses below the threshold of awareness, as *the sublimation of sexual desire.*

Word 14: MISANTHROPY (mis-AN-thruh-pee)
Hatred or distrust of humankind; spiteful pessimism about the human race.

The noun *misanthrope* (MIS-un-throhp) denotes a person who hates or deeply distrusts other human beings. And the adjective *misanthropic* (MIS-un-**THRAHP**-ik) means having an aversion (uh-VUR-zhun) to the human race. (*Aversion* is intense dislike or disgust.) These words, and our keyword, *misanthropy,* hatred or distrust of humankind, all come from the Greek *mīsánthrōpos,* hating humankind, which comes in turn from *misein,* to hate, and *ánthrōpos,* a man, human being.

From the Greek *ánthrōpos* we get the combining form *anthropo-,* of or pertaining to human beings, which appears in numerous English words, including *anthropomorphic* (AN-throh-puh-**MOR**-fik), shaped like or resembling a human being; *anthropomorphize* (AN-thruh-puh-**MOR**-fyz), to personify, give human form or feelings to something not human; and *anthropoid* (AN-thruh-poyd), resembling or shaped like a human being.

The familiar word *philanthropy,* from the Greek *philein,* to love, and *ánthrōpos,* a man, human being, is love of humankind—the opposite of our keyword, *misanthropy,* hatred or distrust of humankind.

Word 15: IMPRIMATUR (IM-pri-**MAH**-tur)
Approval, support; also, a mark of approval or support.

Synonyms of *imprimatur* include *license, sanction, authorization, sponsorship,* and *dispensation.*

Imprimatur comes directly from the New Latin word *imprimātur,* which means "let it be printed." Originally an imprimatur was an official license to print and publish granted by the licenser of the press, especially such a license granted by a censor of the Roman Catholic Church.

From this specific sense *imprimatur* broadened to mean approval, license, or support in general, or a mark of approval or support.

Thus, when Oprah Winfrey selected a book for her book club, everyone knew that receiving her imprimatur would make the book a bestseller. And if the American Dental Association puts its imprimatur on a brand of toothpaste, that toothpaste has both the ADA's support and its mark of distinction.

Word 16: CANARD (kuh-NARD)
A false, absurd, and often derogatory story or report.

A canard may be a published report, a widely circulated story, or merely a rumor. What makes it a canard is that it is groundless, meaning it has no basis in fact; it has been fabricated, made up, usually to disparage or make fun of someone or something; and it is ridiculous—though not so ridiculous that it won't fool people. The tabloids have always reveled in publishing canards, false or exaggerated reports, about the allegedly scandalous behavior of celebrities, but their preeminence in the business of circulating nonsense is swiftly being rivaled by the obsessively tweeting public.

Canard is the French word for a duck, and, as Robert Hendrickson explains in *The Facts on File Encyclopedia of Word and Phrase Origins,* we use it in English to mean a ridiculously false story because of the French expression *vendre un canard à moitié,* which meant literally to half-sell a duck. Because the implication of the French expression was not to sell the duck at all, its figurative meaning, writes Hendrickson, was "to make a fool out of a buyer, or anyone else, with a false story."

Word 17: PERFIDIOUS (pur-FID-ee-us)
Deliberately betraying another's trust or confidence; treacherous.

The adjective *perfidious* comes from the Latin *perfidiōsus,* faithless, treacherous, dishonest, and has the same meaning in English as its Latin source. The word also usually implies a base and calculated treachery or betrayal. A perfidious person is deliberately dishonest and disloyal; a perfidious government purposely betrays the faith and confidence of its people and its allies. The corresponding noun *perfidy* (PUR-fi-dee) means an act of treachery, a deliberate breach of faith or trust, or deceitfulness, untrustworthiness, as *the perfidy of a cheating spouse.*

Take care not to confuse the adjectives *perfidious* and *insidious. Insidious* applies to deceit or treachery accomplished by stealth or in a sly, devious manner. Insidious ideas spread ill or harm in a subtle way. An insidious plot attempts to deceive or ensnare by secret means. And an insidious disease develops in a gradual, seemingly harmless way. *Perfidious,* on the other hand, is used of any betrayal of trust or confidence, whether secret or open, and always implies deliberate deceit and disloyalty. Perfidious friends will cheat or deceive you at the first opportunity. Perfidious deeds are actions, whether subtle or obvious, that betray another's trust or confidence.

Synonyms of *perfidious* include *traitorous, faithless, dishonorable, deceitful, untrustworthy, unscrupulous,* and *duplicitous* (d[y]oo-PLIS-i-tus). Antonyms include *trustworthy, loyal, faithful, steadfast, dutiful, scrupulous,* and *incorruptible.*

Word 18: EPIPHANY (e-PIF-uh-nee)
A moment of sudden and dramatic insight or realization; a revelation.

Epiphany comes from the Greek *epipháneia,* a manifestation, apparition, especially the appearance of a divinity. Originally an epiphany was an appearance of a divine being, for as a proper noun *Epiphany* (note the capital *E*) is the Christian festival of Twelfth Night, celebrated on January 6, the twelfth day after Christmas, and commemorating what Christians believe was the manifestation of Christ's divine nature to the world through the three wise men called the Magi (properly pronounced MAY-jy). *Epiphany* may still denote the appearance of a deity, but more often it applies to any sudden and dramatic moment of insight or realization.

In modern usage, when you have an epiphany you experience "a sudden, intuitive perception of . . . the essential meaning of something," a perception "usually initiated by some simple, homely, or commonplace occurence or experience," says *The Random House Dictionary.* The corresponding adjective is *epiphanic* (EP-i-**FAN**-ik), which is often used in literary criticism to mean pertaining to or marked by an epiphany, a moment of dramatic insight or realization.

Word 19: PRATTLE (PRAT'l, rhymes with *rattle*)
To talk in a foolish, childish, or simpleminded way; to chatter or babble.

The verb to *prattle* probably comes from a Middle Low German word that meant to chatter, babble, or cackle, and is closely related in etymology and meaning to the verb to *prate,* which was originally used of chickens to mean "to make the loud clucking noise associated with laying an egg" (*OED*). In modern usage to *prate* is most often used to mean to talk at great length, especially in a boastful or pompous manner, while to *prattle* is most often used to mean to talk at great length, especially in a foolish or pointless way.

To *blather* (BLATH-ur, rhymes with *rather*) is another close synonym of *prattle.* To *blather* suggests excessive talking that is of no consequence or even nonsensical, while to *prattle* suggests excessive talking that is childish or gossipy. *Blathering* and *prattling* both denote excessive talking, but blathering is trivial and tedious while prattling is silly or simpleminded.

Prattle may also be used as a noun to mean babble or chatter, as *the prattle of a preschool playground,* or it may mean a babbling sound, as *the prattle of birds* or *the prattle of the creek.*

A *prattler* is a person who talks foolishly and constantly, a babbler. Other words for this kind of nonstop talker include *chatterbox, blabbermouth, blatherer, windbag, magpie* (after the chattering bird); *palaverer* (puh-LAV-ur-ur), from the verb to *palaver,* to talk profusely (*profuse,* pronounced pruh-FYOOS, means in abundance or without restraint); and *blatherskite* (BLATH-ur-skyt), which combines the verb to *blather* with the suffix *-skite,* an alteration of *skate,* a contemptible person, as in *cheapskate,* a miser.

Word 20: PLEBEIAN (ple-BEE-in)
Of or pertaining to the common people; hence, popular, common, vulgar.

Plebeian comes from the Latin *plēbēĭus,* which meant of the common people. This Latin *plēbēĭus* comes in turn from *plebs,* the common people, the masses, the mob, and for more than four centuries *plebs* has been used in English with this same meaning. In ancient Rome, the plebs were the common people and a plebeian was a member of the plebs, the masses. The plebeians, or commoners, were social opposites of the patricians (word 9 of this level), the ancient Roman nobility or upper class. Also from the Latin *plebs,* the common people, comes the unusual English word *plebiscite* (PLEB-i-syt), which means a direct vote of all the people on some matter of great public importance, such as self-determination in government.

When *plebeian* entered English in the 16th century, it was first a noun meaning a member of the Roman plebs and an adjective meaning of or belonging to the Roman plebs. But the noun soon came to be used of any person of low social standing, and the adjective was also soon applied to anyone of ordinary birth or rank to mean belonging to or characteristic of the working classes. And since the late 18th century the abbreviated form *pleb* has been used to mean an uncultured person.

Synonyms of *plebeian* include *lowborn, blue-collar, proletarian* (PROH-luh-**TAIR**-ee-in), *lowbrow, unsophisticated,* and *unrefined.* Antonyms include *aristocratic, patrician, highborn, blue-blooded, highbrow,* and *highfalutin.*

Review Quiz for Keywords 11–20

Consider the following statements and decide whether each one is true or false. **Answers appear on page 247**.

1. If you don't have time to read all of something, you can read a précis of it.
2. Binomial nomenclature is the system of names used in taxonomy.
3. Something subliminal is emerging from the subconscious mind.
4. Philanthropy is the opposite of misanthropy.
5. Something you disapprove of would not get your imprimatur.
6. Unsuspecting people tend to believe canards.
7. Perfidious friends are just as bad as enemies.
8. An epiphany is a sudden impulse to do something.
9. It's interesting to listen to people who prattle.
10. A person of high birth or rank is plebeian.

The Style File: *Like* versus *As If*

"I'm confused about the use of *it looks like*," writes Catherine Athearn. "Is it correct to say, 'It looks like it's going to rain this afternoon,' or should we say, 'It looks as if it's going to rain this afternoon'?"

In *The Careful Writer,* Theodore M. Bernstein writes that "*like* cannot stand for *as if,* except for a few idiomatic phrases such as 'The car looks like new' and 'They cheered like crazy.' But it is not proper to write, 'He spent money like it was going out of style' [make that *as if it were going out of style*], or 'The Russians advocated disarmament like they meant it.' "

That has long been the reigning opinion among usage authorities: *like,* as in "It looks like it's going to rain," is not appropriate in careful writing—or what is often called "edited writing," meaning that someone who knows something about Standard Written English has checked the piece for proper grammar and style. In casual speech, however, this common use of *like* is forgivable. And of course you may either say or write, with impunity (word 6 of Level 2), "It looks like rain."

Regarding the choice between *as if* and *as though* in this context, most usage experts agree that they are interchangeable.

Now let's return to the *Word Workout* vocabulary.

Word 21: GULL (rhymes with *dull*)
To cheat, trick, deceive, take advantage of.

The verb to *gull* is of uncertain origin. The word may also be used as a noun to mean a person who is easily cheated or taken advantage of. Just as you can fool a fool and dupe a dupe, you can gull a gull—trick or deceive a foolish, unwary, or overly trusting person. Gulling gulls is the specialty of swindlers and con artists, who call their victims *marks*.

The related adjective *gullible,* which means easily fooled, cheated, or deceived, combines the verb to *gull* with the suffix *-ible,* which means capable of being, as in *tangible,* capable of being discerned by the sense of touch or realized by the mind, from the Latin *tangĕre,* to touch; and *credible,* capable of being believed, from the Latin *credĕre,* to believe, trust, the source also of the English *creed,* a set of beliefs or principles. Also from the Latin *credĕre,* to believe, comes the adjective *credulous* (KREJ-uh-lus), a close synonym of *gullible* that means too inclined to believe, willing to accept something as true without questioning.

Synonyms of the verb to *gull* include to *dupe, defraud, swindle, hoodwink, fleece, bamboozle,* and *cozen* (KUZ-'n, like *cousin*).

Word 22: COMPENDIOUS (kum-PEN-dee-us)
Condensed, abridged; containing the substance of a subject in brief form; briefly but comprehensively expressed.

Concise and *succinct* (suhk-SINGKT, with the first *c* like *k*) are synonyms of *compendious.* Antonyms include *comprehensive, extensive, thoroughgoing, sweeping, exhaustive,* and *voluminous.*

Compendious dates back in English to before 1400 and comes from the Latin *compendium,* literally that which is weighed together, hence a saving or shortcut. Since the late 16th century this Latin *compendium* has been used in English to mean a summary, condensation, or abridgment of a larger work or of some area of knowledge. In 1713 the English poet Alexander Pope wrote, "Indexes and Dictionaries . . . are the Compendium of all Knowledge," and that is still how the word is best used today: "Cuevas describes the book as a compendium of conversations . . . about his life" (*Los Angeles Times*). But since about the mid-20th century people have also been using *compendium* to mean a complete list of something, or a collection, compilation, as in "an annual compendium of the UK's best food destinations" or "a two-hour-long compendium of 26 short films." This twist of meaning has sparked concern and objection among authorities on usage and has also affected the adjective *compendious,* which many people now use to mean big, comprehensive, all-embracing.

"*Compendious* means 'abridged, succinct,' not 'voluminous,' as writers often mistakenly believe," says *Garner's Modern American Usage.* "Perhaps the error stems from the idea that a compendium is, at best, a fairly comprehensive abridgment. But properly speaking, the emphasis falls on the *abridgment,* not on *comprehensive.*"

What's the difference between a compendium and an abridgment? A compendium may consist of previously published material or be a condensed summary of any broad subject, while an abridgment is always a shorter version of a longer piece of writing.

Word 23: RHAPSODIZE (RAP-suh-dyz)
To express oneself with extravagant emotion or enthusiasm.

A *rhapsody* (RAP-suh-dee), the noun corresponding to the verb to *rhapsodize,* was originally an epic poem, or a portion of it, "of a suitable length for recitation at one time" (*OED*). *Rhapsody* has also been used of a miscellaneous literary collection or of any miscellaneous collection, especially a muddled one, as in this sentence from Frank McCourt's 2005 memoir *Teacher Man:* "They produced a rhapsody of excuses, ranging from a family epidemic of diarrhea to a sixteen-wheeler truck crashing into a house."

Since the early 17th century *rhapsody* has also been used of any highly emotional piece of writing with an irregular or disconnected form, or of any ecstatic or intense expression of feeling; and since the early 19th century the word has been used in music, in perhaps its best-known sense today, of a highly emotional or exuberant instrumental composition with an irregular and seemingly improvisational form. Two of music's best-known rhapsodies are Franz Liszt's *Hungarian Rhapsodies* (nineteen of them composed from about 1846 to 1886) and George Gershwin's *Rhapsody in Blue* (1924), which introduced elements of American jazz to the classical concert stage.

To *rhapsodize* was originally to recite rhapsodies, selections from epic poems. But by the late 1700s *rhapsodize* had acquired its modern sense: to speak or write with extravagant emotion or enthusiasm: "She rhapsodized about the food at her favorite restaurant"; "The professor rhapsodized on the poetry of Dylan Thomas."

The adjective is *rhapsodic,* of the nature of a rhapsody, hence highly enthusiastic or emotional, as *a rhapsodic, visionary novel.*

Word 24: OXYMORON (AHK-si-**MOR**-ahn *or* AHK-see-**MOR**-ahn)
An expression or figure of speech that combines two contradictory words; a concise and pointed phrase that seems self-contradictory. In *Crazy English,* Richard Lederer defines *oxymoron* as "a figure of speech in which two incongruous, contradictory terms are yoked together in a small space."

For the plural, dictionaries give only the Greek *oxymora,* but *Garner's Modern American Usage* notes that the anglicized *oxymorons* "is now about 60 times as common as *oxymora* in print sources, and ought to be accepted as standard." The adjective is *oxymoronic* (AHK-si-muh-**RAH**-nik), being or resembling an oxymoron.

By derivation the word *oxymoron* is itself an oxymoron. It comes from the ancient Greek *oxymōros,* which meant literally sharp-dull or figuratively keenly stupid, for in Greek *oxys* meant sharp, acute, keen, and *mōros,* the source also of the English *moron,* meant dull or foolish.

Oxymorons abound in literature, as in Shakespeare's *sweet sorrow,* Milton's *darkness visible,* and Keats's *little noiseless noise.* Alfred, Lord Tennyson penned a memorable pair of oxymoronic lines in "Lancelot and Elaine": "His honor in dishonor stood, / And faith unfaithful kept him falsely true."

Many common expressions are also oxymoronic. Consider these examples: *student teacher, executive secretary, sure bet, baby grand, jumbo shrimp, inside out, random order, working vacation, death benefit, benevolent despot,* idiot savant,† deafening silence, industrial park, urban village, white chocolate, good grief, whole piece, conspicuously absent, plastic silverware, guest host,* and *pretty ugly.*

Lederer notes that oxymorons can also be found in place names

---

* **Benevolent** (buh-NEV-uh-lint) means charitable, desiring good for others, and a **despot** (DES-put) is a tyrant, dictator.
† A **savant** (suh-VAHNT) is a learned person, expert, pundit (word 10 of Level 4). An **idiot savant** is "a person with generally impaired intellectual and social functions who is extremely gifted in a particular way" (*OED*).

such as *Little Big Horn* and *Old New York,* as well as in single words such as *bittersweet, firewater, spendthrift,* and *wholesome. Pianoforte* (or sometimes *fortepiano*)—the original name of the musical instrument now called simply a piano—is also a one-word oxymoron because in music the Italian *piano* means soft and *forte* (pronounced FOR-tay) means loud. Even personal names can sometimes be oxymoronic, such as the baseball player *Angel Pagan.*

"Among language aficionados," says Garner, "collecting and inventing cynical oxymorons is a parlor game; they enjoy phrases that seem to imply contradictions," such as *legal brief* and *military intelligence.* "If you are willing to stretch the oxymoronic concept and editorialize unabashedly," writes Lederer, "you will expand your oxymoronic list considerably." Among Lederer's examples in this vein are *student athlete, educational television, nonworking mother, postal service,* and *business ethics.* What "editorializing oxymorons" like these can you think of?

Word 25: PROVENANCE (PRAHV-uh-nints)
The origin, source, or derivation of something.

Provenance comes from the Latin *prōvenīre,* to come forth. The word may refer specifically to "the history of the ownership of a work of art or an antique, used as a guide to authenticity or quality" (*OED*), but in general usage it is applied to the origin or source of almost anything, whether something physical, such as an object or artifact, or something intangible (in-TANJ-i-bul), such as a word, statement, or idea. (*Intangible* means incapable of being perceived by the sense of touch, impalpable.)

Fans of organic produce are concerned about the provenance of their food, preferring a local origin to a faraway one. Fans of fine wine also take great interest in the provenance of their selections. A virtuoso violinist would be thrilled to own an instrument whose provenance could be traced to the legendary Italian violinmakers Giuseppe Antonio Guarneri (1683–1745) or Antonio Stradivari (1644?–1737). And historians might disagree about the provenance of a manuscript, arguing over who its author was or when it was written, as in this citation: "The provenance of the papyrus fragment is a mystery, and its owner has asked to remain anonymous" (*The New York Times*).

Word 26: LAISSEZ-FAIRE (LES-ay-**FAIR**, rhymes with *guess way there*)

Noninterference with the affairs of others or with individual freedom of action.

Laissez-faire entered English about 1825, a combination of the French *laissez,* the imperative of the verb *laisser,* to let, allow, permit, and *faire,* to do. Thus, by derivation *laissez-faire* means to let people do as they choose or think best. In English it is used of a political or economic policy of noninterference based on the belief that government should meddle as little as possible in people's affairs.

In modern usage *laissez-faire* is roughly synonymous with *free-market economics* and is related to the political philosophy of libertarianism, which argues that people should be allowed to exercise their free will with a minimum of government intervention or regulation. As defined here, *laissez-faire* is a noun, but it is often used attributively (meaning as an adjective) to modify another noun, as *a laissez-faire economy,* one in which government takes a hands-off approach to business and industry. Advocates of online freedom have a laissez-faire attitude toward the Internet, believing that we should be allowed to post and copy and share anything, regardless of ownership or copyright.

Word 27: PRETERNATURAL (PREE-tur-**NACH**-ur-u̱l)

Supernatural, beyond what is considered normal or natural; hence, exceptional, extraordinary.

Preternatural comes from the Latin phrase *praeter nātūram,* beyond or outside nature, and the notion of being beyond the ordinary course of nature, being abnormal or supernatural, has long been central to the word. *Preternatural* may still be used in this way, as *a story about the preternatural return of someone who has died.* But in recent decades the word has tilted away from this sense and become a synonym of *extraordinary,* as *a preternatural gift for music.*

"*Preternatural,* which for centuries served as a synonym for *supernatural,* now serves a separate purpose as a powerful word of praise, meaning 'surpassing the normal, extraordinary,'" writes Mark Davidson in *Right, Wrong, and Risky.* To illustrate that point, Davidson quotes John Updike's comment on Max Beerbohm:* "He early developed a preternatural poise and grace as a writer and a caricaturist."

But *preternatural* can still mean extraordinary or exceptional, beyond what is considered normal or natural, without conveying special praise. Consider these examples: a preternatural stillness in the woods; a preternatural beam of light penetrating the darkness; the preternatural speed of jet plane breaking the sound barrier; and a mother's preternatural ability to know what her children are feeling.

Word 28: DISABUSE (dis-uh-BYOOZ)
To free from error, falsehood, deception, or misunderstanding; to set straight.

The verb to *disabuse* comes from the French *désabuser,* to undeceive, free from illusion. It combines the privative prefix *dis-,* not, and the verb to *abuse,* to use something badly or improperly so as to injure or damage it. Thus to *disabuse* is literally not to abuse, to reverse or nullify the effects of abuse or exploitation.

When you disabuse, you free someone of an illusion or a false idea; you correct a mistaken notion or clear up a misconception. In colloquial (kuh-LOH-kwee-ul, informal) terms, to disabuse is to set someone straight.

Properly, you do not disabuse the *mind* of a person who embraces an error or false idea, and you do not disabuse the error or false idea itself. In careful usage, you always disabuse *people* of

---

* John Updike (1932–2009) was an American fiction writer, poet, and critic. Max Beerbohm (BEER-bohm, 1872–1956) was an English essayist, critic, and caricaturist.

their errors and misunderstandings: "Millie politely tried to disabuse Ronald of his exaggerated opinion of his abilities on the
tennis court"; "Doctors today often have to disabuse patients who
have diagnosed themselves on the Internet"; "It is our duty as
citizens of a democracy to disabuse ourselves of our prejudices."

Word 29: COURTESAN (KOR-tuh-zun)
A female prostitute, especially one whose clients are noble or men of
wealth and power.

Courtesan comes through French from an Italian word that originally meant a woman attached to a royal court. It is the sort of
word that conjures the olden days when ambitious and often ruthless aristocrats engaged in political and sexual intrigue, plotting
their paths to power while secretly slipping into bed with each
other. The courtesan was not usually herself a member of the nobility but rather a court-mistress who serviced courtiers (KOR-
tee-urz), attendants at the court of a king or other royal person.
Later the term broadened to denote a prostitute who serviced
wealthy, famous, or powerful men.

In modern usage, *whore* is the general and most vulgar term
for someone who has sex for money. *Prostitute,* because it's from
Latin, is a more refined and socially acceptable word for the same
thing. *Courtesan* is the most elevated term of the three, a high-
class prostitute, as this citation from Edward Sharpham's 1607
play *The Fleire* illustrates: "Your whore is for every rascal, but
your Curtizan is for your Courtier." (*Courtesan* was formerly often spelled with *cur-* rather than *cour-* and pronounced KUR-
tuh-zin.)

Let's take a look at some other words for so-called fallen women.
The word *harlot* (HAHR-lut), which dates back to the 13th
century and was originally used of a man to mean a rogue or villain, has since the 15th century been used of a woman as a milder
term for *whore* or *prostitute.* But unlike those two common words,
harlot, which occurs often in the Bible and older literature, is now
less common.

Strumpet (rhymes with *trumpet*), *trull* (rhymes with *dull*), and *tart* are unusual synonyms of *prostitute, whore,* and *harlot.* A *trollop* (TRAH-lup) may be either a woman who has sex for money or a sexually promiscuous woman, while a *slattern* (rhymes with *pattern*) is either an untidy, dirty woman or a wanton (WAHN-tun) woman, a slut. (*Wanton* in this context means lewd, lustful, sexually unrestrained.)

Yet another synonym of *prostitute* is the rare word *meretrix* (MER-uh-triks), which comes directly from the Latin *meretrix,* a prostitute, the source also of the English adjective *meretricious* (MER-uh-**TRISH**-us), which means attractive in a flashy or cheap way, falsely alluring, tawdry, gaudy.

The words *concubine* and *paramour* are close cousins of our keyword *courtesan.* A concubine (KAHNG-kyuh-byn)—from the Latin *con-,* together, and *cubāre,* to lie down, go to bed—is a mistress, a woman who lives and makes love with a man to whom she is not married. *Paramour* (PAR-uh-moor) has been used since the 14th century to mean either a lover, sexual partner, or an illicit or secret lover, a companion in adultery.

Let's close this wanton discussion with an amusing anecdote about William Lyon Phelps (1865–1943), an American literary scholar who taught English at Yale for forty-one years. According to legend, Phelps was correcting a student's essay when he came across this line: "The woman fell down the stairs and lay prostitute at the bottom." In the margin Phelps wrote, "Young man, you must learn to distinguish between a fallen woman and one who has merely slipped." (The hapless—unlucky, unfortunate—student confused the noun and verb *prostitute* with the adjective *prostrate,* which means lying facedown on the ground, often in humble submission.)

Word 30: **DEBAUCH** (di-BAWCH)
To corrupt or seduce, lead away from virtue or responsibility.

Synonyms of *debauch* include *pervert* (pur-VURT), *debase, deprave,* and *despoil* (di-SPOYL).

The verb to *debauch* comes from the French *débaucher,* to lead astray, entice away from duty. In modern usage it means to corrupt morally or to entice into sensual indulgence, as *to debauch an innocent young woman with flattery and gifts.* The noun is *debauchery* (di-BAW-chuh-ree), excessive indulgence in sensual pleasure, especially eating, drinking, and sex: "The ancient Greeks and Romans were infamous for their debauchery."

Intemperance is a close synonym of *debauchery. Temperance, sobriety,* and *abstinence* are antonyms of *debauchery.*

Debauched, the past tense and past participle of the verb, is often used as an adjective to mean either corrupted morally, as *a debauched lifestyle,* or showing the ill effects of excessive indulgence in sensual pleasures, as *debauched with strong drink.* A debauched person, one given or addicted to extreme sensual indulgence, is called a *debauchee* (deb-aw-SHEE or deb-aw-CHEE).

Review Quiz for Keywords 21–30

Decide if the pairs of words below are synonyms or antonyms. **Answers appear on page 248.**

1. *Gull* and *hoodwink* are . . . synonyms or antonyms?
2. *Compendious* and *exhaustive* are . . .
3. *Criticize* and *rhapsodize* are . . .
4. *Oxymoron* and *incongruity* are . . .
5. *Provenance* and *destination* are . . .
6. *Noninterference* and *laissez-faire* are . . .
7. *Preternatural* and *supernatural* are . . .
8. *Deceive* and *disabuse* are . . .
9. *Courtesan* and *concubine* are . . .
10. *Deprave* and *debauch* are . . .

Difficult Distinctions: *Diffuse* and *Defuse*

In dispensing advice on how to handle a mother with advanced Alzheimer's who makes inappropriate remarks—such as "You are extremely fat"—Philip Galanes, the Social Q's columnist for *The New*

York Times, says it's probably best to say something simple like " 'I'm sorry for my mother. She isn't well.' That should diffuse the situation." Good advice, perhaps. But he should have written *defuse.*

This mistake is increasingly common, perhaps because the pronunciation of the verbs *diffuse* and *defuse* is often identical (di-FYOOZ). But their meanings are far apart. To *diffuse* is to spread or distribute widely, disperse, disseminate (word 4 of Level 1). To *defuse* is to remove the fuse from, and so to make less harmful, dangerous, or difficult.

If your intended meaning is to spread out, scatter, or disseminate, use *diffuse.* Lamps diffuse light. The sun diffuses fog. And kindergarten teachers diffuse rudimentary knowledge while their sniffling, sneezing pupils diffuse germs.

If your intended meaning is to make something less harmful or troublesome, use *defuse.* You can defuse a bomb, render it harmless, or defuse a ticklish or potentially explosive situation.

Now let's return to the *Word Workout* vocabulary.

Word 31: BRAGGADOCIO (BRAG-uh-DOH-shee-oh)
Empty and arrogant boasting or bragging.

Braggadocio is an eponymous word—a word created from a name—in this case from the boastful character Braggadocchio in Edmund Spenser's epic poem *The Faerie Queene* (1590). It was probably a pseudo-Italian coinage based on the verb to *brag,* which dates back to the 14th century.

Braggadocio is most often used to mean arrogant and empty boasting, as in these contemporary citations: "Despite my brash online braggadocio—it's true. I am shy" (mashable.com); "The arm punching, the braggadocio . . . they're for buffoons. Most men have no truck with it" (*Vancouver Sun*). "From braggadocio to vulnerability, from manic excitement to angry defiance, his is a versatile and commanding performance" (oxfordstudent.com). But *braggadocio* is also sometimes used to mean a braggart, an arrogant boaster, as when Thomas Carlyle, in 1832, wrote, "He . . . had much of the sycophant, alternating with the braggadocio."

Synonyms of *braggadocio* include *bluster, swagger, vainglory, gasconade, rodomontade,* and *fanfaronade.* Let's take a closer look at the last four of these words.

Vainglory (VAYN-glor-ee; the adjective *vainglorious* is word 37 of Level 7) comes from the Middle Latin *vāna glōria,* literally empty glory or fame. *Vainglory* is boastful and pretentious vanity, a tendency to take unwarranted and excessive pride in one's accomplishments or abilities.

Gasconade (gas-kuh-NAYD) comes through the French *gasconner,* to boast, from the proper noun *Gascon,* a person from Gascony (GAS-kuh-nee), France, "the inhabitants of which were reputedly very boastful," says *The Random House Dictionary.* Gasconade is not merely boasting but extravagant boasting, extreme exaggeration, as in this sentence from 1903 by the American short story writer O. Henry: "Whosoever entered [had to] listen to the imp's interminable gasconade concerning his scandalous career."

Rodomontade (RAHD-uh-mun-TAYD), like *braggadocio,* is an eponymous word. It comes from Rodomont, a boastful warrior king in Boiardo's *Orlando Inamorato* (1482) and Ariosto's *Orlando Furioso* (1516), both famous epic poems of the Italian Renaissance. The name comes in turn from the Italian *rodomonte,* which means literally one who rolls away mountains. By derivation, rodomontade is the arrogant boasting of someone who claims he can move mountains.

Finally, the pleasant-sounding *fanfaronade* (FAN-fuh-ruh-NAYD) is related to the familiar English *fanfare,* which may mean a flourish of trumpets or a showy, noisy display, a big fuss. *Fanfaronade* comes ultimately from the Spanish *fanfarrón,* a braggart, and means arrogant, boastful talk, ostentatious bragging. The corresponding noun *fanfaron* (FAN-fuh-rahn) means a braggart.

Our keyword, *braggadocio,* means empty and arrogant boasting or bragging.

Word 32: FLAGELLATE (FLAJ-uh-layt)
To whip, flog, lash, scourge (SKURJ, rhymes with *urge*).

To *flagellate* and the unusual verb to *fustigate* (FUHS-ti-gayt) are similar in sound and sense, but denote different kinds of violence. To *fustigate,* from the Latin *fustis,* a stick, is to beat with a stick, to cudgel. To *flagellate,* from the Latin *flagellare,* to whip, is to strike with a strap or rod.

To *flog,* to *scourge,* and to *flagellate* all mean to whip, literally or figuratively.

To *flog,* which may also come from Latin *flagellare,* to whip, means to punish or torture by whipping or beating: "The horse thief was flogged"; or to promote or talk about something excessively: "They flogged their proposal until everyone was sick of it."

The noun *scourge* is a strip of animal hide used as a whip; the word comes from the Latin *excoriare,* to strip off the hide, the source of the English verb to *excoriate* (ek-SKOR-ee-ayt), to strip off the skin, flay, and so to rebuke or denounce harshly. To *scourge* is to whip with or as if with a scourge, to punish severely. A vicious master will scourge a slave; a tyrant or an epidemic can scourge—or be the scourge of—a population; and a critic can write a scourging review, lashing out with spiteful words.

The verb to *flagellate* and the noun *flagellation* (FLAJ-uh-**LAY**-shin), whipping, often connote punishment motivated by self-hatred or masochism. Historically, a *flagellant* (FLAJ-uh-lint) was a member of a medieval European sect of fanatics who whipped themselves in public to atone for sin. Though condemned by the church, the practice continued until the 16th century. Because of this history, *flagellate* is often used of self-inflicted punishment or violence, either literal or figurative—"After the burglary she couldn't stop flagellating herself for not remembering to lock the back door"—and since the late 19th century *flagellation* has also referred to sexual gratification derived from whipping or being whipped.

The word *self-flagellation* is commonly used today to mean extreme self-criticism, as "The public will tolerate a celebrity obsessed with self-promotion, but they will soon grow tired of one addicted to self-flagellation."

Word 33: INSURGENT (in-SUR-jint)
A person who rises in opposition to a government or to established authority or leadership; a rebel.

Insurgent may also be used as an adjective to mean rising in revolt, rebellious. Thus, you can have *an insurgent attack* or *an attack by insurgents.* The word comes from the present participle of the Latin *insurgĕre,* to rise up, and in English it always suggests rebellion or opposition to authority, often by force of arms.

The nouns *insurgence* and *insurgency* both denote an uprising, but there is a fine distinction between these words. An *insurgence,* explains *Garner's Modern American Usage,* is "an act or the action of rising against authority," as *government forces quashed yesterday's insurgence,* while an *insurgency* is "the state or condition of being in revolt," as *an insurgency in the northern provinces that has gone on for a month.*

An *insurgency* and an *insurrection* (IN-suh-**REK**-shun) both suggest rising in opposition on a small scale or for a brief time. A *revolt* is larger, longer, and somewhat more organized. A *rebellion* is even larger and fairly well organized. And if a rebellion led by insurgents succeeds in overthrowing an established authority or government, it becomes a *revolution.*

Word 34: PANACHE (puh-NASH, *not* puh-NAHSH)
Grand or flamboyant confidence of style or manner.

Synonyms of *panache* include *elegance, verve, flair, dash,* and *flourish.*

English borrowed *panache* in the 16th century from a Middle French word that meant a tuft or plume of feathers, and its original meaning was an ornamental tuft or plume of feathers, especially on a hat, helmet, or other headdress. *Panache* may still be used in this sense, as *a cockatoo with a colorful panache,* but since about 1900 the figurative implications of this ostentatious plume have overtaken the word, and it has been used almost exclusively to mean a grand and showy confidence of style or action.

Anything that you can do with grand style and self-assurance you can do with panache. A sexy Hollywood star in a flamboyant gown strolls down the red carpet with panache. Great orators deliver spellbinding speeches with panache. A good waiter at a fancy restaurant will serve your dinner with panache. And Vladimir Horowitz (1903–1989), the virtuoso pianist, performed Chopin's romantic waltzes with panache, majestic elegance and style.

Word 35: OMNIBUS (AHM-ni-bus)

Pertaining to, containing, or covering many different things or items at once.

Omnibus comes through French from the Latin *omnibus,* for all, which comes in turn from *omnis,* all. From this Latin *omnis* English has adopted the combining form *omni-,* used at the beginnings of words to mean "all." For example, *omnipotent* (ahm-NIP-uh-tint) means all-powerful; *omnivorous* (ahm-NIV-uh-rus) means all-devouring, eating all kinds of foods; *omniscient* (ahm-NISH-int) means all-knowing; *omnipresent* (ahm-ni-PREZ-int) means present everywhere, in all places at once; and *omnifarious* (ahm-ni-FAIR-ee-us) means of all sorts or kinds, as *omnifarious opinions.*

Omnibus entered English about 1828 as a noun for what we now more concisely call a *bus,* a large public vehicle for transporting many passengers by road. By 1840 the noun *omnibus* had also come to be used to mean something that contains or covers a large number of things or items or, specifically, a book containing reprinted works by a single author or a volume containing works by various authors on a particular topic or theme.

By 1842 *omnibus* had become an adjective used to modify an immediately following noun in phrases such as *an omnibus show,* one featuring all kinds of acts; *an omnibus account,* one that accommodates all kinds of assets; *an omnibus motion,* a legal motion that makes a number of requests; and, most often, *an omnibus bill,* a piece of legislation that covers or contains many different items.

Word 36: MILITATE (MIL-i-tayt)
To weigh heavily, operate or work (against).

Militate comes from the Latin *mīlitāre,* to serve as a soldier, the source also of the English adjective *militant,* which may mean either engaged in warfare or fighting, as *the militant opposition,* or aggressively persistent or combative, especially in support of a cause, as *militant animal rights activists.*

You may militate for or in favor of something, as "to militate for the Syrian president's departure" (*Foreign Policy Journal*). But in modern usage *militate* is almost always paired with the word *against* to mean to weigh heavily in opposition, operate or work against, as *entrenched customs that militate against change,* or *strong evidence that militates against a ruling in their favor.*

Take care not to confuse the verbs *militate* and *mitigate.* To *mitigate* is to lessen in intensity, make less severe, and should never be followed by *against:* "Twitter has taken some steps to mitigate the spike in traffic and ensure that the site is not knocked offline again" (*PC World*). *Militate* means to operate, work, or weigh heavily: "Almost everything in modern society militates against our falling in love hard or long. It militates against love as risk, love as sacrifice, love as heroism" (Christina Nehring, *The Atlantic*).

Word 37: NIHILISTIC (NY-i-LIS-tik)
Rejecting all established institutions, laws, morality, and religious beliefs, "often from a sense of despair and the belief that life is devoid of meaning" (*OED*).

The adjective *nihilistic* and the noun *nihilism* (NY-i-liz'm) come from the Latin *nihil,* nothing, the source also of the English noun *nil,* which may mean nothing, zero, as *her efforts amounted to nil,* or consisting of nothing, as *the results were nil.*

In philosophy, nihilism is an extreme form of skepticism—a denial of reality, any purpose to existence, and any objective basis for truth. Historically, nihilism was the doctrine of certain Russian revolutionaries in the late 19th century who held that all political, economic, and social institutions should be destroyed by acts of terrorism and assassination. And in psychiatry, nihilism is a delusional belief that everything is unreal, and that the self, or individual consciousness, has ceased to exist.

In general usage *nihilism* implies a negative, hostile, anarchic view of the world. The nihilist rejects established beliefs, institutions, and traditions and welcomes despair and destruction, including self-destruction. A nihilistic worldview denies the value and purpose of existence and embraces meaninglessness and nothingness.

Writers often use *nihilistic* of anyone who opposes the establishment, who questions the meaning of existence, or who exhibits antisocial or destructive behavior. For example, Anthony Burgess's 1962 novel *A Clockwork Orange,* which depicts the violent, depraved, repugnant* behavior of a gang of British teenagers, has been called nihilistic, and some critics of popular music have argued that songs that appeal to the despairing, self-destructive impulses of teenagers are nihilistic.

Word 38: TORPID (TOR-pid)
Inactive, sluggish, slow, lacking energy.

The adjective *torpid* and the noun *torpor* (TOR-pur, mental or physical sluggishness or dullness) come from the Latin verb *torpēre,* to be sluggish, inactive, or numb. Anything that sorely lacks energy or vigor, or that is inactive or dormant, can be described as torpid. An old person's mind may become torpid, sluggish from inactivity. A torpid audience is one whose members are dull and unresponsive, who yawn and doze. And in medicine a patient's digestion is called torpid when it is slow or inactive.

Synonyms of *torpid* include *inert, apathetic, lethargic, indolent* (word 48 of Level 4), *phlegmatic* (fleg-MAT-ik), *languid* (see *languish,* word 14 of Level 2), *somnolent* (word 16 of Level 2), *enervated, languorous* (LANG-gur-<u>us</u>), *stupefied* (*stupefy* is word 30 of Level 3), and *otiose* (**OH**-shee-OHS). Antonyms of *torpid* include *lively,*

---

* *Depravity* is word 1 of Level 1; *repugnant* is word 4 of Level 2.

energetic, vigorous, animated, frisky, spry, spirited, dynamic, and *vivacious* (word 15 of Level 1).

Word 39: SEMINAL (SEM-i-nul)

Highly influential and creative; so original and important as to influence later development or provide a basis for future works, events, or ideas.

The adjective *seminal* comes through the Latin *sēminālis* from *sēmen,* a seed, that which is sown or planted. This Latin *sēmen,* a seed, is also the source of *disseminate* (word 4 of Level 1), to spread widely, scatter as if sowing seed; *seminary,* a place where people study religion and prepare to become members of the clergy; and *inseminate,* which in its literal sense means to impregnate, inject with semen, as *an artificially inseminated cow,* and in its figurative sense means to implant as if by sowing seed: "Advertising seeks to inseminate desire for a product in as many minds as possible."

Our keyword, *seminal,* literally means like a seed. It is used in this literal way in botany, physiology, and anatomy to mean of, pertaining to, or containing the seed. But since the 17th century *seminal* has also been used figuratively to mean "containing the possibility of future development" (*OED*); hence, so original and important as to influence later development or future events, as *a seminal scientific study that charted the course of all subsequent research.*

Word 40: CRAVEN (KRAY-vin)

Cowardly, utterly lacking courage, contemptibly timid or fearful.

The origin of *craven* is uncertain, but it may go back to an Old French word meaning crushed, overwhelmed, and may be related to the obsolete English adjective *creant* (KREE-int), defeated, vanquished. This obsolete *creant* is in turn related to the contemporary English *miscreant* (MIS-kree-int), which at first meant a person who holds a religious belief regarded as false, but now means an evil, unscrupulous person, a villain; and *recreant* (REK-ree-int), which as a noun means a person who breaks allegiance, a deserter or coward, and as an adjective means cowardly or unfaithful to one's duty.

Synonyms of *craven* include *gutless, spineless, fainthearted, lily-livered, timorous* (TIM-ur-<u>us</u>), and *pusillanimous* (PYOO-si-**LAN**-i-mus). The first five of these synonyms suggest cowardice or fearfulness in general, while *pusillanimous,* like *craven,* is used of cowardly people or actions that are especially dishonorable or disgraceful.

Craven may also be used as a noun to mean a despicable coward, and it has sometimes been used as a verb to mean to make craven or cowardly, deprive of courage or spirit, as when Shakespeare writes in his play *Cymbeline* (c. 1610), "Against self-slaughter / There is a prohibition so divine / That cravens my weak hand."

The expression *to cry craven,* like the familiar expression *to cry uncle,* means to yield, surrender, acknowledge that one has been beaten.

Review Quiz for Keywords 31–40
In each statement below, a keyword (in *italics*) is followed by three definitions. Two of the three are correct; one is unrelated in meaning. Decide which one doesn't fit the keyword. **Answers appear on page 248.**

1. *Braggadocio* is bluster, gasconade, fanfare.
2. To *flagellate* is to scourge, curse, flog.
3. An *insurgent* is a rebel, a rabble-rouser, a revolutionary.
4. *Panache* is self-satisfaction, self-assurance, grand style.
5. An *omnibus* bill has many sections, is full of amendments, covers many items.
6. To *militate* is to make less severe, weigh heavily, work against.
7. A *nihilistic* worldview is utilitarian, anarchic, despairing.
8. Something *torpid* is enervated, vivacious, sluggish.
9. A *seminal* work is original, influential, spiritual.
10. A *craven* person is starving, cowardly, pusillanimous.

Once Upon a Word: Portmanteau Words
Charles Lutwidge Dodgson (DAHD-s<u>u</u>n, 1832–1898), the shy Oxford University mathematician better known by his pen name,

Lewis Carroll, is remembered today as the author of the classic children's books *Alice's Adventures in Wonderland* (1865) and *Through the Looking-Glass* (1871). As lovers of his books know well, Carroll was fond of punning and wordplay, and he was particularly fond of blending two words to create a nonce (NAHNS) word, meaning a word created "for the nonce," the present moment or a particular occasion. Carroll called this blending a *portmanteau word* (PORT-man-**TOH** or port-MAN-toh), after a type of stiff leather case or bag that opened into two parts.

In his famous nonsense poem "Jabberwocky," which appears in *Through the Looking-Glass,* Carroll coined various humorous nonce words—such as *brillig, gimble, vorpal, frabjous,* and *uffish*—along with several portmanteau words, such as *frumious,* a blend of *fuming* and *furious,* and *slithy,* a blend of *slimy* and *lithe.* Two of Carroll's blends in that poem have since gained widespread popularity: *chortle,* created from *chuckle* and *snort,* and *galumph,* a blend of *gallop* and *triumphant.*

Portmanteau words, now better known as blend words, are not just the stuff of children's books but have long been a vital part of the language. Not all blend words catch on, of course, but, as Carroll's creations demonstrate, some stand the test of time and make it into the dictionaries. In fact, some of our most familiar words today were born as blends. For example, *motel,* a blend of *motor* and *hotel,* was coined in the 1920s; *brunch,* a blend of *breakfast* and *lunch,* was originally university slang in England in the 1890s; and *smog,* a blend of *smoke* and *fog,* was introduced in 1905 by a London doctor who was concerned about the heavy pall of coal smoke choking the city.

My best *guesstimate* (a blend of *guess* and *estimate*) is that the English language has absorbed hundreds of blend words since the 19th century. *Slanguage,* a blend of *slang* and *language,* was coined in the 1870s. *Glitterati* (GLIT-uh-**RAH**-tee), a blend of *glitter* and *literati* (LIT-uh-**RAH**-tee), the educated class, was coined in the 1950s and denotes celebrities or fashionable people. *Camcorder,* a combination of *camera* and *recorder,* came along about 1980, and the late 1990s saw the emergence of *bromance,* which is now in the online edition of the *OED.* A blend of *brother* and *romance, bro-*

mance means a close, nonsexual relationship between two hetero-sexual males. Perhaps the best-known bromance in literature is the relationship between Sherlock Holmes and Dr. Watson.

Some blend words are created in such a way that their endings become suffixes used to create later blends. For example, *walk-athon* (1930), *talkathon* (1934), and *telethon* (1949) all use the *-thon* of *marathon* as a suffix. Likewise with *newscast* (1934), *telecast* (1937), and *simulcast* (1948), which use the *-cast* of *broadcast* as a suffix.

Other well-known blend words include *motorcade,* a blend of *motor* and *cavalcade* (KAV-ul-kayd, a grand procession, originally on horseback), which was created about 1910; *bookmobile,* a coin-age from the 1930s that uses the *-mobile* of *automobile* as a suffix; *infomercial,* a blend of *information* and *commercial* that was coined in 1981; and *staycation,* a blend of *stay* and *vacation* that appeared in 2005 and means a vacation spent at or near one's home.

Let's return now to the *Word Workout* vocabulary for ten more keyword discussions.

Word 41: MALADROIT (MAL-uh-DROYT)
Awkward, clumsy, unskillful.

Synonyms of *maladroit* include *incompetent, inept, bungling, tactless, gauche* (GOHSH), and *lubberly* (a *lubber* is a big, clumsy, stupid person). The direct antonym of *maladroit* is *adroit* (uh-DROYT), skillful, clever, and efficient at doing a difficult thing, either with one's hands or with one's brain. Other antonyms include *accomplished, adept, competent, dexterous, proficient, deft,* and *masterly.*

The antonymous adjectives *adroit* and *maladroit* are classic examples of the English language's ingrained bias against the left hand and favoring of the right hand. The two words share the same root, the French *droit,* which means right, the right hand, or straight, correct. In *adroit,* which means literally to the right, we see the positive implication of skillfulness and dexterity associated with the right hand. But in *maladroit,* which begins with the priva-tive prefix *mal-,* bad, ill, and means not adroit, not done with the right hand, we see the implication of bias against the left.

Dexterous, skillful, comes from the Latin *dexter,* right. The English word *sinister,* corrupt, evil, unfavorable, comes from the Latin word *sinister,* left. The English word *gauche,* awkward, crude, or graceless, is the French *gauche,* which means left but also crooked, awkward, clumsy. If you're ambidextrous, skillful with both hands, you literally have two right hands. But if you're ambisinister you are clumsy with both hands because, by derivation, you have two left hands. So there you have it: the English language is unfair to lefties.

Our keyword, *maladroit,* implies awkwardness or clumsiness that may be either physical or intellectual; the maladroit person displays a pronounced lack of skill with either the hands or the mind. A maladroit driver is a poorly skilled and possibly reckless driver. A maladroit surgeon may be the target of malpractice lawsuits. A maladroit lawyer lacks the proper knowledge and expertise to present a persuasive case in court. And a maladroit writer is an intellectually clumsy writer, one who writes awkward sentences and makes elementary mistakes of grammar and usage.

Word 42: GORMANDIZE (GOR-mun-dyz)
To eat greedily and excessively, like a glutton; to gorge.

The familiar word *gourmet* denotes a connoisseur of fine food and drink, a person who appreciates "the delicacies of the table" (*OED*). The words *epicure* (EP-i-kyuur) and *gastronome* (GAS-truh-nohm) are synonyms of *gourmet,* implying somewhat greater expertise and refinement of taste. The not-so-familiar word *gourmand* (guur-MAHND or GUUR-mahnd) also denotes a person who appreciates good food and drink, but one whose taste is much less discriminating and who eats heartily or greedily. The word *glutton* takes hearty eating one voracious step further and is used of someone who habitually overindulges in food and drink.

From the noun *gourmand* we get the verb to *gormandize,* which in most instances means to eat voraciously and excessively, like a glutton. But to *gormandize* is also sometimes used figuratively to mean to devour or gobble up, as in this sentence written by the

American clergyman Henry Ward Beecher in 1887: "To gormandize books is as wicked as to gormandize food."

Word 43: POLEMICAL (puh-LEM-i-kul)
Pertaining to or consisting of an argument or dispute.

Synonyms of the adjective *polemical* include the familiar words *argumentative, controversial, contentious* (kun-TEN-shus), and *disputatious*
(DIS-pyoo-**TAY**-shus), and the unusual word *eristic* (e-RIS-tik),
which comes from the Greek *éristikós,* fond of wrangling or arguing, from *éris,* strife, which is also the name of the goddess of strife
or discord in Greek mythology. *Eristic* means given to or characterized by argument that employs subtle and sometimes specious
(SPEE-shus) reasoning. (*Specious* means using deceptive language
to make something false appear true. A specious argument looks
good on the surface but is flawed underneath.)

Polemics (puh-LEM-iks) is the art or practice of argument or
disputation, and a *polemic* is a strong argument or aggressive verbal
attack, usually against some person, opinion, principle, or doctrine.
A *polemicist* (puh-LEM-i-sist) is a person who engages in polemics
or who issues a polemic. Our keyword, *polemical,* means relating to
polemics or consisting of a polemic. A polemical novel, film, or
play is one in which the author presents a vigorous argument about
some social or political issue. And the U.S. Congress is a polemical
institution in which debates, disputes, and controversy thrive.

Word 44: EPOCHAL (EP-uh-kul)
Highly significant, important, or influential; momentous.

Epochal is the adjective corresponding to the noun *epoch* (EP-uk), a
particular period of time known for its distinctive developments,
remarkable characteristics, or noteworthy events. *Epochal* means
important enough to initiate or characterize an epoch, a distinctive or noteworthy period; hence, highly significant, important,
or influential.

When the Russian composer Igor Stravinsky's *Rite of Spring* was
first performed in Paris in 1913, it was met with riotous disfavor;

yet this epochal composition paved the way for the modern, ex-
perimental music of the 20th century. And if archaeologists ever
uncover the so-called missing link—the hypothetical evolutionary connection between the anthropoid apes and human beings—it will be an epochal discovery.

Word 45: COGNOSCENTI (KAHN-yuh-**SHEN**-tee, *also* KOHN- *or* KAWN-)

Experts in a certain subject, connoisseurs, those "in the know."

English borrowed *cognoscenti* from Italian in the late 18th century;
it is the equivalent of the more familiar word *connoisseur* (KAH-
nuh-**SUR**, *not* -SOO-ur), which English borrowed from French
in the early 18th century. *Cognoscenti* comes ultimately from the
Latin *cognoscĕre,* to learn, get to know, the source also of the English *cognizant,* aware, knowing; *cognition,* knowledge, perception;
and *cognitive,* pertaining to cognition.

   Note that *cognoscenti* is a plural noun, both in Italian and in English; the singular is *cognoscente,* spelled with a final *e* instead of an
i and pronounced the same except with -tay instead of -tee at the
end. *A* cognoscente is an expert, and *the* cognoscenti are experts,
connoisseurs, people with superior knowledge of a subject. It is
often used of connoisseurs of the fine arts and literature, but it may
also be used of an expert in or aficionado of almost anything, such
as *tennis cognoscenti, NASCAR cognoscenti,* or *foreign policy cognoscenti.*

Word 46: IMMOLATE (IM-uh-layt)

To kill or destroy as a sacrifice, especially by fire.

The verb to *immolate* comes from the Latin *immolāre,* to sprin-
kle with sacred meal before sacrificing. The noun is *immolation*
(IM-uh-**LAY**-shun), the act or practice of burning as a sacrifice.

   Immolation is historically associated with the Hindu custom,
now outlawed, called *sati* (suh-TEE, also spelled *suttee*), in which a
wife would show her unwavering loyalty to her deceased husband
by immolating herself on his funeral pyre. Buddhist monks have
also sometimes practiced self-immolation, or self-sacrifice, by set-

ting themselves on fire in public as a form of protest. *Immolate* is usually used literally of the burning of anyone or anything as a sacrifice, but the word may also be used figuratively to mean to offer in sacrifice, as *people who immolate themselves on the altar of love.*

Now a word of caution on usage. First, do not use *immolate* as an intransitive verb meaning to catch fire. *Immolate* is a transitive verb, meaning that something must *be* immolated; it can't just immolate by itself. Second, *immolate* should not be used loosely to mean to kill or destroy for any reason. The notion of sacrificial burning is intrinsic to the derivation and history of the word, and should be respected. Thus, you do not immolate a house, immolate garbage, or immolate the love letters of a former boyfriend; you burn or destroy them. Reserve *immolate* for contexts in which something is destroyed or someone is killed as a sacrifice, especially by burning.

Word 47: HIDEBOUND (HYD-bownd, rhymes with *ride hound*)
Narrow and inflexible in one's opinions; stubbornly stuck in one's ways.

Synonyms of *hidebound* include *narrow-minded, uncompromising, bigoted, close-minded, obstinate, intolerant, adamant, dogmatic, parochial* (puh-ROH-kee-ul), *intractable,* and *obdurate* (AHB-d[y]uu-rit). Antonyms of *hidebound* include *broad-minded, open-minded, tolerant, liberal,* and *latitudinarian* (word 33 of Level 8).

Hidebound was first used of a horse, cow, or other domestic animal to mean having skin that clings tightly to the bones; hence, undernourished or emaciated (word 11 of Level 1). This sense was also applied to human beings, as in this citation from William Wright's 1895 travelogue *Palmyra and Zenobia:* "They had not the hidebound, hunger-pinched appearance of the children of Yabroud." But from the time *hidebound* entered English in about 1600 it has also been used figuratively, in what is today its usual sense, to mean obstinately set in one's opinion or purpose, stubbornly narrow-minded, as *a hidebound traditionalist who resists change of any kind* or *hidebound grammarians who cling to outmoded rules.*

Individuals and groups can be hidebound, narrow and inflexible in their opinions, but certain things, such as laws, traditions, and customs, can also be hidebound, stubbornly inflexible: "The English have always struggled with their hidebound class divisions"; "If so hidebound an institution as the papacy can be changed, what can't be?" (*The New York Times*).

Word 48: MOLDER (MOWL-dur, rhymes with *shoulder*)
To decay, disintegrate, crumble, rot, waste away, become particles or dust.

When you think of the noun *mold* you probably think of the greenish-gray, downy fungi (FUHN-jy, not FUHNG-gy) that grow on things that are damp or decaying. But there's another kind of *mold:* rich, soft, loose soil, full of organic matter and suitable for planting. Such garden soil made from composting leaves is called *leaf mold.* It is from this earthy, crumbly kind of mold that we get the verb to *molder,* to rot or decay: "There is little to lure visitors into the weeds and moldering woods that stretch for miles along Jamaica Bay's northern edges" (*The New York Times*).

Anything old and damp that is left to decay can be described as moldering—for example, moldering fruit, moldering books, moldering wallpaper, moldering clothes, a moldering castle, works of art that molder in a museum's basement, and—hold your nose now—a moldering corpse.

But *molder* can also be used of anything that is figuratively falling apart or wasting away: "Halligan's nomination has been moldering for two years now" (*The New York Times*). A friendship can molder from inattention. A convict can molder for years in prison. A brilliant idea can molder if no one acts on it. And support for or opposition to something can molder, crumble or disintegrate, over time.

Word 49: FRATRICIDE (FRA-tri-syd)
The act of killing one's brother, or a person who kills his or her brother.

In extended use, *fratricide* may also denote the killer or the killing of someone who is like a brother—for example, a countryman, fellow soldier, or close friend.

In law, *fratricide* is defined as the act of killing a brother or sister, or a person who kills a brother or sister, and some contemporary dictionaries give this definition for *fratricide*. This follows the old-fashioned practice of lumping women with men in such words as *mankind* and in well-worn phrases like "all men are created equal." Because this practice is widely considered sexist, most of us now use *firefighter* instead of *fireman, police officer* instead of *policeman,* and *mail carrier* instead of *mailman,* and many prefer the inclusive word *humankind* over the one-sided *mankind.*

So with *fratricide* you should know that by derivation the word refers only to the killer or killing of a brother, because it comes from the Latin *frater,* brother, while the companion term *sororicide* (suh-ROR-i-syd), from the Latin *soror,* sister, denotes a killer or the killing of a sister. Both terms incorporate the combining form *-cide,* which comes from the Latin *caedere,* to cut or kill, and means either a killer or the act of killing.

Let's have a look at some of the other *-cide* words—or killer words—in the language. There are, regrettably, quite a lot of them.

Homicide (properly pronounced HAHM-i-syd, not HOHM-i-syd), from the Latin *homo,* a man or a human being, is the killing or killer of a person, male or female. *Suicide,* from the Latin *sui,* of oneself, is a self-killing or a self-killer. *Infanticide* (in-FAN-ti-syd) is the killing or killer of an infant. *Matricide* (MA-tri-syd), from the Latin *mater,* a mother, is the killing or killer of one's mother. *Patricide* (PA-tri-syd), from the Latin *pater,* a father, is the killing or killer of one's father. And *parricide* (PAR-i-syd), from the Latin *parracida,* a kin-killer, is the killing or killer of a father, mother, or other close relative.

The more familiar *regicide* (REJ-i-syd), from the Latin *rēx, rēgis,* a king, ruler, is the killing or killer of a king; *tyrannicide* (ti-RAN-i-syd), from the Latin *tyrannus,* an absolute ruler, is the killing or killer of a tyrant; and *genocide* (JEN-uh-syd)—which was coined during World War II from the Greek *génos* and the Latin *gĕnus,* both of which meant race or kind—denotes "the systematic and planned extermination of an entire national, racial, political, or ethnic group" (*American Heritage*). The systematic undermining of a person's values and beliefs, as through brainwashing or torture, is called *menticide* (MEN-ti-syd).

There are also many *-cide* words that kill things other than human beings. For example, a *pesticide* kills pests; an *insecticide* kills insects; a *herbicide* (pronounce the *h,* HUR-bi-syd) kills weeds and other unwanted plants; a *bactericide* kills bacteria; a *fungicide* (FUHN-ji-syd) kills *fungi* (FUHN-jy), the plural of *fungus;* and a *vermicide* (VUR-mi-syd), from the Latin *vermis,* a worm, kills worms, especially intestinal worms.

Word 50: SPLENETIC (spluh-NET-ik)
Irritable, ill-tempered; spiteful and morose; given to angry and impatient fits.

You can imagine how many synonyms there are for a word that means irritable or ill-tempered. Here are some of them: *cross; cranky; peevish; churlish* (word 9 of Level 6); *waspish; snappish; petulant* (PECH-uh-lint); *cantankerous* (kan-TANG-kur-us); *choleric* (KAH-luh-rik, literally affected with the disease cholera); *grouchy; sullen; sulky; crabbed* (KRAB-id); *surly; ill-humored; testy; crusty; captious; irascible* (i-RAS-i-bul); *curmudgeonly* (kur-MUHJ-in-lee); *dyspeptic* (dis-PEP-tik, word 11 of Level 7); *acrimonious* (AK-ri-**MOH**-nee-us); *querulous* (KWER-uh-lus); and *atrabilious* (A-truh-**BIL**-ee-us, word 24 of Level 8).

Splenetic comes from the Greek and Latin words for the spleen, and originally meant of, pertaining to, or affecting the spleen, the organ that destroys old red blood cells, filters and stores blood, and produces lymphocytes (LIM-fuh-syts), a type of white blood cell essential to the body's immune system. Because the ancients considered the spleen the seat of various emotions, *splenetic* came to be used of people who had fits of bad temper, angry impatience, or ill will, or who had a melancholy, morose, ill-humored disposition. In 1780 the English philosopher Jeremy Bentham wrote of "the fear of future punishment at the hands of a splenetic and revengeful Deity." And in 1841, in his novel *Barnaby Rudge,* Charles Dickens wrote that "neighbours who had got up splenetic that morning, felt good-humour stealing on them as they heard" the "pleasant music," the "magical tink, tink, tink," of the locksmith.

That is how we continue to use *splenetic* today: to mean gloomy, irritable, and spiteful, given to fits of anger and impatience. The word is commonly applied to people, but it may apply as well to what people say or write, as *the splenetic utterances of a demagogue* [word 12 of Level 4] *with a million followers on Twitter.* It may also apply to anything that seems to manifest spiteful or morose irritability: "Stock markets . . . turned downright splenetic in exchanges from Frankfurt to New York" (*The Deal Pipeline*).

Review Quiz for Keywords 41–50
In this quiz the review word is followed by three words or phrases, and you must decide which comes nearest the meaning of the review word. **Answers appear on page 249.**

1. Is a *maladroit* maneuver awkward, ill-considered, or inappropriate?
2. When you *gormandize,* do you talk at length, eat excessively, or chew thoroughly?
3. Is a *polemical* essay scholarly, humorous, or argumentative?
4. Would an *epochal* event be highly significant, controversial, or unremarkable?
5. Are the *cognoscenti* powerful people, ordinary people, or experts?
6. When you *immolate* something, do you copy it, compete with it, or sacrifice it?
7. Is a *hidebound* person narrow-minded, optimistic, or antisocial?
8. When something *molders,* does it sprout, disintegrate, or burn?
9. Is *fratricide* the act of hating a brother, marrying a brother, or killing a brother?
10. Would a *splenetic* person be vigorous, spiteful, or incoherent?

Once Upon a Word: A Brief Cruise on the Ocean of English
Have you ever wondered why a ship's latrine is called the *head*? What does that body part have to do with the functions we reserve for the bathroom? As it turns out—happily—nothing. The nautical *head* refers to the bow or head of the ship, where the latrine was originally situated. The *head* is a euphemism (word 18 of Level 2) sailors use in the same way landlubbers use the *john,*

which is probably a variation on the 19th-century British dialectal *jack* or *Jack's house,* meaning a privy.

Speaking of the head and the john, let's turn our attention to the *poop,* the superstructure at the stern of a ship. Have you ever wondered what those ancient mariners were thinking when they chose to poop in the head and stand on the poop? Sometimes they even ate and slept in the poop!

Don't be alarmed, for it all makes sense. The landlubber's *poop,* which probably comes from the Middle English *poupen,* to blow a horn, bears no direct relation to the seafarer's *poop,* which comes from the Latin *puppis,* the stern of a ship. There's even a nautical verb to *poop,* meaning to break over the stern of a vessel. "A large tumbling swell threatened to poop us," says the earliest citation for it in the *OED,* from 1748.

Whenever you feel groggy you can blame the 18th-century British vice admiral Sir Edward Vernon, whose men called him "Old Grog" because of the heavy grogram coat he would always wear on deck, no matter the weather. In August of 1740, tired of putting up with unruly, drunken sailors, Vernon issued an order to dilute their rum ration, three parts water to one part rum, with portions served six hours apart. His men responded by dubbing the adulterated mixture *grog.* When it became the official liquor ration for the entire Royal Navy, *grog* came to mean inferior, inexpensive booze, and later it was used even more broadly of any liquor.

If some old salt tells you that *gob,* meaning a sailor, comes from the sealants sailors use to waterproof a ship, don't believe a word of it. This *gob* is not sealant; it's plain old spit. In the second half of the 19th century *gob* was used in British and American English to mean to expectorate. It appears to have first been used of British coastguardsmen who were fond of sitting around together smoking pipes and spitting.

Finally, let's dispel the persistent rumor that *posh*—meaning elegant, fashionable, upper-crust—is an acronym for *port out, starboard home.* As the story goes, *posh* "was formerly stamped on first-class, round-trip tickets of the Peninsular and Oriental Steam Navigation Co., which carried mail and passengers between England and India," writes Hugh Rawson in *Devious Derivations.*

"The acronym, said to date from the years prior to World War I, supposedly entitled the ticket holder to passage in one of the cooler cabins aboard ship, on the port side, facing north, on the outward bound journey, and on the starboard side, again facing north, when returning home." This story, though charming, has never been proved, and the origin of *posh* remains unknown.

Answers to Review Quizzes for Level 5

KEYWORDS 1–10

1. Yes. *Bereft* means forcibly deprived of something needed, wanted, or expected.

2. No. A *nemesis* is an unconquerable avenger, a person or thing that metes out punishment.

3. No. Someone who *equivocates* uses evasive and ambiguous language so as to mislead.

4. No. A *philistine* is an uneducated, uncultured, narrow-minded person.

5. No. *Bacchanalian* means frenzied, riotous, orgiastic, characterized by drunken revelry.

6. No. A *schism* is a split or break, a division of a group into opposing factions.

7. Yes. A *lingua franca* is a common language.

8. Yes. *Winsome* means charming, agreeable, and pleasant in appearance or manner.

9. No. *Patrician* means aristocratic, of high birth or social standing, upper-class.

10. Yes. To *redact* is to edit for publication, especially to remove or adapt text to make something acceptable for publication.

KEYWORDS 11–20

1. True. A *précis* is a brief summary or concise outline.

2. True. *Taxonomy* is an orderly system of naming and classifying things.

3. False. Something *subliminal* is below your level of conscious awareness.

4. True. *Philanthropy* is love of humankind; *misanthropy* is hatred of humankind.

5. True. Your *imprimatur* is your approval or support.

6. True. A *canard* is a false, absurd, and often derogatory story or report.

7. True. *Perfidious* friends are treacherous, disloyal friends—just as bad as enemies.

8. False. An *epiphany* is a moment of sudden, dramatic insight or realization.

9. False. To *prattle* is to chatter, babble, talk in a foolish, childish, or simpleminded way.

10. False. A person of high birth or rank is aristocratic or patrician (word 9 of this level). *Plebeian* means of the common people, ordinary.

KEYWORDS 21–30

1. Synonyms. To *gull* is to cheat, trick, deceive, take advantage of.

2. Antonyms. *Compendious* means condensed, abridged, containing the substance of a subject in brief form. *Exhaustive* means thorough, covering everything.

3. Antonyms. To *rhapsodize* is to express oneself with extravagant emotion or enthusiasm.

4. Synonyms. An *incongruity* is something that disagrees, something incompatible. An *oxymoron* is a self-contradictory expression.

5. Antonyms. *Provenance* is the source or origin of something. A *destination* is a place where something goes or is sent.

6. Synonyms. *Laissez-faire* is noninterference with the affairs of others or with individual freedom of action.

7. Synonyms. *Preternatural* means supernatural, beyond what is considered normal or natural; hence, exceptional, extraordinary.

8. Antonyms. To *disabuse* is to free from error, deception, or misunderstanding.

9. Synonyms. A *courtesan* is a high-class female prostitute. A *concubine* is a mistress.

10. Synonyms. To *debauch* is to corrupt or seduce—the same as to *deprave*.

KEYWORDS 31–40

1. *Fanfare* doesn't fit. *Braggadocio* is empty and arrogant boasting or bragging.

2. *Curse* doesn't fit. To *flagellate* is to whip, flog, lash, scourge.

3. *Rabble-rouser*—a demagogue (word 12 of Level 4)—doesn't fit. An *insurgent* is someone who rises in opposition to a government or to established authority, a rebel, revolutionary.

4. *Self-satisfaction* doesn't fit. *Panache* is self-assurance, grand or flamboyant confidence of style or manner.

5. *Full of amendments,* corrections or changes, doesn't fit. *Omnibus* means pertaining to, containing, or covering many things or items at once.

6. *Make less severe* doesn't fit; to *mitigate* means to make less severe, alleviate. To *militate* is to weigh heavily, operate or work against.

7. *Utilitarian* (word 49 of Level 4) doesn't fit. *Nihilistic* means anarchic, despairing, rejecting established institutions and beliefs.

8. *Vivacious,* lively, energetic, doesn't fit. *Torpid* means inactive, sluggish, enervated.

9. *Spiritual* doesn't fit. *Seminal* means highly original and creative, influencing later works, events, or ideas.

10. *Starving* doesn't fit. *Craven* means cowardly, contemptibly timid, pusillanimous.

KEYWORDS 41–50

1. A maladroit maneuver is awkward, clumsy, unskillful.

2. When you gormandize, you eat greedily and excessively, like a glutton.

3. It's argumentative. *Polemical* means pertaining to or consisting of an argument or dispute.

4. An epochal event is highly significant, important, or influential.

5. The cognoscenti are experts in a certain subject, connoisseurs.

6. You sacrifice it. To *immolate* is to kill or destroy by sacrifice, especially by fire.

7. A hidebound person is narrow-minded and stubbornly inflexible.

8. It disintegrates. To *molder* is to decay, crumble, rot, waste away.

9. *Fratricide* is the act of killing one's brother, or a person who kills his or her brother.

10. A splenetic person is irritable, spiteful, and morose.

LEVEL 6

Word 1: INELUCTABLE (IN-i-**LUHK**-tuh-bul)
Not to be evaded or resisted; unavoidable; inescapable; inevitable.

Ineluctable comes from the Latin *inēluctābilis,* from which one cannot struggle free, combining the privative prefix *in-,* not, with the verb *ēluctāre,* to struggle out of, surmount. By derivation *ineluctable* means not to be struggled free from, unable to be surmounted, or, as Henry Cockeram defined it in his *English Dictionarie* of 1623, one of the earliest works of English lexicography, "not to bee ouercome by any paines." This is still the essential meaning of the word today.

 History is replete (well-stocked, richly supplied) with stories of ineluctable social, political, and economic forces altering and sometimes destroying the lives of individuals. Someone's fate or destiny is often described as ineluctable, unavoidable or inevitable. And in classical Greek drama, the downfall of the main character is the ineluctable consequence of tragic flaws—including hubris (word 40 of Level 1), excessive pride.

Word 2: MORIBUND (MOR-uh-bund)
Dying, close to death, at death's door.

An unusual synonym of *moribund* is the Latin phrase *in extremis* (in-ek-STREE-mis), at the point of death.

 Moribund comes from the Latin *moribundus,* dying, at the point of death, which comes in turn from the verb *morī,* to die, the source also, by a circuitous (sur-KYOO-i-tus, indirect, roundabout) path, of the word *murder.* This Latin *morī,* to die, appears also in the expression *memento morī* (muh-MEN-toh MOR-eye or MOR-ee), which was borrowed directly from Latin and means "remember that you must die"; the phrase is often used of an object, such as a skull, that serves as a reminder of one's mortality.

Moribund may be used in a literal sense to mean dying, as *a moribund houseplant* or *a moribund relative.* But in modern usage *moribund* is also often used in an extended, nonliteral sense to mean in a state of terminal decline, approaching extinction. A dying empire, an obsolescent custom, a failing love affair, and a company going out of business—all are moribund, close to death or on the verge of expiring.

Word 3: BELLWETHER (BEL-weth-ur)
A leader, one who takes the initiative; also, a leading indicator of a trend.

A *wether* (pronounced like *weather*) is a castrated male sheep, and in its original sense a bellwether was a wether with a bell hung on its neck whose function was to lead the flock of sheep. Hence, *bellwether* came to also mean a leader. At first this sense was disparaging, as *the bellwether of a mutiny,* meaning not just a leader but a ringleader, one who leads others in improper or illegal activity. But in modern usage *bellwether* no longer has this negative connotation, and the word is used chiefly in two ways. It may denote "a person or thing that assumes the leadership or forefront" (*Random House*), as *Blackstone is a bellwether investor in the industry.* Or it may denote a leading indicator of a trend, as *Ohio is considered the bellwether state in U.S. presidential elections.*

Word 4: PERMUTATION (PUR-myoo-TAY-shin)
A thorough or fundamental change, or the result of such a change.

Synonyms of *permutation* include *alteration, transformation, transmutation, transfiguration,* and *metamorphosis.*

The noun *permutation* comes ultimately from the Latin *permūtāre,* to change completely, a combination of the intensifying prefix *per-,* thoroughly, completely, and *mūtāre,* to change, alter. In its most general sense, a *mutation* is a change or alteration; for example, a so-called correction in the stock market (meaning a sudden and often steep decline in prices) may cause a mutation in the economy, and cells in the body may undergo mutation and become cancerous. A permutation is a thorough or fundamental mutation, or the result of such a mutation. The Ford Mustang has undergone several design permutations since the classic car was introduced in 1964. And every year the movers and shakers in the world of fashion hope they have found a successful permutation of what was in style before.

Word 5: INTERLOPE (in-tur-LOHP *or* IN-tur-lohp)
To interfere, intrude; to thrust oneself into others' affairs, usually for selfish reasons.

Synonyms of *interlope* include to *meddle, trespass, invade, infringe, encroach,* and the colloquial *butt in.*

The origin of the verb to *interlope* is unclear, but it is probably related to the Middle Dutch *lopen* or *loopen,* to run, and an Old English word meaning to leap. The combining form *inter-* means between, so *interlope* by derivation means to run or leap between, hence to interfere. Originally to *interlope* referred to unlicensed interfering in others' trading rights or unauthorized intruding on their commercial territory, and the word may still be used in this way, as *An interloping company eager to profit from the untapped oil and gas in the region.* But from this specialized meaning developed the modern and more general sense: to intrude on the domain of others or to interfere in their affairs, invariably for selfish gain. Thus, an interloping species is one that intrudes on the habitat of other species and crowds them out. And on the sci-fi TV show *Star Trek* the so-called Prime Directive for the United Federation of Planets dictates that there can be no interloping in alien civilizations.

The noun is *interloper* (**IN**-tur-LOH-pur), someone or something that selfishly interferes or meddles in the affairs of others: "Ever since Martha took in that stray cat he's been an interloper in our house."

Word 6: **HECTOR** (HEK-tur)

To bully or be domineering; to intimidate or torment with words or threats.

The verb to *hector* is an eponym, a word derived from a name. It comes from Hector, the leader and bravest warrior of the Trojans in Greek mythology. In Homer's *Iliad,* which tells the story of the Trojan War, Hector slays Patroclus (puh-TROH-klus), the friend of the greatest of the Greek warriors, Achilles (uh-KIL-eez), who in revenge slays Hector and drags his body behind his chariot around the walls of Troy.

Hector was first used in English as a noun to mean a valiant warrior like Hector. It was later applied to "a set of disorderly young men who infested the streets of London" (*OED*) in the 17th century and was used to mean a swaggering, bullying braggart. It was soon transformed into a verb meaning to bully or to be a bully, as in this quotation from Henry Fielding's 1749 novel *Tom Jones:* "We are . . . not to be hectored, and bullied, and beat into compliance." This is how *hector* is most often used today.

Someone who hectors is domineering and intimidating, using any means short of outright violence—such as shouting, insults, and threats—to instill fear and obedience in others. Army drill sergeants, for example, are infamous for hectoring recruits, but even a parent or teacher who bullies and threatens children can be described as hectoring.

Word 7: **DISSOLUTE** (DIS-uh-LOOT)

Lacking moral restraint; given to immoral behavior.

Synonyms of the adjective *dissolute* include *wanton, lewd, debauched* (*debauch* is word 30 of Level 5), *licentious* (ly-SEN-shus), *dissipated* (DIS-i-pay-tid), and *profligate* (PRAHF-li-git). Antonyms include *prudish, straitlaced,* and *puritanical.*

Dissolute comes from the Latin *dissolūtus,* loose, disconnected, and once meant loose or relaxed. In modern usage, though, *dissolute* means loose in morals and conduct, too relaxed about one's virtue. The dissolute person lacks all restraint and is given to indulgence in immoral behavior, especially sensual pleasures and vices. A dissolute lifestyle is one characterized by overindulgence in and often addiction to something considered immoral, such as drugs, sex, or gambling.

Dissolute may also be used as a noun to mean a dissolute person: "Whether they are from high or low society—trust-fund-squandering preppies slugging gin and tonics in the Hamptons or unwashed, unemployed ne'er-do-wells sticking needles in their arms—dissolutes everywhere are all the same."

Word 8: LINEAMENTS (LIN-ee-uh-mints)
Distinguishing features or distinctive characteristics.

The singular noun *lineament,* which is more often used in the plural, *lineaments,* comes through the Latin *līneāmentum,* a drawn line or a feature, from the Latin *līneā,* a line, the source also of the adjective *linear,* composed of lines, hence straight or sequential, as *a linear narrative* or *linear thinking.*

Lineaments may be used of a part of the body, especially the face, to mean a distinctive contour or outline, or a particular feature or detail, as *a marble bust with the same graceful lineaments as its subject.* Perhaps more often, though, *lineaments* is used generally of any distinguishing features or distinctive characteristics, whether physical, as *the grim and dangerous lineaments of that barren coast,* or figurative, as *the structural lineaments of poetry* or *an apartment with all the lineaments of a sophisticated man with refined tastes.*

Word 9: CHURLISH (CHUR-lish)
Lacking civility and graciousness; rude, ill-mannered, ungracious.

Synonyms of *churlish* include *surly, gruff, boorish, loutish,* and *uncouth.* Antonyms include *polite, gracious, well-bred, refined,* and *courtly.*

The English noun *churl* (rhymes with *girl*) is more than a thousand years old and comes from the Anglo-Saxon *ceorl,* a man or husband. In the Middle Ages, in the feudal system, a churl was a freeman of the lowest rank, just above a slave. Because of this low social position the adjective *churlish,* which is almost as old as *churl,* first meant pertaining to the low rank of a churl, but it soon came to suggest the rustic, earthy, and crude characteristics of a churl, and then the vulgar, low-bred character of a churl. By the early 15th century *churlish* had come to mean lacking civility and graciousness, rude, boorish, surly, and this is the common meaning of the word today.

When Shakespeare, in *Troilus and Cressida,* writes, "He is as valiant as the lion, churlish as the bear, slow as an elephant," he means that the bear is irritable and antisocial. Churlish hosts or churlish guests are rude and ungracious—not nice or accommodating at all. And anyone who has watched the classic TV sitcom *All in the Family* knows that Archie Bunker—the benighted (word 48 of this level) bigot played by Carroll O'Connor—was the embodiment of churlishness, rude, ill-mannered behavior.

Word 10: PREPOSSESSING (PREE-puh-ZES-ing)
Giving a favorable impression; attractive, engaging, pleasing, comely.

The verb to *prepossess* may mean to preoccupy beforehand: "She came to Washington prepossessed with grandiose (word 3 of Level 1) ideas." Or it may mean to influence beforehand, to bias or prejudice, especially in favor of something: "They easily prepossessed the corrupt judge with flattery and bribes." The adjective *prepossessing* originally meant causing bias or prejudice, but that sense is obsolete, and since the 1700s the word has been used to mean creating a good impression, predisposing favorably: "His prepossessing good looks and manners won the hearts of all who met him"; "Rarely is a young writer's first novel as prepossessing and profound as this."

The antonym of *prepossessing* is the perhaps more common *unprepossessing,* not creating a good impression; hence, unattractive, unremarkable, or unpleasant. An unprepossessing person makes a poor impression, perhaps because he or she is dressed poorly, speaks poorly, or has bad breath. And a great restaurant may be located in an undesirable neighborhood on an unprepossessing street.

Review Quiz for Keywords 1–10

Consider the following questions and decide whether the correct answer is yes or no. **Answers appear on page 290**.

1. Is something ineluctable avoidable?
2. If something is moribund, is it likely to survive?
3. Is a bellwether a leader?
4. Is a permutation a transformation?
5. When you interlope, do you interfere?
6. Does someone who hectors offer helpful advice?
7. Would a dissolute person exercise restraint?
8. Are lineaments distinguishing features?
9. Is a churlish person unfriendly?
10. Is something prepossessing attractive?

Don't Stupidsize Me

After my vocabulary-building program *Verbal Advantage* came out as a book in 2000 (it was originally an audio course), I was invited to be a guest on *salon.com,* answering questions in a forum called Table Talk. It was a lively discussion. At one point a participant commented that many of the keywords in the book struck her as "trivia questions more than elements of a working vocabulary." And she asked, "As much fun as it is to know a word like *sciamachy* [sy-AM-uh-kee, fighting with a shadow or an imaginary opponent], do you really think it should be part of everyday discourse?"

That's a fair question, I told her. Too many people use big words to show off or to intimidate others, which is obnoxious, and what's the point of learning words that nobody else will understand? But then I reminded her that nine-tenths of the words in an unabridged dictionary are not part of everyday discourse, and at least half of those are not so technical or obscure that no one uses them. They're just not common. Should lexicographers not bother to include them? (Sometimes they don't, to make room for trendy new words.) Should we not bother to learn some of them, if only because they're uncommonly interesting? And why should something as unimaginative and boring as everyday discourse dictate—or circumscribe—what words are worth learning?

To a writer all words are useful, whether they are used today, tomorrow, next year, just once, or never. Just having a word in your vocabulary is enough; it's like having had a memorable experience. For example, my experience with the adjective *chryselephantine* (KRIS-el-uh-**FAN**-tin), made of gold and ivory, gave me untold delight, while my experience with the verb to *impact* was unpleasant enough to make me swear off it permanently.

What writer wouldn't squirm and curse if confined to the vocabulary of everyday discourse? That's like having to eat fast food and drink sugary soda at every meal. Such an unappealing diet of unremarkable words can do only one thing: stupidsize me.

This isn't an argument against simple diction, which has its merits. It's an argument against the arbitrary notion that we should always use simple words and that difficult words have no place in our discourse. Writers who reject uncommon words condemn themselves to the frustration of trying to build a house with only a screwdriver. And they forfeit, foolishly, the right to partake in the treasure of our tongue.

Here are the next ten keywords in Level 6:

Word 11: ELEGIAC (EL-i-**JY**-ik)

Of the nature of an elegy; hence, expressing grief, sorrow, or lamentation.

Synonyms of *elegiac* include *mournful, tearful, melancholy, funereal, rueful* (word 25 of Level 1), and *plaintive* (word 9 of Level 2).

Elegiac is the adjective corresponding to the noun *elegy*. An *elegy* (EL-i-jee) is a type of poem that expresses grief or mourning. In *The Making of a Poem,* Mark Strand and Eavan Boland explain that "an elegy is a lament. It sets out the circumstances and character of a loss. It mourns for a dead person, lists his or her virtues, and seeks consolation beyond the momentary event." Although the elegy is a public poem of lament, expressing the grief of a community or culture, the best elegies express not only communal lamentation but the poet's private grief as well.

Elegiac expression is not limited to poetry. A novel, a memoir, a play, or a film can be elegiac, expressing grief over the loss of a person or thing. A great deal of music is also elegiac, mournful, melancholy, expressive of loss.

Elegiac is sometimes mispronounced EL-i-**JAY**-ik, as if the word were spelled *elegaic*. Take care to spell it *elegiac* and say EL-i-**JY**-ik.

Word 12: UKASE (yoo-KAYS *or* YOO-kays, like *you case*)
An authoritative order, command, or proclamation.

Ukase entered English about 1730, coming through French from Russian. It originally meant an absolute decree or edict by the czar of Russia or his government, and this is still the word's specific historical meaning. But in the 19th century the meaning broadened and *ukase* was used of any proclamation having the force of law, and in this sense it is broadly synonymous with the words *edict* and *decree*. However, in modern usage *ukase* also often suggests an arbitrary or subjective order or command issued by an authority: "The professor's ukase on late papers—that they would get an F, with no extensions or exceptions—took some students by surprise." A ukase may also come from an authority whose final authority may be questionable: "During the contract negotiations the union rejected management's ukase, calling it unacceptable."

Word 13: ASPERITY (uh-SPER-i-tee)
Harshness, roughness, or sharpness of manner, temper, or tone.

Asperity comes from the Latin *asperĭtās,* which comes in turn from *asper,* rough. The Latin *asperĭtās* had several meanings. It was used of the sense of touch to mean roughness or unevenness. It was used of hearing to mean sharpness or sourness. And it was used of character or manner to mean harshness, severity, fierceness. All these senses survive in the English noun *asperity*.

You may use *asperity* to mean a roughness or unevenness, as *the asperity of unfinished wood,* or a slight, uneven projection from a surface, as *the asperities of the tongue.* You may use it to mean harshness or sharpness of sound, as *the piccolo's asperity* or *the asperity of her mother's scolding voice.* And you may use it to mean hardship, difficulty, rigor, as *the economic asperity of a long recession* or *the asperity of New England winters.* But most often *asperity* is used to denote a harshness, roughness, or sharpness of manner, temper, or tone: "Herman's editor insisted on softening his unrestrained asperity toward his literary rivals"; "Portia was infamous for treating her friends and enemies with equal asperity."

Synonyms of *asperity* include *bitterness, acerbity, crabbedness, petulance, surliness, irascibility,* and *captiousness.* Antonyms of *asperity* include *cheerfulness, graciousness, courteousness, cordiality,* and *affability.*

Word 14: DELECTATION (DEE-lek-**TAY**-sh<u>i</u>n)
Enjoyment, delight, great pleasure.

Delectation comes through the Latin *dēlectātio,* delight, pleasure, from the verb *dēlectāre,* to delight, take delight in, the source also of the adjective *delectable* (d<u>i</u>-LEK-tuh-b<u>u</u>l), delightful, pleasing, delicious, as *a delectable feast* or *a delectable story.*

Delectation entered English in the late 14th century, and the *OED* explains that initially the word was used of all kinds of pleasure, both worldly and spiritual, but since the 18th century *delectation* has been applied chiefly "to the lighter kinds of pleasure." Thus, we speak of "entertainments provided for the public's delectation," or "fresh local seafood and vegetables for the delectation of the guests."

Delectation may also be used of anything that delights, or as a more literary synonym of *delight:* "She spoke for a full hour, to the delectation of all present"; "That summer working on the dairy farm he was so isolated, bored, and bereft (word 1 of Level 5) of books that watching TV was his only diversion and delectation."

Word 15: **BOOTLESS** (BOOT-l<u>i</u>s)
Useless, unproductive, unprofitable.

Synonyms of *bootless* include *fruitless, vain, inefficacious* (in–EF–i–
KAY-sh<u>u</u>s), *unavailing* (uhn–uh–VAYL–ing), and *nugatory* (word
31 of Level 9).

The adjective *bootless* may mean literally without boots, and
therefore shoeless, unshod, discalced (word 22 of Level 10). But
in the sense we are concerned with here, *bootless* goes back to the
Old English *bōt,* a remedy, which gave us the noun *boot* meaning
advantage, profit, use, familiar in the phrase *to boot,* meaning to
good advantage or in addition, and formerly used in the phrases *it
is no boot,* meaning it is no use, and *to make boot of,* meaning to
profit or gain by, as when Shakespeare, in *Antony and Cleopatra,*
writes, "Give him no breath, but now make boote of his distrac-
tion."

Bootless combines this archaic *boot,* advantage, profit, use, with
the privative suffix *-less* to mean of no advantage, unprofitable,
useless. In modern usage *bootless* is the equivalent of *to no avail,*
meaning to no profitable use or advantage. We speak of bootless
attempts, bootless efforts, bootless words, or a bootless enterprise.
"Each quarter," writes Jason Hirthler at CounterPunch.org,
"hundreds of thousands of workers become so dispirited by their
bootless search for work that they simply quit looking."

Word 16: **EXPLICATE** (EKS-pl<u>i</u>-kayt)
To present a detailed explanation or analysis of.

The verb to *explicate* comes from the Latin *explicāre,* to unfold,
unroll, disentangle. By derivation, when you explicate you unfold the meaning of something, disentangle its difficulties and make
them plain.

To *explain* is the general term for making something clear or
understandable. To *explicate* implies explaining in much greater
detail and depth, unfolding the meaning or mysteries of something. You can explicate a literary text, explicate a scientific theory, explicate a philosophical principle, explicate a complex piece

of music, or explicate the peculiar trends and obsessions of popular culture. The noun *explication* is the act of explicating, presenting a detailed explanation or analysis of something. To be a good teacher you must be adept at explication.

Synonyms of *explicate* include *interpret, expound,* and *elucidate* (word 22 of Level 1). Antonyms of *explicate* include *complicate, muddle, adumbrate* (ad-UHM-brayt or AD-um-brayt), and *obfuscate* (ahb-FUHS-kayt or AHB-fuh-skayt).

Word 17: PEJORATIVE (pi-JOR-uh-tiv *or* -JAHR-uh-tiv)
Having a negative meaning or force; uncomplimentary.

Synonyms of *pejorative* include *belittling, disparaging, derogatory, depreciatory* (di-PREE-shee-uh-tor-ee), and *deprecatory* (DEP-ri-kuh-tor-ee).

The adjective *pejorative* comes from the Late Latin *pējōrāre,* to make or become worse, which in turn comes from *pejor,* worse, the comparative form of the adjective *malus,* bad, evil, the source of *maleficent* (muh-LEF-i-sint), harmful, evil. The verb is *pejorate* (PEE-juh-rayt), to make worse, cause to deteriorate, as *to pejorate an already bad situation.* The noun is *pejoration* (PEE-juh-**RAY**-shin), a lessening in worth or status, devaluation, as *the pejoration of a once-popular theory.*

In linguistics, the nouns *pejoration* and *amelioration* (uh-MEEL-yuh-**RAY**-shin), often called *melioration,* denote opposite tendencies in semantic change—in the meaning of a given word. When, over time, a word acquires a less favorable or less pleasant meaning or connotation, it is said to have undergone pejoration. And when, over time, a word acquires a more positive or favorable meaning or connotation, it is said to have undergone amelioration (from the Latin *melior,* better). A pejorative word, one with negative implications, conveys contempt or condemnation, while an ameliorative word, one with positive implications, conveys acceptability and approval.

For example, *knave* once meant a boy, *boor* once meant a farmer, and *villain* once meant a peasant, but after centuries of pejoration a knave is now an untrustworthy, deceitful man, a boor is now a rude, churlish (word 9 of this level) person, and a villain is now a criminal or scoundrel, the opposite of a hero. Meanwhile, centuries of amelioration have taken the simple adjective *nice* from meaning foolish, silly, stupid when it entered English in the 14th century to meaning pleasant, agreeable, friendly today.

Word 18: LABYRINTHINE (LAB-uh-RIN-thin)

Like a labyrinth or maze; consisting of many windings and turnings; hence, complicated, intricate, involved, knotty.

Synonyms of *labyrinthine* include *tortuous* (TOR-choo-us), *convoluted* (KAHN-vuh-loo-tid), *meandering* (*meander* is word 7 of Level 3), *sinuous, serpentine* (SUR-pin-teen or -tyn), and *circuitous* (sur-KYOO-i-tus).

The adjective *labyrinthine* and the more familiar noun *labyrinth* (LAB-uh-rinth) come to us from the famous story in Greek mythology about the hero Theseus (THEE-syoos or THEE-see-us) and the Minotaur (MIN-uh-tor) of Crete, a monster with the head of a bull and the body of a man, which ate nothing but human flesh. Theseus used a magic ball of thread that rolled ahead of him through the labyrinth and led him to the Minotaur, which he killed with his bare hands. He then retraced his steps out of the labyrinth by following the thread again.

Labyrinthine is sometimes spelled *labyrinthian* and pronounced in five syllables, LAB-uh-RIN-thee-in. It shouldn't be. Take care to use the preferred spelling with *-thine* at the end and the preferred pronunciation, which has four syllables: LAB-uh-RIN-thin.

Word 19: LEONINE (LEE-uh-nyn)

Relating to or resembling a lion.

The adjective *leonine* comes from the Latin *leōnīnus,* of or resembling a lion, which comes in turn from *leo, leōnis,* a lion. This Latin *leo,* of course, is where we get the name of the constellation *Leo* and the name of the fifth sign of the zodiac in astrology. *Leonine* dates back in English to the 14th century, when Chaucer, in "The Monk's Tale," wrote, "So was he full of leonine courage." Later writers used *leonine* to attribute lion-like characteristics to human beings, referring to a man's leonine aspect, a woman's leonine beauty, or a person's leonine nature. A thick mane of hair on a person's head, especially a full head of white hair, is often described as leonine.

You'll learn some more animal adjectives in a moment, after this set of keywords.

Word 20: DOCTRINAIRE (dahk-tri-NAIR)
Inflexibly or fanatically wedded to certain ideas or beliefs and intent on imposing them on others.

A *doctrine* is a system of belief or a set of principles that people teach and advocate as the truth. The adjective *doctrinaire* means not only rigidly attached to your beliefs or principles but also intent on imposing them on others. A doctrinaire person takes a narrow-minded, inflexible view of a subject and expects others to accept that view unquestioningly.

The adjectives *dictatorial, dogmatic,* and *doctrinaire* are close in meaning. *Dictatorial* means like a dictator, an absolute ruler; hence, insisting on strict obedience in a domineering manner. *Dogmatic*—from the noun *dogma* (DAWG-muh), an authoritative and often rigid set of opinions or beliefs—means asserting your opinion in an arrogant, overbearing way. *Doctrinaire* means having inflexible and often fanatical opinions or beliefs and trying to impose them on others.

Other synonyms of *doctrinaire* include *uncompromising, authoritarian, imperious* (word 15 of Level 3), *obdurate* (AHB-d[y]uu-rit), and *intransigent* (in-TRAN-si-jint).

Review Quiz for Keywords 11–20
Consider the following statements and decide whether each one is true or false. **Answers appear on page 291.**

1. Elegiac language is mournful.
2. A ukase is a strong suggestion.
3. A boss should treat employees with asperity.
4. Something you do for your own delectation is pleasurable.
5. A bootless attempt is a successful attempt.
6. To explicate is to remove from a difficult situation.
7. A pejorative remark is complimentary.
8. Something labyrinthine is complicated or convoluted.
9. A person with leonine looks resembles a horse.
10. A doctrinaire person has inflexible beliefs.

Once Upon a Word: Animal Adjectives

You just learned the word *leonine*, relating to or resembling a lion, and you're probably familiar with the adjectives *feline* (FEE-lyn), *canine* (KAY-nyn), *avian* (AY-vee-in), *equine* (EE-kwyn), and *bovine* (BOH-vyn), which mean, respectively, like a cat, like a dog, like a bird, like a horse, and like a cow. But here are some animal adjectives you may not know that may come in handy, especially when describing people with animal qualities:

ursine (UR-syn): like a bear
ovine (OH-vyn): like a sheep
porcine (POR-syn): like a pig or swine
corvine (KOR-vyn): like a crow
saurian (SOR-ee-in): like a lizard
hircine (HUR-syn, like *her sign*): like a goat
lupine (LOO-pyn) and *vulpine* (VUHL-pyn): like a wolf
anserine (AN-suh-ryn): like a goose
struthious (STROO-thee-us): like an ostrich
selachian (suh-LAY-kee-in): like a shark
bufoniform (byoo-FAHN-i-form): like a toad
blattoid (BLAT-oyd): like a cockroach
ophidian (oh-FID-ee-in): like a snake
vermiform (VUR-mi-form): like a worm
pavonine (PAV-uh-nyn): like a peacock

Let's return now to the *Word Workout* vocabulary for ten more keyword discussions.

Word 21: PRESCIENCE (PREE-shints *or* PRESH-)
Knowledge of events before they happen or of things before they exist; foreknowledge or foresight.

Precognition and *preapprehension* are fancy synonyms of *prescience.*

Prescience comes from the Latin verb *praescire,* to know beforehand, which in turn comes from *prae,* before, and *scire,* to know, understand, the source of the familiar word *science* and of the unusual word *sciolist* (SY-uh-list), a person of superficial learning; hence, an intellectual fake or pretender to knowledge.

By derivation *prescience* means knowledge beforehand, foreknowledge, foresight. Since about 1400, when Chaucer wrote his *Canterbury Tales,* the word has been used in exactly that sense either of the divine foreknowledge of God or of the faculty of foresight in human beings, as in this sentence: "Peabody is known for his prescience in seeing the coming collapse in the mortgage market" (MotleyFool.com).

The adjective is *prescient* (PREE-shint or PRESH-), having foreknowledge, knowing about things or events before they happen: "Reexamined in light of the current headlines, the concerns raised by the study seem quite prescient" (*Foreign Policy*).

Word 22: LOCUTION (loh-KYOO-shun)
A particular word, phrase, expression, or idiom, especially one used by a specific person or group.

Locution comes from the Latin *locūtio,* speech, pronunciation, which comes in turn from the verb *loqui,* to speak, the source of numerous English words, including *eloquent,* speaking or writing in a vivid, forceful, and moving way; *loqacious* (loh-KWAY-shus), extremely talkative; *colloquial,* pertaining to informal speech or conversation; *interlocutor* (IN-tur-**LAHK**-yuh-tur), which combines *inter-,* between, and *loqui,* to speak, and means a person one speaks with, who takes part in a conversation; *circumlocution* (word

44 of Level 3), roundabout or indirect expression; *obloquy* (AHB-luh-kwee), abusive language or speech; and *grandiloquent* (gran-DIL-uh-kw<u>i</u>nt), full of grand, lofty, high-flown words.

Locution may refer to any word, phrase, or expression: "*Old sport* is an old-fashioned and stuffy locution." Or a locution may be a specific word or phrase associated with a particular person or group: "*Trouble and strife* is a Cockney locution for *wife*"; "[She] has spent the past twenty-eight years working with dementia patients—or, in her preferred locution, with people who have trouble thinking" (*New Yorker*). A locution can even be an abbreviation or initialism, such as *etc.* for *et cetera* or LOL for *laugh out loud*.

Word 23: OLFACTORY (ahl-FAK-tur-ee, with ahl- as in *olive*)
Of or pertaining to the sense of smell, or to the act of smelling.

The adjective *olfactory* comes from the Latin *olfăcĕre*, to smell or sniff, detect by smelling, from *olēre*, to smell, and *făcĕre*, to do. Your olfactory organ (sometimes called your *olfactories*) is your nose, and the noun *olfaction* (ahl-FAK-shin) is the sense of smell or the act of smelling.

Olfactory, which entered English in the 17th century, was once chiefly a medical and scientific term, but these days the word is used freely in journalism and fiction: "Unmistakable olfactory clues led me to discover that Wilf, my 11-week-old cairn terrier, had defecated in the fireplace at some point during the morning" (Felicity Cloake, *The Guardian*); "None of the evil roommates appeared to be home, though traces of them, both visual and olfactory, were everywhere" (Michael Chabon, *The Mysteries of Pittsburgh*, 1988).

Word 24: LOGOPHILE (LAHG-uh-fyl *or* LAWG-, like *log a file*)
A lover of words.

The noun *logophile* is a blend of the combining forms *logo-*, word, speech, which comes from the Greek *logos*, word, and *-phile*, a lover of, enthusiast for, which comes from the Greek *philos*, loving, dear, beloved.

Logophiles come in many forms—from the connoisseur of style and usage, to the etymologist, to the cruciverbalist (a crossword puzzle expert), to the aficionado of wordplay. Your humble author likes to bill himself as a writer, editor, broadcaster, and logophile, a lover of words.

Logophile, which was borrowed from French and has been used in English since the 1950s, still has no dictionary-sanctioned corresponding adjective. But the obvious choice, favored by those who use the word *logophile,* is *logophilic* (LAHG-uh-**FIL**-ik).

Word 25: PERTURB (pur-TURB)

To trouble or upset mentally, distress or disturb greatly; also, to throw into great disorder or confusion.

Synonyms of *perturb* meaning to trouble or distress greatly include to *agitate, disquiet, harry, fluster, unsettle, discompose,* and *disconcert* (dis-kun-SURT). Synonyms of *perturb* meaning to throw into disorder or confusion include to *confound* (word 34 of Level 2), *flummox, flabbergast, befuddle,* and, once again, *discompose* and *disconcert.* Antonyms of *perturb* include to *pacify, mitigate, mollify,* and *assuage* (uh-SWAYJ).

The verb to *perturb* comes from the Latin *perturbāre,* to disturb thoroughly, throw into complete confusion, a combination of the intensifying prefix *per-,* which means completely, thoroughly, and the verb *turbāre,* to disturb, confuse.

The adjective is *perturbed,* made anxious or uneasy, disturbed, overwrought: "It was after midnight, and she was perturbed that her daughter hadn't come home from the party." The noun is *perturbation,* the state of being perturbed, agitation, disquiet, uneasiness: "The thought of being buried alive threw him into a terrible perturbation." The agent nouns* *perturber* (pur-TUR-bur) and *perturbator* (**PUR**-tur-BAY-tur) denote a person or thing that causes perturbation, a disturber or troublemaker, as *a perturber of the environment* or *a perturbator of the peace.*

---

* An agent noun designates a person who performs an action. Agent nouns usually end in *-er* or *-or.* Thus, a *thinker* is one who *thinks,* and an *actor* is one who *acts.*

What's the difference between to *perturb* and to *disturb*? Both mean to trouble the mind of, upset, or to throw into disorder or confusion. The difference is one of degree. To *disturb* is to cause mild or moderate distress or confusion. To *perturb* is more intense: to cause great distress or agitation, throw into severe disorder or confusion.

If you cannot be perturbed, you are *imperturbable,* extremely calm and steady, impassive. The noun *imperturbability* means the quality of being imperturbable.

Word 26: DISSIMULATE (di–SIM–yuh–layt)
To disguise or hide under a false appearance; to conceal the truth, the facts, or one's thoughts, feelings, or motives by some pretense.

The verbs to *dissimulate* and to *dissemble* (di–SEM–bul) are close synonyms; both come from the Latin *dissimulāre,* to conceal, disguise, pretend that things are not as they are. Both words mean using pretense, deceit, or hypocrisy to conceal the truth or disguise the real nature of one's motives or feelings. But *dissemble* suggests making an insincere show to make others believe that something false is true, while *dissimulate* suggests constructing a false or contrary appearance to disguise the reality or truth of something. Thus, when the press exposes a scandal, those involved will often dissemble to protect themselves. But while that scandalous behavior is still going on and has yet to be exposed, those involved will often dissimulate, try to hide the truth or facts under a false appearance.

The noun is *dissimulation,* the act of dissimulating, hiding truth or reality by some pretense.

Word 27: BAUBLE (BAW–bul)
A showy, inexpensive ornament; a trinket, knickknack, trifle.

The noun *bauble* dates back to the 14th century and is probably descended from an Old French word for a child's toy or plaything. *Bauble* is related to the word *bibelot* (BEE–buh–loh or BIB–loh), which was borrowed from modern French in the 19th century and denotes a small decorative object, often of beauty or rarity. By contrast, a *bauble* is a showy, cheap, often gaudy ornament or decoration, "a piece of finery of little worth" (*OED*), such as a piece of inexpensive jewelry. Historically, *bauble* has also been used to denote the scepter or baton carried by a jester, or court fool, in the Middle Ages.

Trinket, knickknack, and *trifle* are the most familiar synonyms of *bauble.* More unusual synonyms include *gewgaw* (GYOO-gaw), *gimcrack* (word 49 of Level 7), *kickshaw, brummagem* (BRUHM-uh-ju̱m), and *bagatelle* (BAG-uh-**TEL**).

Word 28: CONTRARIAN (ku̱n-TRAIR-ee-i̱n)

A person who takes a contrary position or opposing view, especially someone who opposes or rejects the opinion of the majority or established practice.

The noun *contrarian* and the adjective *contrary* come from the Latin *contrārius,* opposite, against, opposed. To be *contrary* (KAHN-trair-ee) is to be opposite or opposed in various ways—in direction, position, nature, character, or opinion—and the word often implies a stubborn unwillingness to listen or obey, as *a contrary child. Contrarian* may also be used as an adjective to mean opposing prevailing opinion or established practice, as *a contrarian social observer who rails against the tyranny of the majority.*

It is the nature of the contrarian to habitually take an opposing view and reject prevailing opinion or practice. If everyone's going one way, the contrarian goes the other. The word is often applied specifically to an investor who flouts conventional wisdom and buys when others sell or sells when others buy. *Contrarianism* (ku̱n-TRAIR-ee-i̱n-iz'm) is habitual opposition, the tendency to reject majority opinion or established practice.

Word 29: LUMMOX (LUHM-u̱ks)

A clumsy and stupid person, usually a large and heavy one; an oaf.

Ah, how the language doth abound with words for awkward, clumsy, stupid, blundering, and ill-mannered people. Perhaps that's because there are so doggone many of them! (If that doesn't make me sound misanthropic, reread word 14 of Level 5.)

There are the common words *blockhead, bonehead, dolt, dunce, numbskull, imbecile, nincompoop, ignoramus* (IG-nuh-**RAY**-mus), and *clod,* whose unusual cousin is *clodpate* (a combination of *clod* and *pate,* which means the head). There are the less common *simpleton, dullard, dunderhead, addlepate, puzzlepate,* and *witling.* There are the rude and surly *boor* and *churl* (discussed in word 9 of this level). There's the *galoot* (guh-LOOT), who may be eccentric and foolish as well as awkward and stupid. And from the rustic region of clumsy stupidity come the *bumpkin, clodhopper, yokel* (YOH-kul), and *hayseed.*

We know that our keyword, *lummox,* was born in the United States and has been documented in print since the 1820s, but its origin is obscure. Some dictionaries label it informal or colloquial, but don't let that discourage you from using it. *Informal* doesn't mean suitable only in casual speech; it means merely that a word is not likely to occur in especially formal writing, such as a scholarly journal, but it's acceptable in other kinds of writing, particularly when you want to convey a relaxed and familiar tone. The Nobel Prize–winning American novelist John Steinbeck, who knew a thing or two about writing in a natural, unaffected voice, used *lummox* in this way in his 1952 novel *East of Eden.* "Those great lummoxes," he wrote, "would chew a little thing like you to the bone."

Word 30: FECUND (FEK-und *or* FEE-kund)
Fruitful, productive; producing or capable of producing abundant offspring or vegetation. Also, extremely productive or creative intellectually or artistically.

Prolific (proh-LIF-ik) and *fertile* are close synonyms of *fecund.* Antonyms include *unproductive, infertile, barren, sterile, impotent* (IM-puh-tint), and *effete* (i-FEET).

The adjective *fecund* comes from the Latin *fēcundus,* fruitful, abundant. The noun is *fecundity,* productiveness or the ability to produce young. The verb is *fecundate* (FEK-un-dayt), to make fecund or fruitful, or, in biology, to fertilize or impregnate.

Fecund soil or a fecund region is abundantly fruitful, producing many crops. A fecund couple or fecund marriage produces many children. And a fecund artist or a fecund imagination is abundantly inventive or creative.

Review Quiz for Keywords 21–30
Decide if the pairs of words below are synonyms or antonyms. **Answers appear on page 291**.

1. *Foreknowledge* and *prescience* are . . . synonyms or antonyms?
2. *Gesture* and *locution* are . . .
3. *Olfactory* and *nasal* are . . .
4. *Word-lover* and *logophile* are . . .
5. *Mollify* and *perturb* are . . .
6. *Dissimulate* and *disclose* are . . .
7. *Bauble* and *gewgaw* are . . .
8. *Gadfly* and *contrarian* are . . .
9. *Lummox* and *galoot* are . . .
10. *Fecund* and *barren* are . . .

Once Upon a Word: Are You a Logophile?
As you learned in *logophile,* word 24 of this level, the combining form *logo-* comes from the Greek *logos,* word. If you're a logophile, a lover of words, you'll love the following "word-words."

To begin with, a *logomaniac* (LAHG-uh-**MAY**-nee-ak) is someone who is nuts about words; a *logolept* (LAHG-uh-lept) is someone who has seizures about words; and *logorrhea* (LAHG-uh-**REE**-uh) is excessive talkativeness, verbal diarrhea.

Logomachy (luh-GAHM-uh-kee) is a war of words or a battle about words (from the Greek *mache,* battle). Anyone who contends verbally—for example, a lawyer, a politician, or a critic—is a *logomachist* or *logomacher* (stress on *-gom-*). To *logomachize* (luh-GAHM-uh-kyz) is to engage in a war of or about words.

A *logogogue* (LAHG-uh-gahg) is a person—not unlike your humble author—who legislates or makes pronouncements about words. Logogogues tend to like logomachy, and they sometimes suffer from logorrhea.

Finally, one of my favorite dictionaries, *Webster's New International,* second edition, defines *logodaedaly* (LAHG-uh-**DED**-uh-lee) as "verbal legerdemain," using one of my favorite words, *legerdemain* (LEJ-ur-duh-**MAYN**), sleight of hand, artful trickery. The *-daedaly* half of *logodaedaly* is related to Daedalus, the ingenious Athenian architect and inventor who designed the labyrinth for the Minotaur of Crete (mentioned in *labyrinthine,* word 18 of this level). *Logodaedaly* denotes an ingenious, intricate, or cunning use of words.

Here are the next ten keywords in Level 6:

Word 31: HOI POLLOI (HOY-puh-**LOY**)
The common people, the general population, the masses.

In ancient Greek *hoi polloi* meant "the many," and English has borrowed the phrase virtually unchanged in sense. In modern usage, whenever writers want to refer to ordinary people in the aggregate, as opposed to the few who have power, wealth, and privilege, they use *hoi polloi:* "You should always be wary when big-time Wall Streeters come asking for money from the hoi polloi" (*Time*); "In Pittsburgh . . . both the hoi polloi and the high and mighty are constantly brought back down to earth" (*Pittsburgh Post-Gazette*); "Since the birth of leisure travel, aristocrats have been devising creative ways to isolate themselves from hoi polloi" (*The New York Times*).

Because the Greek *hoi* meant "the," not a few authorities on usage—including me—have lamented that using *the* with *hoi polloi* is redundant, meaning literally *the the masses.* But, as you can see from the first two of the examples just cited, there is no denying that *the* is frequently paired with *hoi polloi* in edited writing, and in a 2002 survey a whopping 78 percent of the *American Heritage Dictionary's* usage panel admitted using this redundant *the.*

Whether you choose to embrace this questionable usage or eschew (es-CHOO, avoid, shun) it, you should take special care to avoid the increasingly common misuse of *hoi polloi* to mean the elite, upper crust, or privileged few, the opposite of its proper meaning. This is doubtless a confusion of sound between *hoi polloi,* the common people, the masses, and *hoity-toity,* which means haughty, snobbish. Here's one example of the mistake: "Word . . . spreads through the L.A. police force and criminal underworld and on to the Jazz-Age hedonists of the Hollywood hoi polloi" (The Stranger.com). Make that *the Hollywood elite* or *upper crust* instead.

Word 32: FELICITOUS (fi-LIS-i-tis)

Especially apt or appropriate in action, manner, or expression; "admirably suited to the occasion" (*OED*).

Felicitous comes from the Latin *fēlīcitās,* happiness, good fortune, success, ultimately from *fēlix,* happy, favorable, bringing good luck. From the same source comes the noun *felicity* (fi-LIS-i-tee), which may mean great happiness, bliss, as *marital felicity,* or skill, appropriateness, and grace in expression, as *her felicity with language* or *his felicity as a painter. Felicity* may also refer to an especially skillful, appropriate, and well-chosen expression: "Jordan was impressed with the many felicities he heard from the Toastmasters that evening."

Felicitous is chiefly used of verbal expression to mean well-suited to the occasion, skillfully apt or appropriate. We speak of a felicitous writer or speaker with a felicitous command of English idiom and the ability to find the felicitous word or turn of phrase, the one most appropriate for the occasion. But it's not unusual for writers to describe the action or manner of something as *felicitous.* You can have felicitous timing, perfectly suited to the moment. You can have a felicitous mix of music at a concert, with selections especially appropriate for the audience or mood. You can have a felicitous pairing of wine with food. You could even have a felicitous coincidence or outcome, where what might have happened badly turns out to be appropriate and welcome.

The antonym of *felicitous* is *infelicitous,* inappropriate or ill-timed, ill-suited to the occasion, awkward, malapropos (MAL-ap-ruh-**POH**). Like *felicitous, infelicitous* is often used of verbal expression, as *an infelicitous remark* or *infelicitous prose.* But almost anything that is ill-timed, inappropriate, unhappy, or unfortunate can be infelicitous, as *an infelicitous phone call, an infelicitous choice of outfit,* or *an infelicitous marriage.*

Word 33: PAEAN (PEE-un)

A song of praise, joy, thanksgiving, or triumph; hence, a tribute or expression of praise.

The noun *paean* comes directly from the Latin *paeān,* a hymn. The *OED* notes that the paean was originally a solemn song or chant, usually of victory, addressed at first to Apollo—the god of the sun, of prophecy, of music, and of poetry—and later to other gods. From this historical sense soon developed the general sense in which the word is most often used today: a glowing tribute or expression of high praise.

   Paean is usually used of a work that praises or honors its subject—whether serious, as *President Obama's paean to the late Senator Ted Kennedy* or *a paean to the pristine grandeur of Yosemite National Park,* or not so serious, as *a paean to the joys of karaoke* or *a paean to the nobility of bacon.* But the word is also frequently used to denote praise for a person or thing you wouldn't expect to be praiseworthy, as *a paean to living fast and dying young* or *a paean to poor parenting.* That usage is acceptable because praiseworthiness is in the eye of the beholder, and *paean* merely denotes an expression of praise. What is not acceptable usage, though, is writing *a paean of praise,* which is redundant because the idea of praise is implicit in *paean.*

   As you may have noticed from these examples, *paean* must be followed by *to* unless it stands alone syntactically, as in this citation: "The humble coffee bean harvested, roasted and ground is worthy of a modern-day paean" (*New Statesman*).

Word 34: SERENDIPITY (SER-un-DIP-i-tee)

The ability to make, or the act of making, desirable and fortunate discoveries by accident.

The adjective is *serendipitous* (SER-un-DIP-i-tus), characterized by serendipity, making fortunate and desirable discoveries by accident.

Perhaps it was serendipity that in 1754 led the English novelist and essayist Horace Walpole to write a letter in which he coined the word *serendipity* from a Persian fairy tale called "The Three Princes of Serendip." The heroes of the tale, Walpole wrote, "were always making discoveries, by accidents and sagacity, of things they were not in quest of."

Surely we've all had memorable moments of serendipity: you find a twenty-dollar bill on the sidewalk; your friend tells you there's a nice house down the street for sale, and you wind up buying it; or you decide at the last minute to go to a party where you meet your future spouse. The two keys to serendipity are (1) that you aren't looking for what you discover, and (2) the discovery is good.

The British writer William Boyd, in his 1998 novel *Armadillo,* proposed an antonym for *serendipity* that was based on the name of a bleak Russian archipelago in the Arctic Ocean. "Think of another world in the far north, barren, icebound, cold, a world of flint and stone. Call it Zembla," he wrote. "Ergo: *zemblanity* [zem-BLAN-i-tee] . . . the faculty of making unhappy, unlucky and expected discoveries by design."

Word 35: EPISTOLARY (i-PIS-tul-er-ee)
Pertaining to letters; contained in, consisting of, or carried on by letters.

The adjective *epistolary* and the noun *epistle* (i-PIS'l), a letter, especially a formal one, come through the Latin *epistula,* a letter, written communication, from the Greek *epistolé,* a message, letter. In the New Testament of the Bible, the Epistles of Paul the Apostle, meaning his open letters, comprise all the books from Romans to Hebrews. An epistolary collection is a collection of letters, often formal or instructive ones. And the epistolary novel, which is written in the form of letters, is a venerable (VEN-ur-uh-bul) literary form. (*Venerable* means worthy of deep respect or reverence.)

Before the advent of email, when people wrote letters by hand or on a typewriter, sent them by what is now disparagingly (or sometimes nostalgically) called "snail mail," and then waited, often for weeks, for a reply, the act of composing letters was sometimes called the epistolary art.* In those days long-distance friendships and love affairs were by necessity epistolary, carried on by letters.

Word 36: GUSTATORY (GUHS-tuh-TOR-ee)
Of or pertaining to tasting or eating, or to the sense of taste.

The adjective *gustatory* comes from the Latin *gustare,* to taste, partake of, enjoy. The noun is *gustation* (guh-STAY-shin), the action of tasting or the sense of taste. And from the Latin noun *gustus,* taste, flavor, comes the familiar word *gusto* (GUHS-toh), hearty enjoyment, keen appreciation, either of eating and drinking or in general: "At the wedding they dined with gusto, then danced with even greater gusto."

Gustatory is a neutral word that may be used of almost anything having to do with tasting, eating, or the sense of taste. A gustatory experience can be pleasant or unpleasant, a gustatory delight or a gustatory disaster. You can have gustatory refinement, gustatory memories, or a gustatory adventure. Here's an interesting use of the word from *The New York Times:* "[The] crowds witnessed miracles of gustatory excess: towers of breakfast cereal, a snarling bear made of prunes, palaces built from corn."

The Latin phrase *de gustibus non est disputandum* (day GUUS-tibuus nohn est DIS-puu-**TAHN**-duum)—sometimes shortened to *de gustibus*—means there is no disputing about tastes. In other words, taste is a personal matter, not worth arguing about.

Word 37: COSSET (KAHS-it)
To pamper, coddle, treat as a pet, spoil with kindness and affection.

The verb to *cosset* comes from the noun *cosset,* which originally meant a pet lamb, one brought up without its dam, or mother sheep, and later was applied to human beings to mean a spoiled

---

* Email has, at the very least, transformed the epistolary art, and probably rendered it obsolescent. Because email communications are typically brief and informal, they can hardly be called epistles. So, some years ago (c. 2000), I coined a word for our distinctly unliterary electronic letters: *emissives,* from the noun *missive* (word 14 of Level 7), a written communication or message.

pet. The noun is now rare but the verb is going strong. Today we use *cosset* of anything we treat or that treats us as a pet, that pampers or is pampered. An athletic coach may cosset certain players. A mother may cosset a child. A good host cossets the guests. And the organizers of a fund-raiser must slavishly cosset donors.

The adjective is *cosseted,* pampered, spoiled, overindulged, as *a cosseted child* or *the cosseted passengers in first class.*

Word 38: RIPOSTE (ri-POHST)
A quick and sharp reply or response; a retaliatory answer or action; a counterstroke.

Riposte comes through French ultimately from the Latin *respondēre,* to give an answer to, reply. When it entered English in the early 18th century, a riposte was a retaliatory maneuver in fencing, a quick thrust of the sword made after parrying an opponent's lunge. The word may still be used in this way, of literal fencing, but today it is more often used of figurative fencing, of quickly delivered words or actions that are sharp and retaliatory. When John Montagu, the fourth Earl of Sandwich* (1718–1792), predicted that his dissolute (word 7 of this level) political rival, John Wilkes (1727–1797), would "die either of a pox or on the gallows," Wilkes let fly with this immortal riposte: "That depends, my lord, whether I embrace your mistress or your principles."

The words *reply, rejoinder, retort, rebuttal,* and *riposte* are related in meaning. *Reply* is the most general, denoting any answer or response, or sometimes a thorough response to all points and questions raised. A *rejoinder* (ri-JOYN-dur) is an answer to a reply, and often a quick, clever answer to another's comment or objection: "Mark thought he had Pamela on the ropes, but her rejoinder nonplussed him." (*Nonplus* is word 14 of Level 3.) A *retort* (ri-TORT) is a prompt reply, often witty or cutting, that counters a charge or turns an argument against the person who

---

* The eponymous source of the word *sandwich*. It all began when the earl got hungry late one night while gambling and asked a servant to bring him roast beef between slices of bread.

made it: "Opposing members of the legislature yesterday hurled accusations and retorts across the aisle like cannon fire." A *rebuttal* (ri-BUHT-ul) is a counterargument, a formal response that counters an accusation or charge by presenting evidence or proof to the contrary. Our keyword, *riposte,* because of its connection to fencing, implies an especially swift and cutting reply or retort, a retaliatory counterstroke with words or action: "James was not intimidated by the big man's insults and threats, and he followed up his withering verbal riposte with a knee-buckling fistic riposte." (*Fistic,* which rhymes with *mystic,* means pertaining to boxing or to fighting with the fists. The noun *fisticuffs* means fighting with the fists.)

Word 39: PATOIS (PA-twah)
A regional dialect; a regional or rural form of a language that differs considerably from the standard written form of the language. By extension, any informal speech characteristic of a particular social group or occupation.

Patois comes directly from the French *patois,* which meant literally clumsy speech. Originally *patois* referred to any dialect of France or of French-speaking Switzerland that differed enough from standard written French so as to confound (word 34 of Level 2) those who didn't speak it. From this use *patois* came to denote any dialect or regional form of a language, as *the Dutch patois of South Africa* or *Brooklyn patois,* or any informal language used by a particular social or occupational group, as *the patois of taxi drivers* or *prison patois.*

The words *jargon, argot,* and *patois* are all used of specialized and often unintelligible language. *Jargon* (JAHR-gun) is difficult to understand because it is highly technical and often pretentious, as *medical jargon, legal jargon,* and *business jargon.* An *argot* (AHR-goh or AHR-gut) is a specialized and often secret vocabulary used by a particular group for private communication. Argots (AHR-gohz) are associated chiefly with subcultural groups, as *the argot of adolescence* and *underworld argot.* By derivation *patois* implies a regional or local form of speech that is difficult to understand because its vocabulary, idioms, and grammar differ markedly from that of the standard written form of the language. But today *patois* is also often used, like *argot,* of informal speech used by a particular group for private communication.

Word 40: ANIMADVERSION (AN-i-mad-**VUR**-zhun)
An unfavorable, censorious (word 33 of Level 3), or hostile comment; also, adverse or hostile criticism, or the act of criticizing unfavorably.

Animadversion comes from the Latin verb *animadvertĕre,* which in its neutral sense meant to take notice of, pay attention to, but which also had a negative sense: to take notice of a fault, to blame, censure. It is this sense that informs the English noun *animadversion* and the etymologically related words *animosity,* resentment, hostility, and *animus* (word 20 of Level 4), a deep-seated dislike or feeling of ill will.

Animadversion* may be used in two ways. It may denote a particular remark that is severely critical or hostile: "For an hour he listened to their animadversions, trying not to lose his temper." Or it may refer to adverse criticism in general or the act of criticizing unfavorably: "Some British critics have lamented that American book reviewers rarely indulge in animadversion"; "This newspaper has never felt that it is above criticism, especially from politicians and other public officials who take the brunt of our animadversion" (*Jamaica Observer*).

The corresponding verb *animadvert* (AN-i-mad-**VURT**) means to comment unfavorably, express strong criticism or disapproval of. Throughout this book I have not been reluctant to animadvert on common errors of English usage and pronunciation.

Review Quiz for Keywords 31–40
In each statement below, a keyword (in *italics*) is followed by three definitions. Two of the three are correct; one is unrelated in meaning. Decide which one doesn't fit the keyword. **Answers appear on page 292.**

1. *Hoi polloi* means the privileged few, the common people, the masses.

2. *Felicitous* means well-suited, especially apt, inappropriate.

3. A *paean* is a tribute, an award, an expression of praise.

4. *Serendipity* is a lucky discovery, an unexpected discovery, an unwanted discovery.

5. *Epistolary* means pertaining to novels, pertaining to correspondence, pertaining to letters.

6. *Gustatory* means pertaining to eating, pertaining to swallowing, pertaining to tasting.

7. To *cosset* is to swaddle, pamper, coddle.

8. A *riposte* is a lunge, counterstroke, sharp reply.

9. *Patois* is regional dialect, jargon, nonsense words.

10. *Animadversion* is adverse criticism, unfounded criticism, a censorious remark.

Difficult Distinctions: *Torturous* and *Tortuous*

Torturous (TOR-chur-<u>us</u>) means causing or involving torture or great suffering; extremely painful. *Tortuous* (TOR-choo-<u>us</u>) means winding, circuitous, full of twists and turns. Driving at night in the fog along a *tortuous* (winding) road can be a *torturous* (painful) experience. The *tortuous* path to economic recovery can be *torturous* for those at the bottom of the wage-earning barrel. And a book replete with *tortuous* language can be *torturous* to read.

This sentence misuses the winding word for the painful word: "This was a case of years of tortuous [*torturous*] abuse" (South-CoastToday.com). This sentence gets it right: "Dr. Zats is no stranger to the sometimes torturous footwear high fashion can ask of working women" (Reuters).

Difficult Distinctions: *Discreet* and *Discrete*

The word *discreet,* ending in *-eet,* and the word *discrete,* ending in *-ete,* are soundalikes with different meanings. *Discreet,* the better known of the pair, means tactful, prudent, circumspect, showing careful judgment: "She told him the news in a discreet whisper." *Discrete* means separate, detached, or unrelated, as *discrete* *issues on the agenda* or *physicists experimenting with discrete atomic particles.*

Here is the last set of ten keyword discussions in Level 6:

Word 41: EXEGESIS (EK-si-JEE-sis)
Critical explanation or interpretation of a text.

Exegesis comes directly from the ancient Greek *exēgēsis,* an interpretation, explanation. The adjective is *exegetic* (EK-si-JET-ik), pertaining to exegesis, critical explanation. The noun is *exegete* (EK-si-jeet), a person skilled in exegesis, one who undertakes a critical interpretation of a text.

Explanation is the general word for any statement meant to make something clear or understandable. *Elucidation* (i-LOO-si-DAY-shin)—from the same source as the adjective *lucid,* clear, easily understood—is the act of casting light on something obscure or hard to understand. *Explication* (EK-spli-KAY-shin) is a detailed explanation or analysis of something, by derivation an unfolding of the meaning. *Exegesis* denotes a detailed analysis of a text, a critical and scholarly interpretation of a piece of writing. The word is often used of an interpretation of the Bible or a passage from it.

Word 42: DOYENNE (doy-YEN)
A woman who is a senior member of a group; a highly skilled and knowledgeable woman with extensive experience in a given field.

Doyenne and its masculine counterpart, *doyen* (pronounced the same), a senior male member of a group, come through French from the Latin *decānus,* a dean, literally the leader of ten. In modern usage both words denote highly skilled, experienced, and respected people who are leaders or senior members of a group or profession. Wherever you could use the word *dean* to denote an experienced member or leader of a group, you can use *doyen* or *doyenne* to imply even greater knowledge, skill, and seniority. For example, Bill Clinton is a doyen and Hillary Clinton is a doyenne of American politics. Joyce Carol Oates is a doyenne of American letters, and Meryl Streep is a doyenne of Hollywood.

The suffix -*enne* occurs in loanwords from French, forming feminine nouns corresponding to masculine nouns ending in -*en* or -*an*. "The few English words that end in -*enne* . . . usually carry little implication of inferiority," says *The Random House Dictionary*. Thus, English has *comedienne* for a female comedian; *tragedienne* for a female dramatic actor; *Parisienne* for a female native or inhabitant of Paris; *equestrienne* for a female horseback rider; and *doyenne* for a female leader, a woman who is a senior member of a group.

Grande dame (grahnd-DAHM or gran-DAM), which also comes from French and means literally a great lady, is a close synonym of *doyenne*. A grande dame is an elderly woman of great dignity and prestige, or the preeminent doyenne of a particular field. The British actress Judith Dench was given the title *Dame,* the equivalent of knighthood for a woman, because she is a grande dame of the stage and screen.

Word 43: ACIDULOUS (uh-SIJ-uh-lus)
Somewhat sour, sharp, or harsh in taste or manner; also, sour-tempered, bitter.

Acidulous comes from the Latin *acidulus,* slightly sour, from *acidus,* sour. By derivation *acidulous* suggests a somewhat sour or acidic taste, as the acidulous pulp of the grapefruit or an acidulous cigar.

But *acidulous* perhaps more often suggests not a sour taste but a sour quality or manner. When used of expression, of someone's comments or tone in speech or writing, *acidulous* implies a much greater degree of sourness or sharpness. Acidulous criticism is sour-tempered, and therefore harsh, bitter, and often sarcastic. The advice of an acidulous mother-in-law is sharp and biting.

Synonyms of *acidulous* in this figurative sense include *caustic, scathing, mordant, acrimonious,* and *virulent* (VIR-[y]uh-lint).

Word 44: GELD (GELD, *g* as in *go,* rhymes with *weld*)
To deprive of strength, force, vitality, or some essential part.

The verb to *geld* entered English about 1300 and was used of animals such as horses and pigs to mean to castrate, deprive of virility, emasculate, as in this quotation from James Boswell's *Life of Samuel Johnson,* published in 1791: "A judge may be a farmer, but he is not to geld his own pigs." The noun *gelding* denotes a castrated male animal, especially a horse.

To *geld* may still be used in this way, but since about 1500 the word has also been used figuratively to mean to impair the strength or power of, weaken, enfeeble, or deprive of some essential element or part. Lawmakers can geld a piece of legislation, a bad editor can geld a book, and a thief can geld your wallet of its cash.

Word 45: BATHOS (BAY-thahs *or* -thaws)
In writing or speech, a ludicrous descent from the elevated or lofty to the commonplace or ridiculous; anticlimax.

Bathos comes directly from the Greek *báthos,* depth. In 1727, the English poet and essayist Alexander Pope plucked the word from Greek and used it as the opposite of *the sublime,* meaning that which is supreme, exalted, or raised on high. By derivation and in modern usage, *bathos* refers to writing or speech whose tone is elevated but whose subject matter is commonplace, specifically a passing from the sublime to the ridiculous. Bathos is the proper tone for a comedic novel or for mock-heroic poetry, but when a serious novel or poem veers into bathos, descending from the lofty to the ludicrous, from the sublime to the ordinary, the sudden and unsatisfying anticlimax can alienate the reader. This sort of descent from the elevated to the commonplace has earned *bathos* the attendant meanings of excessive sentimentality or triteness, inanity, as *the predictable bathos of a soap opera.*

Bathos is the opposite of *pathos* (PAY-thahs or -thaws), the quality or power in life, literature, or art to arouse feelings of sympathy or compassion, as *the pathos of Shakepearean tragedy. Ba-*

thos is insincere or exaggerated pathos, comically sentimental and overdone emotion. The corresponding adjectives are *pathetic,* arousing pathos, pity or compassion, and *bathetic,* characterized by *bathos,* anticlimax, triteness, or sentimentality.

Word 46: OVERWEENING (OH-vur-**WEE**-ning)
Excessively self-confident or conceited; having an exaggerated opinion of oneself. Also, excessive, exaggerated, immoderate.

Synonyms of *overweening* include *arrogant, self-important, overbearing, presumptuous* (word 2 of Level 1), *high-handed, overconfident, egotistical, imperious* (word 15 of Level 3), *supercilious,* and the informal *hoity-toity.*

Overweening comes from the verb to *overween,* to think too highly of oneself, be arrogant or conceited, a combination of *over-,* too much, excessive, and the obsolete verb to *ween,* to think, suppose, believe. An overweening coworker is excessively self-confident, always trying to take charge and impress everyone. An overweening relative is arrogant, overbearing, and presumptuous. Overweening students have an exaggerated opinion of themselves.

Overweening may also be used of something excessive, exaggerated, or immoderate that also implies self-importance, arrogance, or conceit. Overweening pride, to paraphrase the proverb, often leads to a fall. Overweening ambition can make people arrogant and tempt them to compromise their principles. And an overweening expectation of success is an exaggerated expectation arising from overconfidence and conceit.

Word 47: FEBRILE (FEE-br<u>u</u>l *or* FEB-r<u>u</u>l)
Pertaining to, marked by, or caused by fever.

Febrile comes from the Latin *febris,* a fever, the source also of the combining form *febri-,* which means fever and appears in several words used chiefly in medicine: *febrific* (fi-BRIF-ik), feverish; *febrifacient* (FEB-ri-**FAY**-sh<u>i</u>nt), something that causes fever (from the Latin *facere,* to make or do); and *febrifuge* (FEB-ri-fyooj), a medicine or agent that dispels or reduces fever, also called an *antipyretic* (AN-tee-py-**RET**-ik). The *-fuge* in *febrifuge* comes from the Latin *fugāre,* to drive away, put to flight, the source also of the English adjective *fugacious* (fyoo-GAY-shus), fleeting, passing swiftly away.

Febrile heat can cause dehydration, fever, and ultimately heat-stroke. A febrile condition is one caused or marked by fever. And *febrile* may also be used figuratively to suggest a fever or feverishness, as *a febrile imagination* or *febrile desire.*

Word 48: BENIGHTED (bi-NYT-id)
In a state of mental or moral ignorance or darkness; unenlightened.

The adjective *benighted* comes from the archaic verb to *benight,* to darken, obscure, as *clouds that benight the sky. Benighted* may mean to be overtaken by night or darkness, as "The demise of room service would be . . . hell for the benighted business traveller" (*Irish Independent*). But far more often *benighted* means to be in figurative darkness—namely, a state of intellectual, moral, or cultural ignorance and backwardness.

The peasants of the Middle Ages were benighted because they couldn't read and write and knew nothing of the world beyond their hamlets and villages. A benighted government is ignorant of and unconcerned with the needs and desires of the people. In my vocabulary-building novel *Test of Time,* I used *benighted* to describe the backward, unenlightened state of the entire human race: "After a hundred-odd years of 'progress,' those miserable, benighted creatures called human beings were still making the same stupid mistakes in their sorrowful march from cradle to grave."

Because it denotes a lack of light, which figuratively implies a lack of awareness, the word *unenlightened* is probably the closest synonym of *benighted.* Other synonyms include *primitive, backward, crude, unsophisticated, unrefined, uncultured,* and *uncultivated.* Antonyms of *benighted* include *educated, learned* (LUR-nid), *lettered, enlightened, refined, cultivated, genteel* (jen-TEEL), and *urbane* (ur-BAYN).

Word 49: TURPITUDE (TUR-pi-t[y]ood)
Shameful wickedness, vileness, baseness of character; also, an evil or
depraved act.

The noun *turpitude* comes from the Latin *turpis,* morally foul, disgraceful, shameful, base. Synonyms of *turpitude* include *immorality,
corruption, depravity* (word 1 of Level 1), *vileness, baseness, degeneracy,
sordidness, iniquity* (word 2 of Level 4), *perfidiousness* (*perfidious* is
word 17 of Level 5), and *improbity* (im-PROH-bi-tee). Antonyms
of *turpitude* include *trustworthiness, integrity, scrupulousness, uprightness, incorruptibility, impeccability, rectitude,* and *probity.*

Turpitude may mean wickedness, vileness of character, as when
Shakespeare writes in *Antony and Cleopatra,* "My turpitude thou
dost so crown with gold." Or it may denote a shamefully evil act,
as *the turpitude of the Holocaust.* But the word appears most often in
the phrase *moral turpitude,* a legal concept that *Black's Law Dictionary* defines as "conduct that is contrary to justice, honesty, or morality" and "shocking to the moral sense of the community."

Word 50: IMPRECATION (IM-pri-**KAY**-shin)
A curse, or the act of cursing.

The noun *imprecation* comes from the Latin *imprecāri,* to invoke
harm or call down evil upon, the precise modern meaning of the
verb to *imprecate,* to invoke harm or evil on someone, to curse. A
person who imprecates is an *imprecator,* and the adjective is *impre-
catory* (IM-pri-kuh-tor-ee), of the nature of or containing a curse.

An *imprecation* may be a curse, a calling down of evil or misfortune on someone, including oneself, as in this couplet from the
18th-century English poet Alexander Pope: "With imprecations
thus he fill'd the air, / And angry Neptune heard th' unrighteous
prayer." Or *imprecation* may be the action of imprecating, cursing,
invoking evil or calamity, as in this sentence from George Put-
tenham's *Arte of English Poesie,* published in 1589: "This was done
by a manner of imprecation, or as we call it by cursing and banning of the parties, and wishing all evil to alight upon them."

Synonyms of *imprecation* include *malediction, execration* (EK-si-**KRAY**-shin), and the archaic *malison* (MAL-i-zun), an etymological contraction of *malediction*.

Review Quiz for Keywords 41–50

In this quiz the review word is followed by three words or phrases, and you must decide which comes nearest the meaning of the review word. **Answers appear on page 293.**

1. Is an *exegesis* a mass departure, a critical interpretation, or the removal of something objectionable?

2. Is a *doyenne* a woman who is widowed, who is elderly, or who is a senior member of a group?

3. Is something *acidulous* somewhat sour, somewhat spoiled, or somewhat sugary?

4. Is to *geld* to blend, to add ornamentation, or to deprive of strength or force?

5. Is *bathos* a crisis, an anticlimax, or the resolution of the plot?

6. Would someone *overweening* be excessively fond, excessively self-confident, or excessively curious?

7. Does *febrile* mean pertaining to February, to fever, or to wild animals?

8. Is a *benighted* person unenlightened, immoral, or unmanageable?

9. Is *turpitude* moral purity, shameful wickedness, or festering guilt?

10. Is an *imprecation* a suggestion, an accusation, or a curse?

A Pronunciation Primer

Did you know that *primer,* meaning an introductory book or treatise, is properly pronounced PRIM-ur, with a short *i* as in *print?* The word is often mispronounced PRY-mur, with a long *i* as in *prime,* but that's the proper pronunciation for the word that's spelled the same way but means an undercoat of paint.

There may be no *prime* in *primer,* but it's always prime time for a primer on pronunciation. So here's a compendious (word 22 of Level 5) list of commonly mispronounced words with their proper, preferred pronunciations:

There is no *day* in *academia.* It's ak-uh-DEE-mee-uh.

There is no *flew* in *affluent*. It's AF–loo–int.

There is no *door* in *ambassador*. It's am–BAS–uh–dur.

There is no *thigh* or *hide* in *apartheid*. It's uh–PAHRT–hayt (like *apart hate*), also uh–PAHRT–hyt (like *apart height*).

There is no *beast* in *bestial*. It's BES–chul.

There is no *lay* in *Chilean*. It's CHIL–ee–in (like *chilly in*).

There is no *sewer* in *connoisseur*. It's kahn–uh–SUR.

There is no *cue* in *coupon*. It's KOO–pahn.

There is no *die* in *dais*. It's DAY–is.

There is no *day* in *deity*. It's DEE–uh–tee.

There is no *ant* in *defendant*. It's di–FEN–dint.

There is no *dip* in *diphthong*. It's DIF–thahng.

There is no *shoe* in *eschew*. It's es–CHOO.

There is no *X* in *espresso*. It's es–PRES–oh.

There is no *spear* in *experiment*. It's ek–SPER–uh–mint.

There is no *foe* or *foil* in *foliage*. Say it in three syllables: FOH–lee–ij.

There is no *foe* in *forward*. It's FOR–wurd (like *for word*).

There is no *wine* in *genuine*. It's JEN–yoo–in.

There is no *hand* or *chief* in *handkerchief*. Hang it all, it's HANG–kur–chif.

There is no *render* in *heartrending*. It's **HAHRT**-REN-ding (three syllables).

There is no *hole* or *haul* in *Holocaust*. It's **HAHL**-uh-KAWST.

There is no *home* in *homicide*. It's **HAHM**-i-SYD.

There is no *noise* in *Illinois* (it's very quiet there). Make it IL–uh-**NOY**.

There is no *pair* in *incomparable*. It's in–KAHM–pur–uh–bul.

Do not stress the *grew* in *incongruous*. It's in–KAHNG–groo–wus.

Do not stress the *flue* in *influence*. It's IN–floo–ints.

There is no *pit* in *interpret*. Put two *r*'s in it: in–TUR–prit.

There is no *eye* in *Iraq*, but you may put a *rock* or *rack* in it: i–RAHK or i–RAK.

There is no *clue* in *Ku Klux Klan*, because they're clueless. It's KOO–kluhks–.

There is no *berry* in *library*. It's LY–brer–ee.

There is no *mash* in *machination.* It's MAK-i-**NAY**-shin.

There is no *ore* in *mayoral.* It's MAY-ur-ul.

There is no *moment* in *memento.* It's muh-MEN-toh.

There is no *cue* in *nuclear.* Please, people: it's N(Y)OO-klee-ur.

There is no *owner* in *onerous.* It's AHN-ur-us.

There is no *tang* in *orangutan.* It's uh-RANG-uh-tan.

There is no *ray* in *orator.* It's OR-uh-tur.

There is no *store* in *pastoral.* It's PAS-tur-ul.

There is no *play* in *pleasure.* It's PLEZH-ur.

There is no *pose* in *possess.* It's puh-ZES.

There is no *purr* in *prerogative.* It's pruh-RAHG-uh-tiv.

There is no *rye* in *ribald,* which means humorous in a mildly indecent, coarse, or vulgar way. It's RIB-'ld (rhymes with *scribbled*).

There is no *sphere* in *spherical.* It's SFER-i-kul.

There is no *Tia* in *Tijuana.* It's tee-HWAH-nuh or tee-WAH-nuh.

There is no *anus* in *Uranus.* It's YUUR-uh-nus.

There is no *aerial* in *venereal.* It's vuh-NEER-ee-ul.

There is no *bray* in *vertebrae.* It's **VUR**-tuh-BREE.

There is no *war* in *wash.* It's WAHSH.

There is no *zeal* in *zealous.* It's ZEL-us.

There is no *zoo* in *zoology.* It's zoh-AHL-uh-jee.

And, as an astonishing number of educated people fail to realize, there is no *noun* in *pronunciation.* Make sure to put a *nun* in it: pruh-NUHN-see-**AY**-shin.

You'll find more on these and many other commonly mispronounced words in my *Big Book of Beastly Mispronunciations.*

Answers to Review Quizzes for Level 6
KEYWORDS 1–10

1. No. *Ineluctable* means not to be evaded or resisted, unavoidable, inevitable.

2. No. *Moribund* means dying, close to death.

3. Yes. A *bellwether* is one who takes the initiative; also, a leading indicator of a trend.

4. Yes. A *permutation* is a thorough or fundamental change, a transformation.

5. Yes. To *interlope* is to interfere, intrude, thrust oneself into others' affairs.

6. No. To *hector* is to bully or be domineering, to intimidate or torment.

7. No. *Dissolute* means lacking moral restraint, given to immoral behavior.

8. Yes. *Lineaments* are distinguishing features or distinctive characteristics.

9. Yes. *Churlish* means rude, ill-mannered, ungracious.

10. Yes. *Prepossessing* means attractive, engaging, pleasing, comely.

KEYWORDS 11–20

1. True. *Elegiac* means expressing grief, sorrow, or lamentation.

2. False. A *ukase* is an authoritative order or command.

3. False. A boss should treat employees with courtesy and respect, not *asperity,* which means harshness, roughness; sharpness of manner, temper, or tone; or hardship, rigor.

4. True. *Delectation* is great pleasure, enjoyment, or delight.

5. False. A *bootless* attempt is a useless, unprofitable, vain attempt.

6. False. To *extricate* is to remove from a difficult situation. To *explicate* is to present a detailed explanation or analysis of.

7. False. *Pejorative* means having a negative meaning or force; uncomplimentary.

8. True. *Labyrinthine* means like a labyrinth or maze; hence, complicated, intricate.

9. False. *Leonine* means relating to or resembling a lion.

10. True. A *doctrinaire* person is inflexibly or fanatically wedded to certain ideas or beliefs and intent on imposing them on others.

KEYWORDS 21–30

1. Synonyms. Both *foreknowledge* and *prescience* mean knowledge of events before they happen or of things before they exist.

2. Near antonyms. A *gesture* is a motion with some part of the body. A *locution* is verbal: a particular word, phrase, expression, or idiom.

3. Near synonyms. *Nasal* means pertaining to the nose and *olfactory* means pertaining to smelling or the sense of smell.

4. Synonyms. A *logophile* is a lover of words.

5. Antonyms. To *mollify* is to soothe, pacify. To *perturb* is to trouble or distress greatly.

6. Antonyms. To *disclose* is to make something known, especially something secret. To *dissimulate* is to disguise or hide under a false appearance.

7. Synonyms. Both *bauble* and *gewgaw* denote a showy, inexpensive ornament; a trinket.

8. Near synonyms. A *gadfly* (word 50 of Level 3) is a person who continually pesters, criticizes, or provokes others. A *contrarian* is a person who habitually takes a contrary position or opposing view.

9. Synonyms. *Lummox* and *galoot* both denote a clumsy, stupid, usually big, and often foolish person.

10. Antonyms. *Barren* means not fertile or productive. *Fecund* means fruitful, productive.

KEYWORDS 31–40

1. *The privileged few* is the opposite of *hoi polloi*, the common people, the masses.

2. *Inappropriate* is the opposite of *felicitous*, especially apt or well-suited.

3. A *paean* may accompany an award, but it is an expression of praise, a tribute.

4. *Serendipity* applies to discoveries that are lucky and unexpected, not unwanted.

5. You can write an *epistolary* novel, but the word means pertaining to letters or correspondence.

6. *Pertaining to swallowing* doesn't fit. *Gustatory* means pertaining to tasting or eating.

7. *Swaddle* doesn't fit. To *cosset* is to pamper, coddle, spoil with affection.

8. *Lunge* doesn't fit. A *riposte* is a response to a lunge, a counterstroke or sharp reply.

9. *Nonsense words* doesn't fit. *Patois* is regional dialect, jargon, or informal speech.

10. *Unfounded criticism* doesn't fit. *Animadversion* is adverse criticism or a censorious remark.

KEYWORDS 41–50

1. *Exegesis* is a critical interpretation or explanation of a text.
2. A *doyenne* is a woman who is a respected senior member of a group.
3. Something *acidulous* is somewhat sour in taste or harsh in manner; also, sour-tempered, bitter.
4. To *geld* is to deprive of strength, force, vitality, or some essential part.
5. *Bathos* is anticlimax, a ludicrous descent from the lofty to the commonplace.
6. Someone *overweening* is excessively self-confident or conceited; *overweening* means having an exaggerated opinion of oneself.
7. *Febrile* means pertaining to, marked by, or caused by fever.
8. A *benighted* person is unenlightened, in a state of mental or moral ignorance or darkness.
9. *Turpitude* is shameful wickedness, vileness; also, an evil or depraved act.
10. An *imprecation* is a curse or the act of cursing.

LEVEL 7

Word 1: SIMPER (SIM-pur)
To smile in a silly, self-conscious way.

The verb to *simper* and the noun *simper,* a silly, self-conscious smile, probably come from the Danish dialectal word *simper,* which meant affected or coy. In modern usage *simper* does often imply affectation or coyness, as *a coquettish simper* or *a simpering bridesmaid. Simper* also strongly implies silliness and often simplemindedness; for example, fools are often described as simpering, smiling in an absurd and obvious way, and a simpering manner is a silly, self-conscious manner. To *simper* may also mean to express with a simper, as *to simper an apology.*

Dictionaries often give *smirk* as a synonym of *simper.* Although both words denote smiling, *simper* suggests smiling in a silly, self-conscious, or simpleminded way: "Browning's role is so under-written that all she is required to do is simper" (*The Guardian*). *Smirk* usually suggests smiling in a smug, scornful, or self-righteous way: "The council members ignored the public's testimony and instead smirked and snickered among themselves."

Word 2: DENUDE (di-N[Y]OOD)
To strip, make naked, lay bare; hence, to strip or deprive of (a possession, quality, etc.).

The verb to *denude* comes from the Latin *dēnūdāre,* to lay bare, make naked, uncover, also to rob, plunder. The ultimate source is

295

the Latin *nūdus*, naked, bare, from which also come the English *nude* and *nudity.*

To *denude* is to strip of all covering or clothing or to strip of some important quality, characteristic, attribute, or possession; in geology, *denude* is used to mean to lay bare or uncover by erosion. The word usually implies a forceful or violent stripping or laying bare. For instance, a denuded hillside is a bare hillside, stripped of vegetation. A denuded orange has been stripped of its covering or peel, and a denuded person has been stripped of clothing. A lumbering operation can denude a mountain of its trees. A company denuded of its assets is a bankrupt company. An editor's job is to denude a writer's style of faults such as redundancy and circumlocution (word 44 of Level 3). And a quotation denuded of its context—deprived of surrounding, clarifying words or historical background—can be not only ambiguous but also willfully misleading.

The noun *denudation* (DEN-yuu-**DAY**-sh<u>i</u>n) means the act of denuding, stripping, depriving, or the state of being denuded.

Word 3: SUI GENERIS (SOO-ee-**JEN**-uh-ris *or* SOO-eye-)
Being the only one of its kind; constituting a class by itself; unique.

Sui generis, which has been English since the 18th century, comes directly from Latin: *suī* means of its own, and *generis* is the genitive of *genus*, kind. That which is sui generis is literally of its own kind, one of a kind.

In *Amo, Amas, Amat and More: How to Use Latin to Your Own Advantage and to the Astonishment of Others*, Eugene Ehrlich observes, "One should take some care in applying *sui generis*, lest the phrase lose its value. Properly used, *sui generis* requires that the person, place, or thing be of an entirely distinctive character." Like the word *unique*, which comes from the Latin *ūnus*, one, and properly is an absolute adjective that should not be qualified by words such as *almost, somewhat,* and *completely,* that which is sui generis should be the only one of its kind, constituting a class by itself, never that which is just more unusual than or different from something else.

If something is unique, it stands alone and has no equal. For example, your daughter is unique because there is no one else exactly like her. Strictly speaking, she cannot be *very* unique or *more* unique than other people; that just means she's special or unusual in some way, but not unique, matchless, peerless, unrivaled. Likewise, if something is sui generis it is the only one of its kind; it occupies a class by itself. In English literature, Shakespeare is sui generis; no one else can match his genius. The Grand Canyon is geologically sui generis; there is nothing else like it in the world. "We humans . . . are the only animals whose brains are known to atrophy as we grow older," writes Patricia Marx in *The New Yorker,* "and . . . we are also sui generis in suffering from Alzheimer's disease."

Word 4: JEREMIAD (JER-uh-**MY**-id)
A prolonged expression of sorrow or grief, or a long, mournful complaint, often laced with outrage; a lengthy and often angry lamentation.

The suffix -*ad* means derived from, concerning, or related to, as in *Olympiad,* derived from Mount Olympus and related to the Olympic Games, or the *Iliad,* Homer's epic poem about the Trojan War, which concerns Ilion (IL-ee-un), the Greek name for the ancient city of Troy. Thus, the suffix -*ad* in *jeremiad* means derived from or related to the Old Testament prophet Jeremiah, the author of Lamentations and Jeremiah. *Jeremiad* is thus an eponymous word, and in his *Dictionary of Eponyms* Robert Hendrickson explains that "Jeremiah's long and sorrowful complaints were a protest against the sins of his countrymen and their captivity."

The Century Dictionary notes that *jeremiad* is often used "with a spice of ridicule or mockery, implying either that the grief itself is unnecessarily great, or that the utterance of it is tediously drawn out and attended with a certain satisfaction to the utterer." Thus, *jeremiad* is a kind of mock-serious word that can be applied to any long and tedious complaint, or to any lengthy and exaggerated lament, that grates on the nerves and patience of those listening: "He has prolonged his complaint into an endless jeremiad," wrote the English essayist and critic Charles Lamb (1775–1834).

Word 5: SOBRIQUET (SOH-bri-kay)

A descriptive name or nickname, especially an affectionate, humorous, or fanciful one.

Sobriquet entered English from French in the 17th century; before that, its origin is uncertain. The unusual corresponding adjective is *sobriquetical* (SOH-bri-**KET**-i-kul), of the nature of a sobriquet.

Nickname, from the Middle English *eke,* also, and *name,* is the general term for a descriptive name given to a person, place, or thing: *The Big Apple* is the nickname of New York City. A nickname is sometimes also called a pet name, and the fancy word for a pet name is *hypocorism* (hy-PAHK-ur-iz'm). A hypocorism is a kind of endearment, a word or expression that shows affection. Lovers use hypocorisms like *sweetie* and *honey,* and parents typically shower their kids with hypocorisms—often personalized ones like *Joojy-Pie,* the one I use for my younger daughter, Judith.

Our keyword, *sobriquet,* denotes a nickname that is usually affectionate and often clever or funny. For example, the legendary baseball slugger Babe Ruth's sobriquet was *Sultan of Swat.* And when Mark Twain burst on the eastern literary scene with his story "The Jumping Frog of Calaveras County," he was given the sobriquet "The Wild Humorist of the Pacific Slope."

Word 6: REGNANT (REG-nint)

Ruling, reigning, dominant; exercising power, authority, or influence.

The adjective *regnant* comes from the Latin *regnāre,* to exercise royal authority, rule as a king or queen, which is also the source, ultimately, of the English verb to *reign,* to rule, exercise power as a monarch. You may use *regnant* to mean ruling or reigning as a monarch, as *the regnant king,* or simply ruling, dominant, exercising power, authority, or influence: "In a democracy the people are regnant"; "We like to think of Jacqueline Kennedy regnant in her pillbox hat" (*Newsweek*).

Regnant may also be used to mean reigning in the sense of having the chief power or being the chief authority: "After twenty years at the State Department she had become the regnant expert on Middle Eastern affairs." You may also use *regnant* to mean prevalent or widespread in a dominant or influential way: "Superstition and illiteracy were regnant in the Middle Ages."

Finally, *regnant* is also sometimes used postpositively—meaning after the noun it modifies instead of before—most often in the phrase *queen regnant,* meaning a ruling queen, one in power: "The husband of a queen regnant has no official position in the British monarchy."

Word 7: HAUTEUR (hoh-TUR)
Arrogance, haughtiness, condescension; a lofty, lordly, or domineering manner.

Synonyms of *hauteur* include *snobbishness, pretentiousness, pomposity, contemptuousness, imperiousness,* and *superciliousness.*

The noun *hauteur* and the adjective *haughty* are etymological cousins whose closest antecedent is the French *haut,* high. And both *haughty* and *hauteur* strongly imply high-and-mightiness, lordliness of manner. But while *haughtiness* is either an instinctive or an affected arrogance, *hauteur* so boldly aspires to the heights of arrogance, and so fully expects others to view condescension as its birthright, that, depending on the context, the effect can be arresting, even intimidating—or downright farcical.

Think of the stereotype of the grim and gaunt waiter in a fancy French restaurant—in France—who alternately sneers at and ignores foreign customers: that's hauteur. Think of the lordly posture of proud flamenco dancers in a vibrant duet: that's hauteur. Think of the 19th-century Irish playwright and poet Oscar Wilde, who, when passing through customs on a visit to the United States, said, "I have nothing to declare but my genius": that's hauteur. Or if you'd prefer an example from popular culture, there's the maliciously condescending Cruella de Vil in Disney's *101 Dalmatians*. That "cruel devil" is the embodiment of hauteur!

Word 8: PATERFAMILIAS (PAY-tur-fuh-**MIL**-ee-u̲s *or* PAT-ur- *or* PAH-tur-)

A man who is the head of a household or the father of a family; by extension, a man who is the leader of a tribe, community, or movement.

The plural of *paterfamilias* is *patresfamilias* (PAY-treez-fuh-**MIL**-ee-u̲s).

Paterfamilias comes from the Latin *paterfamiliās,* a father or head of a household, from *pater,* father, and *familia,* a household. Its female counterpart is *materfamilias* (MAY-tur-fuh-**MIL**-ee-u̲s), a woman who is the head of a household or the mother of a family, from the Latin *mater,* mother, and *familia,* a household.

In Roman history the paterfamilias was a male head of a household who had absolute legal power over his extended family, servants, and slaves. English adopted the word from Latin in the 15th century and used it in a less authoritarian sense to mean any male head of a household or father of a family, as in this 1754 quotation from *The Gray's Inn Journal:* "I am here a Kind of Pater-familias with all my little Brood of Hens and Chickens around me." The word eventually broadened to denote a male leader of any group, community, or enterprise: "Ernest Hemingway was the paterfamilias of the so-called Lost Generation, the American expatriate writers who lived in Europe after World War I."

The words *paterfamilias* and *patriarch* (PAY-tree-ahrk) both denote a father or male leader. But *patriarch,* which dates back in English to before 1200, originally meant a high-ranking bishop in the early Christian church or "one of the scriptural fathers of the human race or of the Hebrew people" (*Merriam-Webster's Collegiate*). Later, *patriarch* came to mean a founding father of some group or institution, or the oldest or most respected member of a group: "Ralph Waldo Emerson was the patriarch of the American school of transcendental philosophy." Thus, the role of the patriarch is generally more dignified than that of the paterfamilias, and the person who occupies it more venerable; the paterfamilias leads a family or group but may or may not command its respect.

Word 9: APOGEE (AP-uh-jee)

The point at which a heavenly body or object orbiting the earth is at its greatest distance from the earth; by extension, the highest point, the climax or culmination.

Apogee comes from the Greek *apogaion,* far from or away from the earth, from *apo-,* away, off, apart, and *gaia,* a variant of *gē,* the earth. You can see this Greek *gē* in the many English words beginning with the combining form *geo-,* meaning pertaining to the earth or ground, such as *geology, geometry,* and *geophagy* (jee-AHF-uh-jee), the practice of eating dirt, chalk, or clay, from *geo-* and the Greek *phagein,* to eat.

Apogee was originally used in the astronomical system devised by Ptolemy (TAHL-uh-mee) of Alexandria, a second-century mathematician, geographer, and astronomer who posited that the earth was the stationary center of the universe around which the sun, moon, and stars revolved. In modern astronomy *apogee* is used of things that actually orbit the earth, such as the moon or a satellite, but it is also used of the point in any orbit that is farthest from the body being orbited, as *the apogee in the earth's revolution around the sun.* The opposite of the apogee is the *perigee* (PER-i-jee), the point at which something orbiting the earth is nearest to the earth.

Apogee is often used figuratively to mean the highest point, the climax or culmination of something, as *the apogee of Mayan civilization in the 8th and 9th centuries,* or *she is at the apogee of her career.* In this figurative sense *apogee* is synonymous with the words *summit, pinnacle, apex, acme, vertex,* and *zenith.* The antonym of all these highest-point words is the *nadir* (NAY-dur), the lowest point.

Word 10: MIEN (MEEN, like *mean*)

A person's bearing, air, or manner, especially when it reveals character, personality, attitude, or feeling; one's demeanor, deportment, or carriage.

The noun *mien* is a shortening of the obsolete noun *demean,* bearing, behavior. Over time, the word's spelling changed from *mean* to *mien* to distinguish the two words.

A person's mien can show several things. It can indicate a feeling or mood, as *a downcast mien, a wistful mien,* or *a haunted mien.* It can indicate an attitude or manner, as *a humble mien* or *a haughty mien.* And it can indicate a person's bearing or behavior, as *an imposing mien* or *a widowlike mien.* "Fops at all corners, ladylike in mien," wrote the English poet William Cowper (KOO-pur) in 1775. (A *fop* is a vain, effeminate man overly concerned with his dress and manners.) The context in which *mien* appears often reveals something about a person's character or personality: "At seventy, white of beard and hair, Turrell combines the mien of a courtly Western rancher with that of a loquacious youthful enthusiast" (Peter Schjeldahl, *The New Yorker*).

The nouns *deportment, demeanor,* and *mien* are close in meaning. According to *Merriam-Webster's Collegiate Dictionary, deportment* "suggests actions or behavior as formed by breeding or training," as *deportment appropriate to a formal event. Demeanor* "suggests one's attitude toward others as expressed in outward behavior," as *her unwelcoming demeanor* or *the doctor's calm and reassuring demeanor.* Our keyword, *mien,* "is a literary term referring both to bearing and demeanor," says *Merriam-Webster.* Your mien is how you carry yourself, how you behave, and what that reveals about you to others.

Review Quiz for Keywords 1–10

Consider the following questions and decide whether the correct answer is yes or no. **Answers appear on page 336.**

1. Does a simpering person need to be comforted?
2. Can you denude an orange?
3. Are two similar things sui generis?
4. Is a jeremiad pleasant to listen to?
5. Is a sobriquet a kind of epithet?
6. Is a regnant woman going to have a baby?
7. Do humble people exhibit hauteur?
8. In Roman history, was a paterfamilias a male slave?

9. Is the apogee the lowest point?

10. Does a person's mien often reveal character or personality?

Difficult Distinctions: *Appraise* and *Apprise*

The verbs to *appraise* and to *apprise* are often confused, usually with the former misused in place of the latter. For example, in *Right, Wrong, and Risky,* Mark Davidson cites a CNN newscaster who "reported accusations that Defense Secretary Donald Rumsfeld had not been kept sufficiently 'appraised' by U.S. military leaders. About a minute later the newscaster noted that he should have used the word *apprised*."

To *appraise* (uh-PRAYZ, almost like *upraise*) is to officially decide the worth or price of, evaluate, estimate, judge. Local governments appraise property so they can levy taxes. And you can appraise an antique, a piece of artwork, or a rare manuscript, determine its worth or price. To *apprise* (uh-PRYZ, like *a prize*) is to inform or notify. You apprise someone of the latest news, or you can be apprised of what's happening. Parents want their teenage children to keep them apprised of their whereabouts.

Here is the next set of ten keywords in *Word Workout:*

Word 11: DYSPEPTIC (dis-PEP-tik)

Irritable and gloomy; grouchy and morose; ill-humored and pessimistic.

The adjective *dyspeptic* comes from Greek, combining *dys-,* bad, ill, or difficult, and *pepsis,* digestion. The noun *dyspepsia* (dis-PEP-see-uh) is bad digestion, indigestion. The antonyms of *dyspepsia* and *dyspeptic* are *eupepsia* (yoo-PEP-see-uh), good or normal digestion, and *eupeptic* (yoo-PEP-tik), having good digestion.

The combining form *dys-* is used in medicine to form words denoting an impaired or abnormal condition. For instance, the familiar word *dyslexia* refers to various linguistic learning disabilities, including reading disorders. *Dyspnea* (DISP-nee-uh) is difficult or labored breathing; *dysphagia* (dis-FAY-juh) is difficulty swallowing; *dysosmia* (dis-AHZ-mee-uh) is an impairment of the sense of

smell; *dysmenorrhea* (DIS-men-uh-**REE**-uh) is difficult and painful menstruation; and *dysgraphia* is an inability to write caused by
a lesion, or, informally, writer's cramp or writer's block.

   Dyspeptic may be used literally to mean suffering from dyspepsia, indigestion, but it is probably more often used figuratively to mean exhibiting the emotional symptoms of dyspepsia,
such as gloominess and irritability. Dyspeptic people, also
called dyspeptics, tend to be grouchy and pessimistic, as *a dyspeptic neighbor* or *a dyspeptic movie critic.* But *dyspeptic* may be applied not only to people but also to things. For example, any
kind of expression—a book, an essay, a speech, a comment, and
even a digital missive (word 14 of this level)—can be dyspeptic,
ill-humored and morose: "Senator Chuck Grassley is well known
as one of Congress's most heroic users of social media, sending legendarily illegible, frequently dyspeptic tweets" (*The Huffington Post*).

Word 12: ANAPHORA (uh-NAF-uh-ruh)

In rhetoric, a figure of speech in which a word or phrase is repeated at
the beginning of successive clauses, sentences, or verses, as in these lines
from Psalm 23 in the King James Bible: *He maketh me to lie down in green
pastures: he leadeth me beside the still waters. He restoreth my soul.*

The noun *anaphora* comes from the Greek *anapherein,* to bring or
carry back. The adjective is *anaphoric* (AN-uh-**FOR**-ik).

   One of the most famous examples of anaphora is Winston
Churchill's thrilling speech to the House of Commons on June
4, 1940, at the height of the Battle of Britain during World War
II. Here is an excerpt from its conclusion: "We shall not flag or
fail. We shall go on to the end. . . . We shall fight on the beaches,
we shall fight on the landing grounds, we shall fight in the fields
and in the streets, we shall fight in the hills; we shall never surrender."

   Another famous use of anaphora is Martin Luther King's repetition of the phrase *I have a dream* in his speech for the March on
Washington, August 28, 1963. What most of us don't remember
about that great speech is how King also used several other phrases

anaphorically, including *One hundred years later, We refuse to believe, We cannot be satisfied,* and *Let freedom ring.*

As you have probably surmised—to *surmise* (sur-MYZ) is to come to a conclusion by using one's intuition or imagination—anaphora is common in speechwriting. It is also a common device in poetry, where the repetition of an initial word or phrase can be incantatory.* Anaphora also contributes to the solemn, earnest tone of the Bible, and Julius Caesar's famous declaration, *I came, I saw, I conquered,* may be the most terse use of anaphora in history.

In rhetoric—the art of using words effectively—the opposite of anaphora is the figure of speech called *epistrophe* (i-PIS-truh-fee), repetition of a word or phrase at the *end* of successive verses, clauses, or sentences. Abraham Lincoln used epistrophe at the close of the Gettysburg Address: ". . . and that government of the people, by the people, for the people, shall not perish from the earth." And in George Bernard Shaw's 1912 play *Pygmalion,* Alfred Doolittle utters this memorable combination of anaphora and epistrophe: "I'm willing to tell you. I'm wanting to tell you. I'm waiting to tell you."

Word 13: PHILANDER (fi-LAN-dur)
Of a man, to flirt with and seduce women without having any serious intentions.

Philander comes from the Greek *philandros,* one who loves, a combination of *philo-,* loving, and *andro-,* a man, male. "In Renaissance literature, [*Philander* was] a common name for a flirtatious male character who has many love affairs," says *Merriam-Webster's Encyclopedia of Literature.* From the name we get the verb to *philander,* to court many women but commit to none. *Philandering,* as a noun, is the act of engaging in multiple casual romantic encounters.

Philander is usually used either of adulterous men who have

---

* *Incantatory* (in-KAN-tuh-tor-ee) means having the magical or spellbinding effect of an *incantation,* the chanting of certain words as a charm or spell.

casual sex outside marriage or of flirtatious single men who consider themselves, to use a current slang term, *players*. According to the online Urban Dictionary, a *player* is "a male who is skilled at manipulating ('playing') others, and especially at seducing women by pretending to care about them, when in reality they are only interested in sex." (That definition could also serve for the noun *philanderer*, a man who flirts with and seduces women.) But occasionally the verb to *philander* is used figuratively of intellectual flirtation or seduction, as in this 1951 quotation from *International Organization:* "They philandered with the forces of fascism in the vain hope that the latter would move eastward and crush communism."

Word 14: MISSIVE (MIS-iv)
A letter; a written message or communication.

The noun *missive* comes from the Latin *mittere,* to send, the source of many English words including *submission,* literally something sent in; *missile,* literally an object sent out forcefully; *emission,* a discharge, literally something sent out; and *intermittent,* happening at intervals, occasional, literally sent out between.

A missive may be any sort of letter or written message longer than a brief note, whether handwritten, typed, or digitized. But *missive* may also denote a more formal written announcement, similar to a press release: "Steve Jobs has posted a 1,700-word missive on Apple's website." In this sense *missive* is synonymous with the words *bulletin, dispatch,* and *communiqué* (kuh-MYOO-ni-**KAY**). Other synonyms of *missive* include *epistle* (i-PIS'l, discussed in *epistolary,* word 35 of Level 6), and *billet-doux* (BIL-ay-**DOO**), a love letter, which was borrowed directly from French, where it meant literally a sweet note. A tweet,* a posting on the social networking service Twitter, is also a missive—or an *emissive,* my proposed word for an email message or other electronic communication.

* The noun *tweet,* meaning a message of 140 characters or fewer sent via Twitter, was admitted into the *Oxford English Dictionary* in 2013.

Word 15: PENULTIMATE (pe-NUHL-ti-mit)
Next to the last; second to last; being the last but one.

Penultimate comes from the Latin *paene ultima,* in which *paene* means almost, nearly, and *ultima* means the last. By derivation, that which is penultimate is almost the last. Specifically, it means next to the last, as *the penultimate chapter of the book.*

Penultimate may be used generally of anything that is second-to-last, as *the penultimate day of our vacation* or *the penultimate episode of a TV show.* But it also has a specific use in prosody (PRAH-suh-dee), the study of poetic meter and versification, where it denotes the second-to-last syllable of a word, the last syllable but one. This next-to-last syllable is also sometimes called the *penult* (PEE-nult). For example, the penultimate syllable, or penult, in the word *penultimate* is *-ti-.* And the antepenultimate (AN-tee-pe-**NUHL**-ti-mit) syllable is the one before, *ante-,* the penultimate, hence the third to last: *ver-* is the antepenultimate syllable of *versify.*

Penultimate is often misconstrued as being an emphatic synonym of *ultimate,* which means the last or the utmost. These two words are, most emphatically, not synonymous. Reserve *penultimate* for when you mean not the last but the next to last.

Word 16: ZEITGEIST (TSYT-gyst, rhymes with *slight diced*)
Literally, the spirit of a time or age; the general trend of thought or feeling, or the intellectual or cultural climate, of a particular period or generation.

Zeitgeist is a mid-19th-century German loanword formed from the German *Zeit,* time, and *Geist,* spirit—the same *Geist* as in *poltergeist* (POHL-tur-gyst), a spirit or ghost that makes noises, from the German *poltern,* to knock, make noise.

The zeitgeist is the spirit of a given time, the general trend of its thought and feeling, as *the anti-rational zeitgeist of the Romantic era, the freewheeling zeitgeist of the 1960s,* and *the zeitgeist of greed in the 1980s.* Novelists, playwrights, and filmmakers often try to capture and sometimes influence the zeitgeist, the general trend of

thought or feeling, in their creative work. *Zeitgeist* can also sometimes refer to the prevailing intellectual or cultural mood of a
particular group in a particular time, as *the zeitgeist of the millennial
generation* or *the zeitgeist of Silicon Valley.*

Until recently, *zeitgeist* was printed in italics with a capital *Z*,
but it is now a fully English word that should be printed in lowercase letters and roman type.

Word 17: SENTENTIOUS (sen-TEN-shus)
Full of, or given to using, aphorisms or maxims, or short, meaningful
sentences. By extension, abounding in or given to pompous moralizing;
self-righteous.

Way back in the discussion of *adage* (word 23 of Level 1) I noted
that an *aphorism* (AF-ur-iz'm) is a general truth or shrewd observation expressed in a terse, forceful, thought-provoking way,
while a *maxim* (MAKS-im) is a guiding principle or rule of conduct that expresses a general truth drawn from experience. Here's
an aphorism from Mark Twain: "The lack of money is the root of
all evil." And here's a maxim from Mark Twain: "Irreverence is
the champion of liberty and its only sure defense."

The adjective *sententious*—which comes through the Latin
sententiōsus, full of meaning, from *sententia,* opinion, thought,
meaning, the source of the English *sentence*—means having lots of
aphorisms and maxims, as *a sententious book,* or given to using lots
of aphorisms and maxims, as *a sententious clergyman.* Poets and
prophets are often sententious; professors and philosophers generally are not.

The pompous Polonius in Shakespeare's *Hamlet* is sententious,
and probably because sententious people can be prone to moralizing, like Polonius, *sententious* came to be used to mean self-
righteous and moralistic, or pompously formal, as in this 1850
citation from Washington Irving's *Mahomet:* "His ordinary discourse was grave and sententious"; and this one from Charles
Kingsley's 1855 historical novel *Westward Ho!:* "a long sententious
letter, filled with Latin quotations."

Synonyms of *sententious* include *terse, pithy, succinct, aphoristic,* and *epigrammatic* (EP-i-gruh-**MAT**-ik). Challenging antonyms of *sententious* include *circumlocutory* (discussed in *circumlocution,* word 44 of Level 3), *prolix* (PROH-liks), *tautological* (TAW-tuh-**LAHJ**-i-kul), and *pleonastic* (*pleonasm* is word 6 of Level 8).

Word 18: INTERDICT (IN-tur-**DIKT**)
To prohibit or forbid, especially by formal command or authoritative decree.

Synonyms of *interdict* include to *ban, bar, outlaw, disallow, embargo,* and *proscribe.* Antonyms of *interdict* include to *permit, legalize, authorize,* and *sanction.*

To *interdict* comes through the Latin *interdictum,* a prohibition, from the verb *interdīcere,* to stop by coming between, from *inter-,* between, and *dīcere,* to speak.

When the verb to *interdict* entered English in the late 13th century it was an ecclesiastical term meaning to place under an *interdict* (IN-tur-dikt), which today means any official prohibition, as from a court, but which originally was an authoritative decree of the Roman Catholic Church prohibiting a person or place from receiving religious benefits and privileges. Since the early 16th century to *interdict* has been used in its modern sense, to forbid or prohibit, especially by formal command: "A member of the Royal Virgin Islands Police Force has been interdicted from duty amid allegations of indecent assault" (*BVI Beacon*). Since the mid-20th century *interdict* has also been used to mean to impede or destroy, as *to interdict the enemy's supply lines,* or to interrupt or intercept, as *to interdict a shipment of illegal drugs.*

To *forbid, prohibit,* and *interdict* all mean to stop or disallow something. Generally speaking, an individual forbids while an institution or government prohibits. Thus, parents may forbid staying out late and a teacher may forbid talking in class, while businesses prohibit smoking and the law prohibits driving without a license. To *interdict* may apply to an individual or to an institution, but it is the most formal and authoritative of these three words.

The noun is *interdiction* (IN-tur-**DIK**-shin), the act or an instance of interdicting: forbidding, prohibiting, impeding, or intercepting.

Word 19: MALAISE (muh-LAYZ)
A vague and general feeling of physical discomfort or mental uneasiness.

Malaise is borrowed directly from the French *malaise,* discomfort, uneasiness, a combination of *mal-,* bad, and the Middle French *aise,* the source of the English *ease.*

When *malaise* entered English in the mid-18th century it was used of a vague and general feeling of physical weakness or discomfort, often signaling the onset of an illness, and the word is still used this way today, as in this quotation from 1981: "In milder cases, there is just a feeling of malaise, with some shivering, pallor . . . and nausea" (Oliver Sacks, *Migraine*). But over time the word came to be used more broadly and figuratively to include mental uneasiness or discomfort, as *the malaise of an unhappy marriage,* or a vague and general state of unhealthiness, as *an economy suffering from chronic malaise.*

Word 20: PROGENY (PRAH-juh-nee)
Offspring, children, descendants, spawn.

Progeny comes from the Latin *prōgeniēs,* offspring, descendants. The word is usually construed as plural, denoting someone's children or offspring, as *the philanderer's legitimate and illegitimate progeny.* (*Philander* is word 13 of this level.) But *progeny* is occasionally used to mean a single child or descendant: "The investigation determined that she was her progeny."

Progeny has also often been used figuratively to mean a person's "spiritual, intellectual, or artistic descendants" (*OED*): "These mendicant monks are the progeny of St. Francis." (*Mendicant* is word 24 of Level 4.) In this sense *progeny* is synonymous with *successors, followers,* and *disciples. Progeny* may also denote something that results from something else, the product, issue, or outcome, as when the lexicographer Samuel Johnson, in 1750, wrote, "Falsehood was the progeny of Folly."

But most often *progeny* is used to mean the offspring or descendants of human beings, animals, or plants. Lovers of horse racing wonder if the progeny of a great racehorse will be great too. Saplings are the progeny of trees. And the hope of every generation of humankind is to make the world a better place for its progeny.

A *progenitor* (proh-JEN-i-tur) is a creator of progeny, hence, an ancestor, precursor, or originator.

Review Quiz for Keywords 11–20

Consider the following statements and decide whether each one is true or false. **Answers appear on page 337**.

1. Dyspeptic people tend to be cheerful and carefree.
2. Anaphora is the repetition of a word or phrase at the end of successive verses, clauses, or sentences.
3. To philander is to have many love affairs.
4. A missive could be a message sent in a bottle.
5. The penultimate syllable is the final syllable.
6. If you contradict the zeitgeist, you contradict the spirit of the age or times.
7. A sententious person is circumlocutory.
8. The FDA can approve or interdict the sale of any food or drug.
9. A malaise is a feeling of uncertainty or perplexity.
10. Your children's children are not your progeny.

Figures of Speech That Every Writer Should Know

In Level 1 you learned about the figure of speech called alliteration, and a few keywords ago I introduced you to anaphora and epistrophe. Now let's take a look at some other common figures of speech that you can put in your rhetorical toolbox.

Assonance (AS-uh-nints) is partial rhyme or harmony of vowel sounds at the beginning of neighboring words, as in *the lady had a baby* or *now comes the cover of night*. The opposite of assonance is *consonance* (KAHN-suh-nints), harmony of the final consonant sounds in neighboring words, as in *And then it rained and ruined everything* or *an intricate and delicate contrivance.*

Anadiplosis (AN-uh-di-**PLOH**-sis) is the repetition of an ending at the next beginning, as in *When I love, I love fully,* or as in this line from Ecclesiastes 9:10 in the Bible: "Whatsoever thy hand findeth to **do, do** it with thy might."

Antithesis (an-TITH-uh-sis) is the juxtaposition (placing side by side) of sharply contrasting or directly opposed ideas, as in *Give me liberty or give me death*—which, with its repetition of *give me* in successive clauses is also an example of anaphora.

Asyndeton (uh-SIN-duh-tahn) is the omission of a conjunction that would normally join words or clauses, as in the title of Elizabeth Gilbert's bestselling memoir *Eat, Pray, Love,* which is missing *and* before *Love.* By contrast, *polysyndeton* (PAH-lee-**SIN**-duh-tahn) is the addition of conjunctions, especially *and,* where they are not normally required, as in *to work and hope and struggle and never give up.*

Finally, *dissonance* (DIS-uh-nints) or *cacophony* (kuh-KAHF-uh-nee) is the use of harsh-sounding words or a harsh combination of sounds, as in *a horrid screech that split the air, and then the sickening thud and crunch of bone.*

Learning to recognize these figures of speech and use them in your own writing will make what you have to say more interesting, more musical, and more memorable.

Here are the next ten keywords in Level 7:

Word 21: BELIE (bi-LY)

To give a false impression or representation of, to misrepresent or disguise; or to show to be false or mistaken, to contradict.

The verb to *belie* dates back more than a thousand years to Old English, where it meant to deceive by lying. In Middle English to *belie* came to mean to tell lies about, to slander. This sense is now archaic. Since the 16th century *belie* has been used to mean to misrepresent or be misleading: "His youthful looks belie his age"; "Recent train wrecks belie improving rail safety record" (Associated Press). And since the 17th century *belie* has also been used to mean to show to be false or mistaken: "The facts belie such easy answers" (*The Wall Street Journal*); "The record turnout belied predictions of widespread voter indifference."

Take care not to use *belie* as a synonym of *reveal* or *indicate,* as *her accent belied her New England roots.* This erroneous usage is almost the opposite of the word's true meaning: to misrepresent or disguise, or to show to be false or mistaken.

Word 22: FACTOTUM (fak-TOH-tum)
A person employed to do all kinds of work, a handyman, jack-of-all-trades; hence, an employee or assistant who has many different duties or responsibilities.

Factotum comes from the Late Latin *factōtum,* a combination of *fac,* the imperative of *facere,* to do, make, and *tōtum,* everything, the whole. This word for a person who is handy at all kinds of work can come in handy to describe either a person skilled in various trades, who can do all sorts of odd jobs and manual labor, or someone who handles a variety of tasks or shoulders numerous responsibilities. Thus, if you're not a do-it-yourself expert it's helpful to have a factotum to do the upkeep on your house; but if you are a do-it-yourself expert then you're probably your own factotum, a jack-of-all-trades. And business owners always appreciate having a factotum, an employee willing to take on many more duties than are listed in the job description.

Word 23: JINGOISM (JING-goh-iz'm)
Overzealous and aggressive patriotism, or an aggressive and belligerent foreign policy.

The noun *jingo* denotes "a person who professes his or her patriotism loudly and excessively, favoring vigilant preparedness for war and an aggressive foreign policy," says *The Random House Dictionary.* This use of *jingo,* explains *Webster 2,* "arose in England, where the word was originally a nickname for a supporter or praiser of Lord Beaconsfield's* action in sending a fleet to Turkish waters to oppose Russia's advance in 1878. It is derived from the chorus of a popular music-hall song of the times: " 'We don't want to fight, but *by Jingo!* if we do, / We've got the ships, we've got the men, and got the money too.' "† The jingoes or jingoists, as they were called, were zealous, militant patriots who believed that might is always right. An 1881 article in *Gentleman's Magazine* observed that "the Jingo is the aggregation of the bully. An individual may be a bully; but, in order to create Jingoism, there must be a crowd."

Jingoism is "a blind, flag-waving nationalism that refuses to acknowledge any failings whatsoever of our society" (*The Wall Street Journal*). The adjective is *jingoistic,* which means either characteristic of jingoes, overzealous patriots, or expressive of jingoism, belligerent patriotism.

The eponymous word *chauvinism* (**SHOH**-vuh-NIZ'm) is a close synonym of *jingoism.* In my book *Verbal Advantage* I recount the story of a 19th-century Frenchman named Nicolas Chauvin, who "was a veteran of the Napoleonic wars and a fervent follower of the emperor. After the defeat and exile of Napoleon, Chauvin became so zealous in his demonstrations of patriotism and allegiance to the fallen emperor that people began to ridicule him. . . . The French coined a word for his blind love of country, which soon made its way into English."

Word 24: GAINSAY (gayn-SAY *or* GAYN-say)
To deny, contradict, or oppose; to declare to be untrue.

Synonyms of *gainsay* include to *dispute, disavow, disown, repudiate, controvert,* and *abnegate* (AB-ni-gayt).

The verb to *gainsay* begins with the Anglo-Saxon prefix *gain-,* which corresponds to the more common prefix *re-,* from Latin, and signifies "opposition, return, or reversal" (*OED*). By derivation, when you gainsay you speak against something, either to deny or contradict it. To gainsay a charge or accusation is to de-

---

* The aristocratic title of Benjamin Disraeli (1804–1881), England's prime minister at the time.
† The phrase *by jingo* is probably an old euphemism (word 18 of Level 2) for *by Jesus.*

clare it to be untrue. The past tense is *gainsaid* (gayn-SED or GAYN-sed). Facts or evidence that cannot be gainsaid cannot be denied or opposed by argument.

Garner's Modern American Usage observes that "originally *gainsay* was the popular word and *contradict* the erudite [learned, scholarly] one. Today just the opposite is true." *Contradict,* the more learned word from Latin, has nearly supplanted (word 17 of Level 2) *gainsay,* the once-popular word from Anglo-Saxon. To *gainsay* is now more common in British English than in American, but it would not be inappropriate for an American to use it in a formal or dignified context.

Word 25: NEOLOGY   (nee-AHL-uh-jee)
The invention of new words, phrases, usages, meanings, or expressions.

Neology is borrowed from French; the combining form *neo-* means new, and the combining form *-logy* designates sciences, disciplines, or spheres of knowledge.

Neology is the coining of new words and meanings. A *neologism* (nee-AHL-uh-jiz'm) is a newly minted locution (word 22 of Level 6) or a new meaning of a word. To *neologize* (nee-AHL-uh-jyz) is to invent new words. And the people who coin new words are called *neologists* (nee-AHL-uh-jists). The rest of the population is the court of no appeal, which decides whether these creations will thrive or expire.

Here's one example of how swift and arbitrary that judgment can be. In the mid-19th century, when people needed a word for someone who collects postage stamps, somebody proposed *timbromaniac* (from the French *timbre-poste,* a postage stamp). That's a perfectly good word, I suppose, but the moment somebody else came up with the more elegant word *philatelist* (fi-LAT-uh-list), poor old *timbromaniac* was licked.

Since Geoffrey Chaucer, way back in the 14th century, borrowed from French to create the words *attention, duration, fraction,* and *position,* there have been some great English neologists and some great successes in English neology. Sir Thomas More published a book in 1516 whose title has endured as the word for an ideal society, a paradise on earth: *utopia.* The poet John Milton was looking the other way when, in 1667 in his epic poem *Paradise Lost,* he coined the word *pandemonium* (literally, the place of all the demons) for Satan's palace in hell. Milton also gave us *earth-shaking, impassive, infinitude, lovelorn,* and *sensuous.* Sir Francis Bacon gave us *placid* in 1626; Sir Thomas Browne gave us *hallucination* in 1629; John Dryden gave us *witticism* in 1677; and, because somebody had to do it, Alexander Pope gave us *anticlimax* in 1710.

Thomas Jefferson was belittled by the British for inventing the useful word *belittle.* Samuel Johnson, who published a landmark dictionary in 1755, coined the humorous word *fiddledeedee,* unaware that his creation would achieve dubious immortality in the Disney version of *Pinocchio.* And Jonathan Swift, in his 1726 satirical romance *Gulliver's Travels,* introduced the word *yahoo* to denote "a member of a race of brutes . . . who have the form and all the vices of humans."

Where would Emily Post and Miss Manners be had Lord Chesterfield not politely plucked the word *etiquette* from French in 1750? And where would the pocket-protector crowd be had Theodor Seuss Geisel, known to millions as Dr. Seuss, not invented the word *nerd* in his 1950 book *If I Ran the Zoo?*

Neology, the invention of new locutions and meanings, is essential to the growth and survival of a language. Even if you've never coined a word you are still part of the process of embracing or rejecting words as they come along, giving them life and breath or giving them a shove in the direction of the dustbin.

Word 26: EXCRESCENCE (eks-KRES-ints)
An outgrowth, lump, enlargement, or projection, especially when abnormal.

Challenging synonyms of *excrescence* include *protuberance* (proh-T[Y]OO-bur-ints) and *intumescence* (IN-t[y]oo-**MES**-ints), from the Latin *tumēre,* to swell, the source of the English *tumor.* The adjective is *excrescent* (eks-KRES-int), forming an excrescence, growing abnormally or superfluously out of something else.

The noun *excrescence* comes from the Latin *excrescĕre,* to grow out, spring up, from *ex-,* out, and *crescĕre,* to grow, spring forth, the source of the English *crescent,* which as an adjective means growing, as *a crescent moon,* and the noun *crescendo* (kruh-SHEN-doh), which in music means a gradual increase in volume.

An excrescence may be a benign and harmless growth or projection, such as a mole, pimple, or blister; or it may be an abnormal growth, especially an abnormal swelling or lump, such as a wart, cyst, boil, pustule (PUHS-chool), wen, or tumor. The bumpy taste buds on your tongue are normal excrescences, but polyps in your colon—even when benign—are abnormal excrescences. As you age your bones can develop excrescences, bumps or projections, from calcium deposits. And on certain animals, horns are normal excrescences.

Sometimes *excrescence* is used figuratively of any unwanted or disfiguring enlargement or addition, as *the gaudy excrescence of her wedding ring* or *the excrescence of the federal bureaucracy.*

Word 27: CORBEL (KOR-bul, rhymes with *warble*)
A bracket; specifically, in architecture, a projection from within a wall that supports a weight, such as a girder.

Corbel comes from the Late Latin *corvellus,* the diminutive of *corvus,* a raven. What does a bracket have to do with a big black bird? The answer isn't clear, but the *OED* notes that corbels were originally cut on a slant so that they would look like a bird's beak. In medieval architecture corbels were often elaborately carved, which may have led Sir Walter Scott to write, in his 1805 poem "Lay of the Last Minstrel," that "[t]he corbels were carved grotesque and grim," but in modern architecture corbels are usually functional rather than ornamental.

A *gargoyle* (GAHR-goyl) and a *corbel* are both architectural projections. A gargoyle is a spout—in the form of a grotesquely carved human or animal figure with an open mouth—that projects from a roof gutter and throws rainwater clear of the building. A corbel is a bracket—generally of wood, stone, or brick—projecting from the vertical face of a wall to support some horizontal weight, such as a beam, a cornice, or an arch.

Word 28: SEDULOUS (SEJ-uh-lus)

Involving or characterized by careful and persistent effort; requiring or accomplished by painstaking attention or application.

Sedulous comes through the Latin *sēdŭlus,* busy, diligent, careful, from *sē dolō,* literally without guile or trickery. By derivation the sedulous person works honestly and carefully to accomplish the task at hand.

Sedulous is often applied to people and creatures: the sedulous student burning the midnight oil; the sedulous lawyer working late writing a brief; the sedulous beaver building a dam; or the sedulous bumblebee tirelessly collecting pollen. The word may also be used of actions to mean done in a persistent, painstaking way: *sedulous attention, sedulous investigation, sedulous preparation, sedulous listening.*

Synonyms of *sedulous* include *busy, industrious, diligent, painstaking, persevering, unremitting, indefatigable* (word 21 of Level 2), and *assiduous* (uh-SIJ-oo-us). Antonyms of *sedulous* include *lethargic, languid, indolent* (word 48 of Level 4), *phlegmatic* (fleg-MAT-ik), *slothful, shiftless,* and *otiose* (OH-shee-ohs).

Sedulousness, the noun, means diligence, industriousness, careful and persistent effort: "The captain told the crew, 'This long and difficult mission will require your unwavering sedulousness, if we are to succeed.'"

Word 29: MAUNDER (MAWN-dur)

To talk in a rambling, dreamy, or meaningless way; to speak incoherently or foolishly. Also, to move or act in an aimless, idle, or dreamy manner.

The origin of the verb to *maunder* is uncertain.

There are various ways to use *maunder* in the sense of speaking in a rambling or incoherent manner. You can simply *maunder:* "She saw the old folks maundering in wheelchairs in the hallways of the nursing home." You can *maunder over* something: "It's odd to see some brawny guy maundering over some ugly little dog."

You can *maunder on:* "Judith stopped listening as her father maundered on." You can *maunder about:* "After a few drinks he started maundering about his troubles." And you can *maunder on about:* "Ruth fidgeted while Anita maundered on about her failing marriage."

Maunder may also be used to mean to move or act in an idle, dreamy way, as *to maunder through the woods* or *to maunder down the primrose path.*

Here's a sentence that accomplishes the neat trick of using the rambling, aimless *maunder* in both its talking and its moving senses: "His columns frequently wander and maunder, heading this way and that, but never actually arriving anywhere" (Jeffrey Shallit, pandasthumb.org).

Word 30: SALTATION (sal-TAY-shin, *not* sawl-)
The act of leaping or jumping, or a leap, jump; hence, the act of dancing, or a dance.

Saltation comes from the Latin *saltāre,* to dance, the frequentative of the verb *salīre,* to leap, jump, bound, spring. *Saltation* has specific uses in the sciences of geology and evolutionary biology, but in general literary use it means the act of leaping or jumping or the act of dancing: "Still keeping time to the music like Harlequin in a pantomime, he thrust a letter into our hero's hand, and continued his saltation without pause or intermission" (Sir Walter Scott, *Waverley,* 1893); "Life must be taken with a grain of saltation: let the spirit dance a measure or two ere it collapse" (Christopher Morley, *Pipefuls,* 1920).

The adjective *saltatory* (SAL-tuh-tor-ee) means pertaining to or adapted for saltation, leaping or dancing, and the adjective *saltant* (SAL-tint) means leaping or dancing. The unusual verb to *saltate* (SAL-tayt) means to leap or jump.

Review Quiz for Keywords 21–30
Decide if the pairs of words below are synonyms or antonyms.
Answers appear on page 338.

1. *Belie* and *prove* are . . . synonyms or antonyms?
2. *Factotum* and *jack-of-all-trades* are . . .
3. *Jingoism* and *chauvinism* are . . .
4. To *gainsay* and to *confirm* are . . .
5. *Neology* and *verbicide* are . . .
6. *Excrescence* and *protuberance* are . . .
7. *Corbel* and *bracket* are . . .
8. *Sedulous* and *indolent* are . . .
9. To *maunder* and to *ramble* are . . .
10. *Saltation* and *torpor* are . . .

The Greatest Neologist

The English language's greatest neologist was a man who contributed at least 1,500 items to our wordstock, along with countless idioms and expressions that are so famous they have become cliché. He was an Elizabethan playwright and poet who, had his father not decided to move the family to Stratford-on-Avon shortly before his birth, would be known to us today as the Bard of Snitterfield.

William Shakespeare was, quite simply, a world–champion wordmaker. As Jeffrey McQuain and Stanley Malless tell us in *Coined by Shakespeare,* we encounter his words every day, from *assassination* to *zany.* Shakespeare's creations are so firmly embedded in the language that, like the conveniences of modern life, you can't imagine a time when they didn't exist.

How would we make love had Shakespeare not given us the words *embrace, courtship, undress,* and *kissing*? Where would our economy be without *employer, manager, investment,* and *retirement*? Where would religion be without *pious* and *sanctimonious*? Where would journalism be without *reword, misquote,* and *critic*? Where would criticism be without *fashionable, monumental,* and *worthless*? And where would all of English literature be had Shakespeare not given us such simple and beautiful words as *gloomy, hurry, generous, unaware,* and *lonely*?

Shakespeare was also the English language's greatest phrase-maker: "There has never been anyone to match him," says Bill

Bryson in *The Mother Tongue*. For ever and a day (*Taming of the Shrew*), Shakespeare laid it on with a trowel (*As You Like It*) and showed us in one fell swoop (*Macbeth*) and with no apparent foul play (*King John*) what it was like to be in a pickle (*The Tempest*), to be fancy-free (*Midsummer Night's Dream*), to beggar all description (*Antony and Cleopatra*), to be eaten out of house and home (*Henry IV, Part 2*), and to wear your heart on your sleeve (*Othello*). With the milk of human kindness (*Macbeth*) he took us on a wild-goose chase (*Romeo and Juliet*), gave us short shrift (*Richard III*), and sent us packing (*Henry IV, Part I*). He made our hair stand on end (*Hamlet*) because he was as merry as the day is long (*Much Ado About Nothing*) and as pure as the driven snow (*The Winter's Tale* and *Macbeth*). Surely his words will never become too much of a good thing (*As You Like It*) or vanish into thin air (*Othello*).

And that's the long and the short of it—an idiom that the Bard, in *The Merry Wives of Windsor*, originally wrote as "this is the short and the long of it." As the 19th-century Irish poet and playwright Oscar Wilde dryly observed, "Now we sit through Shakespeare in order to recognize the quotations."

Now let's return to the *Word Workout* vocabulary for another ten keyword discussions.

Word 31: ANODYNE (AN-uh-dyn)
A medicine, drug, or agent that relieves pain; hence, anything that soothes the mind or feelings or that alleviates anxiety or distress.

The noun *anodyne* comes from the Greek *anódynos,* painless, a combination of the privative prefix *an-,* without, and *ódyne,* pain. Originally an *anodyne* was a medicine or drug that alleviated pain: laudanum (LAWD'n-um), a tincture or preparation of opium, was once a popular anodyne. But perhaps because emotional pain is as prevalent as physical pain, *anodyne* was soon used of other things that alleviated anxiety or distress: "Listening to beautiful music can be an anodyne for grief"; "Devouring a pint of ice cream every night is not a sensible anodyne for stress."

The unusual word *nepenthe* (nuh-PEN-thee) is a close synonym of *anodyne*. *Nepenthe* comes from the Greek *nēpenthēs,* banishing pain and sorrow, and means a magical drug or drink that makes you forget your sorrows or misfortune. In his epic poem *The Faerie Queene* (1590–1609), Edmund Spenser writes, "Nepenthe is a drink of sovereign grace, / Devised by the gods, for to assuage / Heart's grief, and bitter gall away to chase." And in Edgar Allan Poe's "The Raven" (1845), the depressed narrator moans, "Quaff [KWAHF], oh quaff this kind nepenthe and forget this lost Lenore!" (To *quaff* is to drink a beverage, especially an intoxicating one, deeply and heartily.)

Our keyword, *anodyne,* may also be used as an adjective to mean relieving pain, soothing to the mind or feelings, or not likely to offend or arouse ill will: "For some people canned background music in public places is irritating and invasive, while for others it is anodyne."

Word 32: AUTODIDACTIC (AW-toh-dy-**DAK**-tik)
Self-taught; acquiring knowledge by oneself.

Autodidactic is the adjective corresponding to the noun *autodidact* (AW-toh-**DY**-dakt). An *autodidact* is a self-taught person, one who has gained knowledge or skill without the benefit of a teacher or formal education.

The combining form *auto-,* self, comes directly from the Greek *autós,* self, and appears in many English words, such as *autograph,* literally self-writing; *automatic,* literally moving by oneself; *autocracy,* government by one person with sole power; and the unusual *autochthonous,* combining *auto-* with the Greek *chthón,* earth, land, to mean literally of the land itself, hence native, aboriginal, indigenous (in-DIJ-i-nus).

Autodidactic combines *auto-,* self, with the adjective *didactic,* designed to teach, instructive. Throughout history, many great writers, artists, and musicians have been autodidactic, self-taught, and even some eminent scholars and scientists were autodidacts— for example, the 18th-century English lexicographer Samuel

Johnson, who, for lack of money, had to abandon his studies at Oxford after only a year, and the prolific American inventor Thomas Edison, who as a youth had just three months of formal schooling.

Word 33: JOCUND (JAHK-und, first syllable like *jock,* not *joke*)
Merry, cheerful, mirthful, filled with high spirits, lively and lighthearted.

The adjective *jocund* comes from the Late Latin *jocundus,* an alteration of the Latin *jūcundus,* pleasant, delightful, from the verb *juvāre,* to help, benefit, or to please, delight. In English *jocund* may be used either of people or of things to mean characterized by merriment and mirth, full of high spirits. A gathering or a greeting can be jocund, full of good cheer. Someone's expression or manner can be jocund, merry and lively: in Shakespeare's *Henry IV,* Sir John Falstaff is a jocund reveler. And even music can be jocund, as in this sentence from *The Duke's Children* (1879) by the English novelist Anthony Trollope: "It was a sweet and jocund air, such as would make young people prone to run and skip."

Because of their similar sound, the adjectives *jovial, jocose, jocular,* and *jocund* should be carefully distinguished in meaning. *Jovial* (JOH-vee-ul), which comes from the Roman god Jove, or Jupiter, who was renowned for his love of feasting and merriment, means literally like Jove, good-humored, friendly, and convivial: *jovial conversation. Jocose* (joh-KOHS) and *jocular* (JAHK-yuh-lur) both hail from the Latin *jocus,* a joke (the source of the English *joke*), and both mean humorous, witty, or habitually given to joking, as *a jocose drunkard* or *a jocular play on words.* Our keyword, *jocund,* may suggest wit or playful humor, but it primarily suggests cheerful merriment and high spirits; that which is jocund is lively, lighthearted, and exhilarating: *their hilarious and jocund banter.*

The corresponding nouns are *joviality* (JOH-vee-**AL**-i-tee), *jocosity* (joh-KAHS-i-tee), *jocularity* (JAHK-uh-**LAR**-i-tee), and *jocundity* (joh-KUHN-di-tee).

Word 34: SIMULACRUM (SIM-yuh-**LAY**-kr<u>u</u>m)
An image or representation, or an insubstantial or unreal likeness; a
semblance.

English borrowed *simulacrum* in the late 16th century directly
from the Latin *simūlācrum,* an image, likeness, portrait, effigy.
The standard plural of *simulacrum* follows the Latin: *simulacra*
(SIM-yuh-**LAY**-kruh).

A simulacrum may be, like its Latin source, an image or likeness of a person, as *a simulacrum of the Greek god Apollo;* a representation of a thing, as *the play's set is a simulacrum of a subway station;* or
a representation of a concept, as *a convincing simulacrum of reality.* Or
a simulacrum may be a vague, unreal, insubstantial image or likeness, a semblance. For example, to anyone who appreciates good,
real food, Kraft macaroni and cheese is a simulacrum of the genuine article. An android is a simulacrum of a human being. And the
strange "phantom limb" so often described by amputees is a simulacrum, a vague and shadowy mental image of the absent limb.

Simulacrum is sometimes mispronounced with *lock* in the penultimate (word 15 of this level) syllable; dictionaries do not record this
variant. And despite what you may see in your dictionary, the penultimate syllable shouldn't be *lack* either. Most authorities recognize
only the traditional pronunciation with *lay:* SIM-yuh-**LAY**-kr<u>u</u>m.

Word 35: LAMBENT (LAM-b<u>i</u>nt)
Lambent has three senses: (1) moving or playing lightly over a surface,
flickering; (2) softly radiant or bright; or (3) expressed in a light and
brilliant style.

I have listed these three senses of *lambent* in their order of development, not in their order of frequency. Sense 1 dates from the
17th century, sense 2 from the early 18th century, and sense 3, the
most extended one, from the late 19th century.

Lambent comes from the Latin verb *lambĕre,* which meant to
lick, lap, or wash and was used of water or fire. In its original
sense, *lambent* suggests fire, flame, or light that flickers, shimmers,
or plays lightly over a surface, as *lambent candles, lambent stars,* or

lambent moonlight on the water. In its second sense, *lambent* suggests something softly bright or radiant, either emitting or suffused (word 17 of level 3) with light, as *a lambent jewel, lambent eyes,* or *the lambent screen of her Kindle.* And in its third sense, *lambent* is used figuratively to suggest a light, playful, brilliant style, as *lambent flashes of wit* or *the lambent melodies of Mozart's comic operas.*

Word 36: SUPERVENE (SOO-pur-**VEEN**)
To happen afterward as an additional, unrelated, or unexpected consequence. Also, to follow closely or come shortly after, especially as a consequence; to ensue.

The verb to *supervene* comes from the Latin *supervenīre,* to come down on top of, or to come up unexpectedly, a combination of *super-,* over, above, beyond, and *venīre,* to come. By derivation, when something supervenes it comes from above or beyond; the word "suggests the following or beginning of something unforeseen or unpredictable" (*Merriam-Webster's Collegiate*). Specifically, what supervenes happens or follows, usually soon after, as an additional, unrelated, or unexpected consequence. If Congress passes a bad law, a lawsuit challenging its constitutionality may supervene. Farmers are suprised when a bad harvest supervenes after a favorable growing season. A headache may supervene a night of partying, or heartburn may supervene overeating. And pneumonia often supervenes in the final stages of a severe illness.

The noun is *supervention,* the act or an instance of supervening, following after as a consequence.

Word 37: VAINGLORIOUS (vayn-GLOR-ee-<u>us</u>)
Boastful, excessively proud of or vain about one's abilities or achievements.

The adjective *vainglorious* and the noun *vainglory* (VAYN-glor-ee) come from the Middle Latin *vāna glōria,* literally empty glory or fame. *Vainglory* is boastful pride, excessive and pretentious elation over one's accomplishments; *vainglorious* means characterized by or given to vainglory.

Vainglorious people behave as if they are smarter, more talented, and more important than everyone else, and they typically do not surround themselves or consort with people who might challenge that view. Celebrities whose heads have been puffed up by fame can be vainglorious, taking unwarranted and excessive pride in their status and achievements. And to some people, the owners of fancy sports cars are vainglorious—obnoxiously proud of and boastful about their expensive vehicles.

Take care not to confuse the adjectives *glorious* and *vainglorious*. *Glorious* is positive and means worthy of great praise or honor. *Vainglorious* is negative and means boastful, full of pride. Thus, a glorious novel is quite different from a vainglorious one.

Word 38: PETRIFACTION (PE-tri-**FAK**-shin)

The act or process of turning into stone, or something like stone; also, the state of being hardened or turned into stone.

The noun *petrifaction* and the verb to *petrify* come ultimately from the Latin *petra,* a stone, rock, and *facere,* to do, make. To *petrify* may mean to convert into stone or something like stone, as *petrified wood*. It may mean to harden, deaden, or immobilize, as *his emotions were petrified*. Or, in its best-known sense, it may mean to stun or paralyze with fear: "The horror movie petrified the child." *Petrifaction* is the act or process of petrifying in any of these senses, or the state of being petrified, hardened, paralyzed, or turned to stone.

Petrifaction is used literally in science and medicine of any conversion into stone or a stony substance, such as fossilization or calcification. It is also used to mean a hardening, deadening, or immobilization, a figurative turning into stone: "As Manny got older his inflexible political opinions underwent even greater petrifaction"; "Her shocking words caused petrifaction in the audience."

Word 39: FECULENT (FEK-yuh-lint)

Foul, filthy, filled with waste matter; hence, disgusting, offensive, revolting.

The adjective *feculent,* the noun *feculence,* and the noun *feces* (FEE-seez), excrement, waste matter discharged through the anus, all come from the Latin *faex, faecis,* which meant the dregs of any liquid, especially wine, or, figuratively, the dregs or lowest order of society.

In modern usage *feculent* is used literally of anything that is filled with waste matter, such as dregs, garbage, or excrement, and also figuratively of anything that is foul or filthy as if filled with disgusting waste matter. Thus, in the literal sense you can have feculent streets or feculent water, and in the figurative sense you can have feculent words, feculent lies, a feculent movie, or feculent music. This sentence illustrates the literal use: "The odor that rose up from the muck was horrible—stifling and feculent" (John Dalton, *Heaven Lake*). And this sentence illustrates the figurative use: "These fellows were simply the feculent scum . . . of civilization." (William Cowper Brann, 1898).

Word 40: SOLOMONIC (SAH-luh-**MAH**-nik)
Showing great wisdom and good judgment, especially in difficult situations; wise, reasonable, and fair.

Solomonic is an eponymous word derived from the name *Solomon,* a biblical king, the son and successor of David, who led the ancient Hebrews in the 10th century B.C. According to legend, Solomon was an exceptionally wise man. The Old Testament (1 Kings 3) recounts how God appears to Solomon in a dream and says, "Ask what I shall give thee." When Solomon does not ask for riches or a long life but instead for "a wise and an understanding heart," God is pleased with his humility and grants the request.

Straightaway, Solomon's wisdom and judgment are tested. Two women come to the new king with a baby that they both claim to be the mother of. To silence their bickering Solomon asks for a sword, and when it arrives he says, "Divide the living child in two, and give half to the one [mother], and half to the other." Fair enough—on paper, at least. But when they are about to cleave the poor baby, the true mother cries out, begging Solomon to let the child live and give it to the fraudulent mother, while the fraudulent mother coldly says, "Let it be neither mine nor thine, but divide it." With that, the king knew which woman was the true mother and he gave the child to her. And when the Israelites heard of his shrewd decision, "they saw that the wisdom of God was in him to do judgment." That is why today *Solomonic* is used to mean suggestive of the wisdom of Solomon, showing fairness and good judgment.

Synonyms of *Solomonic*, which is still customarily printed with a capital *S*, include *judicious, prudent, sage, sapient* (SAY-pee-int), *shrewd, sagacious, astute,* and *perspicacious* (word 44 of Level 4).

Review Quiz for Keywords 31–40

In each statement below, a keyword (in *italics*) is followed by three definitions. Two of the three are correct; one is unrelated in meaning. Decide which one doesn't fit the keyword. **Answers appear on page 338**.

1. An *anodyne* is a charm, a drug, a medicine.
2. If you are *autodidactic* you are self-trained, self-involved, self-taught.
3. A *jocund* person is merry, cheerful, self-assured.
4. A *simulacrum* is a copy, a likeness, a semblance.
5. To be *lambent* is to flicker, be gentle, be softly radiant.
6. To *supervene* is to happen afterward, happen suddenly, ensue.
7. A *vainglorious* person is powerful, proud, boastful.
8. *Petrifaction* is the state of being hardened, the process of becoming stone, the process of becoming old.
9. Something *feculent* is foul, stifling, revolting.
10. To be *Solomonic* is to be fair, firm, wise.

The Style File: Don't Think to Yourself

Nearly every day I read or hear a sentence like this one written by Jimmy Golen of The Associated Press: "And he thought to himself, 'We're next.'"

Unless you're thinking out loud, you always think *to yourself*. There is no other way to think. In any such construction involving thinking—or wondering, reflecting, musing, and ruminating—adding the preposition *to* and a reflexive pronoun such as *myself, yourself,* or *herself* is redundant. The good stylist lets the verb stand alone. So don't *think in your head* or *wonder to yourself.* Just think and wonder.

Here are the next ten keywords in Level 7:

Word 41: LEITMOTIF (LYT-moh-TEEF)

In a piece of music, a short, recurring theme or melodic passage associated with a person, thing, idea, or situation; by extension, any recurring idea, feature, or theme.

Leitmotif is a German loanword that means literally a leading motif. A *motif* (moh-TEEF) is a distinctive subject, central theme, or dominant feature in a work of art, literature, or music: "Resilience is the motif in these remarkable women's stories." In music, a motif is a brief melodic theme or passage from which more complex passages are developed. By contrast, a leitmotif is a short recurring musical theme or passage that evokes a particular person, situation, thing, or idea—a kind of musical quotation.

The leitmotif is often associated with the 19th-century German composer Richard Wagner (VAHG-nur), who used it often in his lengthy operas. But Wagner did not invent the leitmotif for it occurs in earlier compositions, including Mozart's comic opera *Così fan tutte* (1790). In *Peter and the Wolf* (1936), Sergei Prokofiev's beloved symphonic fairy tale for children, each character has a theme that is initially played in full, then briefly repeated throughout the composition as a leitmotif to musically illustrate the narrator's story. The flute plays the leitmotif of the bird; the oboe that of the duck; the clarinet that of the cat; the French horn that of the wolf; the bassoon that of the grandfather; and the strings play Peter's leitmotif, which is often evoked in just six notes.

In current usage *leitmotif* is also used more generally of any recurring theme, idea, or feature: "Curry is a leitmotif in the cuisine of India and Thailand"; "Obama promised many things and set lofty goals—'change' was his leitmotif" (*The Huffington Post*).

Word 42: SCARAMOUCH (SKAR-uh-mooch *or* -moosh)
A cowardly rascal or buffoon; a scamp.

Scaramouch, with a capital *S,* is the name of a stock character in farce and commedia dell'arte (kuh-MAY-dee-uh-del-**AHR**-tay, Italian popular comedy of the 16th to 18th centuries), a foolish, cowardly, boastful rascal who is continually flogged by the character Harlequin. With a lowercase *s, scaramouch* is a term of contempt for any boastful rascal or cowardly buffoon—not necessarily someone who is regularly beaten, but someone who perhaps deserves to be. In the Irish writer Justin Huntly McCarthy's 1901 play *If I Were King,* a character asks, "Why are the women all sunflowers to this scaramouch?"

The unusual word *poltroon* (pahl-TROON), from the Old Italian *poltrone,* a cowardly idler, is a colorful synonym of *scaramouch.* But a poltroon is a scaramouch squared: not just a boastful, cowardly buffoon but a wretched, worthless coward.

Word 43: EFFLORESCE (EF-luh-**RES**)
To bloom, blossom, burst forth into flowers. Figuratively, to flower, flourish, thrive.

The verb to *effloresce,* the adjective *efflorescent* (EF-luh-**RES**-int), and the noun *efflorescence* (EF-luh-**RES**-ints) all come from the Latin *efflōrescĕre,* to blossom, break into bloom, a combination of *ex-,* out, and *flōrescĕre,* to begin to blossom, come into flower. The ultimate source is the Latin *flōs, flōris,* a flower, blossom, the source of various English words, such as *floral,* pertaining to or consisting of flowers, and its fancier synonym, *floriated,* decorated with flowers; *florist,* a seller of flowers; *floriculture,* the growing of flowers; and *floriferous* (flaw-RIF-ur-us), bearing flowers.

By derivation, something that effloresces doesn't just bloom; it bursts into bloom. In New England, where I grew up, the crocuses, those welcome harbingers (word 38 of Level 4) of spring, push up through the half-frozen soil and effloresce, bloom swiftly and spectacularly. And in my backyard in Southern California, where I live now, the agapanthus (AG-uh-**PAN**-th<u>u</u>s) effloresce in June, breaking into a brilliant display of globular (GLAHB-yuh-lur) flowers that look like miniature fireworks. (*Globular* means globe-shaped, spherical.)

You may also use *effloresce, efflorescent,* and *efflorescence* of anything that flowers figuratively, that develops swiftly and flourishes or thrives. The tremendous growth in the vocabulary of English during the Elizabethan era (1533–1603) was an effloresence, a period of great flowering, for the language. An efflorescent artist is a blossoming, thriving artist, one who is bursting with creative output. And it is every parent's hope that their children will grow up and effloresce, flourish and succeed.

Word 44: SKEIN (SKAYN, rhymes with *train*)
"A length of thread or yarn wound in a loose long coil" (*American Heritage*). By extension, (1) anything suggesting the coils or twists of a skein; (2) a flock of wild fowl in flight; and (3) any succession of related things: a series.

Skein may come from the Vulgar Latin *scamniare,* to wind yarn. In its original sense, which dates from the 15th century, a skein is "a loosely coiled length of yarn or thread wound on a reel" (*Merriam-Webster's Collegiate*), as *a skein of wool, cotton, or silk.*

By the early 17th century *skein* had come to be used figuratively to mean something suggesting the coils of a skein, a complex tangle or web, as *a skein of lies, a skein of red tape,* or "a skein of Afghan tribal politics that we will never understand" (*The Wall Street Journal*). "For love is but a skein unwound / Between the dark and dawn," wrote the Irish poet W. B. Yeats in 1932. *Skein* has also been used of a flock of geese, ducks, or other wildfowl in flight, and from this use, perhaps, we get the word's most recent and extended sense: a series of similar or related things, as *watching a skein of boxcars pass by on the railroad tracks* or *her life has been a skein of tragedies.*

Word 45: INTERSTICE (in-TUR-stis)

A small or narrow space, gap, opening, or break between closely spaced things or parts.

The noun *interstice* comes from the past participle of the Latin verb *intersistĕre,* to pause, make a break, a combination of *inter-,* between, and *sistĕre,* to cause to stand, set, place. By derivation an interstice is something that stands between or creates a break between things, hence, a small or narrow gap or opening, as *an interstice in the clouds through which a single sunbeam shone;* "We all looked on with horrified amazement as we saw . . . the woman, with a corporeal body as real at that moment as our own, pass through the interstice where scarce a knife blade could have gone" (Bram Stoker, *Dracula*).

Interstices (in-TUR-sti-seez), the plural, are often small spaces or breaks between closely spaced things or parts. Picket fences and Venetian blinds have interstices. The interstices in tilework are filled with grout. Even your thoughts have interstices—breaks or intervals where your mind is not focusing on anything in particular.

Synonyms of *interstice* include *cleft, slit, rift, chink, crevice, cranny,* and *lacuna* (luh-K[Y]OO-nuh). The adjective is *interstitial* (IN-tur-**STISH**-ul), of the nature of an interstice, or forming or situated in an interstice, a small space or gap.

Word 46: COMMENTARIAT (KAH-mun-**TAIR**-ee-it)

The news media, seen as a class; especially, those members of the news media whose role it is to comment on politics and current events.

Commentariat is a freshly minted word, a neologism, coined in the United States in the 1990s. It is a portmanteau word, a blend of *commentary* and *proletariat,* the working class. Although *commentariat* is so wet behind the ears that it is not yet listed in some current dictionaries, you can bet that it will be soon, because in recent years its use has exploded. Today it appears frequently both in print and online. Here's one example from *The Wall Street Journal:* "He was actively opposed by a majority of the Congress and a commentariat that argued for everything from withdrawing immediately to partitioning the country."

The words *commentariat* and *punditocracy* are close in meaning. *Punditocracy* (PUHN-dit-**AH**-kruh-see), which was coined in the 1980s, is based on *pundit* (word 10 of Level 4), an expert who is called on to express opinions to the public. The punditocracy comprises members of the news media as well as experts who opine (word 13 of Level 2) publicly on various subjects of general interest. Initially the commentariat designated those members of the news media who opine on politics and current events, but the word is showing signs of differentiating itself from *punditocracy* by suggesting a broader and more plebeian (word 20 of Level 5) group that includes nonprofessionals, as *the online commentariat,* the people who broadcast their opinions on websites and blogs.

Word 47: PEREGRINATION (PER-i-gri-**NAY**-shin)
Travel from one place to another; a journey, especially one on foot.

Peregrination comes from the Latin *peregrīnātio,* a traveling or a staying in foreign countries, from *peregrīnus,* foreign, strange. Originally a peregrination was the spiritual journey of a person's life, one's sojourn (word 35 of Level 2) on earth. Later *peregrination* was used as a synonym of *pilgrimage,* as *a peregrination to Rome.* But the dominant meaning in modern usage, which took root in the 16th century, is a traveling or journey from one place to another, especially one made on foot.

A peregrination may be fairly short, as *a week of peregrination in the Cotswolds.* But it is usually long, as *his six-month peregrination around Europe.* And sometimes a peregrination is very long, as *several decades of persistent peregrination in the remotest parts of the world.* The word is also often used in the plural, *peregrinations,* to mean travels, wanderings, ramblings: "His book is an entertaining travelogue, an amusing account of his peregrinations."

The verb is *peregrinate* (PER-i-gri-nayt), to travel, journey, as *to peregrinate from the East Coast to the West.* The adjective is *peregrine* (PER-i-grin), traveling, wandering, as *a peregrine minister* or *a peregrine spirit.* The peregrine falcon, literally a wandering hawk, is prized for its swift and powerful flight.

Word 48: FILIGREE (FIL-i-gree)

Ornamentation, embellishment; anything very delicate, intricate, and fanciful.

Filigree comes from the Latin *filum,* a thread, and *grānum,* a grain or seed. Originally, filigree was ornamental jewelry work made of grains or beads; later, filigree was made of delicate threads of fine gold, silver, or other metal wire formed into lacy, intricate scrolls and patterns. Earrings, bracelets, rings, necklaces, buttons, goblets, window glass, the frames of paintings or mirrors, fabrics, containers, silverware, pens, and even doors, cabinets, and gates were applied with the delicate, intricate, and fanciful ornamentation of filigree. Eventually *filigree* also came to be used figuratively of any sort of delicate, fanciful ornamentation, whether fabricated or natural, as *a filagree of poetic images* or *a filigree of frost on frozen branches,* or of any fine and showy embellishment, as *the harp's rich, cascading filigree.*

You may also use *filigree* as a verb to mean to adorn with or as if with filigree, or as an adjective, spelled either *filigree* or *filigreed,* to mean delicately, intricately, and fancifully decorated, as *a filigree pattern* or *filigreed language.*

Word 49: GIMCRACK (JIM-krak)

Showy but useless, trivial, or worthless.

The origin of *gimcrack* is obscure. The word may be used as a noun meaning "a cheap and showy object of little or no use" (*American Heritage*), as *the gimcracks they give for prizes at the county fair.* Or it may be used as an adjective to mean "flimsy or poorly made but deceptively attractive" (*New Oxford American Dictionary*), as *the gimcrack prizes at the county fair.*

Gimcrack cookware, gimcrack jewelry, or gimcrack furniture— also called *borax*—may be good-looking but is cheaply and poorly made. Gimcrack prose or a gimcrack theory is showy and attractive on the surface but trivial or worthless on closer inspection. And Americans are obsessed with the gimcrack glamour of Hollywood, otherwise known as Tinseltown.

Synonyms of *gimcrack* include *shoddy, tasteless, gaudy,* and *trumpery* (TRUHM-puh-ree). The noun is *gimcrackery* (JIM-krak-uh-ree), cheap and showy ornaments, useless trifles, trinkets, knickknacks, or baubles (word 27 of Level 6).

Word 50: IMMITIGABLE (i-MIT-i-guh-bul)
Not able to be mitigated; that cannot be lessened or softened in force or intensity.

The verb to *mitigate* means to lessen in intensity, make less severe, and the adjective *mitigable* means capable of being mitigated, able to be softened or soothed. Because *immitigable* begins with the privative prefix *im-,* not, it means not mitigable, unable to be made less intense or severe. These words come ultimately from the Latin *mītigāre,* to soften, calm, soothe.

Anything that cannot be mitigated—moderated or alleviated—is immitigable. Immitigable pain cannot be lessened and immitigable sorrow cannot be relieved. A judge's immitigable sentence cannot be lessened or appealed. Immitigable darkness is constant darkness. Immitigable stubbornness is unrelenting; it never gives up. And immitigable hunger is insatiable, unable to be satisfied.

Unappeasable and *implacable* (im-PLAK-uh-buul) are synonyms of *immitigable.*

Review Quiz for Keywords 41–50
This time the review word is followed by three words or phrases, and you must decide which comes nearest the meaning of the review word. **Answers appear on page 339**.

1. Is a *leitmotif* a funny story, a recurring theme, or an ingenious plot?
2. Is a *scaramouch* a lover, a joker, or a rogue?
3. When something *effloresces,* does it break apart, break into bloom, or break into song?

4. Is a *skein* a small flaw, a tangle, or a shameful secret?

5. Is an *interstice* a narrow space, a point of connection, or an unspoken contract?

6. Is the *commentariat* the voters, the speechwriters, or the news media?

7. Is a *peregrination* a question, a journey, or an ordeal?

8. Is *filigree* an ancestral line, fine ornamentation, or a foolish fancy?

9. Is something *gimcrack* first-rate, eccentric, or worthless?

10. Would *immitigable* destruction be partial, avoidable, or unstoppable?

Once Upon a Word: *Semordnilap*

"Dear Wordmaster," writes James Phelan on my website. "My son has a boy whose name is Aidan. A neighbor has a child named Nadia, which is the reverse of Aidan. Is there a name for this?"

I would call that delightful coincidence a "name semordnilap" (sem-ORD-ni-lap). *Semordnilap*—a word that has long been used in recreational linguistics but that has not yet found its way into a dictionary for lack of more general use—is the word *palindromes* spelled backward. A palindrome (PAL-in-drohm) is a word, phrase, or sentence that says the same thing when read either forward or backward, as in *A man, a plan, a canal, Panama* and *Go hang a salami, I'm a lasagna hog.* A word-unit palindrome reads the same, word for word, forward and backward, as in *All for one and one for all.* By contrast, a semordnilap is a word that means one thing when read forward and another when read backward; for example, *part* turned around becomes *trap, wolf* becomes *flow, wood* becomes *doom,* and *straw* becomes *warts. Bob* and *Eve* are name palindromes; *Aidan* and *Nadia* is a name semordnilap. Another example of a name semordnilap is *Harpo* and *Oprah.*

Answers to Review Quizzes for Level 7
KEYWORDS 1–10

1. No. A *whimpering* person needs to be comforted. To *simper* is to smile in a silly, self-conscious, and often affected or simpleminded way.

2. Yes. To *denude* is to strip, make naked, or to deprive of something.

3. No. *Sui generis* means not like anything else, one of a kind, in a class by itself.

4. No. A *jeremiad* is a prolonged expression of sorrow or grief, or a long, mournful complaint, often laced with outrage.

5. Yes. Both a *sobriquet* and an *epithet* are descriptive names or nicknames.

6. No. A *pregnant* woman is going to have a baby. *Regnant* means ruling, reigning, dominant; exercising power, authority, or influence.

7. No. *Hauteur* is the opposite of *humility*—arrogance, haughtiness, condescension.

8. No. A *paterfamilias* is a man who is the head of a household or the father of a family; by extension, a man who is the leader of a tribe, community, or movement.

9. No. The *apogee* is the highest point, climax; originally, the point at which a heavenly body or object orbiting the earth is at its greatest distance from the earth.

10. Yes. Your *mien* is your bearing, air, or manner, especially when it reveals character, personality, attitude, or feeling.

KEYWORDS 11–20

1. False. *Dyspeptic* people are irritable and gloomy, grouchy and morose.

2. False. *Anaphora* is repetition of a word or phrase at the *beginning* of successive verses, clauses, or sentences. *Epistrophe* is repetition of a word or phrase at the end.

3. True. To *philander* is to flirt with and seduce many women.

4. True. A *missive* is a letter, a written message or communication.

5. False. *Penultimate* means next-to-last, not last.

6. True. *Zeitgeist* means the spirit of the age or times.

7. False. *Circumlocutory* means speaking indirectly or in a roundabout way. *Sententious* means full of, or given to using, aphorisms or maxims, or short, meaningful sentences.

8. True. To *interdict* is to prohibit or forbid, especially by command or decree.

9. False. *Malaise* is a vague, general feeling of discomfort or uneasiness.

10. False. Both your own children and your descendants are your *progeny.*

KEYWORDS 21–30

1. Antonyms. To *belie* is to misrepresent or disguise, or to show to be false or mistaken.

2. Synonyms. A *factotum* is a person employed to do all kinds of work, a handyman, jack-of-all-trades; hence, an employee or assistant who has many different duties.

3. Synonyms. Both *jingoism* and *chauvinism* mean overzealous, aggressive patriotism.

4. Antonyms. To *confirm* is to prove, verify. To *gainsay* is to deny or contradict.

5. Antonyms. *Verbicide,* as defined by the writer and physician Oliver Wendell Holmes (1809–1894), is "violent treatment of a word with fatal results to its legitimate meaning"; by derivation *verbicide* is the killing of a word. *Neology* is the invention of new words, phrases, usages, meanings, or expressions.

6. Synonyms. An *excrescence* is an outgrowth, lump, enlargement, or projection, especially when abnormal.

7. Synonyms. A *corbel* is a bracket that projects from a wall and supports a weight.

8. Antonyms. *Indolent* (word 48 of Level 4) means lazy, idle, inactive. *Sedulous* means involving or characterized by careful and persistent effort; diligent, painstaking.

9. Synonyms. To *maunder* is to talk in a rambling, dreamy, or meaningless way; or to move or act in an aimless, idle, or dreamy manner.

10. Antonyms. *Torpor* (see *torpid,* word 38 of Level 5) is a state of mental or physical sluggishness or dullness. *Saltation* is the act of leaping or jumping, a leap or jump; hence, the act of dancing, or a dance.

KEYWORDS 31–40

1. *Charm* doesn't fit; an *amulet* is a charm. An *anodyne* is a drug or medicine that relieves pain or anxiety.

2. *Self-involved* doesn't fit. *Autodidactic* means self-taught, self-trained.

3. *Self-assured* doesn't fit. *Jocund* means merry, cheerful, mirthful.

4. *Copy* doesn't fit. A *simulacrum* is a likeness or representation, a semblance.

5. *Be gentle* doesn't fit. *Lambent* means (1) moving or playing lightly over a surface, flickering; (2) softly radiant or bright; or (3) expressed in a light and brilliant style.

6. *Happen suddenly* doesn't fit. To *supervene* is to happen afterward as an unrelated or unexpected consequence, or to follow closely or come shortly after, ensue.

7. *Powerful* doesn't fit. *Vainglorious* means boastful, excessively proud.

8. *The process of becoming old* doesn't fit. *Petrifaction* is the act or process of turning into stone, or something like stone; also, the state of being hardened or turned into stone.

9. *Stifling* doesn't fit. *Feculent* means foul, filthy; hence revolting, disgusting.

10. *Firm* doesn't fit. *Solomonic* means fair, wise, reasonable, just.

KEYWORDS 41–50

1. A *leitmotif* is a short, recurring theme or melodic passage associated with a person, thing, idea, or situation; by extension, any recurring idea, feature, or theme.

2. A *scaramouch* is a cowardly, boastful rascal or rogue.

3. When something *effloresces* it breaks into bloom or flourishes, thrives.

4. A *skein* is a long loose coil of thread or yarn; by extension, anything suggesting the coils or twists of a skein, such as a complex web or tangle.

5. An *interstice* is a small or narrow space, gap, opening, or break between closely spaced things or parts.

6. The *commentariat* is the news media, especially those members whose role it is to comment on politics and current events.

7. A *peregrination* is a journey, travel from one place to another, especially on foot.

8. *Filigree* is fine ornamentation, anything very delicate, intricate, and fanciful.

9. Something *gimcrack* is showy but useless, trivial, or worthless.

10. *Immitigable* destruction would be unstoppable because it cannot be lessened or softened in force or intensity.

LEVEL 8

Word 1: PANOPLY (PAN-uh-plee)
An impressive array or splendid display.

Panoply comes from the Greek *panoplía*, from *pan-*, all, and *hopla*, arms, armor, the plural of *hoplon*, a weapon, tool, or piece of armor, especially the heavy shield worn by the *hoplites* (like *hop lights*), the heavily armed foot soldiers of ancient Greece.

A panoply may be a full suit of arms and armor, as *the panoply of a knight;* or, by extension, a panoply may be a protective or complete covering, as *the quilled panoply of the porcupine* or *a panoply of ice.* The word is also often used of any splendid display of full ceremonial attire and accessories, as in *the panoply of a military parade,* or "Last came the knightly Normans . . . with all the panoply of chivalry" from Sir Walter Scott's 1821 novel *Kenilworth.*

From these earlier and still current uses of the word has come the most popular sense: any magnificent array or striking display. You can have a panoply of shiny medals or colorful flags. You can have a panoply of heavenly stars or a panoply of Hollywood stars. You can have a panoply of tantalizing appetizers or desserts, or a panoply of high-priced lawyers or political consultants. You can even use *panoply* of an impressive or striking array of some intangible thing, as *a panoply of reforms,* or "a panoply of grim secrets" (*The Guardian*).

Word 2: RECHERCHÉ (ruh-shair-SHAY; *also, and chiefly British,* ruh-SHAIR-shay)

Sought out with great care; hence, very rare, obscure, exotic, exquisite, or refined.

Recherché comes from the past participle of the French verb *rechercher,* to search for carefully, investigate, the source also of the English *research.* Although *recherché* entered English about 1700 and is no longer printed in italics (which indicates a foreign borrowing), the word retains a French acute accent over the final *e.*

Recherché is used of things that must be sought out or procured with care and effort, and that are therefore rare, exotic, or obscure. The word is frequently used of fine art, as *a recherché collection of pre-Columbian figurines;* of fine food and wine, as *a recherché banquet that began with oysters, caviar, and champagne;* and of language, as *a recherché expression.* William F. Buckley Jr. was renowned, and often criticized, for displaying his large and often recherché vocabulary on his television show *Firing Line.* And Mark Twain had some satirical fun with the word when, in his 1869 travelogue *The Innocents Abroad,* he described an impressive group of Egyptian donkeys as "the best we had found anywhere, and the most recherché. I do not know what 'recherché' is, but that is what these donkeys were, anyhow."

Because *recherché* implies a rare and sophisticated knowledge or taste, it is often applied to something or someone who is overly elegant or refined, to the point of being affected, precious, or pretentious. For example, in his 1914 novel *The Titan,* Theodore Dreiser describes a member of Chicago's business elite as being "a small, polite, recherché soul, suggesting mansions and footmen and remote luxury . . ."

Word 3: VERTIGINOUS (vur-TIJ-i-nus)
Dizzy, or causing dizziness.

Synonyms of the adjective *vertiginous* include *giddy, lightheaded, disordered,* and *reeling.* Antonyms of *vertiginous* include *sober, steady, clearheaded, composed, unruffled, self-possessed,* and *imperturbable.*

Vertiginous comes from the Latin *vertīgo,* a turning or whirling round, which comes from *vertere,* to turn, the source of *revert,* literally to turn back, *convert,* literally to turn with, and *vertigo* (VUR-ti-goh), the technical term for dizziness.

Vertiginous is perhaps most commonly used to mean affected with vertigo, dizzy, or causing dizziness: "She spun around until she was vertiginous"; "They gasped when they reached the vertiginous edge of the cliff." It may also be used of a figurative dizziness or giddiness: "The prospect of gaining sudden wealth makes some people vertiginous." But the word has two other meanings in general use.

Vertiginous may be used to mean unstable, unsettled, or inconstant, apt to change quickly, as *a vertiginous economy* or *the court of public opinion is notoriously vertiginous.* It may also be used to mean whirling, spinning, rotating or revolving, as *the vertiginous motion of the earth on its axis* or *a vicious, vertiginous tornado.*

Word 4: KISMET (KIZ-met *or* KIZ-mit)
Fate, destiny, fortune; one's lot or portion in life.

The noun *kismet* entered English in the mid-19th century, coming through Turkish and Persian from the Arabic *qisma,* portion, lot, fate, from *qasama,* to divide, allot.

The words *fate, destiny, fortune, karma,* and *kismet* all refer to what happens to a person in this life or the next.

Fate is an inevitable and often predetermined condition or outcome, especially a bad one resulting in destruction or death: "The fate of the Confederacy was sealed when Vicksburg fell" (Ulysses S. Grant).

Destiny suggests an "invincible power conceived of as controlling human life and the operations of the universe" (Funk & Wagnalls *Standard Dictionary*): "I felt as if I were walking with destiny," wrote Winston Churchill in *The Gathering Storm* (1948), "and that all my past life had been but a preparation for this hour and this trial."

Fortune is the result of mysterious and incomprehensible controlling forces, good or bad. You can seek your fortune in life; you can be "fortune's fool," like Shakespeare's Romeo; or, like his Hamlet, you can "suffer the slings and arrows of outrageous fortune."

In Hinduism and Buddhism, *karma* is the force created by a person's actions, regarded as determining his or her fate either in this life or in reincarnation. In current usage *karma* is often used loosely and informally to mean merely good or bad luck.

Dictionaries define our keyword, *kismet,* as synonymous with *fate* or *destiny,* but while the latter words suggest an inevitable outcome determined by some controlling force, *kismet* is more like *karma* in suggesting an unknown or unexpected outcome, often a lucky and advantageous one, determined by one's actions or by chance. In other words, your destiny can deal you a bad hand and fate can seal your doom, while kismet can give you the talent you need to succeed and put you in the right place at the right time. If that happens, be sure to thank your lucky stars—otherwise known as *kismet.*

Word 5: TEMPORIZE (TEM-puh-ryz)

To act evasively or be indecisive so as to gain time; to stall or hedge.

The verb to *temporize* comes from the Medieval Latin *temporizāre,* to hang back, delay, wait for one's time. By derivation, temporizing is the act of delaying or hanging back until a more favorable time.

Temporize neatly captures in one word what various common idioms express in several. For example, *to drag one's feet, to sit on the fence, to sleep on it, to bide one's time,* and *to see which way the wind blows* are all ways of saying to *temporize,* to delay acting so as to gain time.

Temporizing is a way of life in politics and diplomacy, where ideological opponents or participants in negotiations often act evasively and draw things out so as to gain time: "As elected officials posture and temporize, families are bankrupted by health-care costs and forgo treatment they can't afford" (*Newsweek*). Temporizing is also often a popular official strategy in dealing with the ever-changing winds of the economy: "For a while, the Treasury [Department] can temporize with creative accounting, shifting money from one pile to another" (*The Wall Street Journal*). But you can temporize on a more mundane level as well—for example, in your relationships at work and at home—by acting evasively so as to gain time, avoid a conflict, or put off a decision.

Word 6: PLEONASM (PLEE-uh-naz'm)

The use of more words than are necessary to express an idea; also, an example of this.

The rhetorical term *pleonasm* comes through Latin from the Greek *pleonasmos,* abundance, which comes in turn from *pleonazein,* to be excessive, and *pleion,* more. The adjective is *pleonastic* (PLEE-uh-**NAS**-tik), and the rare word *pleonast* (PLEE-uh-nast) denotes a person addicted to pleonasm.

The familiar word *redundancy* is the generic term for needless repetition in the use of words. Like *redundancy, pleonasm* can refer to any superfluous repetition. More specifically, it denotes a word or phrase that can be deleted without altering the meaning, or "the use of words whose omission would leave one's meaning intact" (*Webster 2*). "We know we have a pleonasm," writes Arthur Quinn in *Figures of Speech: 60 Ways to Turn a Phrase,* "when we can eliminate words without changing meanings."

Everywhere you look you will find pleonasms embedded in our speech and writing, from the substandard *where is it at?* and *more preferable* to the ubiquitous *free gift* and *close proximity.* Pleonasm takes root in the innocently redundant habits of childhood, as in *My friend, she told me* (a double subject), and reaches full flower in the countless excesses of adulthood that we utter without thinking, such as *hot water heater, future plans, past history, added bonus, three a.m. in the morning,* and *the reason . . . is because* (*because* means "for the reason that").

There are scores of pleonastic set phrases in the language—such as *write down, tiny bit, tiny little, none at all, temper tantrum,* and *up in the air*—that only a pedant* would fret about. But there are also many common word combinations that careful users of the language would find objectionably pleonastic. Consider the excess verbiage (VUR-bee-ij: three syllables, not two) in the phrase *excess verbiage*—have we forgotten that *verbiage* means an overabundance of words? Now consider the superfluous words in such familiar phrases as *safe haven, lag behind, my personal opinion, filled to*

---

* A *pedant* (PED'nt) is a person who "lays an undue stress on exact knowledge of detail or of trifles, as compared with larger matters or with general principles" (*The Century Dictionary*).

capacity, best ever, brief summary, pick and choose, ultimate goal, root cause, pizza pie, and *empty hole.* We say and print those and many other pleonasms countless times a day.

Many pleonastic phrases—such as *any and all, fit and proper, aid and abet, save and except, sole and exclusive, null and void, terms and conditions, cease and desist,* and *various and sundry*—have been adopted from legal jargon. Other common pleonastic twins that usage authorities condemn include *if and when, unless and until, compare and contrast, first and foremost,* and the much-despised *each and every.*

Let's close this discussion with a short list of hackneyed (word 1 of Level 4) phrases that are indefensibly pleonastic: *final conclusion; end result; new recruit; temporary reprieve; necessary requirement; advance warning* (or *planning*); *opening gambit; compete* (or *meet* or *interact*) *with each other; true* (or *actual* or *real*) *fact; passing fad; fresh new* (*idea, look,* etc.); *new beginning* (or *innovation*); *general consensus; congregate together; continue to remain; endorse on the back;* and *dwindling down,* which my wife gleefully caught me saying long ago, in my pleonastic youth.

Word 7: VERISIMILITUDE (VER-i-si-**MIL**-i-t[y]ood)
The appearance of or resemblance to truth or reality.

The noun *verisimilitude* comes from the Latin *vērisimilitūdō,* probability, which comes in turn from *vērī,* the genitive of *vērum,* the truth, reality, and *similis,* like, resembling. From the same source comes the uncommon adjective *verisimilar* (VER-i-**SIM**-uh-lur), which means having the appearance of truth, as *a verisimilar story.*

If it is true that art imitates life, then artists must be concerned with verisimilitude, the quality in their work that makes it seem lifelike, real, and believable. The sculptures and frescoes of the neoclassical artist Michelangelo Buonarroti (1475–1564) are brilliant examples of verisimilitude, so convincing in their resemblance to reality that we overlook how the people and things portrayed are much larger than life. Writers of realistic fiction and drama must also strive for verisimilitude, creating characters who seem like real people and settings that evoke recognizable places. Modern filmmakers employ all manner of special effects to achieve verisimilitude, and video game designers pride themselves on the level of verisimilitude they can give their animated digital creations.

Word 8: CABAL (kuh-BAHL *or* kuh-BAL)
A group of secret plotters, a conspiracy; also, the plot or scheme of such a group.

The noun *cabal* comes from the Hebrew *qabbālāh,* tradition, literally something received or handed down, the source also of the English *cabala* (KAB-uh-luh or kuh-BAH-luh), an esoteric and mystical system of interpreting Scripture, developed by rabbis, that arose in the 7th century and lasted into the 18th. "Cabalistic interpretation of Scripture was based on the belief that every word, letter, number, and even accent contained mysteries interpretable by those who knew the secret," says the *Columbia Encyclopedia.* "The system degenerated into juggling with letters and formulas and became the basis of much medieval magic."

Cabal was initially a variant of *cabala,* but since the mid-17th century *cabal* has been used of any small group of plotters who conspire against a government or against someone in authority. In 1865, the actor and Confederate sympathizer John Wilkes Booth led a cabal that plotted the assassination, on April 14, of President Abraham Lincoln.

The word *cabal* was also famously applied to five cabinet ministers of Charles II, king of England from 1660 to 1685. Although this group did not conspire against the throne, people were much taken by the fact that the first letters of their names—Clifford, Arlington, Buckingham, Ashley, and Lauderdale—happened to spell *cabal.*

Word 9: POSTPRANDIAL (pohst-PRAN-dee-ul)
Happening or done after a meal, especially after dinner.

Postprandial comes from the Latin *post,* after, and *prandium,* a meal, repast. The word may refer to any meal, but it is usually used of dinner: *a postprandial speech, a postprandial snifter of brandy, a postprandial stroll,* or, for the elderly, *a postprandial nap. Anteprandial,* beginning with the Latin *ante,* before, means happening or done before a meal. And *prandial,* as you might guess, means of or pertaining to a meal, relating to dinner or dining, as *a prandial invitation* or *prandial expenses.*

Word 10: ONOMATOPOEIA (AHN-uh-MAT-uh-**PEE**-uh)
The formation or use of a word in imitation of the sound that a thing or an action makes.

Onomatopoeia comes from the Greek *onomatopoíia,* the making of words, a combination of *onoma,* a name, and *poiein,* to make, the ultimate source of the English word *poet.* The adjective is *onomatopoeic* (AHN-uh-MAT-uh-**PEE**-ik)

When I was a kid I loved to read comic books about superheroes battling supervillains in a mythic clash between good and evil. Because comics don't have soundtracks, the illustrator would include big, bold words with exclamation points to depict the sounds of the struggle: *Wham! Bash! Crunch! Pow! Kaboom!* I didn't know it then, but all these smashing words were classic examples of onomatopoeia.

"The sound must seem an echo of the sense" proclaimed the 18th-century English poet Alexander Pope, providing us with a concise guideline for creating onomatopoeic words, ones formed in imitation of a sound. Today, the English language contains a vast number of onomatopoeic words, most of them short and vivid like the sounds they represent. Many imitate the sounds that animals make: the *buzz* of a bee; the *bowwow* of a dog; the *croak* of a frog; the sibilant (word 9 of Level 4) *hiss* of a snake; and the lyrical *cock-a-doodle-doo* of a rooster. Many others imitate sounds in nature, such as *crack, thud, clunk, pop, plop,* and *whoosh,* or the sounds that objects make, such as the *ding-dong* of a bell; the *clackety-clack* of a keyboard; the *tick-tock* of a clock; the *bang* or *rat-a-tat-tat* of a gun; and the *beep!* of almost every dadblamed thing in this digitized age. Still others imitate sounds human beings make that convey meaning, such as *shush, pssst, brrrr, ahem, hmmm, pshaw,* and *phew.*

Onomatopoeia is commonly mispronounced with *monna* in the middle: *ono-MONNA-poeia.* Take care to put a *mat* in the word: *onna-MAT-opoeia.*

Review Quiz for Keywords 1–10

Consider the following questions and decide whether the correct answer is yes or no. **Answers appear on page 384**.

1. Would a panoply be impressive?
2. Is something recherché exotic or obscure?
3. Does something vertiginous make you impatient?
4. Can you determine or shape your kismet?
5. If you temporize, do you stall?
6. Is *completely surrounded* a pleonasm?
7. Do abstract expressionist paintings have verisimilitude?
8. Is a cabal a group of plutocrats?
9. Would a postprandial cigar be smoked after dinner?
10. Is onomatopoeia the formation of words from names?

Style File: Find the Pleonasms

In each of the following sentences there's a common pleonasm that eluded a copyeditor. If you can spot them all, you have a fine eye for superfluous words.

1. "Federal and local authorities surrounded a small bank in Buena Park where an armed gunman was said to be holding at least one hostage" (*Los Angeles Times*).
2. "Banks began offering cards with a variety of different interest rates and fees" (*The New York Times*).
3. "He has . . . just recently released his first documentary film" (Reuters).
4. "The band performed three original numbers that they had written" (San Diego public radio).
5. "Lynchburg is presently facing a $500,000 free-speech complaint" (*Lynchburg News & Advance*, Virginia).
6. "Up until now, premium producers like Mercedes-Benz have had an easier time weathering economic storms" (*BusinessWeek*).
7. "Their home is still in the process of being renovated after Hurricane Katrina" (Associated Press).
8. "They continued on for 600 miles" (*The Washington Times*).

9. "A keyless chuck is included with it" (*Pittsburgh Post-Gazette*).

10. "Both author and illustrator focus in on the boy as he wonders aloud what life will be like for him when he's grown" (*The New York Times*).

EXPLANATIONS

1. A gunman is a person armed with a gun. Strike *armed*.

2. The word *variety* means "a number of different things thought of together" (*Webster's New World College Dictionary*), so pairing it with *different* is pleonastic.

3. Pairing *just* with *recently* is pleonastic. Use one or the other.

4. The last four words, *that they had written,* are repetitive and superfluous. Or you could keep them and delete *original*.

5. *Presently facing* is pleonastic; *facing* conveys the meaning by itself.

6. *Until* means "up to the time of," so pairing it with *up* is redundant. Make it *until now* or *up to now*.

7. The phrase *in the process of* adds nothing but baggage to the sentence.

8. *On* after *continue* or *proceed* is pleonastic because those verbs mean to go on.

9. Strike *with it* and let *included* do its work alone.

10. When you focus, you concentrate your attention *on* something. The word *in* is unnecessary after *focus*. If you mean to bring into close-up, as with a photographic lens, use *zoom in on* instead.

Now let's return to the *Word Workout* vocabulary for Level 8.

Word 11: DUDGEON (DUHJ-un)
A feeling or a sudden fit of anger, resentment, or indignation.

The origin of *dudgeon* is unknown.

In modern usage *dudgeon* usually appears after the adjective *high*—"She stormed out of the meeting in high dudgeon"—or sometimes after *great*: "Nothing could mollify her great dudgeon." But you can also express your dudgeon, nurse your dudgeon, and go home in a dudgeon. Here's a citation from *The Wall Street Journal* for the unmodified *dudgeon*: "The boxing world is in a dudgeon about these recommendations."

The nouns *umbrage, pique, huff,* and *dudgeon* all suggest "an emotional response to or an emotional state resulting from a slight or indignity," says *Merriam-Webster's Collegiate Dictionary*.

Umbrage (UHM-brij), from the Latin *umbra*, shade, suggests a person "shadowed in offended pride, retreating into the darkness of proud indignation."★ *Umbrage* usually appears in the phrase *to take umbrage*, meaning to take offense because of an insult or slight to one's dignity or pride: "She took umbrage at his rude manner." You may also *feel* umbrage, resentment, or *give* umbrage, offense, but these locutions are less common. (*Locution* is word 22 of Level 6.)

Pique (pronounced like *peek*), from the French *piquer*, to prick, suggests a temporary feeling of anger or resentment because of an insult to one's vanity or self-respect. You can be in a pique, have a fit of pique, or just feel pique: "John's pique over Morty's insolent remarks put Rachel in a pique too, and they both soon left the party in a double fit of pique."

A *huff* is a peevish or petulant (word 35 of Level 4) fit of sulking or brooding anger, usually prompted by a small, insignificant slight: "They were in a huff over the umpire's questionable call"; "The argument ended with him marching off in a huff."

Our keyword, *dudgeon*, may suggest a feeling of anger or resentment prompted by some real or imagined offense, but it often suggests a fit of self-righteous anger or indignation: "The chairman resigned from the committee in high dudgeon."

Word 12: HEGEMONY (hi-JEM-uh-nee)
Leadership, dominance, preponderant influence or authority.

The noun *hegemony*, which entered English in the 16th century, comes from the Greek *hegemon*, leader, which for a little over a century has also been an English noun meaning a leader or ruling power, a person or nation that exercises hegemony. A 1904 issue of *The Forum* contained this sentence: "The hegemon [HEJ-e-mahn] of the Western hemisphere is the United States."

Hegemony, leadership, dominance, is commonly exercised by a nation, state, or confederation. In ancient Greece, the city-states

---

★ From *A Dictionary of Contemporary American Usage* by Bergen and Cornelia Evans.

of Athens and Sparta continually vied for hegemony, and for centuries Britain, France, and Spain fought for hegemony in Europe. But hegemony may also be exercised by a dominant social, cultural, or ideological group. For example, liberals and conservatives battle for political hegemony, the United States and China compete for economic hegemony, Yale and Harvard contend for intellectual hegemony, and Amazon.com has achieved hegemony in the online retail world.

The adjective is *hegemonic* (HEJ-i-**MAH**-nik), which may mean either ruling, leading, predominant, as *the hegemonic power in the region,* or pertaining to or characterized by hegemony, as *a nation with hegemonic ambitions.*

Word 13: PREMONITORY (pre-MAH-nuh-tor-ee)
Giving warning; serving to notify beforehand.

The adjective *premonitory* and the better-known noun *premonition* (PREE-muh-**NISH**-un) come from the Latin *praemonēre,* to forewarn, advise beforehand. A *premonition* may be a forewarning, but it is usually used to mean a feeling of anticipation or anxiety about a future event; *presentiment* (pri-ZEN-ti-ment) is a close synonym of *premonition.* An *admonition,* from the Latin *admonēre,* to warn, remind, is a strong but gently expressed warning or reminder. And the adjective *monitory* means giving an admonition, serving to warn or remind: "He heard the chill, monitory wail of an air raid siren" (Eileen Dunlop, *The House on the Hill,* 1987).

Premonitory adds to *monitory* the implication of warning or alerting someone well before an anticipated event. You can detect premonitory symptoms of a disease or experience the premonitory tremors of an earthquake. A premonitory speech or letter warns of something to come—usually something adverse or disastrous. And a premonitory dream gives forewarning, serving to notify you of some future event.

Word 14: RETRONYM (RE-truh-nim)
"An adjective-noun pairing generated by a change in the meaning of the noun, usually because of technology" (Richard Lederer, *Crazy English*).

Retronym combines *retro-,* back or backward, and *-onym,* a word or name, from the Greek *onoma,* name. The word was coined in the 1970s by Frank Mankiewicz, the president of National Public Radio, who was intrigued by the proliferation (proh–LIF–uh–**RAY**-shin, rapid growth or spread) of what William Safire, the longtime language columnist for *The New York Times,* once described as noun phrases "created to denote things that have been overtaken by events."

When the world changes, the English language changes right along with it, and retronyms are an obvious manifestation of that change, especially when it is driven by advances in technology. For example, we used to have a guitar, but now we have the retronyms *electric guitar* and *acoustic guitar.* We used to have books, but the advent of *paperback books* begot the phrase *hardcover books,* and now we also have *ebooks.* We used to have plain old milk, but now we have *whole milk, reduced-fat milk,* and *fat-free* or *skim milk.* And we used to have mail, but now we have *email, voice mail,* and *snail mail.*

The word *telephone* has spawned a slew of retronyms in recent years. Once there were only *telephones,* but then the *rotary phone* was supplanted (word 17 of Level 2) by the *touch-tone phone,* which was supplanted by the *cordless phone,* which may be supplanted by what was first a *mobile phone,* then a *cellphone,* and then a *smartphone.*

Retronyms can also reflect societal as well as technological reforms. For example, when people began to challenge and redefine the traditional concept of marriage, we invented the retronyms *gay marriage, same-sex marriage,* and *heterosexual marriage.*

Word 15: RECUSE (ri-KYOOZ)
To remove or disqualify oneself as a judge, authority, or participant to avoid any suspicion of bias or conflict of interest.

The verb to *recuse,* which dates back to the 14th century, comes ultimately from the Latin *recusāre,* to object to, protest against, refuse, reject. *Recuse* is used chiefly in law in either of two ways. It may mean to object to or challenge a judge (or sometimes an attorney or juror) as unqualified to hear a case because of prejudice or conflict of interest: "The defense filed a motion to recuse the trial judge." More often, though, and especially in American usage, to *recuse* means to remove oneself from a position of judgment or authority to avoid the perception of personal interest or partiality: "When it came to light that Councilmember Burns owned shares in Smarmo Corporation, which is bidding for the city contract, she recused herself from the deliberations."

In *Coming to Terms,* William Safire observes that *recuse* "has a more legal connotation than *disqualify,* is more pointed than *excuse* and contains a reason that is not available in *remove* or *withdraw.*"

The corresponding noun is *recusal* (ri-KYOO-zul), the removal of oneself as a judge, authority, or participant because of actual or perceived bias or conflict of interest. A *recusant* (REK-yuh-zint) is a person who refuses to submit to authority or obey a law or command, or, historically, an English Roman Catholic who refused to attend services of the Church of England between 1570 and 1591.

Word 16: PENURY (PEN-yuh-ree)
Extreme poverty.

Synonyms of *penury* include *privation* (word 16 of Level 3), *indigence,* and *destitution.* Antonyms of *penury* include *affluence* (AF-loo-ints; stress the first syllable, not the second), *prosperity,* and *opulence* (AHP-yuh-lints).

Penury comes from the Latin *pēnūria,* a lack, want, especially a lack of the necessities of life. *Pēnūria* comes in turn from the Greek *peina,* hunger.

Penury has been used to mean severe poverty since before 1500. Here's how the Anglo-Irish writer Maria Edgeworth used *penury* in her 1801 novel *Belinda:* "Her father had a small place at court, lived beyond his fortune, educated his daughter . . . as if she were to be heiress to a large estate; then died, and left his widow absolutely in penury." And here's a contemporary citation from *The Huffington Post:* "It can mean the difference between owning a home or renting, sending your kids to college versus sending them to flip burgers, and a decent retirement versus penury in old age."

The adjective is *penurious* (p<u>e</u>-NYOOR-ee-<u>u</u>s), living in or characterized by penury, extreme poverty.

Word 17: ROUÉ (roo-AY, rhymes with *do say*)
A lecherous, dissolute man, one devoted to immoral behavior and sensual pleasure. (*Dissolute* is word 7 of Level 6.)

English borrowed the noun *roué* directly from French in the late 18th century. The word means literally a person broken on the wheel, for it was formed from the past participle of the French verb *rouer*, to break on the wheel, which goes back to the Latin *rota*, a wheel, the source of the English *rotate, rotary,* and *rotavirus*, any of a group of wheel-shaped viruses that cause intestinal distress.

Why is a roué, a dissolute man, by derivation someone broken on the wheel? The word was first applied to the profligate companions of Philippe II (Duke of Orleans and Regent of France from 1715 to 1723), who, because of their dissolute and depraved lifestyle, were said to deserve this punishment. Because of this derivation, *roué* was for a long time applied chiefly to dissipated young men of wealth and privilege, as in this sentence from the 1847 novel *Jane Eyre* by Charlotte Brontë (properly BRAHN-tee, not -tay): "I knew him for a young roué of a vicomte [French for *viscount*, pronounced VY-kownt]—a brainless and vicious youth." However, the *OED* notes that in current usage a roué is often a debauched elderly man, so it appears that young roués, if they survive their early excesses, can grow up to be old ones—not unlike Mick Jagger and Keith Richards, those rickety roués of the Rolling Stones.

Synonyms of *roué* include *playboy, rake, lecher,* and *libertine* (**LIB**-ur-TEEN).

Word 18: LUDDITE (LUH-dyt)
A person fanatically opposed to technological innovation, especially to any machine or labor-saving device perceived to replace workers.

The eponymous noun *Luddite*, which is still printed with a capital *L*, comes from the name Ned Ludd, "a Leicestershire village idiot . . .

who in the late eighteenth century broke several stocking frames belonging to his employer," says the *Morris Dictionary of Word and Phrase Origins*. "The name was taken by a group of workers who, between 1811 and 1816, tried to halt what came to be called the Industrial Revolution by smashing new labor-saving textile machinery."

In his *Dictionary of Eponyms,* Robert Hendrickson explains that "the masked bands of workers who made night raids on English factories were protesting layoffs, low wages, and poor quality goods, all caused by the large-scale introduction of textile machines to replace handicraft. . . . Today a *Luddite* is anyone who fears and would eliminate automation—not only for the unemployment it creates, but for its effect on the quality of life. . . . In our rebellion against an impersonal society the word is used much more sympathetically than before."

In other words, in hindsight the Luddites were prescient about the consequences of technology. (*Prescience* is word 21 of Level 6.) Sociologically speaking, the Industrial Revolution made the individual subordinate to the machine. That's something to keep in mind before you use the word *Luddite* for a person who is mistrustful of progress or who is reluctant to embrace technological change. Better to reserve the word for someone unreasonably or fanatically opposed to any kind of innovation.

Word 19: SCHADENFREUDE (SHAHD-'n-FROY-duh)

Malicious joy in the misfortune of others; pleasure derived from another's troubles.

Schadenfreude is a German loanword, a combination of the German *Schaden,* harm, and *Freude,* joy. Though it has been used in English since the 19th century, it is still sometimes (unnecessarily) printed with a capital *S.*

In *They Have a Word for It,* Howard Rheingold asks, "Why do people laugh at cartoons that show people slipping on banana peels? What is so funny about the way the Three Stooges bonk one another? One of the peculiar defining characteristics of the human race seems to be related to our strange and sometimes sadistic sense of humor."

In contemporary America, where no opportunity to make a buck is overlooked, people have made a thriving business out of schadenfreude. From tabloids that revel in exposing the foibles and misfortunes of celebrities to TV shows featuring home videos of embarrassing and often injurious mishaps, other people's pain has become our pastime and our guilty pleasure. And now you have a word for that: *schadenfreude*.

Word 20: COSTIVE (KAHS-tiv *or* KAW-stiv)
"Slow or reluctant in speech or action" (*New Oxford American Dictionary*).

The adjective *costive* comes from the Latin *constipāre,* to press or crowd together, the source of the English verb to *constipate,* which originally meant to crowd or press together but which now means to confine the bowels.

When it entered English about 1400, *costive* meant constipated, suffering from constipation, and this meaning is still in good standing, as a *costive diet* or a *costive animal.* But the word is also often used figuratively to mean uncommunicative, unforthcoming, slow or reluctant to speak or act: "She sat down at the narrow dining-table, and he seated himself opposite, with the costive feeling of one who cannot find words that will ring true" (John Galsworthy, *The Silver Spoon,* 1926); "Gradually, the British withdrew into a private and costive and repressed universe where eventually they could say . . . 'We don't rule [India] anymore. We preside over it'" (Christopher Hitchens, *The Atlantic,* 2008).

Review Quiz for Keywords 11–20
Consider the following statements and decide whether each one is true or false. **Answers appear on page 385.**

1. When you're in a dudgeon, you're confused.
2. A nation that exercises hegemony has leadership or sway over other nations.
3. A premonitory phone call informs you of something bad that's happened.

4. *Electric car* is a retronym.

5. When you recuse yourself, you assert your innocence.

6. Someone living in penury is serving time in jail.

7. If your husband is a roué, he's faithful to you.

8. People who are fanatically opposed to new technology are Luddites.

9. Schadenfreude is the experience of feeling someone else's pain.

10. A talkative person is costive.

Difficult Distinctions: *Forbidding* and *Foreboding*

The adjective *forbidding* (for-BID-ing), from the verb to *forbid,* is used of that which forbids or strongly discourages approach. Something forbidding may appear hostile, menacing, or sinister, as *a forbidding stranger, a forbidding scowl,* or *forbidding storm clouds.* Something forbidding may also be uninviting because it is bleak or grim, as *a rocky, forbidding coastline* or *a forbidding fortress.* Or something forbidding can be dangerous or threaten to obstruct or hinder progress, as *a dense, forbidding jungle.*

The word *foreboding* (for-BOH-ding), which begins with the combining form *fore-,* beforehand, comes from the verb to *forebode,* which may mean to predict or give an omen of, foretell, portend, as *to forebode evil,* or to anticipate a future event, especially a bad or unfortunate one: "The moment she saw him she foreboded mischief." As a noun *foreboding* is a synonym of *premonition* (PREE-muh-NISH-un) and means a sense or sign of impending evil or misfortune, as *a foreboding of coming trouble* or *an atmosphere of dread and foreboding.* As an adjective *foreboding* means ominous, portending evil or misfortune, as *the foreboding music of Alfred Hitchcock's movies.*

The common mistake, easily found on Google News, is to use the adjective *foreboding,* ominous, to mean *forbidding,* uninviting, dangerous, or menacing. For example, in *a foreboding challenge, foreboding woods,* and *the creepy and foreboding Roderick Usher, foreboding* should properly be *forbidding.*

Here are the next ten keywords in Level 8:

Word 21: **GALLIMAUFRY** (GAL-i-**MAW**-free)
A jumbled or confused mixture.

The plural is *gallimaufries* (GAL-i-**MAW**-freez).

Gallimaufry comes from Middle French *galimafree,* a stew or sauce, a word of unknown origin that is probably a conflation★ of *galer,* to amuse oneself, make merry—the source of the English adjective *gallant*—and *mafrer,* to gorge oneself. Although *gallimaufry* has been used to mean "a dish made by hashing up odds and ends of food" (*OED*), that sense is now rare and the figurative meaning, a jumbled or confused mixture, has prevailed since the mid-16th century.

Gallimaufry is one of many colorful English words for miscellaneous mixtures. Its synonyms include *hodgepodge, medley, miscellany, mishmash, pastiche, salmagundi, mingle-mangle, mélange, potpourri, olio, olla podrida,* and *farrago.* Let's take a closer look at these interesting words.

The word *hodgepodge* (HAHJ-pahj) is an alteration of *hotchpotch,* a thick soup or stew of vegetables and meat. It may refer to any diverse mixture, as *a hodgepodge of humanity,* but it may also refer to "a clumsy mixture of ingredients" (*OED*), a thoughtless jumble, as *a hodgepodge of architectural styles.*

A *medley* (MED-lee) may be any mixture of dissimilar or diverse elements, but specifically the word refers to a musical composition consisting of short pieces or passages from a variety of sources.

Miscellany (MIS-ul-ay-nee) is the noun corresponding to the adjective *miscellaneous.* Like a medley, a miscellany may be any miscellaneous collection of things, or the word may refer specifically to a literary work composed of writings by different authors on various topics.

Mishmash (pronounced to rhyme with *fish hash*), which is sometimes spelled *mishmosh* (and pronounced to rhyme with *pish-posh*), comes from Middle English but is probably related to the German *Mischmasch* and the Yiddish *mish-mash.* There is no question that Jewish culture has done much to popularize the word in the United

---

★   *Conflation* is the noun corresponding to the verb *to conflate,* word 19 of Level 4.

States. In *The Joys of Yinglish,* Leo Rosten defines it not just as a jumble or hodgepodge, as dictionaries often do, but as "a mess," "a fouled-up state of things," "confusion galore." When you think of a mishmash, think of a chaotic mixture, a muddle, as *a book that presents a mishmash of ideas seemingly chosen at random.*

Pastiche (pas-TEESH) comes through French from the Italian *pasticcio,* a pie made from a mixture of meat and pasta. In English, *pastiche* may refer to an artistic work—such as a novel, painting, or musical composition—that borrows various styles, selections, or motifs from other works, or it may refer to an artistic work that humorously imitates or parodies a particular style or another artistic work.

A *salmagundi* (SAL-muh-**GUHN**-dee) is, by derivation, a kind of salad made of chopped meat or fish, eggs, anchovies, onions, sometimes other vegetables, and oil. Since the 18th century *salmagundi* has also been used figuratively of any diverse mixture or medley, as "Her memoir is a salmagundi of experience seasoned with wit and wisdom."

Mingle-mangle combines the verbs to *mingle,* to mix or associate with, and to *mangle,* to injure, spoil, or ruin. Like *gallimaufry* and *hodgepodge, mingle-mangle* usually refers to a confused or jumbled mixture. The English language, which has freely and often haphazardly borrowed its vocabulary from dozens of foreign languages, is a mingle-mangle of words and tongues.

The noun *mélange*—may-LAH(N)ZH, with a nasalized French *n*—is related to the verb to *meddle,* which once meant to mix or mingle. In current usage a *mélange* is any mixture, blend, or collection, especially one composed of unrelated or inharmonious elements: "The Indian-style pizza is a spicy mélange of garam masala, ginger, turmeric, paprika, spinach, cilantro and green onions" (*San Jose Mercury News*).

A *potpourri* (poh-puh-REE) was originally a stew made with a mixture of meats; by derivation the word means a rotten pot (from French *pourrir,* to be rotten). That sense became obsolete and *potpourri* came to denote various things: a mixture of fragrant dried flower petals and spices used to perfume a room or closet; a musical medley; a literary miscellany; and finally, any mixture or miscellaneous collection of things or people, as *an interesting pot-pourri of art objects from all over the world.*

Both *olio* (OH–lee-oh) and *olla podrida* (AHL-uh-puh-**DREE**-duh) come from the Spanish *olla,* a pot or stew, and an *olla podrida* is literally a rotten pot, like a *potpourri.* Both words may denote a spicy Spanish or Portuguese stew of meat and vegetables, but more often they are used of any diverse mixture and are virtually interchangeable with *hodgepodge, medley,* and *potpourri.*

Farrago (fuh-RAY-goh) comes from a Latin word meaning mixed fodder for animals, a jumbled assortment of grains. In modern usage *farrago* may refer to any mixture, especially a confused or jumbled mixture, as "the farrago of errors known otherwise as Wikipedia, which . . . is regarded by many as a reliable research tool" (David Penberthy, *Herald Sun,* Australia).

Our keyword, *gallimaufry,* may apply either to things or to people and refers to "any inconsistent or ridiculous medley" (*The Century Dictionary*), as *a gallifmaufry of useless and discarded objects,* or *a galli-maufry of lies, tall tales, and superstition.* But *gallimaufry* (and *farrago*) can be neutral too, as in this excerpt from I. Moyer Hunsberger's introduction to *The Quintessential Dictionary:* "My wife and all seven of our offspring provided a veritable farrago of advice, a galli-maufry of helpful ideas, and omniscient encouragement as this dictionary was being compiled."

Word 22: ANALECTS (AN-uh-lekts)

Selected written passages, extracts, or fragments from an author or various authors; especially, a collection of such written passages: an anthology.

In classical Latin, the word *analecta* was used for a slave whose job was to clean the table after a meal, collecting any crumbs or scraps of food left behind. Originally in English *analects* followed this derivation literally; in his *Universal Etymological English Dictionary* of 1721, Nathan Bailey defined the word as "fragments gathered from Tables." But in postclassical Latin *analecta* came to mean a collection of literary fragments or extracts—after its own source, the Greek *analégein,* to pick up, gather up, collect—and it is this sense that has survived in the English *analects:* a selection, or a collection, of literary passages, extracts, or fragments by one author or several.

In modern usage the plural noun *analects* (the singular *analect* is so rare that most dictionaries don't list it) is most closely associated with *The Analects of Confucius,* a compilation of the maxims, aphorisms, and teachings of the Chinese philosopher Confucius, dating from the 4th century B.C. But *analects* can denote any collection of literary passages and tidbits, especially a miscellaneous or anecdotal collection, as *the analects of the sages* (a *sage* is a very wise person).

The Latin plural *analecta* is still sometimes used, but *Garner's Modern American Usage* says the English form *analects* is preferred.

Word 23: PARTURITION (PAHR-chuu-**RISH**-in *or* PAHR-tyuu-**RISH**-in)
Childbirth; the act or process of bringing forth offspring.

The noun *parturition* comes from the Latin *parturīre,* to be in labor. The word is chiefly used in medicine and biology, although it occurs occasionally in other nonfiction and in literature, as in this sentence from the 1973 novel *The Rachel Papers* by Martin Amis: "Mother's was a . . . generally rather inelegant parturition." The word may also be used figuratively of something that resembles childbirth; the long labor of writing a book, for example, is a kind of parturition.

The adjective *parturient* (pahr-T[Y]UUR-ee-int) means pertaining to childbirth or bearing offspring. The phrase *parturient amnesia* has been proposed for the act of forgetting, or the ability to forget, the pain of labor and delivery. In my book *There's a Word for It,* I wrote that "parturient amnesia is the oblivion that preserves our species, for without it, how many women would choose to have another child?"

The medical term *parturifacient* (pahr-t[y]uur-i-**FAY**-shint) may be a noun meaning a medicine or agent that induces or accelerates labor, or an adjective that means inducing or accelerating labor. In both these senses *parturifacient* is synonymous with *oxytocic* (AHK-si-**TOH**-sik), which comes from the Greek *oxys-*, sharp, quick, acute, and *tokos,* childbirth.

Word 24: ATRABILIOUS (A-truh-**BIL**-ee-u̲s)
Gloomy and irritable; peevishly melancholy.

Synonyms of *atrabilious* include *sullen, morose, surly, crabbed* (KRAB-id), *splenetic* (word 50 of Level 5), *hypochondriacal* (HY-poh-ku̲n-**DRY**-uh-ku̲l), *saturnine* (**SAT**-ur-**NYN**), and *dyspeptic* (word 11 of Level 7). Antonyms include *mirthful, exuberant, vivacious* (word 15 of Level 1), *sanguine* (SANG-gwin), and *jocund* (word 33 of Level 7).

The adjective *atrabilious* comes from the Latin *ātra bīlis,* black bile, which in ancient and medieval physiology was one of the four humors, or bodily fluids, thought to determine a person's health or disposition. If you were full of *blood,* also known as the sanguine humor, you were cheerful and confident. If you were full of *choler* (pronounced like *collar*), also known as yellow bile, you were passionate or hot-tempered. If you were full of *phlegm* (FLEM)—from which we get the word *phlegmatic* (fleg-MAT-ik), having a sluggish or apathetic temperament—you were either cool and indifferent or dull and sluggish. And if you were full of *melancholy,* also known as black bile, you were gloomy, miserable, or dejected.

By derivation, *atrabilious* means full of melancholy or black bile, and therefore gloomy or depressed. But the word, which entered English in the 17th century, has taken on another dimension in modern usage, suggesting not only a melancholy or morose disposition but also an irritable, dyspeptic one. An atrabilious temperament is gloomy but also sour or surly, melancholy but also cross or cantankerous, glum but also peevish or petulant, as in this sentence from *The Huffington Post:* "No doubt the usual cavalcade★ of atrabilious right-wing commentators will work overtime to . . . distort Obama's remarks."

Atrabilious may be used of people or, figuratively, of things. "The

---

★ *Cavalcade* (KAV-ul-kayd) comes from the Old Italian *cavalcare,* to ride on horseback, and the Latin *caballus,* a horse, the source also of the English *cavalier,* a horseman or mounted soldier. A cavalcade is a procession of people riding on horses or in horsedrawn carriages, or, by extension, any impressive procession or series.

Professor did not like Mr. Simpson," wrote the British-American writer Frank Harris (1856–1931) in his 1895 short story "Gulmore, the Boss." "The atrabilious face, the bitter, thin lips, and grey eyes veined with yellow, reminded him indefinably of a wild beast."

Word 25: TRANSMOGRIFY (tranz-MAHG-ri̱-fy)
To change or transform, especially in a strange, grotesque, or preposterous way.

The origin of the verb to *transmogrify* is uncertain. Coined sometime in the mid-17th century, it is probably a humorous pseudo-Latinism, meaning a word that looks like Latin but isn't, and in modern usage *transmogrify* usually implies a change or transformation that is humorous in a preposterous, bizarre, and sometimes grotesque way, as when the frog in the famous fairy tale is transmogrified into a prince.

To *transmute, transfigure, metamorphose,* and *transmogrify* all mean to change or transform.

To *transmute,* from the Latin *mūtāre,* to change, alter, shift, is to change completely from a lower state to a higher or more refined one: the medieval alchemists tried to transmute lead into gold.

To *transfigure* is closely associated with chapter 17 of the Gospel of St. Matthew, which tells how Jesus "was transfigured before them: and his face did shine as the sun, and his raiment was white as the light." Because of this *transfigure* often implies a change in outward appearance, especially one that glorifies or exalts: "A smile broke over his face, one of those powerful smiles that transfigure the very features of some men" (Ann S. Stephens, *The Old Homestead,* 1855).

To *metamorphose* (MET-uh-**MOR**-fohz), the verb corresponding to the noun *metamorphosis,* suggests a complete and usually striking change, often one effected by magic or supernatural means: "Incantations are muttered, a wand is waved, and your body begins to metamorphose into a horse" (*The Wall Street Journal*).

Our keyword, to *transmogrify,* implies a great transformation that is strange and often preposterous: "I was afraid to walk across the green shag broadloom because I thought there was a chance it would transmogrify into the Indian Ocean and drown me" (Samantha Bee, *i know i am, but what are you?*).

Word 26: SCREED (rhymes with *speed*)
A long and tedious speech or piece of writing.

The noun *screed* comes from the Middle English *screde,* a torn fragment, the source also of the word *shred,* a cut or torn-off fragment or strip. Originally *screed* was a synonym or variant of *shred;* later it was used of a strip or parcel of land and of a bordering edge, such as the frill of a cap. The modern use of *screed* in plastering and concrete work to mean a strip of plaster, wood, or metal used as a guide or leveling device probably came from these archaic senses.

The figurative use of *screed* to mean a long, monotonous discourse arose in the late 18th century, probably from the association of a narrow or torn-off strip with the idea of a long roll or list. In modern usage a screed is often roughly the same as a rant (word 9 of Level 1), a diatribe (word 1 of Level 2), or a harangue, denoting not only a lengthy and boring speech, essay, or book but also one that is angry or impassioned. As you can infer from that, *screed* is usually used pejoratively (*pejorative* is word 17 of Level 6), as *an illiterate, racist screed* or *a rambling, witless screed.* But once in a while you see it used, almost ironically, in a positive context: "In 1950, Dr. Seuss published a charming little animal-liberation screed titled *If I Ran the Zoo*" (vanityfair.com).

Word 27: MATUTINAL (muh-T[Y]OO-ti-nul)
Pertaining to, happening, or performed in the early morning or the period after waking.

The *OED* shows that *matutinal* has also occasionally been used to mean "rising early; active or alert in the morning," as in this surprisingly modern-sounding citation from 1834: "Our household was not the most matutinal in the world" (George Payne Rainsford James, *The Life and Adventures of John Marston Hall*).

Matutinal comes from the Latin *matutinus,* early in the morning or pertaining to the morning. *Matutinal* is related to the word *matins* (MAT'nz), which in the Christian church denotes early morning prayer. *Vespers*—from the Latin *vesper,* the evening or the evening star—are prayers or worship performed in the early evening. *Vespertine* (VES-pur-tin or -tyn) means belonging to or occurring in the evening. *Matutinal* means belonging to or occurring in the morning.

Matutinal may be used of almost anything pertaining to or done in the early morning. A novelist or poet might write of the matutinal crowing of a rooster or the matutinal dew on the grass, while a humorist might write of the matutinal consumption of coffee and doughnuts, or the matutinal ritual of oral hygiene, with its noisy gargling, throat-clearing, and expectoration (ek-SPEK-tuh-**RAY**-shin, a fancy word for spitting). Your matutinal routine is your morning routine, the things you do each day after waking up. This would likely begin with a few moments of *pandiculation* (pan-DIK-yuh-**LAY**-shin), yawning and stretching before getting out of bed.

Diurnal and *quotidian* (kwoh-TID-ee-in) both mean daily, happening or recurring each day—though *quotidian* may also mean ordinary, commonplace, of an everyday nature. *Nocturnal* means relating to or happening at night, and also active at night, as a nocturnal animal. *Matutinal* means relating to, occurring, or done in the early morning.

Word 28: CRAPULENT (KRAP-yuh-lint)
Suffering the ill effects of excessive eating or drinking; sick from overindulgence.

The adjective *crapulent* entered English in the 17th century; its cousin *crapulous,* with which it is interchangeable, is about a century older but less common in modern usage. Both words, along with the noun *crapulence,* sickness resulting from overindulgence in food or drink, come through the Latin *crāpula,* drunkenness, and especially its uncomfortable aftereffects, ultimately from the Greek *kraipálé,* a hangover. (In case you're wondering, the slang word *crap* does not share this source but comes from the Middle English *crappe,* chaff, rubbish, residue.)

If you eat or drink alcohol excessively you may become crapulent, which can involve not only the traditional headache of a hangover but also abdominal cramps, nausea, vomiting, and diarrhea. People, of course, get crapulent or suffer from crapulence, but certain things can be described as crapulent too; for example, in 2013, when the celebrity TV chef Paula Deen was disgraced for using racist language, one writer called her "the queen of crapulent food, sure to induce gout and diabetes."

Word 29: IPSO FACTO (IP-soh FAK-toh)
By the fact itself; by the very nature of the fact or deed.

Ipso facto is a 16th-century borrowing from Latin that means literally by the fact itself, *ipso* being the ablative of *ipse,* itself, and *facto* being the ablative of *factum,* fact. This Latin *ipse* occurs also in another phrase borrowed from Latin, *ipse dixit* (IP-see DIK-sit), literally he himself said it (from the Latin *dīcere,* to say, speak). In English we use *ipse dixit* of an assertion made without proof: "For a long time people believed the tobacco industry's ipse dixit that smoking wasn't harmful or addictive."

Ipso facto, by the fact itself, is a more formal way of saying *necessarily, in itself,* or *by its very nature:* "H. L. Mencken, who began his career as a police reporter in Baltimore, wrote that he quickly encountered what he called the 'police mentality': Every person accused or suspected of a crime is ipso facto guilty of that offense" (Jack Wardlaw, *The Times-Picayune,* New Orleans).

Word 30: DEBOUCH (di-BOOSH *or* di-BOWCH)
To emerge, issue, or march from a narrow or confined place into the open.

The verb to *debouch* comes from the French *déboucher,* to emerge, a combination of *de-,* out, and *bouche,* a mouth or opening. When *debouch* entered English in the mid-1700s it was a military word used to describe troops that marched from a confined area, such as a gorge or a defile, a narrow passage, into open ground: "We saw the column of infantry debouching into Minden plain," reported *The London Magazine* in 1760.

The word was soon applied to other things that emerged or issued from a mouth or outlet into an open or wider space: a stream debouching into a lake; cars debouching from narrow streets into wider avenues or highways; commuter throngs debouching from the bowels of the subway onto the street; angry wasps debouching from a disturbed nest. Here's a contemporary citation from *The Wall Street Journal* that anyone who remembers the terror and destruction of 9/11 can relate to: "The emergency-exit stairs at One World Trade Center will debouch to the street rather than into the lobby to head off a mayhem collision of firefighters and panicking tenants."

Review Quiz for Keywords 21–30

Decide if the pairs of words below are synonyms or antonyms. **Answers appear on page 386.**

1. *Salmagundi* and *gallimaufry* are . . . synonyms or antonyms?
2. *Selections* and *analects* are . . .
3. *Parturition* and *childbirth* are . . .
4. *Atrabilious* and *sanguine* are . . .
5. *Metamorphose* and *transmogrify* are . . .
6. *Screed* and *diatribe* are . . .
7. *Vespertine* and *matutinal* are . . .
8. *Sober* and *crapulent* are . . .
9. *Ipso facto* and *necessarily* are . . .
10. *Confine* and *debouch* are . . .

Once Upon a Word: English Is a Spanish Omelet

The olla podrida of English is heavily spiced with Spanish. (*Olla podrida* is discussed in *gallimaufry,* word 21 of this level.) From California to Texas to Florida—all Spanish names—English is a Spanish omelet. People live in cities and towns with Spanish names like San Antonio, Santa Fe, Las Vegas, and Los Angeles.

They drive on streets with Spanish names and live in Spanish-style houses in developments with (often mangled) Spanish names. They admire Hispanic flora and enjoy Hispanic food. Spanish surrounds them and, whether they realize it or not, they speak it every day.

In the 16th century, when Spain was exploring and conquering the New World, Spanish exerted its earliest influence upon English. By 1600, English had acquired *alligator, anchovy, banana, cannibal, cocoa, hurricane, mosquito, potato, sassafras, sherry, sombrero,* and *tobacco.* By 1700, English had adopted *cargo, barricade, escapade, siesta, matador, toreador, tomato, chocolate, vanilla,* and *cockroach.* By 1750, English had gained the geological term *mesa,* and by 1780, the word *stevedore* (from *estibador,* one who packs or loads cargo), which preceded *longshoreman,* its Anglo-Saxon equivalent, by more than twenty years. By 1850, English had appropriated the now-familiar *canyon, bonanza, loco,* and *vigilante.*

As 19th-century American pioneers pushed west into territory long dominated by Spain and later Mexico, the idiom of the cowboy grew out of the vernacular of his counterpart, the vaquero (vuh-KAIR-oh). From the vaqueros the cowboys adopted the words *ranch, rodeo, lasso* and *lariat, chaps, poncho, serape, stampede, desperado,* and *buckaroo,* an anglicization of *vaquero.*

The buckaroos learned new names for creatures: *burro* for a donkey, *pinto* for a piebald horse, *cinch* for a bedbug, and *coyote* for a wild dog. They ate *frijoles, chiles, tamales,* and *enchiladas.* And if a buckaroo drank too much *mescal* or *tequila,* he might wind up in the *calaboose* or *hoosegow*—the jail. Other borrowings from the heyday of the Old West include *hacienda, patio, arroyo, hombre, amigo,* and *pronto.*

"The Spanish contributions to the American vocabulary are far more numerous than those of any other Continental language," observes H. L. Mencken in *The American Language.* Think about that the next time you're sitting on the patio of your hacienda sipping sherry, taking a siesta, eating some vanilla ice cream with sliced bananas, or gazing at a stampede of mosquitoes in the canyon.

Now let's return to the *Word Workout* vocabulary.

Word 31: IMMURE (i-MYOOR)

To enclose within walls, shut in, confine; hence, to imprison or entomb.

The verb to *immure* comes from the medieval Latin *immūrāre,* to wall in, from *mūrus,* a wall, especially a wall around a city. *Immure* was once used to mean to surround with a wall, but since the word entered English in the late 15th century it has chiefly been used figuratively to mean to enclose within walls, or as if within walls, to imprison. "Thou wert immured, restrained, captivated, bound," wrote Shakespeare in 1598 in *Love's Labours Lost.*

Immure may also be used to mean to entomb in a wall. The most famous immurement (i-MYUUR-mint) in English literature occurs in Edgar Allan Poe's story "The Cask of Amontillado," which ends with these lines: "I forced the last stone into its position; I plastered it up. Against the new masonry I re-erected the old rampart of bones. For the half of a century no mortal has disturbed them. *In pace requiescat!*" (Latin for *rest in peace,* more commonly rendered as *requiescat in pace.*)

Word 32: CORRIGENDUM (KOR-i-JEN-dum)

An error to be corrected in a text or printed work.

Corrigendum is a mid-19th century borrowing of the Latin *corrigendum,* something to be corrected, which comes in turn from the verb *corrigere,* to correct, amend, put straight, the source also of the English words *correct* and *correction.* Although *corrigendum,* the singular, is the typical dictionary headword, meaning an error discovered in print that needs to be corrected, the plural form, *corrigenda* (KOR-i-JEN-duh), meaning a list of errors in a printed work along with their corrections, is considerably more common. Typically, when a new printing or edition of a book is being prepared, an author or editor will submit corrigenda, a list of errors to be corrected, to the compositor. Nowadays, with computers that can make changes in seconds and so much written material being published online, it is much easier to rectify corrigenda, textual errors to be corrected.

Word 33: LATITUDINARIAN (LAT-i-T[Y]OO-di-**NAIR**-ee-in)
Tolerant, broad-minded, especially in religious matters; not insisting on strict conformity or adherence to any doctrine, code, or standard.

The adjective *latitutudinarian* and the noun *latitudinarian,* which means a tolerant, broad-minded person, come from the Latin *lātitūdo,* breadth, extent, the source also of the English noun *latitude.* One meaning of *latitude* is freedom of action, choice, or opinion, as *some parents allow their children considerable latitude.* To be latitudinarian, or to be a latitudinarian, is to favor latitude in opinion or conduct, to be tolerant and open-minded, especially when it comes to religion, for in English history a latitudinarian was "a member of a group of Anglican Christians active from the 17th through the 19th century who were opposed to dogmatic positions of the Church of England and [who] allowed reason to inform theological interpretation and judgment" (*American Heritage*).

In modern usage to be latitudinarian is to be tolerant and broad-minded and not insist on conformity to arbitrary rules or adherence to any one way of thinking: "Some jurists interpret the Constitution narrowly while others are more latitudinarian"; "When Britain quietly made same-sex marriage the law of the land in 2013, observers around the world both hailed and decried the latitudinarian implications of such a move." (To *decry* [di-KRY] is to condemn, express strong disapproval of.)

Synonyms of *latitudinarian* include *liberal, lenient,* and *catholic,* which, when printed with a lowercase *c,* means broad or all-embracing in one's sympathies, interests, or tastes. Antonyms include *narrow-minded, bigoted, biased, intolerant, dogmatic,* and *parochial* (puh-ROH-kee-ul).

Word 34: STENTORIAN (sten-TOR-ee-in)
Very loud, powerful, and far-reaching.

Synonyms of *stentorian* include *thunderous, earsplitting, deafening, screeching, strident, clamorous,* and *vociferous* (word 12 of Level 3). Antonyms include *faint, subdued, harmonious, mellow, melodious, dulcet* (DUHL-sit), and *euphonious* (yoo-FOH-nee-us).

Stentorian is an eponymous word, from the name *Stentor* (STEN-tor), a Greek herald in the Trojan War who, as Homer put it in his epic poem the *Iliad,* had "a voice of bronze . . . as loud as that of fifty men together." By derivation *stentorian* means having or resembling the loud and powerful voice of Stentor.

Stentorian is used chiefly of a very loud or powerful voice, as *a stentorian narrator* or *a stentorian drill sergeant yelling orders.* It is also sometimes used of singing, as *his impassioned, stentorian baritone.* It may also be used of extremely loud sounds, especially voicelike sounds: for example, the word frequently appears in the phrase *stentorian tones. Stentorian* may also be used to mean able to utter a very loud sound, as *a stentorian foghorn* or *stentorian lungs.* Finally, the word is sometimes used figuratively of something that suggests a person speaking in a loud and powerful voice, as *the newspaper's stentorian editorializing.*

The noun *stentor* is used of a person who has a very loud and powerful voice: "The officer of the watch . . . gave the right orders, in the voice of a stentor" (Charles Reade, *A Simpleton*).

Word 35: ABECEDARIAN (AY-bee-see-**DAIR**-ee-<u>in</u>)
A person who is learning the alphabet, or a beginner who is learning the rudiments of something.

You can see and hear the first four letters of the alphabet in the word *abecedarian,* which comes from the Late Latin *abecedārius,* of the alphabet. As a noun, *abecedarian* denotes someone who is learning the alphabet, such as a child in elementary school, or someone who is learning the rudiments or fundamentals in any field of endeavor, as *an abecedarian in the insurance business.* The word may also apply to someone who teaches the alphabet or the rudiments of a subject: "Jenna was a home-schooled child, and her mother was her abecedarian."

As an adjective, *abecedarian* has several senses. It may mean of or pertaining to the alphabet, as *an abecedarian book,* one that teaches the alphabet; of or pertaining to someone who is learning the alphabet, as *her abecedarian pupil;* or elementary, rudimentary, or immature, as *abecedarian instructions* or *an abecedarian interpretation.*

Word 36: JUVENILIA (JOO-vuh-**NIL**-ee-uh *or* -**NIL**-yuh, *not* -**NEEL**-)
Artistic works or compositions, especially literary ones, produced in one's youth.

The plural noun *juvenilia,* which must be used with a plural verb, comes from the Latin *juvenīlis,* youthful, and *juvenis,* a young person, the source of the English *juvenile.*

A poet's juvenilia are the verses written in her youth, which may or may not have literary merit. The essays you wrote in high school and college, even if you're not a professional writer, are your juvenilia. And parents often proudly, and sentimentally, cling to their grown-up children's★ juvenilia, the drawings and scribblings and crude objets d'art they produced in their youth. (By the way, the term *objets d'art,* pronounced AWB-zhay **DAHR**, comes from French and means art objects, usually small creations or curios of some artistic worth. The singular is *objet d'art,* without the pluralizing *s* but pronounced the same way.)

Juvenilia may also denote a collection of literary or artistic works produced in someone's youth. And in the second half of the 20th century *juvenilia* also came to be used of literary or artistic works suitable or designed for young people: "They publish picture books and chapter books and other juvenilia."

Word 37: HIDALGO (hi-DAL-goh)
A gentleman by birth; specifically, a member of the lower or minor nobility in Spain.

The noun *hidalgo* was borrowed from Spanish in the late 16th century and is a contraction of the phrase *hijo de algo,* literally a son of something—namely, a son of a man of worth and esteem. In Spain and Spanish America the hidalgos were roughly the equivalent of the gentlemen and squires of England, who were members of the landed gentry, meaning that they had some land and money and privileges but were at the bottom tier of the aristocracy. According

---

★　Some years ago I won first place in a neologizing contest for the Word Fugitives column in *The Atlantic* by coining the word *offsprung* for one's grown-up children.

to *The Century Dictionary,* "The special privileges formerly possessed by the hidalgos . . . made them as a class self-important, haughty, and domineering, though many of them were not otherwise distinguished from the class below them."

Word 38: ELEEMOSYNARY (EL-uh-**MAHS**-i-ner-ee)
Charitable; pertaining to or supported by alms or charity.

The oddly spelled *eleemosynary* comes from the Greek *eleēmosynē,* pity, compassion, the source also of the English word *alms* (AHMZ), which goes back to Old English and means anything given as charity. An eleemosynary act is an act of charity. An eleemosynary institution—such as a school, church, or humanitarian organization—is one devoted to charity, to distributing alms, although not infrequently an eleemosynary institution may itself be dependent on charity. Doctors Without Borders, the Nobel Prize–winning international medical relief organization, is an eleemosynary institution supported by thousands of donors around the world, including me.

Some authorities sanction a seven-syllable pronunciation, EL-ee-uh-**MAHS**-i-ner-ee, but this is rarely heard today. And the recent editions of *Merriam-Webster's Collegiate Dictionary* record the eccentric variant EL-uh-**MOH**-si-ner-ee, which is not attested elsewhere and is best avoided.

Word 39: PLANGENT (PLAN-jint)
Resounding, reverberating; having a loud, resonant sound, especially a plaintive one. (*Plaintive* is word 9 of Level 2.)

The adjective *plangent* comes from the Latin verb *plangere,* which meant either to strike noisily or to beat the breast as a sign of grief, to bewail, lament. Because of this derivation, *plangent,* which entered English in the 17th century, has been applied both to loud, resonant sounds and to loud, mournful sounds that pull at your heartstrings.

Thus, *plangent* can describe the piercing sound of the bell calling the cowhands in to dinner as well as the sound of church bells tolling for a funeral. A plangent cry can be simply loud and resonant or it can reverberate with deep emotion. The strident fanfare of a trumpet is plangent, as are the wistful, tender, plangent reverberations of a classical guitar. In this sentence from *A Woman of Thirty,* the 19th-century French novelist Honoré de Balzac (ahn-uh-RAY du BAWL-zak) captures both these senses of *plangent*—loud and resonant and also resounding with plaintive feeling: "Ah! that full, deep voice, charged with plangent vibration, was the voice of one who had suffered indeed."

Word 40: LAGNIAPPE (lan-YAP *or* LAN-yap)

A bonus, gratuity, or tip; specifically, a small gift or bonus item given to a customer with a purchase as a way of saying, "Thank you for your business."

The noun *lagniappe* was born in the southern United States, coming through Louisiana French from the Spanish *la ñapa,* a corruption of the Quechua (KECH-wuh) word *yapa,* meaning that which is added. By derivation, *lagniappe* means a little something extra. The word is recorded in English from the mid-19th century; in 1883 Mark Twain noted its Louisiana origins in *Life on the Mississippi.*

You may use *lagniappe* in its original sense: a small gift or petty gratuity given by a retailer to a customer along with a purchase: "A stack of coasters received as lagniappe with a purchase of Iron City Beer long ago, graced an end table" (Richard W. Browne, *Brannon's Choice*). This sense could easily be extended to include the insignificant gifts—such as buttons, coffee mugs, and tote bags—that nonprofit organizations typically give as a thank-you for donations. Or you may use *lagniappe* figuratively to mean a bonus or unexpected benefit, as the American humorist S. J. Perelman (PER-ul-man, beginning with *peril,* not *pearl*) did in 1947 in his collection *Westward Ha!:* "Since the ship was calling there anyway, the trip would be pure lagniappe, an extra dash of stardust unforeseen in our program."

Review Quiz for Keywords 31–40

In each statement below, a keyword (in *italics*) is followed by three definitions. Two of the three are correct; one is unrelated in meaning. Decide which one doesn't fit the keyword. **Answers appear on page 386**.

1. To *immure* is to enclose within walls, tie up, imprison.
2. A *corrigendum* is a correction made, a mistake to be fixed, an error to be corrected.
3. *Latitudinarian* means tolerant, bigoted, broad-minded.
4. A *stentorian* tone is deafening, thunderous, melodious.
5. An *abecedarian* is a beginner, an amateur, a person learning the alphabet.
6. *Juvenilia* are youthful creations, unfinished creations, early artistic works.
7. A *hidalgo* is a minor aristocrat, a gentleman by birth, a high-ranking nobleman.
8. An *eleemosynary* institution is charitable, religious, supported by alms.
9. Something *plangent* is responsive, resonant, resounding.
10. A *lagniappe* is a gift, a note, a bonus.

A Punctuation Primer

The British put their commas and periods outside their quotation marks, but in American style they belong inside—with no exceptions. Thus: "I always put my commas inside my quotation marks," the careful writer said. "And I put all my periods there too."

People also often wonder whether periods should go inside or outside parentheses. When the words in parentheses are part of a larger sentence, even if they constitute a sentence themselves, the period goes outside the closing parenthesis: *You can't go home again* (*wrote Thomas Wolfe*). When a word, a phrase, or a full sentence is enclosed in parentheses and is not part of a larger sentence, the period goes inside the closing parenthesis: (*You bet.*) (*I'm not kidding.*)

Colons and semicolons always go outside parentheses and quotation marks, but question marks can go inside or outside quotation marks, so you have to be on your guard. If the quotation is itself a question, the question mark goes inside the quotation mark: *"What can I get for you tonight?" the waiter asked.* If the sentence itself is a question, and the quoted matter is merely part of it, the question mark goes outside the quotation mark: *Who said "I came, I saw, I conquered"?*

When you need to quote something within a quotation, use single quotation marks: *Any person with even a vestige of taste has to ask, "What are shows like 'Family Guy' and 'South Park' doing on TV? Don't we know what 'humor' means anymore?"*

Word 41: ACOLYTE (AK-uh-lyt)
An assistant, attendant, or devoted follower.

The noun *acolyte* comes from the Greek *akólouthos,* an attendant, follower. Originally, an acolyte was an altar attendant, a person who assisted a member of the Christian clergy by performing minor duties, such as lighting candles, during the service. *Acolyte* has been used in this ecclesiastical sense since Old English, but since the 17th century it has also been used more generally of any assistant or devoted follower. You can be an acolyte of a person, as *Robin is Batman's acolyte* or *the esteemed poet was surrounded by her acolytes.* Or you can be an acolyte of some doctrine, as *an acolyte of the libertarian philosophy of Ayn Rand.*

Word 42: CHATOYANT (shuh-TOY-int)
Changing in luster or color, like a cat's eye in the dark.

Chatoyant comes from the French verb *chatoyer,* to shimmer, glisten, change luster like a cat's eye. (The French word for a cat is *chat.*)

In jewelry work, *chatoyant* refers to a gem that has been cut so as to show a single streak or narrow band of wavy, reflected light. This streak of light in chatoyant jewels can seem to float or undulate and vary in color, much like a cat's eye in the dark. Silk and satin are often described as being chatoyant because of their rich, flowing, and variable sheen or luster. In his 1861 novel *Elsie Venner,* Oliver Wendell Holmes described the dance floor at a formal ball as a "frothy, chatoyant, sparkling, undulating sea of laces and silks and satins." Human eyes have often been likened to those of a cat, as in this quotation from 1916: "Either because they possessed a chatoyant quality of their own . . . or by reason of the light reflected through the open window, the green eyes gleamed upon me vividly like those of a giant cat" (Sax Rohmer, *The Devil Doctor*). You may use *chatoyant* of anything that shimmers and changes in color like silk or like a cat's eye in the dark.

Word 43: DOPPELGÄNGER (**DAHP**-ul-GANG-ur)

A counterpart or ghostly double of a living person; a second self; alter ego.

The unusual nouns *wraith* (rhymes with *faith*) and *fetch* are synonyms of *doppelgänger*.

Doppelgänger entered English in the mid-19th century as a loanword from German, where it meant literally a double-goer or double-walker. "In German folklore," says *Merriam-Webster's Encyclopedia of Literature*, a doppelgänger is "a wraith, or apparition, of a living person, as distinguished from a ghost. The concept of the existence of a spirit double . . . is an ancient and widespread belief. To meet one's double is a sign that one's death is imminent. The doppelgänger became a popular symbol in 18th- and 19th-century horror literature, and the theme took on considerable complexity."

The *American Heritage Dictionary* notes that a prominent characteristic of a doppelgänger is that it "haunts its fleshly counterpart." One of the best-known explorations of the theme of a doppelgänger haunting its fleshly counterpart is Edgar Allan Poe's story "William Wilson," published in 1839.

Word 44: SUPERNUMERARY (SOO-pur-**N[Y]OO**-muh-rair-ee)

Exceeding what is usual or required; beyond what is needed or useful.

The adjective *supernumerary* comes from the Latin *supernumerārius*, which the *OED* tells us was used of soldiers who were appointed to a legion after its numbers had been filled, and in military usage *supernumerary* traditionally applies to additional officers attached to a regiment or battalion to replace those who are sick, injured, or killed in action. It may also be used of a person who is associated with but does not formally belong to an organization or staff, who merely assists in times of need. A supernumerary firefighter helps in an emergency, and a supernumerary teacher is called upon when there's a shortage of regular teachers.

In Late Latin *supernumerārius* came to mean extra, additional, and since the 17th century we have used *supernumerary* to mean exceeding what is usual, needed, or prescribed. Supernumerary ornamentation is excessive, superfluous. Your wisdom teeth are supernumerary and must usually be extracted. And to a king hoping to produce a male heir, a daughter might seem supernumerary, beyond what is needed or required.

Supernumerary is also sometimes used as a noun to mean an additional person, especially an actor who appears in a nonspeaking role, also called a walk-on or an extra.

Word 45: REBARBATIVE (ri-BAHR-buh-tiv)
Repellent, disagreeable, objectionable; causing annoyance or irritation.

The adjective *rebarbative* comes from the modern French *rébarbatif,* repellent, disagreeable, the ultimate source being the Latin *barba,* a beard—a derivation that, because beards can be scratchy, reinforces the notion of annoyance and irritation in *rebarbative,* which entered English in the 1890s.

In current usage *rebarbative* is used chiefly of people and things that are unpleasant, offensive, or repulsive. You wouldn't say that someone has a rebarbative nose, but you could say that he has a rebarbative voice, or that he made rebarbative comments, or that his personality or attitude is rebarbative. A blog can be rebarbative, annoying, because its blogger is rebarbative, disagreeable. Rebarbative views are objectionable views, and rebarbative behavior is repellent, even sickening behavior.

Word 46: LOUCHE (LOOSH)
Disreputable or indecent; of questionable character, taste, morality, or propriety.

Synonyms of *louche* include *shifty, sleazy, dubious, shady,* and *seedy.* English borrowed *louche* in the early 19th century directly from the French *louche,* which means literally cross-eyed, squint-ing, and figuratively suspicious, fishy, and which comes in turn from the Latin *luscus,* one-eyed, blind in one eye.

In English *louche* is frequently used of shady people with dubi-ous reputations or questionable motives, such as the louche Brit-ish journalist Peter Fallow in Tom Wolfe's 1987 novel *Bonfire of the Vanities,* or Mata Hari, the Dutch exotic dancer and spy for the German secret service during World War I who "betrayed im-portant military secrets confided to her by the many high Allied officers who were on intimate terms with her" (*Columbia Encyclo-pedia*). She was executed by the French in 1917.

Louche is also often used of seedy or disreputable places, such as a red-light district or a low-life bar. *Louche* may also refer to actions, qualities, or things that are of questionable or indecent character, such as louche conduct, louche conversation, or a louche dress. "In pre-Las Vegas America, when gambling was illicit and had a louche charm, the natural domain of the disreputable was the poker table, the race track and the pool hall" (*The Wall Street Journal*).

Word 47: INTERREGNUM   (IN-tur-**REG**-n<u>u</u>m)
A pause or interruption in continuity; a lapse or interval.

Interregnum, which entered English in the late 16th century, comes from the Latin *interregnum,* literally a period between reigns, as of a ruler or monarch, a combination of *inter,* between, and *regnum,* rule, royal power or authority. The word is still used today in the specific sense of the interval between when a sovereign's reign ends and a successor assumes the throne, or the period between when a leader's term ends and a successor takes office. The inter-val between when a Roman Catholic pope dies or resigns and a new pope is chosen is called the interregnum, and the so-called lame-duck period between the end of an incumbent president's term and the inauguration of a new president is an interregnum, as "the interregnum between the outgoing Bush administration and the incoming Obama White House" (*The Huffington Post*).

Interregnum may also apply to a period in which a state has no ruler or leader and only a provisional government, or to a period of freedom from control or authority. But in current usage the word is perhaps most often used in the broad sense of a lapse, pause, interruption, or interval in something normally continuous: "Most parents, I suspect, look forward to that short interregnum between child-rearing hours and their own bedtime" (*The Guardian*); "Why not take advantage of this interregnum to borrow money at cheap rates and stimulate the economy and make necessary investments?" (*The Washington Post*).

The recommended plural is the English *interregnums,* not the Latin *interregna.*

Word 48: ALEMBIC (uh-LEM-bik)
Anything that works a change or transformation, or that purifies or refines.

Alembic comes ultimately from the Arabic *al-anbīq,* a combination of *al-,* the, and *anbīq,* a vessel for distilling. An alembic was originally an apparatus used in chemistry for distillation, consisting of two vessels connected by a tube and usually made of glass or copper. This meaning is still in good standing, but *alembic* is perhaps more often used figuratively of anything that causes a change or transformation, such as *the alembic of fate, the alembic of sorrow,* or *the hot alembic of the desert sun.* The word often suggests something that purifies or refines: "For several months before beginning to write the novel the idea percolated in the alembic of her imagination."

The verb to *alembicate* (uh-LEM-bi-kayt) means to change, refine, purify, or transform as if in an alembic: "A good autobiography is the story of a life alembicated into a work of literary art."

Word 49: OLEAGINOUS (OH-lee-AJ-i-nus)
Affectedly polite or flattering in a slimy way; overly and distatefully complimentary.

Oleaginous comes from the Latin *oleāginus,* of the olive tree, from *olea,* an olive. When the word entered English more than four hundred years ago it had the literal meaning of its derivation: oily, greasy, fatty, containing oil or having the nature of oil, as in "the oleaginous scum that pollutes the surface of a river," or "Margarine is an oleaginous substitute for butter." The word was also used to mean yielding or producing oil, as *peanuts are oleaginous*. Both these literal senses are still in good standing.

In the 19th century *oleaginous* came to be used to mean oily, slippery, or slimy in a figurative sense, as *an oleaginous politician* or *an oleaginous funeral director*. Both people and things can be figuratively oleaginous. When flattery or piety is affected and overdone, it's oleaginous. Popular music, created to please the least sophisticated ear, is often oleaginous. And the word may be applied to anyone whose manner is too polite or complimentary, as *an oleaginous used-car salesman* or *an oleaginous waiter*. A critic once described the British actor Hugh Grant, a pretty boy with a history of sexual indiscretions, as "an oleaginous, womanizing lounge lizard." Now that's slimy—and louche (word 46 of this level).

Synonyms of *oleaginous* in its figurative sense include *fawning, smarmy, ingratiating, obsequious,* and *unctuous* (UHNGK-chu̱-wu̱s). The closest of these is probably *unctuous,* which comes from the Latin *ungere,* to anoint, the source of the English word *unguent* (UHNG-gwe̱nt), a medicinal ointment. Like *oleaginous, unctuous* by derivation means oily, fatty, having a greasy or soapy feel, and the word is used today to mean having a slimy or slippery manner. Both the oleaginous and the unctuous person appear agreeable or earnest, but in an affected, self-serving, insincere, and overly flattering way.

Word 50: WASTREL (WAY-stru̱l)

An idle, good-for-nothing person, a ne'er-do-well, or a person who is wasteful and self-indulgent, a spendthrift.

Wastrel combines the word *waste* with *-rel,* "a noun suffix having a diminutive or pejorative force" (*Random House*). Because of this belittling, derogatory derivation, *wastrel* is most commonly used of a wasteful, indolent (word 48 of Level 4), and self-indulgent young person: "His mother calls him 'a lazy pig' and swears a blue streak as she describes the shame of having such a wastrel for a son" (*The Globe and Mail*); "The main male character, Ji-woong, is a handsome wastrel. Unable to get a job, he spends his days goofing around in Seoul" (fandompost.com). Occasionally *wastrel* is used figuratively of something wasteful, lazy, and self-indulgent, as in this 1889 quotation from *The Quarterly Review:* "London is the most conspicuous wastrel of both men and means." *Wastrel* is also often used attributively, meaning as an adjective, as *the wastrel nations of the euro zone* or *those wastrel days of careless youth.*

Wastrel has one other common meaning: an abandoned or homeless child living a vagabond life, a waif, or what used to be called a street urchin.

Review Quiz for Keywords 41–50

In this quiz the review word is followed by three words or phrases, and you must decide which comes nearest the meaning of the review word. **Answers appear on page 387**.

1. Is an *acolyte* an observer, an officer, or an attendant?

2. Does something *chatoyant* change shape, change position, or shimmer?

3. Is your *doppelgänger* your lost love, your ghostly double, or your worst enemy?

4. Are *supernumerary* things excessive, important, or beyond understanding?

5. Would a *rebarbative* remark be stimulating, objectionable, or threatening?

6. Does *louche* mean sophisticated, unpredictable, or disreputable?

7. Is an *interregnum* an interval, an intervention, or an interpretation?

8. Does an *alembic* cause disease, cause a transformation, or cause trouble?

9. Would an *oleaginous* person be nosy, ingratiating, or sedate?

10. Is a *wastrel* a drug addict, a traveling musician, or a ne'er-do-well?

The Style File: First Things First

A headline in *The New York Times Book Review* refers to "the novelist who first conceived of cyberspace." A story in the *Boston Globe* says that "when Southwest first announced it would fly from

Boston to Baltimore for $49 each way, JetBlue added a route there too." And a reporter on NPR's *All Things Considered* says, "When Holder was first appointed over a year ago . . ."

Did you catch the recurring error in these three citations?

The problem is a misuse of the word *first*. When it's understood from the context that something is being done for the first time, or when the verb in the context means doing something for the first time, *first* is redundant.

To *conceive* means to imagine for the first time, to form an idea before anyone else has done so. Thus, the *Book Review*'s headline should have read, "the novelist who conceived of cyberspace." Likewise, to *announce* means to make known or make public, which happens only once, so the *Boston Globe's* copyeditor should have changed "when Southwest *first* announced it would fly" to "when Southwest announced it would fly." And unless you're appointed to a position, then resign and are reappointed to it, you are appointed only once. So the NPR reporter should have said "When Holder was appointed over a year ago," not *first* appointed.

First is always superfluous when it's paired with a verb—such as *start, begin, create, invent, introduce, learn, discover,* and *arrive*—that means doing something for the first time, as in this sentence from *The San Diego Union-Tribune:* "It's been 100 years since Edgar Rice Burroughs first introduced his accidental space traveler, John Carter, to readers." Most of the time deleting *first* will fix the problem, but sometimes the sentence has to be revised. For example, in *The Know-It-All* A. J. Jacobs writes, "Machine guns, when they first were invented, got so hot they had to be cooled by water." Make that "When machine guns were invented they got so hot they had to be cooled by water," or "The first machine guns got so hot they had to be cooled by water."

Answers to Review Quizzes for Level 8
KEYWORDS 1–10

1. Yes. A *panoply* is an impressive array or splendid display.

2. Yes. Something *recherché* is very rare, obscure, exotic, exquisite, or refined.

3. No. Something *vertiginous* makes you dizzy or giddy.

4. No. Your *kismet* is your fate, destiny, or lot in life, and cannot be altered.

5. Yes. To *temporize* is to act evasively or be indecisive so as to gain time; to stall.

6. Yes. *Surrounded* means enclosed on all sides, so adding *completely* to it is pleonastic. *Pleonasm* is the use of more words than are necessary to express an idea.

7. No. Abstract expressionism was an artistic movement of the mid-20th century whose works were nonrepresentational, meaning they did not portray or resemble physical objects in nature. *Verisimilitude* is the appearance of truth or resemblance to reality.

8. No. A *plutocrat* (word 5 of Level 4) is someone whose power comes from wealth. A *cabal* is a group of secret plotters, a conspiracy.

9. Yes. *Postprandial* means happening or done after a meal, especially after dinner.

10. No. *Eponymous* words are formed from names. *Onomatopoeia* is the formation or use of a word in imitation of a sound.

KEYWORDS 11–20

1. False. When you're in a *dudgeon,* you're experiencing a sudden fit of anger, resentment, or indignation.

2. True. *Hegemony* means leadership, dominance.

3. False. A *premonitory* phone call warns you of something that's about to happen.

4. True. A *retronym* is an adjective-noun pairing generated by a change in the meaning of the noun, usually because of technology: e.g., *electric guitar, rotary phone, snail mail.*

5. False. When you *recuse* yourself, you remove or disqualify yourself as a judge or participant to avoid any suspicion of bias or conflict of interest.

6. False. Someone living in *penury* lives in extreme poverty.

7. False. A *roué* is devoted to immoral behavior and sensual pleasure.

8. True. A *Luddite* is someone fanatically opposed to innovation.

9. False. *Schadenfreude* is pleasure or joy derived from other people's misfortune.

10. False. A *costive* person is slow or reluctant to speak or act.

KEYWORDS 21–30

1. Synonyms. A *salmagundi* and a *gallimaufry* are both diverse or jumbled mixtures.

2. Synonyms. *Analects* are selected written passages, extracts, or fragments from an author or various authors.

3. Synonyms. *Parturition* is the medical term for childbirth.

4. Antonyms. *Sanguine* means cheerful. *Atrabilious* means gloomy and irritable.

5. Synonyms. Both *metamorphose* and *transmogrify* mean to change or transform completely. *Transmogrify* implies a strange, grotesque, or preposterous transformation.

6. Synonyms. A *diatribe* is bitter, abusive speech or writing. A *screed* is a long and tedious speech or piece of writing, and often one that is angry or impassioned.

7. Antonyms. *Vespertine* means of the evening. *Matutinal* means of the morning.

8. Antonyms. *Crapulent* means sick from overindulgence in food or drink, hung over.

9. Synonyms. *Ipso facto* means by the very fact itself, necessarily, by its very nature.

10. Antonyms. To *debouch* is to emerge from a narrow or confined place into the open.

KEYWORDS 31–40

1. *Tie up* doesn't fit. To *immure* is not to bind but to enclose within walls, imprison.

2. *A correction made* doesn't fit because a *corrigendum* is an error in a text that has been noted but not yet corrected.

3. *Bigoted,* intolerant, doesn't fit because *latitudinarian* means tolerant, liberal, broad-minded.

4. *Melodious,* tuneful, sweet-sounding, doesn't fit. Something *stentorian* is extremely loud and resounding, often unpleasantly so.

5. *An amateur* doesn't fit. Amateurs are people who by derivation (Latin *amor,* love) do things for the love of it, and although they are not experts or professionals they may have considerable experience and skill. By contrast, an *abecedarian* has no skills. An *abecedarian* is a person learning the alphabet, or, by extension, a beginner at something.

6. *Unfinished creations* doesn't fit. *Juvenilia* are artistic works produced in one's youth, or a collection of such works.

7. *A high-ranking nobleman* doesn't fit. A *hidalgo* is a gentleman by birth and a minor aristocrat.

8. *Religious* doesn't fit. Although an *eleemosynary* institution dispenses charity and may also depend on charity, it need not be religious.

9. *Responsive,* which refers to actions, doesn't fit. *Plangent* refers to sounds that are loud and resounding, and also melancholy.

10. *A note* doesn't fit; it's vague. A *lagniappe* is a small gift or bonus given by the seller to the buyer as a thank-you.

KEYWORDS 41–50

1. An *acolyte* is an assistant, attendant, or devoted follower.

2. It shimmers. *Chatoyant* means changing in luster or color, like a cat's eye in the dark; hence, shimmering, glistening.

3. Your *doppelgänger* is your ghostly double, a counterpart of a living person.

4. They're excessive. *Supernumerary* means exceeding what is usual or required; beyond what is needed or useful.

5. It would be objectionable. *Rebarbative* means repellent, disagreeable, objectionable; causing annoyance or irritation.

6. *Louche* means disreputable, indecent; of questionable character or propriety.

7. An *interregnum* is a pause or interruption in continuity; a lapse or interval.

8. An *alembic* causes a change or transformation, or purifies or refines.

9. An *oleaginous* person is ingratiating, polite or flattering in a slimy, affected way.

10. A *wastrel* is an idle, good-for-nothing person, a ne'er-do-well, or a person who is wasteful and self-indulgent, a spendthrift.

LEVEL 9

Word 1: SANGFROID (sah[n]-FRWAH)
Composure; coolness or calmness of mind, especially in trying circumstances.

Synonyms of *sangfroid* include *self-possession, aplomb* (uh–PLAHM), *equanimity* (EE-kwuh-**NIM**-i-tee), and *imperturbability*. Antonyms of *sangfroid* include *agitation, uneasiness, discomposure, disquiet,* and *perturbation* (discussed in *perturb,* word 25 of Level 6).

The noun *sangfroid* comes directly from French and means literally cold blood (*sang* is French for blood and *froid* is French for cold), the idea being, apparently, that hot-bloodedness implies passion and overreaction while cold-bloodedness implies composure under pressure.

The unusual word *froideur* (frwah-DUR) also incorporates this French *froid,* cold, and denotes an attitude of cold superiority, cool aloofness or haughty indifference. When I think of *froideur* (which is so rare in English that it is still printed in italics), I think of Marie Antoinette (1755–1793), queen of France during the reign of Louis XVI, who, in response to learning that her people were starving from a bread famine, was reputed to have said, with infamous *froideur,* "Let them eat cake."

Sangfroid may be used of any impressive display of composure in difficult circumstances, whether the actions involved are admirable or reprehensible. Thus, a soldier may exhibit sangfroid under fire, and a criminal may exhibit sangfroid while conducting a robbery. A teacher can demonstrate sangfroid in a classroom full of rowdy and insubordinate high schoolers, and an acrobat can show great sangfroid performing on the high wire, but a mafioso can also show sangfroid, coolness of mind or temperament, while brutally murdering a rival.

Word 2: DESUETUDE (DES-wi-T[Y]OOD, rhymes with *guess the feud*)
A state of disuse or inactivity; discontinuance of use or practice.

The noun *desuetude* comes through French from the Latin *dēsuētūdo,* disuse, which comes in turn from the verb *dēsuēscĕre,* to disuse, become unaccustomed to. It is a lovely literary word that is often used in phrases such as *passing into desuetude* or *falling into desuetude* to mean obsolescent, becoming obsolete, entering a state of disuse. But something can also be *in desuetude,* already in a state of disuse or inactivity. For example, a word, a law, or a custom can pass into desuetude or already be in desuetude, discontinuance of use or practice. The word often implies neglect and decay, as *an ancient castle that had long since fallen into desuetude.*

Word 3: SHIBBOLETH (SHIB-uh-leth *or* -lith)
"A word or pronunciation that distinguishes people of one group or class from those of another"; hence, a password. Also, "a word or phrase identified with a particular group or cause"; hence, a catchphrase, watchword, or slogan. (Both definitions quoted are from *The American Heritage Dictionary.*)

Shibboleth comes from an ancient Hebrew word meaning an ear of corn or a stream in flood. "In our language today," says the *Morris Dictionary of Word and Phrase Origins,* "*shibboleth* has the very different meaning of 'test word' or 'watchword,' and behind that change of meaning lies an intriguing bit of Biblical history.

During a battle between the Gileadites and the Ephraimites at the Jordan fords, the men of Gilead took command of the fords and when any of the fugitives of the army of Ephraim asked to pass, they would be asked "Are you an Ephraimite?"

If the answer was no, then in the words of Judges 12:6—"They said to him, 'Say now *Shibboleth*,' and he said '*Sibboleth*,' for he could not frame to pronounce it right. Then they took him and slew him at the passages of the Jordan." Thus the inability to pronounce correctly the Hebrew word . . . was the distinguishing characteristic of the Ephraimites and one which the sons of Gilead were shrewd enough to use as their watchword, giving the word *shibboleth* the meaning it has today.

The Gileadites, it should be noted, slew 42,000 Ephraimites who couldn't say *shibboleth* and sealed their fate by saying *sibboleth* instead. "Perhaps only racial, religious, and national slurs have killed as many men as this word," notes Robert Hendrickson in *The Facts on File Encyclopedia of Word and Phrase Origins*.

In modern usage a shibboleth is a kind of password, specifically "a peculiarity of pronunciation, or a habit, or a mode of dress . . . which distinguishes a particular class or set of persons"★ For example, the consonant combination *th* is a shibboleth that distinguishes native English speakers from many nonnative ones; the so-called half-broad *a* in words like *park, dance,* and *half* is a shibboleth that distinguishes New Englanders; and certain expressions, gestures, and articles of clothing are shibboleths that distinguish members of a street gang.

Shibboleth may also be used to mean a catchphrase or slogan, especially one used repeatedly so as to differentiate those who are adherents to a certain party or cause from those who are not. Senator Joseph McCarthy, in his fanatical crusade against communists in the early 1950s, repeatedly used the rhetorical question and shibboleth "Are you now, or have you ever been, a member of the Communist Party?"

Word 4: CRI DE COEUR (KREE-duh-**KUR**)
An impassioned or anguished outcry, as of distress, protest, or entreaty.

The plural is *cris de coeur,* pronounced the same as the singular.

★ From *A Dictionary of Contemporary American Usage* by Bergen and Cornelia Evans.

English borrowed *cri de coeur* from French in the late 1800s. In French it means literally a cry (*cri*) of (*de*) the heart (*coeur*), and that's precisely how it's used in English. A cri de coeur may express many things—frustration, distress, sorrow, yearning—and it may take many forms—an appeal, a protest, a complaint, or an expression of desire—but it is always an impassioned outcry. To borrow a phrase from the filmmaker Paul Schrader (1946–), a cri de coeur indulges "that need to just lean out the window and yell."

In the *Los Angeles Times* we read of "a desperate cri de coeur aimed at the conscience of society." In *The Daily Beast* we read that "the speech was also a cri de coeur against a system that . . . imposes massive moral and human costs on the United States." In the *Irish Examiner* we learn that "it was really a cri de coeur for decisive action from today's political leaders." And in the *Financial Times* (of London), a writer asks, "Is *Billy Budd* a Christian parable, an exposé of Enlightenment ideals, or a cri de coeur for sexual freedom?"

Word 5: INCUNABULA (IN-kyuu-**NAB**-yuh-luh)
Early printed books, especially those produced before 1501.

Incunabula is a plural noun that comes directly from the Latin plural noun *incunabula,* the straps or bands holding a baby in a cradle, from *incūnāre,* to place in a cradle, and *cūnae,* a cradle. By derivation *incunabula* pertains to something in its infancy, specifically the books produced in the earliest stages of printing from movable type. As you can imagine, incunabula are extremely rare and valuable and fragile because they are so old: "He had repaired all types of books, from Bibles to incunabula, with pages on the point of turning to dust" (*The Huffington Post*).

An *incunable* (in-KYOO-nuh-bul) is a book printed before 1501, a part of the incunabula. Perhaps the best-known incunable is the Gutenberg Bible, considered to be the earliest book printed from movable type, in about 1456.

Word 6: CHEF-D'OEUVRE (shay-DUU[R]-vruh)
A masterpiece, especially one in literature, art, or music.

The noun *chef-d'oeuvre* comes directly from French and means literally a chief piece of work, from *chef,* chief, and *oeuvre* (UU[R]-vruh), work, production, a word that English has also borrowed to mean all the works of a writer, artist, composer, or the like, taken as a whole: "Nigel's knowledge of Jane Austen's oeuvre was decidedly lacking."

Chef-d'oeuvre has been English since the early 1600s, long enough to lose the italics that indicate a foreign borrowing but not its French pronunciation, perhaps because it is such an unusual synonym of *masterpiece,* the commonly used word. But, to borrow a turn of phrase from the American journalist Ambrose Bierce, who disappeared in Mexico in 1914, to call a word unusual means only that it's no longer used by the timid. Most of us may not have the sangfroid (word 1 of this level) to nonchalantly fling *chef-d'oeuvre* into a conversation, but if used in a dignified way in writing about a work of art the word can be a tour de force (TOOR-duh-**FORS**, an exceptional achievement or a stunning display of strength or skill).

The plural is *chefs-d'oeuvre,* with an *s* added after the *f* in the first syllable but pronounced the same as the singular.

Word 7: IAMB (EYE-am, like *I am* with stress on *I*)
In poetry, a metrical foot of two syllables, consisting of a short or unstressed syllable followed by a long or stressed syllable.

The noun *iamb* comes through Latin from Greek, where, according to *The Oxford Companion to the English Language,* it meant "lame: that is, a weak step before a strong step." The adjective is *iambic* (eye-AM-bik), consisting of iambs.

In *penultimate,* word 15 of Level 7, I introduced the word *prosody* (PRAH-suh-dee), the study of poetic meter and versification. In prosody, a *foot* is a group of two or more syllables that constitute a fixed unit of rhythm. The iamb, an unstressed syllable followed by a stressed one, is the most common foot in English poetry and the rhythmic unit closest to ordinary speech.

You can hear iambic meter in English poetry from the sonnets of Shakespeare ("When to the sessions of sweet silent thought / I summon up remembrance of things past") to "I have been one acquainted with the night" by the American poet Robert Frost (1874–1963). Andrew Marvell's "To His Coy Mistress," published in 1681, is iambic ("Had we but world enough, and time, / This coyness, lady, were no crime"), as is Gelett Burgess's nonsense poem "The Purple Cow," published in 1895: "I never saw a purple cow, / I never hope to see one; / But I can tell you anyhow, / I'd rather see than be one."

Poetic lines consisting of five iambic feet are written in *iambic pentameter;* the combining form *penta-,* from Greek, means five, as in *pentagon,* a five-sided figure. Sonnets are written in iambic pentameter. Lines consisting of four iambs, as in "To His Coy Mistress" and "The Purple Cow," are written in *iambic tetrameter* (te-TRAM-i-tur), the combining form *tetra-,* again from Greek, meaning four.

Other common metrical feet in English poetry include the *trochee* (TROH-kee), the *dactyl* (DAK-til), and the *anapest* (AN-uh-pest).

A trochee is the metrical opposite of an iamb: a long or stressed syllable followed by a short or unstressed one, as in Christina Rossetti's "Hurt no living thing" (1872), Dylan Thomas's "In my craft or sullen art" (1946), and the nursery rhyme "Twinkle, twinkle, little star." A dactyl is a long syllable followed by two short ones, as in the lyric from the musical *Oklahoma:* "O what a wonderful morning, / O what a wonderful day." Lots of common names, such as *Jennifer, Evelyn,* and *Christopher,* are dactylic (dak-TIL-ik). An anapest is two short syllables followed by a long one, as in these lilting lines from the children's poem "Spring" by Karla Kuskin (1932–2009): "I'm a gamboling lamb / I'm a light leaping goat / I'm a bud / I'm a bloom / I'm a dove on the wing." (The verb to *gambol* is pronounced like *gamble* and means to skip about, frolic.)

Word 8: FRISSON (free-SOH[N])

A shudder of excitement or quivering thrill that courses through the body.

In the late 18th century English borrowed the noun *frisson* from French, where it means a shudder, shiver, thrill; it may come ultimately from the Latin *frīgēre,* to be cold. *Frisson* has been English long enough to shed its italics, but because it is not in common use it retains its French pronunciation, with *free* for the first syllable and a nasalized *n* at the end. The plural is *frissons,* pronounced free-SOH(N)Z, with a *z* sound at the end.

When the hair stands up on the back of your neck or a chill runs down your spine, it's a frisson. You can get a frisson from reading an action-packed thriller, listening to exciting or transcendent music, jumping into cold water, or watching a horror movie. You can have a frisson of fear, of doubt, of joy, of sexual arousal, and even of despair. Frissons can also be collective, as when a contagious thrill passes through a crowd.

All right, now for a quiz. Here's a sentence from *The Wall Street Journal:* "It began, as these affairs often do, with a frisson of illicit excitement." Can you tell what's wrong with that? Because the idea of excitement is implicit in the meaning of *frisson,* it's redundant to pair *frisson* with *excitement;* an editor should have changed the phrase to "with an illicit frisson." This is a regrettably common mistake made by writers who don't know the word well enough to use it properly and who apparently don't trust their readers to know it either—or to look it up.

Word 9: PRELAPSARIAN (PREE-lap-**SAIR**-ee-in)

Of or pertaining to the time before the Fall of humankind; hence, innocent, carefree, childlike, naive, unspoiled, uncorrupted.

The noun *prelapsarian* comes from the Latin *prae,* before, and *lapsus,* a fall. In the Bible, chapter 6 of Genesis recounts the story of Adam and Eve, who, tempted by the serpent, violated God's commandment and ate the fruit of the tree of knowledge of good and evil. For this transgression, God banished them from the Garden of Eden, also called Paradise.

At heart, this story is a tale of the loss of innocence, writ large for all humankind. And since *prelapsarian* entered English in the 1870s we have used the word to describe any childlike, carefree state of unspoiled innocence reminiscent of Adam and Eve before the Fall. A prelapsarian landscape is a beautiful, pristine landscape. Prelapsarian romance is innocent, childlike love, without the complications of a physical relationship. And some people imagine that there was a prelapsarian state of the language, a time when English was pure and uncorrupted, but that is a myth. Finally, *prelapsarian* may also be used of other kinds of metaphorical falls from innocence, grace, or perfection, as *the prelapsarian days before the stock market collapse.*

Postlapsarian, after the Biblical Fall, is the antonym of *prelapsarian.* It too may be used figuratively to mean no longer innocent, hence spoiled, corrupted, or depraved: "The novel conjures [KAHN-jurs] a postlapsarian world in which people do evil supposedly in the service of some greater good."

Word 10: MÉTIER (may-TYAY *or* MAY-tyay)
A specialty; a field of work or area of activity in which one has special ability or for which one is particularly suited.

The noun *forte,* meaning a strong point or area of expertise—which is properly pronounced in one syllable, like the word *fort,* or in two syllables with the stress on the first syllable, FOR-tay, *not* the second—is a close synonym of *métier.* Other synonyms include *pursuit, calling,* and *vocation* (the fancier word for *calling,* from the Latin *vocare,* to call). Casual synonyms of *métier* include *line* and *dodge:* "If you were to ask me what's my line I'd say I'm in the word dodge."

When it entered English from French in the late 1700s, *métier* meant an occupation, trade, or profession, as in this quotation from Charlotte Turner Smith's 1792 novel *Desmond:* "They wanted . . . to make me a monk; but I had a mortal aversion to that métier." But the word soon became used more specifically to mean a field of work or area of activity at which one excels, and this is its primary sense in modern usage.

Métier, says *Merriam-Webster's Collegiate Dictionary,* "implies a calling or pursuit for which one believes oneself to be especially fitted." Boxing was Muhammad Ali's métier; "the art of the deal" is the businessman Donald Trump's métier; and political maneuvering was the métier of the Italian statesman Nicolò Machiavelli (1469–1527), who wrote *The Prince.* In *Chopin: The Man and His Music* (1900), James Huneker writes, "When asked why he did not compose symphonies or operas, [Chopin] answered that his métier was the piano, and to it he would stick."

Review Quiz for Keywords 1–10
Consider the following questions and decide whether the correct answer is yes or no. **Answers appear on page 433.**

1. Can a soldier exhibit sangfroid under fire?
2. If something falls into desuetude, is it neglected or no longer used?
3. Is a tongue-twister a shibboleth?
4. Can a cri de coeur express frustration, distress, sorrow, or yearning?
5. Are incunabula books printed after 1750?
6. Is Michelangelo's statue of David a chef-d'oeuvre?
7. Is an iamb a metrical foot consisting of a long syllable followed by a short one?
8. Could watching a scary movie give you a frisson?
9. Is a prelapsarian landscape beautiful and pristine?
10. Is your métier your weakness or area of greatest vulnerability?

Once Upon a Word: Le Mot Juste
In the last set of keywords you encountered several borrowings from French—*sangfroid, froideur, cri de coeur, chef-d'oeuvre, tour de force, frisson,* and *métier.* Let's take a moment to look at a few more French locutions (word 22 of Level 6), so you will always have at your fingertips *le mot juste* (le-MOH-**ZHOOST**), the appropriate word for the occasion.

We'll begin with *RSVP,* which often appears in the phrase "Please RSVP." Because *RSVP* is an initialism that stands for *répondez s'il vous plaît,* which means please reply, using *please* with *RSVP* is redundant. I offer this advice *en passant* (ah[n] pa-SAH[N]), in passing, because it's my *raison d'etre* (RAY-zoh[n]-**DE**-truh), my reason for being, to rid the world of redundancy. For me, rooting out redundancy is *de rigueur* (du̲-ri-GUR), strictly required by etiquette, usage, or custom.

If you want to stay *au courant* (oh-kuu-RAH[N]), up-to-date, and never be *passé* (pa-SAY), behind the times, out of fashion, you must cultivate *savoir faire* (SAV-wahr-**FAIR**), tact, diplomacy, an ability to speak and behave appropriately in social situations. Savoir faire will come easily to you if you are a *bon vivant* (BAHN-vee-**VAHNT**), a cultivated person with refined tastes who likes to indulge in fine food and drink. And where better to indulge those refined tastes but at a *soiree* (swah-RAY), a party or social gathering in the evening, at a *pied-à-terre* (pee-AY-duh-**TAIR**), a secondary residence, such as an apartment in a city, for someone who lives elsewhere.

At this *soigné* (swahn-YAY, elegantly appointed or fashionably well-groomed) pied-à-terre you will mingle with members of the *beau monde* (boh-MAHND), high society. Some of them will speak with *éclat* (ay-KLAH), brilliance or conspicuous success, about their *idée fixe* (ee-day-**FEEKS**), their obsession (literally a fixed idea), or some *cause célèbre* (KAWZ-suh-**LEB** or -**LEB**-ruh), which does not mean a celebrated cause or ideal, as some mistakenly believe, but a sensational controversy, such as a legal trial. No doubt there'll be some *soi-disant* (SWAH-dee-**ZAH[N]**), self-styled or self-proclaimed, know-it-alls among them. And of course there'll be a few dull folks who will want to have a *tête à tête* (TAYT-uh-TAYT or TET-uh-TET), a private conversation, with you, and bore you with stories and jokes that are *réchauffé* (RAY-shoh-**FAY**), literally warmed-over, and thus rehashed, unoriginal.

Taken *en masse* (en-MAS), all together, as a group or whole, these French loanwords may seem *de trop* (du̲-TROH), excessive, too much or too many. But don't be daunted. They're all part of the great patchwork quilt of English. And I think you may find, once you've absorbed and begun to use them, that a little assimilated French can sometimes provide not only le mot juste but also be the *pièce de résistance* (pyes dụ RAY-zee-**STAH[N]S**), the chief or prized feature, the showpiece, of your prose.

Now, here are the next ten keywords in Level 9:

Word 11: ABLUTION (uh–BLOO-shịn)
The act of washing or bathing, especially as a religious rite.

The noun *ablution,* which dates back to the early 1400s, comes through the Latin *ablutio,* spiritual purification by baptism or the baptism itself, from the verb *abluere,* to be washed clean, to wash off or away. In various religions, ablution is a ritual performed before prayer. But *ablution* may be used either of the ceremonial and spiritual cleansing of the body or of the act of washing something clean. The English poet John Keats captured both senses in these lines from his sonnet "Bright Star," written in 1819: "The moving waters at their priestlike task / Of pure ablution round earth's human shores."

Here are two contemporary examples of *ablution* used to mean washing or bathing, without any religious connotation: "Designers have spent years trying to perfect an aerated shower head that won't detract from the pleasures of the morning ablution routine" (*The Telegraph,* United Kingdom); "More than 10,000 schools will be provided with new ablution facilities at the beginning of 2014" (www.AllAfrica.com).

Word 12: APOSTASY (uh–PAHS-tuh-see)
Renunciation or abandonment of one's faith or allegiance.

The noun *apostasy* comes from the Greek *apostasía,* a standing away, withdrawal, hence a desertion or defection, the sense in which the word is used today. From the 14th century, when *apostasy* entered English, to the 16th, the word meant a renunciation of religious faith or the act of renouncing one's vows and quitting a religious order.

Then, by extension, *apostasy* also came to be used of any abandonment of one's principles or allegiance to a party or doctrine. In current usage we speak of political apostasy, such as abandoning one party and joining another, and of philosophical or moral apostasy, such as when a person renounces one position in favor of another.

The adjective and noun *apostate* (uh-PAHS-tayt) means either characterized by apostasy or a person who commits apostasy, and the verb *apostatize* (uh-PAHS-tuh-tyz) means to commit apostasy, to renounce or desert one's faith, allegiance, or principles.

Word 13: SUMPTUARY (SUHMP-choo-er-ee)
Pertaining to expenses or expenditures or, especially, to the regulating of them.

The adjective *sumptuary*, which entered English about 1600, comes from the Latin *sumptuārius*, relating to expenses or expenditures, from *sumptus*, a cost or expense, and ultimately from the verb *sūměre*, to take, buy, spend, the source also of the English words *consume* and *consumption*, as well as *presumptuous* (word 2 of Level 1).

The familiar adjective *sumptuous* (SUHMP-choo-us), from the same source as *sumptuary*, means, by derivation, involving great expense, extremely costly, and therefore lavish, luxurious, magnificent, as *a sumptuous feast* or *an opulent mansion with sumptuous furnishings*.

Sumptuary may mean simply pertaining to expenses or expenditures, especially personal ones, as *a sumptuary allowance*, meaning an expense account, or *a household's sumptuary budget*. But the word has most often been used of regulations or laws that govern expenditures on moral or religious grounds, especially personal expenditures that may be considered extravagant or indulgent. Sumptuary laws are often passed to regulate the consumption of luxury items, and sumptuary taxes are imposed typically on things that society considers undesirable or objectionable, such as tobacco. The infamous blue laws of New England, which ban the sale of alcohol on Sundays, are sumptuary laws, as is New York City's controversial proposed ordinance banning the sale of extra-large soft drinks.

Word 14: TATTERDEMALION (TAT-ur-duh-**MAY**-lee-<u>un</u>)
A person who wears tattered or ragged clothing; a ragamuffin (**RAG**-uh-MUHF-in).

The origin of the noun *tatterdemalion* is obscure. When it entered English in the early 1600s it was spelled *tatterdemallion* and pronounced to rhyme with *Italian* and *stallion*. The initial *tatter-* was also often spelled *totter-,* perhaps suggestive of the tottering or staggering of a shabbily dressed vagrant or beggar. But we have settled on *tatter-* as the preferred spelling probably because it suggests either the noun *tatter,* a torn scrap, a shred, as *his clothing was in tatters,* or the adjective *tattered,* torn to tatters or shreds, ragged.

Tatterdemalion has also long been used as an adjective to mean ragged, unkempt, shabby, dilapidated, and may be used of people or things, as *an old, tatterdemalion woman in an old, tatterdemalion gown.*

Word 15: ABJURE (ab-JUUR)
To renounce or reject solemnly or under oath. Also, to abstain from or avoid.

Synonyms of the verb to *abjure* include to *repudiate, recant, retract, forsake,* and *forswear.*

Abjure comes from the Latin *abjurāre,* to deny on oath, from *jurāre,* to swear. The word may be used either to mean to renounce something solemnly or under oath, as *to abjure violence,* or to give up or abstain from something, as *to abjure tobacco.* The word implies "a firm and final rejecting or abandoning often made under oath," says *Merriam-Webster's Collegiate Dictionary.* For example, monks and nuns take vows of celibacy, abjuring marriage and the pleasures of the flesh. You can abjure your religious faith in favor of another religious faith or in favor of no religious faith. You can abjure authority or responsibility for something. And you can abjure your right to do something, such as make a claim or file a lawsuit.

The noun is *abjuration* (AB-juu-**RAY**-sh<u>i</u>n), the act of abjuring, renouncing or rejecting solemnly or under oath.

Word 16: NOBLESSE OBLIGE (noh-BLES oh-**BLEEZH**)
The moral obligation of those of noble birth or high social position to behave in an honorable, kindly, and generous way.

The phrase *noblesse oblige,* which English borrowed from French about 1830, means literally nobility obliges; in other words, privilege entails responsibility. Historically the locution (word 22 of Level 6) refers to the self-imposed responsibility of the nobility to behave benevolently toward those in an inferior social position. But the term is often used in a more general way of the moral obligation that anyone of high social standing has to act honorably and charitably, to help the less fortunate—or, to put that in modern parlance (PAHR-l<u>u</u>nts), "to give back to the community." (*Parlance* is a certain way or manner of speaking, an idiom or vernacular.)

In his 1910 novel *Burning Daylight,* Jack London writes, "He found, with rare and mythical exceptions, that there was no noblesse oblige among the business and financial supermen." And here are some contemporary examples of how writers use *noblesse oblige:* "Scranton's pragmatism, grounded in the spirit of noblesse oblige, was dependent upon his wealth, his family heritage, and, politically, the Republican Party" (www.penlive.com). "At first, the attention Sutter lavishes on Aimee is a kind of chivalry, a high school version of noblesse oblige" (*Baltimore Magazine*).

Word 17: PRIMOGENITURE (PRY-muh-**JEN**-i-chur)
The state of being the firstborn child of the same parents; or, more often, the right of a firstborn, especially the eldest son, to inherit property or title.

The noun *primogeniture* comes from the Middle Latin *prīmōgenitūra,* the right of the firstborn child, which comes in turn from *prīmō,* at first, and *genitūra,* a begetting.

Primogeniture may mean seniority by birth, being the firstborn child in a family, whether male or female. But more often it is a historical term from common law for the rule of inheritance in which land and property descend to the oldest son to the exclusion of all other siblings. Primogeniture developed in the feudal system of medieval Europe, which required military service from all landholders and vassals (VAS-ulz), or feudal tenants. The purpose of primogeniture was to keep a father's land to support his eldest son, who was obligated to the overlord to serve as a knight or vassal for forty days a year. Primogeniture was finally abolished in Britain in 1925. The custom never caught on in the democratic United States, probably because of its feudal and aristocratic origins.

Other words for historical customs of inheritance include *gavelkind* (GAV-ul-kynd), which divided land equally among the decedent's sons or other heirs (a *decedent,* pronounced di-SEE-dint, is a dead or deceased person); and *borough-English,* where the youngest son, or sometimes the youngest daughter, inherited everything. Two fancy synonyms for *borough-English* are *ultimogeniture* (UHL-ti-moh-**JEN**-i-chur), from the Latin *ultĭmus,* most distant, last, and *postremogeniture* (puh-STREE-muh-**JEN**-i-chur), from the Latin *postrēmus,* hindmost, last.

Word 18: XERIC (ZEER-ik)
Pertaining or adapted to a dry environment; having or needing only a little moisture.

The adjective *xeric* comes from the Greek *xērós,* dry, the source of the English combining form *xero-,* dry, which appears in a number of scientific and technical terms such as *xerophthalmia* (ZEER-ahf-**THAL**-mee-uh), abnormal dryness of the eyes. A *xerophyte* (ZEER-uh-fyt) is a plant that can live in dry conditions, and the adjective *xerophilous* (zeer-AHF-i-lus), which means literally loving dryness, means able to thrive in a hot, dry climate. To *xeriscape*

(ZEER-i-skayp) is to landscape an area with drought-tolerant plants and use techniques, such as mulching, that will limit the need for irrigation. A xeric climate is dry, like Southern California, where I live; a xeric region is dry, like a desert or chaparral; xeric conditions are hot and dry conditions; and xeric landscaping needs only a minimal amount of moisture to survive.

Word 19: UXORIOUS (uhk-SOR-ee-us)
Excessively fond of or submissive to a wife.

"Richard was a fond, almost an uxorious husband," wrote Sir Walter Scott in his 1825 novel *The Talisman.* The movie star Paul Newman was famously and charmingly uxorious about his wife, the movie star Joanne Woodward. And President Obama once took some ribbing from Jacob Heilbrun in *The Huffington Post,* who wrote that "the uxorious Obama had more important things to do—attend a Christmas party or Michelle might get mad at him."

The adjective *uxorious* comes from the Latin *uxōrius,* too devoted to one's wife, which comes in turn from *uxor,* a wife, the source also of four other unusual but useful English words: *uxorial* (uhk-SOR-ee-ul), of or pertaining to a wife, wifely; *uxoricide* (uhk-SOR-i-syd), the killing of one's wife or a man who murders his wife; *uxorilocal* (uhk-SOR-i-**LOH**-kul), a term used in anthropology to mean of or pertaining to living with a wife's family or tribe; and *uxorodespotism* (uhk-SOR-oh-**DES**-puh-tiz'm), wifely tyranny.

If *uxorious* is used of a man who is excessively devoted or attentive to his wife, what do we call a woman who does the same with her husband? The unusual word *maritorious,* from the Latin *marītus,* husband, is the companion of *uxorious* and means excessively devoted to a husband.

Word 20: OPPUGN (uh-PYOON)
To attack or oppose by argument or action; to call into question, contradict, dispute.

The verb to *oppugn* comes through the Latin *oppugnāre,* to attack, assault, oppose, which comes in turn from *pugnāre,* to fight, and *pugnus,* a fist, the source also of the English words *pugilist* (PYOO-ji-list), the fancy word for a boxer; *pugilism* (PYOO-ji-liz'm), the fancy word for boxing; and the adjective *pugnacious,* given to fighting, combative, literally ready to fight with the fists.

To *controvert,* the verb corresponding to the noun *controversy,* is to argue against, oppose by reasoning: "The defense tried to controvert the prosecution's allegations." To *oppugn* is to controvert vigorously, to vehemently call into question, to attack or oppose forcefully. You can oppugn someone's judgment, call it into question, or oppugn someone's argument, dispute its merits or its truth. You can oppugn an idea, as *creationists who oppugn the theory of evolution;* you can oppugn an institution, as *political bloggers who oppugn Congress;* or you can oppugn a person, as, "She oppugned him for being an aloof intellectual in an ivory tower."

Review Quiz for Keywords 11–20

Consider the following statements and decide whether each one is true or false. **Answers appear on page 433.**

1. Ablutions are exercises performed in the morning.

2. Someone who renounces one position in favor of another commits apostasy.

3. A sumptuary tax is imposed on the sale of items everyone uses and needs.

4. A tatterdemalion and a ragamuffin are both poorly clothed.

5. When you abjure you object or disagree politely.

6. People of high social standing enjoy certain privileges known as noblesse oblige.

7. The right of the firstborn son to inherit property or title is called primogeniture.

8. A xeric climate is dry, like a desert or chaparral.

9. An uxorious husband is unkind and unfaithful to his wife.

10. When you oppugn someone's judgment, you vigorously call it into question.

Once Upon a Word: Companion Words

If a misogynist (mi-SAHJ-uh-nist) is a hater of women, what do you call a hater of men? That's one of the most frequently asked questions I've encountered in my louche (word 46 of Level 8) career as a word detective. In the discussion of *misanthropy* (word 14 of Level 5) you met the word *misandrist* (MIS-an-drist or mis-AN-drist), from the Greek *mis(o)-,* hate, and *andro-,* man. A misandrist is a hater of men, and the noun *misandry* means hatred of men.

That's just one example of what I call "companion words," unusual counterparts of more familiar words. You recently learned the companion words *uxorious* and *maritorious,* and there are scores of other such gems lurking in the cobwebbed corners of our unabridged dictionaries, waiting to enlighten and delight us.

Earlier in *Word Workout* you met the companion words *fratricide,* the killing of a brother, from the Latin *frater,* brother, and *sororicide,* the killing of a sister, from the Latin *soror,* a sister. So, if to *fraternize* means to mingle or associate as brothers, what's the word for mingling or associating as sisters? It's *sororize* (SOR-uh-ryz).

If a female ballet dancer is a ballerina, what's the comparable word for a male ballet dancer? Entre nous (AHN-truh-**NOO**, just between us), it's *danseur* (dahn-SUR). If a man who keeps a woman is a *keeper,* is there a word for a woman who keeps a man? Yes, she's a *keeperess.* Samuel Richardson used it in his 1748 novel *Clarissa.* If you're experiencing the opposite of *euphoria,* a feeling of great happiness or well-being, what exactly are you experiencing? It's called *dysphoria* (dis-FOR-ee-uh), an unwell feeling or a generally unwholesome condition.

If you're adept with both hands, you're *ambidextrous.* But what if you're *inept* with both hands? The word for that is *ambisinister,* from *ambi-,* both, and the Latin *sinister,* left or left-handed. *Ambisinister* is the perfect substitute for the shopworn expression *all thumbs.*

Have you ever wondered why the word *feminist,* which came along in the 1890s, never generated a companion? Well, actually it did, but it never got any legs. Though it's clearly a useful word, *hominist* (from the Latin *homo, hominis,* man) is so rare that it appears only in the *OED,* which cites the preface to the 1903 play *Man and Superman* by George Bernard Shaw, who apparently coined it.

I hope this brief disquisition (DIS-kwi-**ZISH-**u̲n, a formal discussion of or inquiry into a subject) on companion words has been neither an *eyesore* nor an *earsore,* an annoyance to the ear, a companion word that *The Century Dictionary* and the *OED* label obsolete but that clamors, in a charmingly disagreeable way, to be resurrected from obscurity. Will you be my companion in that worthy effort?

Let's return now to the *Word Workout* vocabulary for Level 9.

Word 21: AGNOSIA (ag-NOH-zhuh)
The inability, or partial inability, to recognize familiar objects through the senses, usually as the result of brain damage.

The noun *agnosia* comes from the Greek *agnōsía,* ignorance, a combination of the Greek privative prefix *a-,* and *gnosis,* knowledge. You can see this same Greek privative prefix *a-* and *gnosis,* knowledge, in the related English word *agnostic,* which is said to have been coined in 1869 by the British scientist Thomas H. Huxley. An agnostic is a person who holds that the essential nature of things is unknown and cannot be known; hence, an agnostic doubts the existence of God or divine power. To be agnostic is to assert the uncertainty of all claims to knowledge, and agnosticism is the doctrine—or belief in unbelief—of the agnostic.

Agnosia is used chiefly in medicine and psychology to denote the lack or a diminution (DIM-i̲-**NYOO**-shi̲n, a decrease or diminishing) of the sensory ability to recognize objects. Auditory agnosia is misperception of or the inability to interpret sound. Localization agnosia is the inability to recognize where one's skin is touched. Optic agnosia is the inability to interpret visual images. Tactile (TAK-ti̲l) agnosia is the inability to recognize objects by touching them. And visual-spatial agnosia is a disturbance of spatial orientation and a misperception of the spatial relations of objects.

Word 22: CASUISTRY (KAZH-oo-i-stree)

Oversubtle and deceptive reasoning; false or dishonest application of moral principles.

The noun *casuistry* comes from the Latin *cāsus,* a case, event, and since the word entered English in the early 1600s it has been used in a neutral way of the resolving of cases of conscience, or of questions of right and wrong in conduct, by the application of general ethical principles, the laws of society, and religious doctrine. But as *The Century Dictionary* observes, "In the history of Christian and Jewish theology, casuistry has often degenerated into hair-splitting . . . arguments, in which questions of right and wrong were construed to meet selfish aims."

That is why *casuistry* has more often been used pejoratively of oversubtle, deceptive, and specious reasoning, or of any quibbling, evasive way of dealing with difficult questions of duty or conscience: "It was legal casuistry to redefine the torture of prisoners with waterboarding . . . as 'enhanced interrogation'" (*The Economist*); "The cause of gay rights . . . is not helped by this kind of slippery, self-interested scholarship, where propaganda and casuistry impede the objective search for truth" (Camille Paglia).

The word *sophistry* (SAHF-is-tree) is a close synonym of *casuistry*. The Sophists of ancient Greece were teachers of rhetoric, politics, and philosophy notorious for their deceptive and oversubtle method of argumentation. Today *sophistry* refers to speech or writing that is clever and plausible but marred by false or deceptive reasoning.

Other synonyms of *casuistry* include *rationalization* and *equivocation* (discussed under *equivocate,* word 3 of Level 5).

Word 23: PARAPRAXIS (PAR-uh-**PRAK**-sis)

In psychology, a minor error or oversight—such as a slip of the tongue or pen, or the mislaying of objects—thought to reveal unconscious motives or wishes.

The noun *parapraxis* combines the Greek *praxis,* an act or action, with the prefix *para-,* abnormal, defective—as in *paranoia,* from *para-,* abnormal, and the Greek *nous,* mind. By derivation *parapraxis* means abnormal or defective action.

Parapraxis is the technical word for what is more commonly known as a *Freudian slip,* an eponymous term from the name of the pioneer of psychoanalysis, Sigmund Freud (FROYD, 1856–1939). A Freudian slip is the seemingly innocent slip of the tongue that seems to reveal an unconscious wish or motive, especially a sexual one.

English has some other interesting terms for slips, or what some observers call "disfluencies." The Latin word *lapsus,* the source of the English *lapse,* meant a slipping or falling, and English has adopted this word, pronounced LAP-sus, to mean a slip or an error. A *lapsus linguae* (LING-gwee) is a slip of the tongue; a *lapsus calami* (KAL-uh-my) is a slip of the pen; and a *lapsus memoriae* (me-MOR-ee-ee) is a slip of the memory.

Word 24: POLYMATH (PAH-li-MATH)
A very learned person; an expert in various subjects.

The noun *polymath* entered English in the early 1600s from the Greek *polymathés,* very learned, which comes in turn from *poly-,* much, many, and *manthánein,* to learn, the source of *mathematics.*

Words close in meaning to *polymath,* though not synonymous, include *pundit* (word 10 of Level 4), *sage* (rhymes with *page*), *savant* (suh-VAHNT), and the rare word *pantologist* (pan-TAHL-uh-jist), a person with universal or very broad knowledge, from *pan-,* all, and *-logy,* a body of knowledge. The unusual word *polyhistor* (PAH-lee-**HIS**-tur), from the Greek *polyístōr,* very learned, is an exact synonym of *polymath.*

The noun *polymathy* (puh-LIM-uh-thee) means encyclopedic knowledge, learning in many fields. The adjective is *polymathic* (PAH-li-**MATH**-ik), pertaining to polymathy or to a polymath, a very learned person, an expert in many subjects.

Word 25: ENCOMIUM (en-KOH-mee-um)
A formal expression of high praise, a rousing tribute.

The preferred plural is *encomiums.*

The noun *encomium* comes from the Greek *enkōmion,* praising a victor, from *enkōmios,* of the victory procession. By derivation an encomium is a formal expression of high praise for the victor in a victory celebration.

Synonyms of *encomium* include *tribute, eulogy,* and *panegyric* (PAN-uh-**JIR**-ik). All three words refer to the bestowing of high praise. *Tribute* implies the expression of praise either through words or actions; a speech, an essay, a poem, a piece of music, or a charitable effort, such as a fund-raiser, can be a tribute to someone or to a cause. Both a *eulogy* and a *panegyric* are lofty public expressions of praise, usually on some formal occasion; according to *Merriam-Webster's Collegiate Dictionary, eulogy* "applies to a prepared speech or writing extolling the virtues and services of a person," as at a funeral, while *panegyric* "suggests an elaborate often poetic compliment."

Although it connotes a formal and often lofty expression of praise, *encomium* also "implies enthusiasm and warmth in praising a person or a thing," says *M-W 11.* Thus, an enthusiastic letter of recommendation or the affectionate tribute to the bride and groom traditionally delivered by the best man at a wedding can be encomiums.

The noun is *encomiast* (en-KOH-mee-ast), a person who praises or delivers encomiums.

Word 26: CHARRETTE (shuh-RET)
An intensive effort to complete an architectural design project before a deadline.

Charrette, which entered English in the 1960s and is still not listed in many dictionaries, is a borrowing of the modern French *charrette,* a cart, little wagon, from *char,* a truck or wagon—the connection apparently being the speed of the cart's wheels representing the speed of the work on the charrette.

In English, the French-derived suffix *-ette* forms diminutives, or littler versions, of the nouns it's attached to: a *kitchenette* is a little kitchen; a *statuette* is a little statue. The suffix *-ette* also forms feminine nouns such as *coquette* (koh-KET), a flirtatious woman, and *grisette* (gri-ZET), a young French woman of the working class.

"Architects have known for centuries that the most creative way to work is to immerse themselves in a problem for an uninterrupted period—often several days," writes Bill Lennertz in the *Lansing State Journal*. "They call this way of working a charrette." Although *charrette* has been used chiefly in architecture of a short, intensive period of planning or design work that may involve other specialists and sometimes the public, the word is ripe for the plucking in a useful wider sense that Wiktionary, the collaborative online dictionary, defines as "a period of intense work, especially group work, undertaken to meet a deadline." This broader sense would cover all kinds of charrettes—from manufacturing and building, to the crafting of legislation, to the performing arts. On not a few occasions I have told people that the intensive effort I made in the summer of 2013 to finish writing *Word Workout* was a literary charrette.

Word 27: DEBRIDE (di-BREED)

In medicine, to clean a wound by removing foreign material and cutting away dead or contaminated tissue.

Debride entered English by a linguistic process called back-formation, in which a new word is formed by removing an inflectional part of a longer word, such as a prefix or suffix. There are many respectable back-formations in modern English, among them the verb to *collide,* from the noun *collision;* the noun *greed,* from the adjective *greedy;* the verb to *diagnose,* from the noun *diagnosis;* and the verb to *sculpt,* from the noun *sculptor.* But many back-formations are rejected or have trouble gaining acceptance. For example, to *burgle,* a back-formation from *burglar,* has never been a serious contender to supplant *burglarize;* to *liase,* a back-formation from *liaison,* still smacks of business and political jargon even though it's almost a century old; and to *enthuse,* a back-formation from *enthusiasm* that dates from the early 19th century, is still at best a casualism, ill at ease in formal writing.

The verb to *debride* is a back-formation from the noun *debridement* (di-BREED-mint),* the cleaning of a wound by cutting away dead tissue and removing foreign material. Athletes who

---

* For more on the pronunciation of this word, see my *Big Book of Beastly Mispronunciations*.

suffer knee or rotator cuff injuries are often candidates for surgery that involves debridement, and any wound that is slow-healing or that festers will heal faster if it is regularly debrided (di-BREE-did), cleaned of dead or contaminated tissue.

Word 28: LAPIDARY (LAP-i-DER-ee)

Having or exhibiting elegance, precision, and refinement of expression.

Lapidary comes from the Latin *lapis, lapidus,* a stone. The word may be a noun meaning a stone-cutter, someone who engraves and polishes tombstones, or a person who cuts, engraves, and polishes precious stones. As an adjective *lapidary* may also mean pertaining to the cutting and engraving of stones, as *the lapidary art,* or engraved or sculpted in stone, especially a stone monument, as *a lapidary maxim.*

But the adjectival sense of *lapidary* that we are most interested in here is its figurative use to mean having an elegant, precise, refined, and often concise manner of expression suggestive of the skill involved in cutting and polishing gemstones or engraving stone monuments. A lapidary style is elegant, refined, and often succinct. Lapidary lines or verses are graceful and polished. A lapidary mind is cultured and brilliant. And lapidary detail is finely observed and precisely recorded.

Word 29: OVIPAROUS (oh-VIP-uh-rus)

Producing eggs that develop and hatch outside the mother's body.

The adjective *oviparous,* which is chiefly used in zoology (zoh-AHL-uh-jee, not zoo-), comes from the Latin *ōviparus,* egg-laying. It is a blend of the combining forms *ovi-,* egg, from the Latin *ōvum,* an egg—the source of the English *oviform* (OH-vi-form), egg-shaped—and *-parous,* which means bearing, producing, and comes from the Latin *parere,* to bring forth, bear, produce.

Viviparous (vy-VIP-uh-rus), which comes from the Latin *vīvus,* living, alive, and the same *-parous,* bearing, producing, means giving birth to living offspring that can survive outside the mother's body, as do human beings and most mammals. *Oviparous* means laying eggs that hatch outside the mother's body. Chickens and other birds are the most familiar oviparous animals, but most reptiles and fish are also oviparous.

Word 30: MARMOREAL (mahr-MOR-ee-ul)
Made of or resembling marble or a marble statue; having the qualities of marble.

The adjective *marmoreal* comes from the Latin *marmoreus,* made of marble, which comes in turn from *marmor,* marble. It is a literary word favored by poets and prose stylists who use it to suggest the whiteness, smoothness, hardness, or coldness of marble. Because marble is both white and smooth and hard and cold, the connotation of *marmoreal* can be either ameliorative or pejorative. (For a review of those terms, see *pejorative,* word 17 of Level 6.) For example, a marmoreal complexion or face can be either attractively white and smooth or unappealingly pallid (word 47 of Level 4), suggesting illness or the paleness of death. The 19th-century English poet Robert Browning used the word in a positive way when he wrote of a "marmoreal neck and bosom." But a movie critic for the *Washington Post* used it negatively when describing a character as "a bloodless, marmoreal being who has no human connections."

Review Quiz for Keywords 21–30
Decide if the pairs of words below are synonyms or antonyms. **Answers appear on page 434.**

1. *Agnosia* and *misperception* are . . . synonyms or antonyms?
2. *Sophistry* and *casuistry* are . . .
3. *Freudian slip* and *parapraxis* are . . .
4. *Polymath* and *ignoramus* are . . .
5. *Encomium* and *panegyric* are . . .
6. *Charrette* and *vacation* are . . .
7. *Befoul* and *debride* are . . .
8. *Lapidary* and *unpolished* are . . .

9. *Mammalian* and *oviparous* are . . .

10. *Marmoreal* and *pallid* are . . .

Difficult Distinctions: *Dieresis* and *Umlaut*

"Could you please settle a debate?" writes Timothy Hernandez of Englewood, Colorado. Of course I can. That's what we language mavens live to do.

"Responding to a question in an online forum," Hernandez explains, "I wrote that the diacritical mark (two dots) placed over the *e* in the name *Chloë* is an umlaut. Two other people said it's more properly called a dieresis. Who is correct?"

Both *umlaut* (OOM-lowt) and *dieresis* (dy-ER-uh-sis) denote the same diacritical mark—two dots placed over a vowel—but the difference between these words lies in how that mark is used. An umlaut is placed over a vowel to show that it has a sound slightly different from how the vowel would be pronounced without the mark. Umlauts, which are common in German, are never used over a vowel next to another vowel. The dieresis, on the other hand, always appears over the second of two adjoining vowels to show that the second, marked vowel should be pronounced separately from the first one.

For example, *cooperate* and *preeminent* were formerly printed with a dieresis (*coöperate, preëminent*) so people wouldn't inadvertently say *koop*-erate and *preem*-inent. Because the diacritical mark over the *e* in *Chloë* appears above the second of two adjoining vowels and indicates that the vowels are pronounced separately (KLOH-ee), it is properly called a dieresis.

Incidentally, a *diacritical mark,* or *diacritic,* is a mark applied to a letter to distinguish it as having a specific sound or way of being pronounced. Common diacritics include the cedilla (suh-DIL-uh) under the *c* in *façade,* which indicates that it should sound like *s* in *sod,* and the acute accents in *résumé,* which show that the word has three syllables and is not pronounced like the verb *resume.* Dictionaries use diacritical marks to show pronunciation, such as the macron (MAY-krahn) for a long vowel sound, as in / sē / for *see,* and the breve (BREEV) for a short vowel sound, as in / pŏt / for *pot.*

Now let's return to the *Word Workout* vocabulary for ten more keyword discussions.

Word 31: NUGATORY (N[Y]OO-guh-tor-ee)

Of no worth, value, or importance; worthless, insignificant. Also, having no force or effect; useless, futile, vain.

Synonyms of *nugatory* in the sense of having no value or worth include *trifling, inconsequential, trivial, piddling,* and *negligible* (NEG-li-gi-bul). Synonyms of *nugatory* in the sense of having no force or effect include *invalid, inoperative, ineffectual, bootless* (word 15 of Level 6), *feckless,* and *inefficacious* (in-EF-i-KAY-shus).

The adjective *nugatory* comes from the Latin *nūgātōrius,* frivolous, insignificant, futile, from the verb *nūgāri,* to trifle, be frivolous, talk nonsense. That which is nugatory either has no intrinsic value or importance or has no force or effect.

Nugatory actions are unimportant or ineffectual; a nugatory argument is worthless or futile; and nugatory excuses are trivial and vain. "As TV and the Internet converge into something generically known as broadband, the distinctions between the two will soon become nugatory from a consumer point of view" (Michael Hirschorn, *The Atlantic*). "Tactical excellence and the considerable courage of frontline troops are forever being rendered nugatory by failed leadership" (*The Washington Post*). In law *nugatory* means invalid, as when a court renders a statute nugatory by declaring it unconstitutional.

The noun *nugacity* (n[y]oo-GAS-i-tee) means either triviality, insignificance, as *the tedious nugacity of everyday life,* or a trivial or insignificant thing or idea, as *the pompous nugacities of the preacher's sermons.*

Word 32: PRESBYCUSIS (PREZ-bi-KYOO-sis)

Loss or impairment of hearing due to old age.

The noun *presbycusis* comes from the Greek *presbys,* which meant old or an old man, and *ákousis,* hearing, which comes in turn from *akouein,* to hear. From the same Greek *akouein,* to hear, come the

English words *acoustic* (uh–KOO–stik), relating to hearing or to the science of sound, and the unusual *acouasm* (uh–KOO–az'm), a buzzing or ringing in the ears, also called *tinnitus* (properly pronounced ti̱-NY-tu̱s to rhyme with *arthritis*), from the Latin *tinnīre*, to ring, tinkle.

You can see the English combining form *presby-,* from the Greek *presbys,* old, in *presbyter* (PREZ-bi̱-tur), which by deriva-tion means an elder; *presbytery* (PREZ-bi̱-ter-ee), a body of pres-byters or elders; and *Presbyterian* (PREZ-bi̱-**TEER**-ee-i̱n), pertaining to various churches that are governed by presbyters or elders. In ophthalmology (in which the first syllable is properly pronounced AHF-, not AHP-), the branch of medicine dealing with the eyes, the word *presbyopia* (PREZ-bee-**OH**-pee-uh) de-notes the gradual development, beginning in middle age, of far-sightedness and a difficulty focusing sharply on things up close.

Our keyword, *presbycusis,* is the medical term for any deterio-ration of the sense of hearing due to advanced age, otherwise known as age-related deafness. Presbycusis often begins with a reduced ability to hear high-pitched sounds. Later, sounds may become distorted and fuzzy and are often quieter overall.

Word 33: CICERONE (SIS-uh-**ROH**-nee)
A guide, especially one who leads and instructs sightseers; hence, a tutor or mentor.

The noun *cicerone* comes through Italian from the name of the fa-mous Roman orator and statesman Cicero (SIS-uh-roh, 106–43 B.C.). Thus, by derivation, the cicerone, or guide, is "thought of as having the knowledge and eloquence of Cicero" (*Random House*). The *OED* says the term was "apparently originally given to learned Italian antiquarians, whose services were sought by visitors seeking information about the antiquities of a place."

Guide is the general term for someone who leads or directs oth-ers. The words *usher, escort,* and *marshal* denote people whose pro-fessional or official duty is to guide or accompany others. The words *tutor, mentor* (MEN-tur, not -tor), and *preceptor* (pree-SEP-tur) denote people who guide by teaching or informing, especially one-on-one. The word *guru* (GUUR-oo), which entered English in about 1820 from the Indian language Hindi (HIN-dee), is a spiritual or religious guide, especially a personal one; by extension, a guru is someone with special knowledge that others rely on or admire, as *a computer guru*. A *docent* (DOH-sint)—from the Latin *docēre,* to lead, the source also of *docile* (DAH-sil), easily led or managed, cooperative—is a tour guide who leads people through galleries and museums, instructing them about what they are viewing.

Our keyword, *cicerone,* is a kind of glorified or scholarly tour guide who has intimate knowledge of places of historical interest and the facts and stories pertaining to them. The word may be used literally of a guide for sightseers, or figuratively of a guide who leads you toward a better knowledge of some subject.

The preferred plural form is the anglicized *cicerones* (SIS-uh-**ROH**-neez), although dictionaries also sanction the Italian *ciceroni* (SIS-uh-ROH-nee).

Word 34: PANSOPHIC (pan-SAHF-ik)
Pertaining to, or possessing, universal wisdom or encyclopedic knowledge.

Pansophic is the adjective corresponding to the noun *pansophy* (PAN-suh-fee), universal wisdom or encyclopedic knowledge. Both words come from the Greek *pan-,* all, and *sophós,* wisdom. You can see this Greek *sophós,* wisdom, in numerous English words including *philosophy,* which means literally loving wisdom; *sophomore,* literally wise-foolish, from the Greek *mōros,* foolish, dull; and *sophrosyne* (suh-FRAHS-uh-nee), which means wise moderation, prudence, discreet good sense.

Pansophy refers in particular to a system of universal knowledge proposed by Comenius (koh-MEE-nee-us), a 17th-century Moravian clergyman and educator whose precepts about teaching and learning seem decidedly modern. "Comenius advocated relating education to everyday life by emphasizing contact with objects in the environment and systematizing all knowledge," says the *Columbia Encyclopedia*. "Teaching was to be in the vernacular rather than in Latin, and languages were to be learned by the conversational method. He [also] worked for a universal system of education offering equal opportunities to women."

Word 35: RUBICUND (ROO-bi-kund)
Red or reddish in color; flushed.

Synonyms of *rubicund* include *ruddy, florid, sanguine, roseate* (ROH-zee-it) like a rose in color; *rufous* (ROO-fus), reddish, from the Latin *rūfus,* red; and *erubescent* (er-uh-BES-int), becoming red, blushing. Antonyms of *rubicund* include *pale, ashen, blanched, bloodless, pallid* (word 47 of Level 4), *wan,* and *cadaverous* (kuh-DAV-ur-us), having the appearance of a cadaver (kuh-DAV-ur), a dead body.

   Rubicund comes from the Latin *rubicundus,* red, flushed, which comes in turn from *rubēre,* to be red, and *ruber,* red, ruddy. From this same source come the English words *ruby,* the familiar red gemstone; the adjective *rubious,* ruby-colored; the noun *rubric,* a title, heading, or part of a text that is printed in red; *rubricate,* to mark or color in red; *rubify,* to redden or make red, as *the sunset rubified the sky;* and *rubeola* (ROO-bee-**OH**-luh), the medical term for measles.

   Rubicund may be used generally of anything that's red or reddish, such as a rubicund apple or rubicund wine, but it is perhaps more often used of the face or complexion to mean red or flushed, as *cheeks rubicund from the cold* or *a rubicund nose,* or of a person who is red-faced, especially from overindulgence in food and drink: "The chef was a corpulent (word 39 of Level 4), rubicund, loquacious little man."

Word 36: PICARESQUE (PIK-uh-**RESK**)
Of or relating to rogues, rascals, or knaves; specifically, of or pertaining to an episodic form of narrative fiction that chronicles the adventures of a roguish but likable hero. "The picaresque style," says the *OED,* "is characterized by social satire and realistic descriptions of scenes from low life."

Picaresque comes from the Spanish *picaresco,* roguish, mischievous, literally of or pertaining to a *picaro,* a rogue, rascal. From the Spanish *picaro* English has also inherited the noun *picaroon* (pik-uh-ROON), a rogue, vagabond, or thief, especially a pirate or brigand (BRIG-und), a member of a band of robbers.

   Synonyms of *picaresque* include *roguish, rascally, prankish, swashbuckling, adventuresome, rakish* (RAY-kish), and *raffish* (RAF-ish).

Synonyms of *picaroon* include *bandit, outlaw, highwayman, desperado,* and *cutthroat.*

In 1829, the Scottish historical novelist Sir Walter Scott astutely called the picaresque novel, which originated in Spain in the 16th century, "a romance of roguery." It was "usually a first-person narrative, relating the adventures of a rogue or lowborn adventurer . . . who drifts from place to place and from one social milieu to another in an effort to survive," says *Merriam-Webster's Encyclopedia of Literature.* "In its episodic structure the picaresque novel resembles the long, rambling romances of medieval chivalry, to which it provided the first realistic counterpart. Unlike the idealistic knight-errant hero, however, the picaro is a cynical and amoral rascal who would rather live by his wits than by honorable work."

Picaresque may be used not only of fiction but of anything that suggests the freewheeling lifestyle of a rogue, rascal, or vagabond. For example, "a picaresque series of exploits that illustrate her ability to live by her wits" (*The New Yorker*); or, "It was a picaresque life, lived in hotels on the fringes of 'normal' society" (*Sunday Independent,* Ireland). When *picaresque* is preceded by *the,* it denotes the mischievous and often amoral qualities of a rogue or rascal: "He loves a trickster; the picaresque amuses him."

Word 37: ENDOGENOUS (en-DAHJ-uh-n<u>u</u>s)
Originating or produced from within.

The adjective *endogenous* combines *endo-,* within—as in *endocardial,* situated within the heart, and *endogamy* (en-DAH-guh-mee), marriage within a tribe or family—with *-genous,* which means originating or producing in a specific manner, as in *indigenous* (in-DIJ-i-n<u>u</u>s), originating in a particular place, hence native.

In biology, *endogenous* means growing or produced within the organism. In pathology, the study of diseases, *endogenous* is used of a disease that originates from within the organism. And in psychiatry, *endogenous* refers to disorders that originate within the individual rather than being caused by external factors, as *endogenous depression.*

The antonym of *endogenous* is *exogenous* (eks-AHJ-uh-n<u>us</u>), originating or produced from without, from *exo-*, outside, external.

Word 38: PERORATE (**PER**-uh-rayt)

To speak at great length, especially in a high-flown or pompous manner; also, to conclude a speech, especially in a forceful or rousing manner.

Synonyms of the verb to *perorate* include to *lecture, declaim, discourse* (dis-KORS), *descant* (des-KANT), and *expatiate* (ek-SPAY-shee-ayt).

   Perorate comes from the Latin *perōrātus,* the past participle of *perōrāre,* which meant either to speak at length, explain or state thoroughly, or to wind up a speech, conclude an oration, from *per-*, thoroughly, and *ōrāre,* to speak, argue, plead. This Latin *ōrāre* is also the source of the familiar words *oration, orator* (OR-uh-tur), and *orate.*

   What's the difference between to *orate* and to *perorate?* It's a difference of degree or intensity caused by the prefix *per-,* which is an intensifier in many words. For example, to *ambulate,* from the Latin *ambulāre,* to walk, means simply to walk or stroll, while to *perambulate* is to walk all about. The adjective *fervid,* from the Latin *fervēre,* to boil, seethe, means passionate or vehement, as *a fervid* debate, while the adjective *perfervid* (pur-FUR-vid) means overheated, boiling over with passionate intensity. And the adjective *tenacious,* from the Latin *tenēre,* to hold, means holding firmly to a belief or course of action, while the adjective *pertinacious* (PUR-ti-**NAY**-sh<u>us</u>) means to be stubbornly and annoyingly tenacious. Thus, to *orate* is merely to lecture or deliver a formal public speech, while to *perorate* is to speak at great length, especially in a pompous or grandiose (word 3 of Level 1) manner.

   The noun is *peroration* (PER-uh-**RAY**-sh<u>i</u>n), which may mean a long and often pompous oration, but which is probably more often used to mean the concluding part of a speech, especially a rousing speech, in which points made earlier are recapitulated.

Word 39: ONYCHOPHAGY (AHN-i-**KAHF**-uh-jee)

The act or habit of biting one's nails; nail-biting.

The noun *onychophagy* links two combining forms: *onycho-,* of or pertaining to the nails, from the Greek *onyx,* a nail, claw; and *-phagy,* eating, devouring, from the Greek *phagein,* to eat. Other words from the Greek *onyx,* a nail, include *onycholysis* (AHN-i̱-**KAH**-luh-sis), a loosening or partial separation of a nail from a finger or toe (from the Greek *lysis,* a loosening), and *paronychia* (PAR-uh-**NIK**-ee-uh), an inflammation of the flesh surrounding a nail: colloquially, an infected hangnail.

Onychophagy is used chiefly in medicine and in psychology, where it refers to habitual nail-biting as a symptom of anxiety or emotional disturbance. In the interest of full disclosure, I must confess that I have a personal stake in this word, since for most of my life I was an inveterate (word 25 of Level 2) onychophagist (AHN-i̱-**KAHF**-uh-jist), a nail-biter, at one point suffering from an excruciatingly painful paronychia caused by my own ruthless onychophagy. And then—and here's the Ripley's -Believe-It-or-Not story—three weeks after 9/11 I realized that I hadn't bitten my nails since that tragic day, and I haven't bitten them since. You'd think that such a horrific and traumatic event would *cause* a nervous habit, but somehow, inexplicably, it broke me of one.

Word 40: DÉJÀ LU (DAY-zhah-**LOO**)
The feeling that you have read something before.

You are probably familiar with the term *déjà vu* (DAY-zhah-**VOO**), which entered English from French about 1900. Literally it means *already seen* and denotes the illusory feeling of having experienced or done something before. From the same French *déjà,* already, and *lu,* read, comes *déjà lu,* which entered English about 1960 and means the sense that you have read something before or in a similar form somewhere else. The *OED* records one more related loan phrase from French: *déjà entendu* (ah[n]-taw[n]-DOO), which means literally *already heard* and denotes the feeling that one has already heard a passage of music before.

Review Quiz for Keywords 31–40

In each statement below, a keyword (in *italics*) is followed by three definitions. Two of the three are correct; one is unrelated in meaning. Decide which one doesn't fit the keyword. **Answers appear on page 435.**

1. *Nugatory* means of no worth, uninteresting, useless.
2. *Presbycusis* is loss of hearing due to old age, ringing in the ears, age-related deafness.
3. A *cicerone* is a taxi driver, a guide, a tutor.
4. *Pansophic* means having exceptional insight, universal wisdom, encyclopedic knowledge.
5. *Rubicund* means reddish, bloodless, flushed.
6. *Picaresque* means pertaining to fools, pertaining to rogues, pertaining to rascals.
7. *Endogenous* means produced from within, coming into existence, originating inside.
8. *Perorate* means to speak incoherently, to speak at great length, to conclude a speech.
9. *Onychophagy* is chewing one's nails, biting one's nails, trimming one's nails.
10. *Déjà lu* is the feeling you have read something before, seen something before, perused something before.

Once Upon a Word: Venery Interesting

"It's a gaggle of geese, a school of fish, and a pride of lions. But what about tigers?" I'm telling you, people email me some amazing questions!

These terms for groups of animals have been called "nouns of multitude," "company terms," "nouns of assemblage," and, most commonly, "group nouns." But connoisseurs of these words also know them by an older phrase, "terms of venery," *venery* here denoting not sexual intercourse but hunting or animals that are hunted (from the Latin *venari,* to hunt).

"The venereal game," as the connoisseurs call it, is the art of inventing these playful and often poetic group nouns, and it has been going on for centuries. One of the earliest and most exhaustive records of group nouns is *The Book of St. Albans* by Dame Juliana Berners (or Barnes), published in 1486. Dame Juliana's book contained a list of 164 group nouns, including *a rafter of turkeys, a murder of crows, a murmuration of starlings, a shrewdness of apes, a leap of leopards, a skulk of foxes, a knot of toads,* and *a cowardice of curs.* It also contained some terms—such as *a pontificality of priests, a superfluity of nuns,* and *an abominable sight of monks*—that venture beyond the animal kingdom and into the human realm.

An Exaltation of Larks by James Lipton is one of the best-known modern books on the subject of group nouns. It discusses the evolution of the venereal game from ancient terms for animals like *a clowder of cats, a sloth of bears, a siege of herons,* and *an ostentation of peacocks* to modern terms for all types of people like *a sneer of butlers, a rash of dermatologists, an indifference of waiters, a wheeze of joggers, an ingratitude of children,* and *a lot of used car dealers.*

Now, what about those tigers? A *streak* of tigers is the term Lipton gives, but an *ambush* of tigers has also been proposed. Take your pick.

Now let's return to the *Word Workout* vocabulary.

Word 41: VERBIGERATE (vur-BIJ-ur-ayt)
To repeat meaningless words or phrases continually and obsessively.

A close synonym of *verbigerate* is the verb to *battologize* (buh-TAH-luh-jyz), which comes from the Greek *battos,* a stammerer, and *logos,* speech, and means to repeat words or phrases needlessly and tiresomely.

The verb to *verbigerate* and the noun *verbigeration,* the obsessive repetition of meaningless words or phrases, come from the Latin *verbigerare,* to chat, talk, converse, a combination of *verbum,* a word, and *gĕrĕre,* to carry on, conduct. A *verbigerator* (rhymes with *refrigerator*) is a person who verbigerates, continually repeats certain meaningless words or phrases.

In pathology, the science of diseases and disorders, verbigeration is the abnormal, unconscious, and often obsessive repetition of non sequiturs (nahn-SEK-wi-turz), words or phrases that do not follow from what has previously been said or are unrelated to the context and therefore meaningless. (*Non sequitur* comes directly from Latin and means "it does not follow.") To a medical doctor or psychiatrist, verbigeration is usually the result of a brain injury or mental disorder, but to the rest of us laypeople it is simply part of the verbal fabric of everyday life.

Toddlers will often latch onto a word or phrase they've picked up from their parents or from TV and repeat it indiscriminately and mercilessly. Elderly people succumbing to senile dementia (SEE-nyl di-MEN-shuh) often verbigerate, even when no one is listening. And then there are those pesky verbigerating teenagers who insert *like* and *y'know* into every sentence, and who grow up to be tedious, verbigerating adults who insert meaningless words and phrases like *anyways* and *irregardless* into every sentence.

For me, the most verbigerated words in the English language are *impact* and *unique,* which have been repeated so often and so unthinkingly by so many people that they have lost all their force and singularity.

Word 42: TENEBROUS (TEN-uh-brus)
Dark, gloomy, obscure.

The adjective *tenebrous,* which dates back to the early 1400s, comes from the Latin *tenebrōsus,* dark, gloomy. The word may be used to mean dark, shut off from the light, either literally or figuratively. A tenebrous castle or a tenebrous climate is a dark and gloomy one. A tenebrous mind is a benighted (word 48 of Level 6) mind, one laboring in a state of intellectual darkness. And a tenebrous argument or a tenebrous philosophy is one that is so obscure as to be impenetrable.

The related adjective *tenebrific* (TEN-uh-**BRIF**-ik), from the Latin *tenebrae,* darkness, and *facere,* to make, means causing or producing darkness. A solar eclipse is tenebrific, as are most economists.

Word 43: AGNATE (AG-nayt)

Related through the male line of descent; related on the father's side.

Agnate comes from the Latin *agnātus,* a male relation on the father's side. The Old Testament of the Christian Bible expends a good deal of ink tracing the agnate offspring, or male line of descent, of various figures: for example, the sons of Noah, the sons of Shem, the sons of Esau. Your agnate relative is either someone whose kinship is traceable only through males, or a male relative on the father's side, a paternal kinsman. *Agnate* may also be used as a noun meaning a relation through the male line.

Perhaps you're wondering if there's a companion word for *agnate* pertaining to women? The adjective *distaff* (DIS-taf) means female, pertaining to women, and the distaff side of a family is the female or maternal branch, also called the *spindle* side, as opposed to the *spear* side, the male or paternal branch. But more closely related to *agnate* is the word *cognate* (KAHG-nayt), from the Latin *cognātus,* born together. In Roman law *cognate* referred to those who were descended from the same ancestor, regardless of sex, but "in Scots and later civil law," says *Black's Law Dictionary,* *cognate* "implies kinship from the mother's side."

Word 44: ULULATE (UHL-yuh-layt *or* YOOL-yuh-layt)

To howl, wail, screech, or shriek.

The verb to *ululate* comes from the Latin *ululātus,* a howling, wailing, shrieking, or yelling, the past participle of the verb *ululāre,* to howl or yell. By derivation, to *ululate* suggests the howling of a dog or wolf, or the screeching of an owl. In fact, in the earliest English dictionary in which *ululate* appears, from 1623, the word is defined as "to howle like a dog or wolf."

Ululate is often used of animal-like howling, wailing, or screeching, as *a pack of hungry, ululating jackals.* But it is also often used of human crying and shrieking, as in this citation from 2009: "In some cultures, the grieving ululate, whip themselves, and rend their clothing" (www.wordnik.com/words/ululate). When used in this way *ululate* is an exact synonym of the verb to *keen,* to wail or lament loudly, especially for the dead. *Ululate* is also sometimes used of any excited howling or yelling, as illustrated by this sentence from *Newsweek:* "We stand in a circle and clap— some of the women even ululate in a sort of joyous yodel."

The noun is *ululation* (UHL-yuh-**LAY**-shin or YOOL-), a howling or wailing. In his 1867 translation of Dante's *Divine Comedy,* the American poet Henry Wadsworth Longfellow wrote, "There sighs, complaints, and ululations loud / Resounded through the air." The adjective is *ululant* (UHL-yuh-lint or YOOL-), howling, wailing, screeching: "The preacher's exhortations whipped the congregation into an ululant frenzy."

Word 45: ZUCCHETTO (zoo-KET-oh)
A skullcap worn by Roman Catholic clerics.

The noun *zucchetto* was borrowed from Italian in the mid-19th century and is related to the Italian *zucca,* which means either a gourd or the head and is the source of the familiar Italian squash called *zucchini* (zoo-KEE-nee). The unusual word *calotte* (kuh-LAHT), which was borrowed from French in the 17th century, is an exact synonym of *zucchetto.* The plural is preferably the anglicized *zucchettos,* not the Italian *zucchetti.*

The *zucchetto* is small and round and made of flexible cloth. You could say that it is the ecclesiastical cousin of the Jewish skullcap called a *yarmulke* (YAHR-mul-kuh, pronounce the *r*). The color of the zucchetto indicates the rank of a cleric in the Roman Catholic hierarchy. Priests wear a black zucchetto; bishops wear a violet or purple one; cardinals wear a red one; and the pope wears a white one.

Word 46: PSEUDANDRY (SOO-dan-dree *or* soo-DAN-dree)
The use of a male name by a woman as a pseudonym or pen name.

The noun *pseudandry* combines *pseudo-,* false, pretended, with *-andry,* male, which comes from the Greek *andrós,* a man, male. A *pseudonym* (SOO-duh-nim), from *pseudo-,* false, and *-onym,* name, is a fictitious name, such as the pen name of an author. A pseudonym or pen name is also called a *nom de plume* (NAHM-duh-**PLOOM**), which is French for pen name.

In the 18th and 19th centuries the few women who wrote for publication usually resorted to pseudandry, the use of a male pen name, because of their inferior social status: women were thought to be less competent than men and it was considered scandalous for a woman to write a book. Pseudandry therefore offered a way to be taken seriously, or at least not to be dismissed outright.

Famous pseudandrists of that period include Mary Ann Evans, who used the nom de plume George Eliot to publish *Middlemarch* and other novels; the Brontë sisters, Charlotte, Emily, and Anne, who used, respectively, the pseudonyms Currer, Ellis, and Acton Bell; the French novelist Lucile Aurore Dupin Dudevant, who achieved fame writing under the pseudonym George Sand; and Louisa May Alcott, author of *Little Women,* who began her career writing under the androgynous (an-DRAH-juh-nus) pen name A. M. Barnard. (*Androgynous,* from the Greek *andrós,* man, and *gyné,* woman, means having qualities or characteristics of both a man and a woman.)

Contemporary female writers who have used androgynous initials in their pen names include Nora Roberts, who has published as J. D. Robb, and Anne Rice, who has published as A. N. Roquelaure. And J. K. Rowling, the androgynously named author of the Harry Potter series, has written under the pseudonym Robert Galbraith.

The counterpart of *pseudandry* is *pseudogyny* (soo-DAH-juh-nee), from *pseudo-,* false, pretended, and the Greek *gyné,* woman, the use of a female name by a man as a pseudonym or pen name.

Word 47: CAESURA (si-ZHUUR-uh)
A break, pause, interruption, hiatus (hy-AY-tus).

Caesura comes directly from the Latin *caesūra,* a cutting, which comes in turn from the verb *caedĕre,* to cut. A *Caesarean section* is so called because the baby must be cut from its mother's womb. The procedure is traditionally associated with Julius Caesar, who was supposed to have been delivered by Caesarean section, but the evidence supporting that story is flimsy.

Caesura has a specific, technical meaning in English prosody, the study of the metrical structure of poetry. In prosody, a caesura is a natural pause or break or breath somewhere in the middle of a poetic line. Thus, the caesura in the opening line of Chaucer's *Canterbury Tales* comes right after *April*: "Whan that April ‖ with his showres soote." And the caesura in the first line of Shakespeare's sonnet 18 is the fleeting pause between *thee* and *to*: "Shall I compare thee ‖ to a summer's day?"

Since about the mid-19th century *caesura* has also been used in a more general sense of any break, pause, or interruption: "The Flavian [FLAY-vee-in] dynasty marks a caesura in the history of Roman first ladies" (Annelise Freisenbruch, *Caesars' Wives*). "He remembers one space offering a welcome caesura from the ormolu and swag" (*The Wall Street Journal*). (*Ormolu,* pronounced OR-muh-loo, is gilded metal.)

Word 48: PHILODOX (FIL-uh-dahks)
Someone in love with his or her own opinions; a person who makes categorical assertions; a dogmatist.

You've run across them your whole life—in school, at work, at parties—those self-referential bores who love to hear themselves talk. Philodoxes think that everything they say is brilliant and that everything they know is right. They are often lovers of argument for its own sake and they are always eager to buttonhole anyone they think will listen. This quality makes the philodox the close cousin of the *macrologist* (ma-KRAHL-uh-jist), the infernally dull conversationalist you get stuck with at a social event and deftly try to pass on to someone else.

The noun *philodox,* which was borrowed from French in 1603, is formed from two Greek elements: *philo-,* loving, and *doxa,* opinion, the source also of *orthodox,* which means literally the right opinion because the combining form *ortho-* means right, correct. Here's a clever citation for *philodox* from the *Berkshire* (Massachusetts) *Eagle* in 1958: "One grows weary of the sickening sophomoric twaddle of our local pansophic philodox." (*Sophomoric* is discussed in *fatuous,* word 6 of Level 3; *twaddle* [TWAHD'l] is silly talk, drivel, nonsense; and *pansophic* is word 34 of this level.)

Word 49: VALETUDINARIAN (VAL-e̲-T[Y]OO-di̲-**NAIR**-ee-i̲n)
A weak or sickly person, an invalid or hypochondriac.

Valetudinarian comes through the Latin *valētūdinārius,* sickly, infirm, from *valēre,* to be strong, well, or vigorous, the source also of the English words *valor* and *valiant.* Cousins with the Latin *valēre,* to be strong, is the adjective *validus,* strong, powerful, the source of the English noun *invalid* (IN-vuh-lid), an exact synonym of *valetudinarian,* a weak or sickly person.

Valetudinarian is often used not only of a sickly person but of a hypochondriac, someone who continually imagines he or she has physical ailments. In Victor Hugo's 1862 novel *Les Misérables,* a character named Joly is a doctor who was "more of an invalid than a doctor. At three and twenty he thought himself a valetudinarian, and passed his life in inspecting his tongue in the mirror."

Valetudinarian may also be used attributively, as an adjective modifying a noun, as *a dissolute, valetudinarian debauchee.* (*Dissolute* is word 7 of Level 6, and *debauchee,* a debauched person, is discussed in *debauch,* word 30 of Level 5.)

Word 50: APOTHEOSIS (uh-PAH-thee-**OH**-sis)
The elevation of a human being to the level of a god; hence, elevation to a transcendent or glorified position, or a glorified or exalted example or ideal.

Synonyms of the noun *apotheosis* include *deification, glorification, exaltation, canonization,* and *consecration.* (*Consecrate* is word 42 of Level 2.)

Apotheosis is a late-16th-century borrowing from Latin and Greek that comes from the Greek *apotheoun,* to make into a god, deify, from *apo-,* formed from, related to, and *theos,* a god. At first *apotheosis* was used of the elevation of a human being to the rank of a god, as when the ancient Romans, by a solemn decree of the senate, would confer divine status upon a deceased emperor. The word was then extended to mean the elevation of any person or thing to a glorified or transcendent position: "Some music critics lament the apotheosis of immature pop stars like Justin Bieber and Miley Cyrus." In the 20th century the word's application was extended even further to mean an exalted or glorified example or ideal, as *the apotheosis of beauty, the apotheosis of courage,* or *the apotheosis of Italian comic opera.*

Sometimes *apotheosis* is used of that which is decidedly *not* glorified or exalted, as if it meant simply the perfect or best example: "Blagojevich is regularly described as the apotheosis of the shady Illinois politician." This erroneous usage should be avoided, and *apotheosis* should be reserved for exalted or glorified examples. *Apotheosis* is also often used to mean the highest point, climax, as *the apotheosis of her career,* but this is another loose usage. When you mean the highest point in the development of something, use *peak, summit, pinnacle, apex, zenith,* or *apogee* (word 9 of Level 7) instead.

The verb to *apotheosize* (uh-PAH-thee-uh-syz) means either to make into a god or to glorify as if to divine honor: "When Dwight D. Eisenhower was elected president in 1952, it was as if the American people had apotheosized him for his role in winning World War II."

Review Quiz for Keywords 41–50

In this quiz the review word is followed by three words or phrases, and you must decide which comes nearest the meaning of the review word. **Answers appear on page 435**.

1. If you *verbigerate,* do you run off at the mouth, repeat meaningless words and phrases continually, or choose your words carefully?

2. Is something *tenebrous* sad, dangerous, or dark?

3. Are your *agnate* relatives on your mother's side, your father's side, or both sides?

4. Does *ululate* mean to eat too much, to garble one's words, or to howl?

5. Is a *zucchetto* a green squash, a skullcap, or a short sword?

6. Is *pseudandry* the use of a female pseudonym by a man, the use of a male pseudonym by a woman, or the use of initials in a pseudonym?

7. Is a *caesura* a break, an operation, or a victory song?

8. Is a *philodox* a virtuous person, a generous person, or a person in love with his or her own opinions?

9. Is a *valetudinarian* a sickly person, a faithful person, or an unreliable person?

10. Does *apotheosis* mean the revelation of divine wisdom, the elevation of a person to the level of a god, or the appearance of a god?

The Wrong Pro-NOUN-ciation

At Merriam-Webster, the storied house of lexicography in Spring-field, Massachusetts, that traces its pedigree to Noah Webster, the editors have been sedulously (*sedulous* is word 28 of Level 7) collecting citations since the 1930s of "all pronunciation variants of a word that are used by educated speakers of the English language." And when they say all, they mean all—including the warts.* If a lapsus linguae happens to come out of an educated speaker's mouth, it goes in the file. This worries me because "it is primarily on the basis of this large and growing file," says their latest dictionary, "that questions of usage and acceptability in pronunciation are answered."

Like other dictionary publishers, Merriam-Webster promises to give us guidance in standard American pronunciation, but their concept of standard American pronunciation seems to be that if you're an American, your pronunciation is standard, no matter how eccentric it may be. Peruse M-W's popular Collegiate dictionaries and you will find many controversial, stigmatized, and downright strange pronunciations—all of them, M-W claims, "falling within the range of generally acceptable variation."

Let's see how that claim holds up.

We'll begin with *accurate,* which M-W gets all wrong. Recent Collegiates bestow their blessing on AK-ur-it and AK-rit, variants that are not standard and never have been. The vast majority of educated speakers consider them slovenly (SLUHV-<u>un</u>-lee, sloppy, careless), which is why the other major current American

---

* This is an allusion to a condensed version of a statement by the English general and statesman Oliver Cromwell (1599–1658), who told an artist who was painting his portrait, "Paint me as I am, warts and all!"

dictionaries ignore them and give only the accurate AK-yur-it, with a *γ*-glide before the *u*.

Since 1961, M-W has endorsed putting an *arch* in *archipelago*, a variant no other dictionary recognizes. Educated speakers simply don't say it that way. They say *ark*—because, as Alfred Ayres explains in *The Orthoëpist*, "When *arch*, signifying *chief*, begins a word from the Greek and is followed by a vowel, it is pronounced *ark*—as in *archangel, architect, archive, archipelago* . . . but when *arch* is prefixed to an English word, it is pronounced so as to rhyme with *march*—as, *archbishop, archduke, archfiend*."

According to M-W, you may count yourself among the ranks of educated speakers if you pronounce *particular* and *particularly* as *puh-tickler* and *puh-tickly* and *pronunciation* as *pro*-NOUN-*ciation*. Other dictionaries do not record these aberrations. M-W is also the only dictionary to recognize SEN-tee-int for *sentient* (SEN-shint, word 48 of Level 2). And for *eschew*, which is properly pronounced es-CHOO, M-W is alone in sanctioning the weird e-SKYOO and the vogue e-SHOO, which it brazenly lists first.

For *foliage*, which is properly pronounced in three syllables, FOH-lee-ij, M-W lists FOY-lij, a major blunder that other dictionaries eschew. It also calls the variant FOH-lij "very common"—as if that alone justifies it. If it were *as* common, and certainly if it were *more* common, a tenable (TEN-uh-bul, able to be defended or upheld) argument could be made for its acceptability. But lots of usages that are "very common" are also very objectionable to lots of people: the mispronunciation *nucular* for *nuclear* (N[Y]OO-klee-ur) comes quickly to mind.

M-W's usage notes apologize for variants that many educated speakers consider substandard and that authorities on pronunciation proscribe. For example, the note for *library* says the variant *liberry* is heard "from educated speakers, including college presidents and professors, as well as with somewhat greater frequency from less educated speakers." If a few college presidents and professors say *liberry*, does that make it less beastly? If your professor, or your child's professor, said *liberry*—or *perfessor*, for that matter—wouldn't you raise a concerned eyebrow? Here, and elsewhere, M-W ignores the plain truth that when educated people use slipshod or stigmatized pronunciations, they lose credibility. They are perceived as "less educated speakers."

Language mavens and lexicographers can agree to disagree. But by sanctioning so many questionable pronunciations, including some that are beyond the pale—like the ludicrous DUHB-yee for the letter *W*—Merriam-Webster misrepresents what Noah Webster famously called "the general practice of the nation" and obliterates the distinction conscientious speakers strive to make between what is and isn't standard.

Answers to Review Quizzes for Level 9

KEYWORDS 1–10

1. Yes. *Sangfroid* means composure, coolness of mind in trying circumstances.

2. Yes. *Desuetude* is a state of disuse or inactivity; discontinuance of use or practice.

3. No. A tongue-twister is simply hard to say. A *shibboleth* is a password, catchphrase, watchword, or slogan.

4. Yes. A *cri de coeur* is an impassioned or anguished outcry that can take many forms.

5. No. *Incunabula* are early printed books, especially those produced before 1501.

6. Yes. A *chef-d'oeuvre* is a masterpiece, especially one in literature, art, or music.

7. No. A *trochee* is a long syllable followed by a short one. An *iamb* is the opposite: a short syllable followed by a long one.

8. Yes. A *frisson* is a shudder of excitement or a quivering thrill.

9. Yes. *Prelapsarian* refers to the time before the Biblical Fall of humankind; hence, innocent, carefree, or unspoiled, uncorrupted.

10. No. Your *métier* is your specialty, work or activity for which you are well suited.

KEYWORDS 11–20

1. False. *Ablution* means the act of washing or bathing, especially as a religious rite.

2. True. *Apostasy* is the abandonment of one's faith, allegiance, or principles.

3. False. Sumptuary taxes are imposed on things society considers indulgent or objectionable, such as tobacco and alcohol. *Sumptuary* means pertaining to expenditures or to the regulating of them.

4. True. A *tatterdemalion* is a person who wears torn or ragged clothing, a ragamuffin.

5. False. When you *abjure* you renounce or reject solemnly under oath.

6. False. *Noblesse oblige* is the moral obligation of those of noble birth or high social position to behave in an honorable, kindly, and generous way.

7. True. *Primogeniture* is the state of being firstborn, or the right of a firstborn, especially a son, to inherit property or title.

8. True. *Xeric* means pertaining or adapted to a dry environment, needing little moisture.

9. False. An *uxorious* husband is excessively fond of or submissive to his wife.

10. True. To *oppugn* is to attack or oppose by argument, call into question, contradict.

KEYWORDS 21–30

1. Synonyms. *Agnosia* is the inability to recognize objects or interpret physical sensations.

2. Synonyms. Both *sophistry* and *casuistry* denote oversubtle and deceptive reasoning.

3. Synonyms. Both *Freudian slip* and *parapraxis* denote a minor error or oversight, such as a slip of the tongue, that seems to reveal an unconscious motive or wish.

4. Antonyms. A *polymath* is a very learned person or an expert in various subjects.

5. Synonyms. Both an *encomium* and a *panegyric* are formal expressions of high praise.

6. Antonyms. A *charrette* is an intensive effort to finish a project before a deadline.

7. Antonyms. To *debride* is to clean a wound. To *befoul* is to make foul or dirty.

8. Antonyms. *Lapidary* means having or exhibiting elegance, precision, and refinement of expression.

9. Antonyms. *Mammalian* means pertaining to mammals, which give birth to live young. *Oviparous* means producing eggs that develop and hatch outside the mother's body.

10. Synonyms. *Pallid* (word 47 of Level 4) means pale, lacking color. *Marmoreal* means resembling marble, either by being attractively white and smooth or unappealingly pale.

KEYWORDS 31–40

1. *Uninteresting* doesn't fit. *Nugatory* means worthless, insignificant, or useless, futile.

2. *Ringing in the ears* doesn't fit. *Acouasm* and *tinnitus* denote ringing in the ears. *Presbycusis* is loss or impairment of hearing due to old age.

3. *Taxi driver* doesn't fit. A *cicerone* is a guide for sightseers or a tutor, mentor.

4. *Exceptional insight* doesn't fit. *Pansophic* means pertaining to or possessing universal wisdom or encyclopedic knowledge.

5. *Bloodless* doesn't fit. *Rubicund* means red or reddish, flushed.

6. *Pertaining to fools* doesn't fit. *Picaresque* means of or relating to rogues, rascals, or knaves; specifically, pertaining to fiction that chronicles the adventures of a roguish hero.

7. *Coming into existence* doesn't fit. *Endogenous* means originating or produced from within.

8. *To speak incoherently* doesn't fit. To *perorate* is either to speak at great length, especially in a high-flown or pompous way, or to conclude a speech in a rousing manner.

9. *Trimming one's nails* doesn't fit. *Onychophagy* is the act or habit of biting one's nails.

10. *Seen something before* doesn't fit. *Déjà vu* is the feeling that you've seen or done something before. *Déjà lu* is the feeling that you've read something before.

KEYWORDS 41–50

1. To *verbigerate* is to repeat meaningless words and phrases continually or obsessively.

2. Something *tenebrous* is dark, gloomy, or obscure.

3. Your *agnate* relatives are on your father's side, through the male line of descent.

4. To *ululate* means to howl, wail, screech, or shriek.

5. A *zucchetto* is a skullcap worn by Roman Catholic clerics.

6. *Pseudandry* is the use of a male pseudonym by a woman. *Pseudogyny* is the use of a female pseudonym by a man.

7. A *caesura* is a break, pause, interruption, or hiatus.

8. A *philodox* is a person in love with his or her own opinions.

9. A *valetudinarian* is a weak or sickly person, an invalid or hypochondriac.

10. *Apotheosis* means the elevation of a human being to the level of a god; hence, elevation to a transcendent position or a glorified example or ideal.

LEVEL 10

Word 1: CHIAROSCURO (kee-AHR-uh-**SKYUR**-oh)
The distribution and gradations of light and shade in a pictorial work of art.

By derivation the noun *chiaroscuro* means clear-dark, for the word is a combination of the Italian *chiaro,* clear, bright (from the Latin *clārus,* clear, distinct), and *oscuro,* dark, obscure (from the Latin *obscūrus,* the source of *obscure*).

In the pictorial arts, *chiaroscuro* refers to "the general distribution of light and shade in a picture . . . that is, the combined effect of all its lights, shadows, and reflections," says *The Century Dictionary.* Any painting, drawing, photograph, or engraving that has strong contrasts between light and shadow is a study in chiaroscuro.

Not surprisingly, this useful word pertaining to the visual arts has been co-opted by other art forms. (To *co-opt* means to take over, appropriate, or to absorb, assimilate.) Movie reviews often refer to chiaroscuro lighting or the chiaroscuro of the cinematography. Music critics may refer to "chiaroscuro harmonies" or note how "the disparity between the dark and light timbres" of a singer's voice is a kind of chiaroscuro. I've even seen a theater review that refers to the players' "chiaroscuro personas," meaning the contrast between the bright and dark sides of their characters. *Chiaroscuro* can also be used of literature in this figurative way to suggest the symbolic struggle between light and darkness or good and evil.

Word 2: CONTEMN (kun-TEM)
To treat or regard with contempt; to scorn or despise.

Synonyms of the verb to *contemn* include to *disdain, spurn, slight, shun, deride* (word 2 of Level 3), *disparage,* and *disrespect*—which, as a verb meaning to have or show no respect for, is not slang, as many mistakenly suppose, but is in fact quite reputable and quite old, dating back to the 17th century.

Antonyms of *contemn* include to *admire, praise, commend, extol* (word 26 of Level 2), *laud, esteem, eulogize,* and *panegyrize* (PAN-i-juh-ryz).

Contemn comes from the Latin *contemnĕre,* to despise, scorn, slight, think meanly of, also the source of the English noun *contempt.* Take care not to confuse *contemn* with the verb to *condemn,* which means to declare to be wrong or evil or to pronounce guilty of a crime. *Contemn,* which the OED calls chiefly a literary word, appears several times in the Christian Bible; for example, Psalm 10, verse 13, asks, "Wherefore doth the wicked contemn God?" meaning "Why do the wicked regard God with contempt?" (In this archaic context *wherefore* means why, as in Shakespeare's "Wherefore [*why*] art thou Romeo?")

To *despise* usually implies loathing or disgust, although it may imply merely strong dislike. To *scorn* and to *disdain* imply arrogant and condescending contempt. To *shun* and to *spurn* imply strong rejection and avoidance of that which is disliked. To *disparage* implies belittling or discrediting that which is disliked, treating it as inferior. To *contemn* implies strong disapproval, a rejecting as unworthy of respect, and may be used either of people or of their actions: "The court struck down the state's law disallowing same-sex marriage, contemning it as unconstitutional and a violation of the defendants' civil rights."

The noun is *contemner* (kun-TEM-nur), one who contemns.

Word 3: APOLOGIA (AP-uh-**LOH**-jee-uh)
An apology; specifically, a defense or justification of one's beliefs, ideas, or actions.

Apologia comes from the Greek *apologia,* a speaking in defense, from *apo,* from, and *logos,* speech, the same source as the common English word *apology.*

What's the difference between an apology and an apologia? Both words may denote a defense or justification of one's beliefs or actions, but an apology is usually spoken while an apologia is usually written, and only the word *apology* may be used of an expression of regret or remorse for having insulted or injured someone else.

In his old age the ancient Greek philospher Socrates was brought before an Athenian court on the charges of corrupting the minds of the young and believing in his own gods rather than those approved by the state. His defense before that court, known as the *Apology*, is perhaps the most famous of *The Dialogues of Plato;* in it, Socrates gives what he would have called an apologia, a detailed explanation of his way of life and a justification of his convictions.

The most famous apologia in English literature is the *Apologia Pro Vita Sua*★—literally a defense of his life—by the Anglican theologian Cardinal John Henry Newman, who converted to Catholicism in 1845 and published his apologia, his religious autobiography and defense of his adopted faith, in 1864.

Word 4: GORGONIZE (GOR-guh-nyz)
"To have a paralyzing or stupefying effect on" (*American Heritage*).

Synonyms of the verb to *gorgonize* include to *hypnotize, mesmerize, paralyze, petrify,* and *stupefy* (word 30 of Level 3).

In ancient Greek mythology, the Gorgons were three ugly and horrible sisters who had wings and claws and who were "so gruesome that all living creatures turned to stone at the sight of them," says *D'Aulaires' Book of Greek Myths.* "Long yellow fangs hung from their grinning mouths, on their heads grew writhing snakes instead of hair, and their necks were covered with scales of bronze."

From these fearsome sisters comes the English verb to *gorgonize,* to have a paralyzing or stupefying effect, or to gaze at with the look of a Gorgon, and so to petrify, turn to stone. In *Maud and Other Poems,* published in 1855, Alfred, Lord Tennyson wrote, "And curving a contumelious lip, / [He] Gorgonized me from head to foot / With a stony British stare." (*Contumelious,* pronounced

★ Pronounced in English AP-uh-**LOH**-jee-uh proh VY-tuh S(Y)OO-uh; in classical Latin, AH-paw-**LAW**-gee-ah proh WEE-tah SOO-ah.

KAHN-t[y]oo-**MEEL**-ee-u̲s, means contemptuous, insulting, and humiliating.)

Word 5: SCHOLIA (SKOH-lee-uh)
Explanatory notes or comments; annotations.

Scholia, and the singular *scholium* (SKOH-lee-u̲m), an explanatory note in a text, come from the Greek *schólion,* a comment.

Annotations and *scholia* are both explanatory notes or comments; *scholia* is the more learned word and may refer specifically to scholarly notes or comments on passages in works written in Latin or ancient Greek.

Footnotes are placed at the bottom of a page. Endnotes are placed at the end of a book or text. Marginal notes, or *marginalia* (MAHR-ji̲-**NAYL**-yuh), are placed in the margins of a text. A *gloss* is a note placed either in the margin or in the text that explains or translates an unusual or obscure word or phrase. Annotations and scholia, explanatory notes or comments, may appear as footnotes, endnotes, or marginalia.

Word 6: CATHECT (kuh-THEKT)
To invest mental or emotional energy in an idea, object, or person.*

The verb to *cathect* is a back-formation—which, as you learned in *debride,* word 27 of Level 9, is a word formed from a longer word by removing a part of it, usually a suffix. In this case the back-formation is from *cathexis* (kuh-THEK-sis), the investing or concentration of mental or emotional energy in an idea, object, or person.

In about 1920 pychoanalysts borrowed *cathexis* from the Greek *káthexis,* a keeping, holding; it was intended as a translation of the German *Besetzung,* a taking possession of, a term used by Sigmund Freud of the libido (li̲-BEE-doh), the psychic energy derived from primitive instincts such as self-preservation and sexual desire. According to Freud, if you are too deeply cathected—mentally and

---

* I have borrowed this definition from A.Word.A.Day (www.wordsmith.org), a popular website and email subscription service run by my logophilic colleague Anu Garg.

emotionally invested in something—you have a psychological complex.

You can cathect, concentrate your emotional or mental energy on something, in good ways or bad. Creative people of all kinds cathect with their creations. A singer must cathect with the song, and a biographer must cathect with the subject of the biography. And lovers who have just fallen in love and are, as we say, mad about each other, are cathected. But such an intense investment of psychic energy can sometimes lead to depression or deviant behavior, as when a cathected person stalks the object of his cathexis or is driven by it to commit a crime.

Take care not to confuse *cathexis* with *catharsis* (kuh-THAHR-sis). Both words come from psychiatry, but *catharsis,* from the Greek *kátharsis,* a cleansing, denotes the release of emotional tension or the purging of the emotions: "Jeremy had a profound catharsis the first time he heard Bach's *Goldberg Variations.*" The adjective is *cathartic.*

Word 7: SORTILEGE (SOR-ti-lij)
Sorcery, magic; specifically, divination conducted by drawing or casting lots.

Divination is the ancient practice of using magic or supernatural means to foretell future events or discover things that are hidden or obscure. Perhaps the most common form of divination is palmreading, for which there are three words: *palmistry* (PAH-mis-tree), *chiromancy* (**KY**-ruh-MAN-see), and *chirognomy* (ky-RAHG-nuh-mee), in which the combining form *chiro-* means hand. Almost as common is *cartomancy* (**KAHR**-tuh-MAN-see), divination with playing cards; *tarot* (TAR-oh) is one popular form of cartomancy. Divination by looking into a crystal ball is called *scrying,* divination by interpreting dreams is called *oneiromancy* (oh-NY-ruh-man-see), and divination by drawing or casting lots is called *sortilege.* If you're wondering what a *lot* is, it's "one of a set of objects, [such] as straws or pebbles, drawn or thrown from a container to decide a question or choice by chance" (*Random House*).

Sortilege comes from the Latin *sortilegus,* which as an adjective meant prophetic, oracular, and as a noun meant a fortune-teller or soothsayer. The Latin *sortilegus* comes in turn from *sors, sortis,* a lot, and the verb *legere,* to gather, collect, or to read, survey. *Sortilege,* which dates back to the 14th century, has been used interchangeably with *sorcery* and *magic,* but in precise usage it refers to divination by drawing or casting lots.

Word 8: TERPSICHOREAN (TURP-si-kuh-**REE**-in)
Of or pertaining to dancing. Also, a dancer.

Do you remember *saltation,* word 30 of Level 7? It means the act of leaping, jumping, or dancing. The adjective *saltatory* (SAL-tuh-tor-ee) means pertaining to or adapted for saltation, and is an unusual synonym of *terpsichorean.*

In ancient Greek mythology there were nine Muses who presided over literature, the arts, and the sciences. All were the daughters of Zeus, the chief god of the Olympians, and Mnemosyne (nuh-MAH-si-nee), the goddess of memory, from whom we get the adjective *mnemonic* (ni-MAH-nik), assisting or pertaining to the memory.

Calliope (kuh-LY-uh-pee) was the leader of the nine Muses, and her specialty was heroic or epic poetry. Erato (ER-uh-toh) was the Muse of lyric and love poetry; Euterpe (yoo-TUR-pee) was the Muse of music; Thalia (thuh-LY-uh) was the Muse of comedy and bucolic (byoo-KAH-lik, rural, rustic) poetry; Melpomene (mel-PAH-muh-nee) was the Muse of tragedy; Urania (yuu-RAY-nee-uh) was the Muse of astronomy; Clio (KLY-oh) was the Muse of history; Polyhymnia (PAH-li-**HIM**-nee-uh) was the Muse of hymns and sacred lyrics; and Terpsichore (turp-SIK-uh-ree) was the Muse of dance.

Terpsichore is the eponymous source of the word *terpsichorean,* which as an adjective means of or pertaining to dancing, and as a noun means a dancer. The TV program *So You Think You Can Dance* is a terpsichorean talent show. The choreographer Twyla Tharp's *Come Fly Away* is a terpsichorean celebration of the music of Frank Sinatra. And the immensely talented terpsichoreans Fred Astaire and Ginger Rogers were perhaps the greatest terpsichorean team of all time.

Word 9: ESPRIT DE L'ESCALIER (e-SPREE duh les-kal-**YAY**)
The perfect response or remark that comes to mind later, after the chance to make it has passed.

Haven't we all had the experience of thinking of a snappy comeback or stinging riposte (word 38 of Level 6) when it's way too late to use it? And haven't you sometimes wondered if there was a word for that? Well, now you know it: *esprit de l'escalier,* which English borrowed from French in the early 1900s, means literally the spirit of the staircase—in other words, inspiration gained upon ascending the stairs to retire to bed, long after the opportunity for a retort has passed. When you're coming home from work and you think of what you *could* have said to your contemptible boss, or when you're cleaning up after dinner and you suddenly know what you *should* have told your insufferable father-in-law, that's esprit de l'escalier.

In recent years, two English equivalents of this French-derived phrase have been proposed: *stairwit,* almost a literal translation of the original, and *retrotort,* a blend of the prefix *retro-,* backward or behind, and *retort.* There is also the German *Treppenwitz* (TREP-en-vitz), a word on the fringe of becoming English whose connotations extend beyond the spirit of the staircase. In *They Have a Word for It,* Howard Rheingold writes that "in addition to referring to the kind of remark that occurs to a person when it is too late, [*Treppenwitz*] also applies to events that appear to be the result of a joke played by fate or history."

The French word *esprit* (e-SPREE) is also an English word meaning liveliness or vivacious wit: "The Howells always invited Marjorie to their Christmas party because everyone loved her infectious esprit." *Esprit* also appears in *bel-esprit* (BEL-e-**SPREE**), a person of intelligence and wit, and in the phrase *esprit de corps* (e-SPREE duh **KOR**), the sense of unity and enthusiasm for a common cause among the members of a group.

Word 10: POPINJAY (PAHP-in-jay)
A person who is vain, conceited, haughty, and fond of idle, pretentious chatter.

The noun *popinjay,* which almost always applies to men, comes from the Middle English *papejay* or *papejai,* which meant a parrot, and is related to the Italian and Spanish words for a parrot, *pappagallo* and *papagayo.* When *popinjay* entered English in the 14th century it was used to mean a parrot and also an ornamental representation of a parrot, as on a tapestry or in heraldry. The modern meaning of *popinjay* appeared in the early 16th century, probably influenced, says the *OED,* by "the bird's gaudy plumage or its mechanical repetition of words and phrases."

Because of this psittacine derivation—*psittacine* (SIT-uh-syn, like *sit a sign*) means resembling or pertaining to parrots—the word *popinjay,* when properly used, always suggests two things about a person: exaggerated vanity and a fondness for empty, pretentious talk. Popinjays are overly concerned with their appearance and have an exaggerated sense of self-importance. They often strut and mince, walk or speak in an affected manner. In his 1819 novel *Ivanhoe,* Sir Walter Scott described a character as being "as pert and as proud as any popinjay." Lest you think this is the sort of word that only 19th-century novelists use, here's a contemporary citation: "Charlie Chaplin enraged Hitler by openly satirising him as a ludicrous popinjay in his 1940 comedy *The Great Dictator*" (*Irish Independent*). And here's one from J. K. Rowling's 2003 novel *Harry Potter and the Order of the Phoenix:* "Has it not occurred to you, my poor puffed-up popinjay, that there might be an excellent reason why the Headmaster of Hogwarts is not confiding every tiny detail of his plans to you?"

Colorful synonyms of *popinjay* include *fop, dandy,* and *coxcomb* (discussed under *epithet,* word 37 of Level 1). Unusual synonyms of *popinjay* include the eponymous *Beau Brummel* (boh-BRUHM-ul), *cockalorum* (KAH-kuh-**LOR**-um), *princox* (PRIN-kahks), and *prickmedainty* (PRIK-mi-dayn-tee).

Review Quiz for Keywords 1–10

Consider the following questions and decide whether the correct answer is yes or no. **Answers appear on page 485.**

1. Does chiaroscuro refer to the contrast between color and shade?
2. Can you contemn someone you dislike or disapprove of?
3. Is a defense of one's beliefs or actions an apologia?
4. When you gorgonize, do you terrorize or defeat?
5. Can scholia appear as footnotes, endnotes, or marginalia?
6. If you are cathected, are you emotionally alienated?
7. Is sortilege a form of divination?
8. Is singing a terpsichorean art form?
9. Is a crushing retort made on the spot an example of esprit de l'escalier?
10. Are a popinjay and a parrot connected etymologically?

Difficult Distinctions: Cache and Cachet

The words *cache* and *cachet,* both borrowings from French, should be carefully distinguished in meaning and pronunciation. *Cache,* pronounced in one syllable like *cash,* denotes a secret storage place or, more often, valuable items that are secretly stored, as *a cache of weapons* or *the pirates' buried cache. Cachet,* pronounced in two syllables, ka-SHAY (rhymes with *parfait*), originally meant an official letter or seal but in modern usage has come to mean a mark of distinction or prestige: "No honor has more cachet than the Nobel Prize"; "When the store stopped catering to the wealthy, it lost its cachet."

Difficult Distinctions: Purposely and Purposefully

When you do something *purposely,* you do it on purpose, intentionally: "He flirted with her purposely"; "She purposely neglected to tell him about the incident." When you do something *purposefully,* you do it with determination to accomplish an objective: "He strode purposefully across the room to confront the loudmouthed bully."

The common mistake is to use *purposefully,* meaning with a specific purpose in mind, with determination, when what is meant is *purposely,* intentionally: "A memorial bears his name and the names of the 39 others on slabs of purposefully [*purposely*] unfinished stone" (*San Francisco Chronicle*).

Word 11: **CATACHRESIS** (KAT-uh-**KREE**-sis)

Misuse of one word for another, or using the wrong word for the context.

The noun *catachresis* comes from ancient Greek, where it meant the misuse or misapplication of a word. In general, *catachresis* denotes any misuse or abuse of words, such as using *reticent* (which means reluctant to speak) to mean *reluctant,* or confusing *supine* (which means lying faceup) with *prone* (which means lying facedown). In rhetoric, the study of effective writing and speaking, *catachresis* denotes any strained or farfetched usage, such as the wresting of a word from its common meaning or a mixed metaphor. Shakespeare's *Hamlet* has two well-known rhetorical catachreses (KAT-uh-**KREE**-seez): "I will speak daggers to her" and "To take arms against a sea of troubles."

English has several words for various slips and blunders of usage, including *gaffe* (word 27 of Level 2), *parapraxis* (word 23 of Level 9), *solecism, malapropism, mondegreen,* and *spoonerism.*

Solecism (SAH-luh-siz'm) comes from the inhabitants of Soloi, an ancient Greek colony in Cilicia (si-LISH-uh), Asia Minor, whose citizens were infamous for their horrible habits of speech. In modern usage a solecism is either a gross grammatical error or a social impropriety (word 10 of Level 3), such as spitting or belching in public.

The word *malapropism* (MAL-uh-prahp-iz'm) comes from Mrs. Malaprop, the name of a character in Richard Brinsley Sheridan's play *The Rivals,* published in 1775. In the play, Mrs. Malaprop, whose name was created from the French loanword *malapropos* (MAL-ap-ruh-**POH**), inappropriate or out of place, has a ludicrous habit of confusing words that are similar in sound, usually substituting a difficult word for a more common one in an attempt to sound educated.

The word *mondegreen* (MAHN-duh-green) was coined in 1954 by journalist Sylvia Wright for the phenomenon of inadvertently transposing what you hear into different words, as when we mishear *a patchy fog* as *Apache fog* or *for all intents and purposes* as *for all intensive purposes.* Wright came up with *mondegreen* for this because she remembered as a child mishearing the lyric of an old Scottish ballad,

"They hae slain the Earl o' Morey / And laid him on the green" as "They hae slain the Earl o' Morey / And Lady Mondegreen."

Finally, a *spoonerism* is a special type of spoken blunder that takes its name from William Archibald Spooner (1844–1930), an Anglican clergyman and warden of New College, Oxford. Also called a transposition pun, a spoonerism is a reversal of the initial letters or syllables of two or more words that creates a nonsensical phrase that seems to make sense: for example, *a blushing crow* for *a crushing blow, a well-boiled icicle* for *a well-oiled bicycle,* and *a half-warmed fish* for *a half-formed wish.*

Word 12: ETIOLOGY (EE-tee-**AHL**-uh-jee)

The study of causes or origins, or the cause of something; specifically in medicine, the study of the causes or origins of diseases, or the cause or origin of a disease.

Etiology, which entered English in the mid-1500s, comes from the Greek *aitiología,* determining the cause of something, from *aitía,* cause, and *-logia,* science or study. *Etiology* is most often used in medicine to mean either the study of the causes or origins of diseases, or, more often, the cause or origin of a disease or disorder, as the etiology of cancer, or the etiology of schizophrenia: "The underlying etiology for autism remains unknown, although genetic and environmental factors . . . are thought to be involved" (www.medscape.com). *Etiology* may also be used to mean the study of causes or origins in general, or it may mean the specific cause of something: "The etiology of the persistent gender gap in physician earnings is unknown and merits further consideration" (www.scienceblog.com).

Word 13: DEMIMONDE (**DEM**-ee-MAHND)

A class of women who live on the fringes of respectable society because of their indiscreet behavior and sexual promiscuity, and who are often supported by wealthy lovers. Hence, by extension, any group whose social respectability or morality is questionable and whose success or status is marginal.

The noun *demimonde* means literally half-world, for the combining form *demi-* means half, as in *demigod* and *demilune* (DEM-i-loon), a crescent or half-moon shape, and the French *monde* means world, coming from the Latin *mundus,* the world, the source of the English adjective *mundane,* of the world, temporal, material as opposed to spiritual, as *mundane affairs.*

When *demimonde* entered English from French in the mid-1800s it was used of women "of doubtful reputation and social standing" (*OED*) who lived on the fringes of respectable society, often as the mistresses and kept women of wealthy lovers. Over time the scope of the word's meaning widened as *demimonde* came to be used of any group that operates on the fringes of society or that seems to inhabit its own world, often a morally questionable one.

Contemporary writers refer to the drug-addled demimonde of New York City's nightclub scene in the 1980s, to the demimonde of strip shows and tattoo parlors in a city's red-light district, or to the lawless, violent demimonde of organized crime. And the so-called noir (NWAHR) fiction of writers such as Raymond Chandler (1888–1959) depicts a demimonde of cynical, hard-boiled detectives who scour the underbelly of society to uncover the sleazy dealings of various louche (word 46 of Level 8) characters.

Word 14: NUMINOUS (N[Y]OO-mi-nus)
Magical, supernatural, mysterious; inspiring awe and reverence, especially in a spiritual or divine way.

The English noun *numen* (N[Y]OO-men) comes directly from the Latin *nūmen,* which in one of its senses meant divine will or command; in English *numen* means a divine power or spiritual force, especially one connected with a particular object or place. The adjective *numinous,* from the same Latin source, means of or pertaining to a numen, hence supernatural or mysterious in a spiritual or transcendent way: "For the rest of her life, Nancy fondly remembered her beloved grandfather's farm as the numinous place where she spent so many blissful summers as a child."

The phrase *the numinous* suggests the awe-inspiring feelings or characteristics associated with religious faith and is roughly equivalent to *the divine* or *the holy.* But the word *numinous* by itself does not always imply divine inspiration; often it suggests a mysterious, magical quality or experience that is spiritually uplifting or sublime, as *a numinous performance, numinous inspiration,* or *the lambent, numinous moon.* (*Lambent* is word 35 of Level 7.)

Word 15: LEXIPHANIC (LEK-si-**FAN**-ik)
Using, or full of, pompous, pretentious words.

Perhaps you're thinking, at this point in Level 10, that *Word Workout* is becoming lexiphanic, full of inflated, overblown words. Indeed it is, and that is the joy of coming to the end of this verbally intensive program, for in this and the previous level I have been sharing with you some of the brightest gems in the bejeweled crown of the language.

The adjective *lexiphanic* comes from the Greek *lexis,* a word or phrase, and the verb *phainein,* to show. This Greek *lexis* is also the source of *lexicology,* the study of the meaning and use of words, and *lexicography,* the compiling of dictionaries or the principles of writing them. Lexiphanic writing or speech is typically hard to understand because it is grandiloquent (gran-DIL-uh-kwint), full of grand, lofty, high-flown words.

The noun *lexiphanicism* (LEK-si-**FAN**-i-siz'm) means showing off with words. And a *lexiphanes* (lek-SIF-uh-neez) is a person who uses big or obscure words as a way of showing off.

Word 16: BRACHIATE (BRAY-kee-ayt)
To move by swinging by the arms from branch to branch, like an ape or monkey.

The verb to *brachiate* and the noun *brachiation* (BRAY-kee-**AY**-shin), the act of swinging through the trees with the greatest of ease, come from the Latin *brāc(c)hium,* which meant an arm or the branch of a tree. Brachiation is the graceful mode of locomotion employed by apes, monkeys, and children playing on a jungle gym.

Word 17: QUIDNUNC (KWID-nuhngk)

A nosy, inquisitive person who likes to gossip about the latest news; a busybody.

The noun *quidnunc*, which entered English about 1700, is formed from the Latin words *quid*, what, and *nunc*, now. The quidnunc asks "What now?" because he or she is a busybody who always wants to know the latest gossip. In his 1978 novel *Chinaman's Chance*, Ross Thomas wrote of "the born gossipmonger, the quidnunc who would almost rather die than be the last to know."

The curious English language contains several interesting words for busybodies and other officious (uh-FISH-us) folks. (*Officious* means meddlesome, nosy, prying, especially in an overbearing way.) A *polypragmon* (PAH-lee-**PRAG**-mun) is a compulsive meddler, someone who is compelled to interfere in others' affairs. A *yenta* (YEN-tuh), which English borrowed from Yiddish, is specifically a female gossip, often a shrewish one. A *badaud* (ba-DOH), which comes from French, is "a credulous, gossiping simpleton," says *Webster 2*, or, colloquially, a rubbernecker. And then there is the freshly minted *scuttlebutthead*, coined by the American journalist Paul Tough, which denotes a person whose chief pleasure in life is being the first to tell everyone the latest news, whether it's a breaking story in the media or a broken heart in the office. That's an exact synonym of our keyword, *quidnunc*.

Word 18: CATECHUMEN (KAT-uh-**KYOO**-min)

A person being taught the basics of a subject; specifically, someone who is being taught the basic doctrine of the Christian church.

The noun *catechumen* dates back to the 14th century. It comes from the Greek *katēchoúmenos*, literally one being taught orally, from *katēcheîn*, to teach orally. From the same source comes the verb to *catechize* (KAT-uh-kyz), to instruct orally by means of questions and answers, and specifically to teach Christian doctrine in this way. Historically, a catechumen is either a convert to Christianity who is learning the basic doctrine of the church in preparation for baptism, or someone who is being taught Christian doctrine in preparation for the rite of confirmation. But in its extended, nonreligious sense, a catechumen is a beginner, someone learning the elementary principles or rudiments of any subject: "Any aspiring cook would jump at the chance to be a catechumen in a great restaurant with a celebrated chef."

English has various words for different kinds of beginners. You've already met the *abecedarian* (word 35 of Level 8), a person who is learning the alphabet or the rudiments of something. A *novice* (NAHV-is) is a probationary member of a religious community or someone new to something who has to learn the basics. A *neophyte* (NEE-uh-fyt) is a person newly converted to a religion or doctrine, hence a beginner or novice. By derivation a *tyro* (TY-roh) is a recruit in the Roman army; in modern usage a tyro is a raw beginner, eager to learn but incompetent. Finally, the words *tenderfoot* and *greenhorn* denote people who lack experience and who may also be naive about what they are getting themselves into.

Word 19: SYBARITE (SIB-uh-ryt)
"A person devoted to luxury and pleasure" (*Random House*).

Sybarite is a toponym (TAHP-uh-nim), a word formed from the name of a place, in this case Sybaris (SIB-uh-ris), an ancient Greek city in southern Italy renowned for its wealth and its inhabitants' devotion to luxury and pleasure.

"The Sybarites were noted among the Greeks for their love of luxury and sensuousness, and to some extent for their effeminacy and wantonness, all qualities associated with the word *sybarite* today," writes Robert Hendrickson in *The Facts on File Encyclopedia of Word and Phrase Origins*. "The fertile land of Sybaris . . . made luxurious living possible, but too many pleasures weakened the people. The neighboring Crotons . . . destroyed Sybaris in 510 B.C., diverting the river Crathis to cover its ruins. It is said that the Sybarites had trained their horses to dance to pipes and that [the] Crotons played pipes as they marched upon them, creating such disorder among their rivals that they easily won the battle."

In modern usage *sybarite* refers to anyone devoted to luxury or to sensual pleasure: "The self-indulgent antics of Hollywood's sybarites are a perennial topic in the tabloid press." The recently coined words *fashionista* and *foodie* denote sybarites who derive pleasure from, respectively, fancy clothing and fine food. But *sybarite* may also refer to someone devoted to nonphysical luxury and pleasure, as *a literary sybarite* or *a sybarite of the contemporary art scene.*

Synonyms of *sybarite* include *voluptuary* (vuh–LUHP–choo-er-ee), *sensualist, hedonist* (HEE–duh–nist), and *debauchee* (discussed under *debauch,* word 30 of Level 5). The adjective is *sybaritic* (SIB-uh-**RIT**-ik). *Sybaritism* (SIB–ur–uh–tiz'm) denotes the habits or practices of a sybarite, a pleasure–loving person.

Word 20: QUISLING (KWIZ–ling)
A traitor, collaborator; a person who betrays his or her country by cooperating with an enemy or an occupying force.

The eponymous noun *quisling* comes from the name Vidkun Quisling (1887–1945), a fascist Norwegian leader who helped Nazi Germany conquer Norway, then became the arrogant and brutal premier of his occupied country. When the Nazis surrendered in 1945, Quisling was arrested, convicted of treason, and shot. His treacherous legacy as a puppet of the enemy made his name synonymous with *traitor.*

Other synonyms of *quisling* include *turncoat, renegade,* and *apostate* (uh–PAHS–tayt, discussed in *apostasy,* word 12 of Level 9). Other eponymous synonyms of *quisling* include *Judas* (or *Judas Iscariot*) and *Benedict Arnold.*

The rare verb to *quisle* (KWIZ'l, rhymes with *fizzle*) means to act as a quisling, to betray one's country by aiding and abetting an enemy or an occupying force.

Review Quiz for Keywords 11–20
Consider the following statements and decide whether each one is true or false. **Answers appear on page 486**.

1. A mispronounced word is a catachresis.
2. Etiology is the study of the symptoms of a disease or problem.

3. A demimonde is a group that operates on the fringes of society.
4. A numinous experience is embarrassing.
5. A lexiphanic person likes to show off with words.
6. When you brachiate you walk from place to place.
7. A quidnunc is misanthropic.
8. A catechumen has lots of experience.
9. The word *sybarite* is a toponym.
10. A quisling is a faithful servant.

Once Upon a Word: Menu English

Had a look at a restaurant menu lately? No doubt you have, and perhaps, like me, you cringed. There they were, all the usual culinary (**KYOO**-li-NER-ee, not KUHL-) redundancies and solecisms, looking up at you from the laminated page with an illiterate sneer like a haughty waiter at a "bistro restaurant," which is a pompous redundancy because the word *bistro* means a small, informal restaurant.

No doubt there was the redundant steak *with au jus* (*au* means with), which you can enjoy after swilling a pleonastic bowl of the *soup du jour of the day* (*du jour* means of the day). Then there was the *penne pasta,* instead of just the *penne,* because the menu writers have decided penne requires special clarification as pasta. But they are not alone. The supermarket people who compose the peculiar language on your grocery receipts also indulge in pasta pleonasm, giving us *spaghetti pasta, linguine pasta,* and so on.

This same redundant reasoning is at work on the word *scampi,* which is invariably billed as *shrimp scampi.* But *scampi* is the plural of the Italian *scampo,* a kind of lobster, and in English *scampi* is a singular noun meaning a large shrimp or a dish of large shrimp sautéed in garlic and butter.

If you're in the mood for a salad, you can order one with *bleu* cheese dressing, which uninspiring restaurants with Continental aspirations prefer to serve instead of the proper English *blue* cheese. You have to wonder, gazing down at the creamy white glop that will travel immediately to your midsection and take up lodging, how the cheese comes into the kitchen *blue* but goes out of it *bleu*. It is a *très* (not *trés*) mysterious frenchification, perhaps influenced by *veal cordon bleu,* in which *cordon bleu* does not have anything to do with cheese but means a first-rate cook.

Finally, there's the so-called restaurant apostrophe—the pluralizing apostrophe that appears on countless menus, which is often miswritten *menu's,* even in the most chic (SHEEK) establishments. An Italian restaurant near me has some especially egregious (i-GREE-jus) specimens: *pizza's, pasta's, appetizer's, soup & salad's,* and *lunch special's.* You can even order a pizza with sauteed *onion's.* Thank goodness the place doesn't have a separate *kid's menu,* which you'll find at scores of family restaurants. Is that a menu for just one kid? Or is it a *kids' menu,* one for all the kids they serve?

Now let's return to the *Word Workout* vocabulary for another ten keyword discussions.

Word 21: CATHOLICON (kuh-THAHL-i-kun)
A cure-all, universal remedy.

The word *panacea* (PAN-uh-**SEE**-uh) is a close synonym of *catholicon. Panacea* comes from the Greek *pan-,* all, as in *panorama,* literally a view all around, and *akos,* cure, and means a cure-all for physical ailments or an antidote for worldly woes.

The Roman Catholic Church is so-called because it regards itself as the one, only, true, and universal church—with the emphasis on *universal* because *catholic* comes from the Greek *katholikós,* universal, general. When printed with a lowercase *c, catholic* means universal, comprehensive, broad in one's sympathies or interests. And *catholicity* (KATH-uh-**LIS**-i-tee) is broad-mindedness, tolerance, liberality in tastes or views.

Our keyword, *catholicon,* also hails from the Greek *katholikós,* universal, general, and means a universal remedy, cure for all ills. The word may be used literally, as in this 1642 quotation from Sir Thomas Browne's *Religio Medici:* "Death is the cure of all diseases. There is no Catholicon or universal remedy I know but this." Or it may be used figuratively, as in this 1734 quotation from Robert North's *Life of Francis North:* "He . . . made his Wit a Catholicon, or Shield, to cover all his weak Places and Infirmities." And if you're really clever, you can use it both literally and figuratively, as Brett T. Robinson did when he wrote, at *salon.com,* that "the iPhone is a catholicon for securing instant gratification. The 'catholic' or universal appeal of the object is a point worth considering."

Word 22: **DISCALCED** (dis-KALST)
Without shoes, barefoot, unshod.

The adjective *discalced* comes from the Latin privative prefix *dis-,* without, and *calceus,* a shoe, which comes in turn from *calx, calcis,* the heel, the source of the verb to *inculcate,* discussed under *indoctrinate* (word 28 of Level 2).

Discalced is the kind of word that native speakers of a Romance language such as Spanish or Italian are more likely to understand than a native English speaker. Why? Because most words in the Romance languages, both common and literary, come from Latin, while English gets its hardest words from Latin and Greek and its simplest words mostly from Anglo-Saxon, which is derived from German. Thus, the common Spanish *descalzo* and the common Italian *scalzo* both mean shoeless, barefoot, and come from the same Latin source as the difficult English word *discalced.*

Historically, *discalced* has been used of the members of certain religious orders, such as friars and nuns, who go about without shoes or who wear sandals. But the word may also be used of any person who is barefoot or temporarily unshod, as in these contemporary examples: "There were several pairs of shoes involved . . . which the otherwise discalced women had a hard time getting on and off" (*Boston Globe*); "Babies must be snatched from mothers, stinky feet must be discalced, nail files must be confiscated, and all your personal belongings must be strewn about" (*The Huffington Post*).

The antonym of *discalced* is *calced* (KALST), wearing shoes, shod.

Word 23: INCONDITE (in-KAHN-dit)
Badly constructed, poorly put together.

Synonyms of the adjective *incondite* include *crude, rough, unpolished, unrefined, ill-arranged,* and *ill-composed.* Antonyms of *incondite* include *elegant, refined, cultivated, genteel* (jen-TEEL), *polished, cultured,* and *urbane* (ur-BAYN).

Incondite, which entered English in the 16th century, comes from the Latin *inconditus,* disorderly, uncouth, from *in-,* not, and the verb *condere,* to put together. Thus by derivation *incondite* means not put together, and that is essentially the word's modern meaning: badly constructed, ill-composed, unpolished, unrefined.

You may use *incondite* of anything that is rough or crude in form, that lacks polish or refinement, such as vulgar speech or behavior. Or you may use *incondite,* as it is perhaps most often used, of literary or artistic works that are badly put together, that are disordered, illogical, or stylistically inelegant. That is how the 19th-century Scottish historian and essayist Thomas Carlyle (kahr-LYL) used it in *Sartor Resartus* (1836) in his critique of the Koran, the sacred text of Islam, which he called "a wearisome confused jumble, crude, incondite . . . stated in no sequence, method, or coherence."

Word 24: AFFLATUS (uh-FLAY-tus)
Inspiration, especially poetic or divine inspiration.

Afflatus may seem like a funny-sounding word until you know its etymology. It entered English in the mid-1600s from the Latin *afflatus,* a breathing on, the past participle of the verb *afflare,* to breathe or blow on, which comes from *ad-,* to, toward, and *flare,* to blow. From the same source come the familiar verbs *inflate* and *deflate,* as well as the unusual noun *flatus* (FLAY-tus), intestinal gas. Unlike *flatus,* the noun *afflatus* is only used figuratively of the so-called breath of inspiration—a word that itself means a breathing in, from the Latin *in-* and *spirare,* to breathe.

The Latin phrase *afflatus divinus* means divine inspiration, and *afflatus* by itself often implies a divine communication of knowledge or the influence of a supernal (soo-PUR-nul) impulse or power. (*Supernal* means coming from on high, heavenly.) *Afflatus* also suggests poetic or artistic inspiration, a strong creative impulse, the kind that is "an impelling mental force acting from within" (*Random House*). "Through me the afflatus surging and surging," wrote the 19th-century American poet Walt Whitman in "Song of Myself" (1855).

The verb is to *afflate* (uh-FLAYT), literally to blow or breathe on, hence to inspire. The adjective is *afflated,* inspired, as *an afflated style* or *an afflated audience.* And an *afflation* is an instance of divine or poetic inspiration.

Word 25: FLANEUR (fluh-NUR)
An idler, loafer, or dawdler.

In the mid-1800s English borrowed the noun *flaneur* from French, where it means, as in English, a stroller, loafer, or lounger, and comes in turn from the French verb *flâner,* to stroll, saunter, loaf or lounge about. By the 1870s English had also adopted the French noun *flânerie* (flahn-REE), which retains the little hat over the *a*—called a circumflex (SUR-kum-fleks)—and means loafing, dawdling, or idleness. "The aimless flânerie," wrote the American novelist and critic Henry James in 1875, "which leaves you free to follow capriciously every hint of entertainment."

Common synonyms of *flaneur* include *lounger, sluggard, trifler, ne'er-do-well, do-nothing, no-account,* and *slacker,* which in its most recent sense, dating from the 1990s, denotes a disaffected, aimless young person who lacks ambition.

Two unusual words for loafers and idlers are *faineant* (FAY-nee-int) and *stalko* (STAW-koh). *Faineant,* which comes from a French phrase meaning to do nothing, may be used as an adjective to mean lazy, good-for-nothing, or as a noun to mean a lazy person, an idler. *Webster 2* defines the word *stalko,* which comes from Anglo-Irish dialect, as "an impecunious [IM-pe-**KYOO**-nee-us] idler posing as a gentleman." (*Impecunious* means penniless, having little or no money.) The earliest citation in the *OED,* from 1804, says *stalko* refers to "men who have nothing to do, and no fortune to support them, but who style themselves esquire."

Our keyword, *flaneur,* originally denoted "a literary type from 19th-century France, essential to any picture of the streets of Paris," says Wikipedia.org. The word "carried a set of rich associations: the man of leisure . . . the urban explorer, the connoisseur of the street." Because of this history, in modern usage *flaneur* does not usually suggest the laziness of the sluggard, the worthlessness of the ne'er-do-well, or the cynical work-shirking of the slacker, but rather a gentlemanly kind of loafer who saunters with idle curiosity from place to place seeking pleasure and entertainment.

Word 26: QUOMODOCUNQUIZE   (KWOH-muh-doh-**KUHNG**-kwyz)
To make money in any way possible.

The verb to *quomodocunquize* is derived from the Latin *quōmŏdŏcunque,* a variant of *quōmŏdŏcumque,* in whatever way, from *quōmŏdo,* in what manner, how.

I'm taking some liberties including *quomodocunquize* as a keyword because, strictly speaking, it's not attested in any dictionaries. The *OED* has one citation, from Sir Thomas Urquhart in 1652, for the present participle *quomodocunquizing,* which it labels obsolete: "Those quomodocunquizing clusterfists and rapacious varlets." (*Clusterfist,* another extremely rare word, means a miser, skinflint, penny-pincher. *Rapacious* is word 10 of Level 2. A *varlet* is a knave, rascal, or scoundrel.)

But I've never been intimidated by so-called obsolete words; a word may no longer be used, but that doesn't mean it's no longer useful. My sentiments are with the eccentric American journalist Ambrose Bierce, author of the satiric *Devil's Dictionary* (1906), who declared that "if it is a good word and has no exact modern equivalent equally good, it is good enough for the good writer."

So I have taken the liberty of extrapolating★ the infinitive *quomodocunquize* from the participle *quomodocunquizing* because

---

★   To *extrapolate,* pronounced ek-STRAP-uh-layt, means "to infer (an unknown) from something that is known" (*The Random House Dictionary*).

we sorely need a word for trying to make money by whatever means possible, and for whatever reason—hunger, desperation, ambition, or naked greed. Clearly *quomodocunquize* "has no exact modern equivalent equally good," so I hope you'll see fit to use this word when the proper occasion arises—perhaps when you next encounter some "clusterfists and rapacious varlets."

Word 27: PASQUINADE (PAS-kwi-NAYD)

A satire, especially a harsh or abusive one, directed against a person and posted in a public place.

The words *pasquinade* and *lampoon* are close in meaning. Both are satires, pieces of writing that use irony and sarcasm to ridicule or scorn a person or an institution, or to expose human stupidity or vice. And both are typically abusive and malicious in tone. But historically a lampoon is published in a traditional manner, for example as a pamphlet, handbill, or circular, while a pasquinade is posted in a public place, in the manner of a poster or placard (PLAK-urd). In the age of the Internet a satirical post on Facebook or an insulting tweet would qualify as a pasquinade.

The first pasquinades "were hung upon an ancient statue unearthed in Rome in 1501, and reerected near the Piazza Navona by Cardinal [Oliviero] Caraffa," writes Robert Hendrickson in *The Facts on File Encyclopedia of Word and Phrase Origins.*

> The mutilated old statue . . . was dubbed Pasquino . . . probably because it stood opposite quarters where a sharp-witted, scandal-loving old man named Pasquino had lived. . . . It became customary on St. Mark's Day to salute and mockingly ask advice from the statue named for the caustic old man, such requests being posted on the statue after a while. These written Latin verses soon took the form of barbed political, religious, and personal satires, often upon the Pope, which were called [in Italian] *pasquinate.*

Eventually, says the *OED,* "the term began to be applied, not only in Rome, but in other countries, to satirical compositions and lampoons, political, ecclesiastical, or personal, the anonymous authors of which often sheltered themselves under the conventional name of Pasquin."

Word 28: XANTHIPPE (zan–TIP-ee)
An ill-tempered, scolding, browbeating woman; a shrew.

Xanthippe is an eponymous word, from the name of the wife of the ancient Greek philosopher Socrates. Legend has made Xanthippe the classic shrew—a quarrelsome, nagging woman—but the *Columbia Encyclopedia* says "the stories have little basis in ascertainable fact." Although Socrates was a brilliant thinker and teacher, he was also a repugnant runt who was hardly God's gift to woman. "Various historians," notes Robert Hendrickson in his *Dictionary of Eponyms,* "argue that [Xanthippe] has been much maligned [word 41 of Level 3], that Socrates was so unconventional as to tax the patience of any woman, as indeed would any man convinced that he has a religious mission on earth."

Xanthippe may be the proverbial shrew, but her name is not the only word in the language for a shrewish woman. A *vixen* (VIK-sin) is a shrew who is not only irritable and quarrelsome but also scheming and malicious. A *virago* (vi-RAY-goh) is an ill-tempered, scolding woman who is big and loud; the word hails from the Latin *vir,* a man, the source of *virile,* manly, because the virago's imposing size and overbearing speech seem more male than female. A *termagant* (TUR-muh-gant, not -jant) is a " boisterous, brawling, or turbulent woman," says *The Century Dictionary,* who doesn't hesitate to use her fists as well as her tongue to make a point; *termagant* was first used as the name of a violent, overbearing character representing a mythical Muslim deity in morality plays of the Middle Ages. Finally, a *harridan,* which may come from the French *haridelle,* an old, thin horse or a large, gaunt woman, is a vicious, disreputable old shrew.

Word 29: POCOCURANTE (POH-koh-kyuu-**RAN**-tee)
Careless, indifferent, nonchalant, apathetic.

Pococurante entered English in the mid-1700s from the Italian *poco curante,* caring little. The word may be an adjective with exactly the same meaning as the Italian, caring little, and so indifferent or apathetic, as *a pococurante manner* or *pococurante conversation.* Or it may be a noun meaning a careless, indifferent, nonchalant person, a trifler, as in this 1779 quotation from the diary of Hester Lynch Thrale, a close friend of Samuel Johnson: "He seems to have no Affections, and that won't do with me—I feel great Discomfort in the Society of a Pococurante."

In *Candide,* the celebrated satirical novel published in 1759 by the French philosopher Voltaire (1694–1778), the naively optimistic Candide travels with a companion to the opulent palace of Count Pococurante, who, true to his name, "received the two travelers quite politely, but without much warmth." The Count proceeds to show them what a wet blanket he is (a *wet blanket* is a person who takes all the pleasure or excitement out of something) by nonchalantly dismissing everything that Candide finds interesting. He says he is bored with attractive women, that he no longer bothers to look at the rare paintings in his collection, that he is unmoved by beautiful music, and disdainful of most of the books in his library. "I say what I think," the Count declares, "and care little whether others agree with me."

Did you notice that *care little*? That's why he's Count *Pococurante,* a man so indifferent to all the riches that surround him that he can only feel superior to or disgusted with them. In short, the Count takes pleasure in not being pleased—and that's a fine modern definition of the word *pococurante.*

Word 30: HOMUNCULUS (hoh-MUHNG-kyuh-l<u>us</u>)
A little man or human being; a diminutive person.

The plural is *homunculi* (hoh-MUHNG-kyuh-ly).

Homunculus comes from the Latin *homunculus,* a little man, the diminutive of *homo,* a man, as in *homo sapiens,* literally intelligent man, the scientific term for human beings. According to the 16th-century Swiss physician and alchemist Paracelsus (PAR-uh-**SEL**-s<u>us</u>), a homunculus was "a tiny human being that may be produced . . . artificially, without a natural mother," as if in an alchemist's flask, says *The Century Dictionary.* "Being produced by art, it was supposed that art was incarnate in it and that it had innate knowledge of secret things" or magical powers. From this fanciful notion an even more fanciful notion developed: that a homunculus was a fully formed but miniature human being supposed to be present in the human sperm cell. Later writers rejected these ideas and used *homunculus* in its etymological sense of a little man or a person who is very small but otherwise normally proportioned.

Familiar synonyms of *homunculus* include *dwarf, pygmy, midget, runt,* and *shrimp.* Less familiar synonyms of *homunculus* include *Tom Thumb,* the diminutive hero of English folklore; *manikin,* a little man—as distinguished from *mannequin,* the dummy for displaying clothing; *mite,* which may denote a small insect, a small coin, a small amount or bit, or a tiny creature; and *Lilliputian* (LIL-i-**PYOO**-shin), one of the diminutive inhabitants of the imaginary land of Lilliput in Jonathan Swift's satirical novel *Gulliver's Travels,* published in 1726.

Antonyms of *homunculus* include *colossus* (kuh-LAH-sus), *titan, behemoth* (word 37 of Level 3), and *leviathan* (discussed in *behemoth*).

Review Quiz for Keywords 21–30
Decide if the pairs of words below are synonyms or antonyms. **Answers appear on page 486**.

1. *Catholicon* and *panacea* are . . . synonyms or antonyms?
2. *Discalced* and *unshod* are . . .
3. *Incondite* and *refined* are . . .
4. *Inspiration* and *afflatus* are . . .
5. *Flaneur* and *sluggard* are . . .
6. *Philanthropize* and *quomodocunquize* are . . .
7. *Pasquinade* and *eulogy* are . . .
8. *Xanthippe* and *shrew* are . . .
9. *Passionate* and *pococurante* are . . .
10. *Homunculus* and *behemoth* are . . .

Once Upon a Word: Pardon My French

English has borrowed many words from French that end with
-eur, including keyword 25 of this level, *flaneur,* an idler, loafer. In
a few borrowings this French suffix creates a noun for a thing or
a quality, as in *liqueur* (li-KUR, not li-KYOOR); *hauteur* (word 7
of Level 7), arrogance, and *froideur* (discussed in *sangfroid,* word 1
of Level 9), cool aloofness; and *pudeur* (pyoo-DUR), modesty,
especially regarding sex (from the Latin *pudēre,* to be ashamed or
to fill with shame, the source also of the English *pudency,* a fancy
synonym of *modesty*). But in most French loanwords this *-eur* is a
suffix that creates an agent noun, meaning a noun denoting a
person who performs an action.

Some of these agent nouns ending in *-eur* are common: words
like *amateur, chauffeur, entrepreneur* (AHN-truh-pruh-**NUR**, not
-NOO-ur, and note the *r* in the antepenultimate syllable), *connoisseur* (kahn-uh-SUR), and *restaurateur*★ (RES-tuh-ruh-**TUR**)
are part of everyday discourse.

Some of them are less familiar, like *masseur* (ma-SUR), a man
who gives massages; *coiffeur* (kwah-FUR), a male hairdresser—
not to be confused with *coiffure* (kwah-FYUR), a hairstyle; *voyeur*
(voy-YUR), a person who gets sexual gratification from spying
on other people, a peeping Tom; *litterateur* (LIT-ur-uh-**TUR**), a
literary person or professional writer; and *agent provocateur* (AY-
jint or A-zhah(n) pruh-VAHK-uh-**TUR**), a person hired to secretly infiltrate an organization and incite its members to some
illegal action.

Then there are some unusual agent nouns ending in *-eur,* known
only to connoisseurs of such verbal delights. Here are some of
them:

An *accoucheur* (a-koo-SHUR) is an obstetrician or a person
who assists in childbirth, from the French *couche,* a bed, couch. A
carillonneur (KAR-uh-luh-**NUR**) is a person who plays a carillon
(KAR-uh-lahn), a set of stationary bells usually placed in a
tower. A *colporteur* (KAHL-por-tur) is a peddler of Bibles and
religious books. A *danseur* (dahn-SUR)—a word you met in the

---

★   *Restaurateur* is often misspelled *restauranteur* and mispronounced RES-tuh-rawn-**TUR**.

discussion of companion words in Level 9—is a male ballet dancer. A *farceur* (fahr-SUR), from the same source as *farce,* is a joker, wag, or humorist. A *friseur* (free-ZUR), from *friser,* to curl, frizz, or wave, is a rare word for a hairdresser. A *jongleur* (zhaw(n)-GLUR) is an itinerant minstrel or juggler. A *persifleur* (PUR-si-flur) is the agent noun corresponding to the noun *persiflage* (PUR-si-flahzh), good-humored banter or jesting. A *rapporteur* (ra-por-TUR) is a fancy word for a person who gives reports. And finally, a *siffleur* (see-FLUR)—one of my favorite words—is a professional whistler.

Now let's leave *La Belle France* and return to the *Word Workout* vocabulary.

Word 31: MORGANATIC (MOR-guh-**NAT**-ik)
Of or pertaining to a marriage between a person of high rank or social standing and a person of a lower rank or social standing.

Historically, the adjective *morganatic* refers to a marriage between a member of the nobility and a commoner in which the aristocrat's titles and property cannot be inherited by the ignoble spouse or the half-noble, half-common offspring. This explains the word's derivation, from the New Latin phrase *matrimonium ad morganaticam,* literally marriage with a morning gift, meaning that the wife and any children she may bear are not entitled to any share of what the husband owns beyond the traditional morning gift, the property the husband gives the wife the morning after their marriage.

Although historically *morganatic* refers to a man of high rank marrying a woman of lower rank, the word has occasionally also been used of a marriage between a high-ranking woman and a low-ranking man. In modern usage *morganatic* could aptly refer to any intimate relationship, married or otherwise, between people of markedly different social status. For example, when some Wall Street Master of the Universe ditches his long-suffering wife and shacks up with the housekeeper, or when a wealthy older woman has an affair with an impecunious young man, that's morganatic.

The noun *hypergamy* (hy-PUR-guh-mee), from *hyper,* over, above, and the combining form *-gamy,* which means marriage or union, denotes a marriage with someone above your social station. Colloquially, hypergamy is called "marrying up."

Word 32: PARALEIPSIS (PAR-uh-LYP-sis)
In rhetoric, the technique of drawing attention to something while claiming to say little or nothing about it.

Paraleipsis—which, since entering English about 1550, has also been spelled *paralepsis* and *paralipsis*—comes from the Greek *paráleipsis,* an omitting, passing over, from *paráleipein,* to leave on one side, omit. By derivation, *paraleipsis* is an intentional passing over so as to draw attention to that which has only been touched upon or omitted.

Garner's Modern American Usage defines *paraleipsis,* which is also known in rhetoric as *occupatio* (AHK-yuh-PAY-shee-oh), as "a brief reference to something done in such a way as to emphasize the suggestiveness of the thing omitted." Garner offers this example: "I'll just mention a few of the outrages committed by the Spanish Inquisition." And *Webster 2* offers this example: "I confine to this page the volume of his treacheries and debaucheries." (The verb to *debauch* is word 30 of Level 5.)

In his *Handlist of Rhetorical Terms,* Richard A. Lanham says that *paraleipsis,* or *occupatio,* occurs when "a speaker emphasizes something by pointedly seeming to pass over it," as when someone introduces a speaker by saying, "I will not dwell here on the twenty books and the thirty articles Professor X has written, nor his forty years as Dean, nor his many illustrious [i-LUHS-tree-us, well known and respected, distinguished] pupils, but only say . . ." Set phrases in the language associated with paraleipsis include *to say nothing of, not to mention,* and *it goes without saying.*

The related rhetorical term *preterition* (PRET-ur-ISH-in) might be defined in colloquial terms as "saying you're not going to say something and then saying it anyway." Preterition is commonly used in debating, and especially in political wrangling, as when a candidate says, "I'm not here to talk about my opponent's reprehensible voting record and failed policies. I'm here to explain my position on the issues."

Word 33: MUMPSIMUS (MUHMP-si-mus)

Someone who obstinately clings to an error, bad habit, or prejudice, even after the foible has been exposed and the person humiliated. Also, any error, bad habit, or prejudice obstinately clung to, especially one in speech or language.

Mumpsimus has its obstinate roots in a 16th-century story of "an ignorant priest," says *The Century Dictionary,* "who in saying his mass had long said *mumpsimus* for *sumpsimus,* and who, when his error was pointed out, replied, 'I am not going to change my old *mumpsimus* for your new *sumpsimus.*' The story evidently refers to the post-communion prayer 'Quod in ore sumpsimus.'"

Mark Twain once said, "You can straighten a worm, but the crook is in him and only waiting." That worm with the crook in him is a mumpsimus, a person who stubbornly adheres to an erroneous or outmoded way of doing something despite all evidence that it is stupid or wrong. Haven't there been a few times in your life when you thought a parent, teacher, or someone else in authority was a mumpsimus?

A mumpsimus may be a person who clings to an error, bad habit, or prejudice or the error, bad habit, or prejudice itself. In *Fifteen Chapters of Autobiography,* the British writer and Liberal politician George William Erskine Russell★ (1853–1919) wrote, "The Liberal Party still clung to its miserable old mumpsimus of laissez-faire [word 26 of Level 5], and steadily refused to learn the new and nobler language of Social Service."

★ A person with four names is called a *quadrinomial* (KWA-dri-**NOH**-mee-ul). As a person with three names, I am a *trinomial* (try-NOH-mee-ul), like Ralph Waldo Emerson and William Jefferson Clinton.

Word 34: BIBLIOPHAGIC (BIB-lee-uh-**FAJ**-ik)
Book-devouring.

The adjective *bibliophagic* and the noun *bibliophage* (BIB-lee-uh-fayj), a person who devours books, come from the Greek *biblios,* a book, and *phagein,* to eat, devour. This Greek *phagein* also appears in *sarcophagus,* which by derivation means flesh-devouring, and *onychophagy* (word 39 of Level 9), nail-biting.

Take a peek sometime in an unabridged dictionary and you'll be surprised, and I hope delighted, to find all sorts of interesting words that begin with the combining form *biblio-,* book. After the familiar *bibliography* and its derivatives, can you think of any other words that begin with *biblio-?* Perhaps *bibliophile,* a lover of books?

A bibliophile has to watch out for three bad *biblios:* the *bibliophobe,* the person who fears books or what's in them; the *biblioklept,* the book thief; and the *biblioclast,* the mutilator or destroyer of books. A bibliophile who needs more books can visit a *bibliopolist* (BIB-lee-**AH**-puh-list), a bookseller, or consult a *bibliothecary* (BIB-lee-**AH**-thuh-ker-ee), the keeper of a library, a blend of *biblio-* and *apothecary* (uh-PAH-thuh-ker-ee), an archaic word for a pharmacist.

Finally, a bibliophile who gets devoured by books can become a *bibliomaniac,* someone who is obsessed with books, or even worse, a *bibliolater* (BIB-lee-**AHL**-i-tur), someone who worships books. And all those insatiably bibliophagic—those incessantly book-devouring—bibliomaniacs and bibliolaters belong to a hyperliterate class that the 20th-century American journalist H. L. Mencken dubbed the *bibliobibuli* (BIB-lee-oh-**BIB**-yuh-ly), meaning people who read too much.

Word 35: CORYBANTIC (KOR-i-**BAN**-tik)
Wild, frenzied, frantic, unrestrained.

The adjective *corybantic* is an eponymous word formed from the proper noun *Corybant* (KOR-i-bant), with a capital *C.* The plural is *Corybantes* (KOR-i-**BAN**-teez). The Corybantes were priests and attendants of the nature and mother goddess Cybele (SIB-uh-lee), who was worshiped by the ancient peoples of Asia Minor. Cybele's rites were celebrated with wild music, wine, and ecstatic dancing, supposedly while Cybele "wandered by torchlight over the forest-clad mountains" (*Webster 2*). In pathology, *corybantism* (KOR-i-**BAN**-tiz'm) is a kind of frenzy or wild delirium in which the patient experiences hallucinations, usually from lack of sleep.

Corybantic, which entered English in the 1600s, means like a corybant, a reckless reveler or frantic devotee (word 14 of Level 1), hence wild, frenzied, madly agitated. In modern usage *corybantic* may apply to dancing or to any sort of frantic, unrestrained behavior, especially wildly self-indulgent behavior, as *the corybantic dancing in the mosh pit* or *her corybantic weekend partying with her friends at the lake.* But the word may also be used more mildly of any intense and uninhibited feeling or action, for example, *corybantic enthusiasm* or *corybantic energy.*

Synonyms of *corybantic* include *agitated, frenetic, hectic, impassioned, delirious, moonstruck, crazed, overwrought, deranged,* and *unhinged.* Antonyms of *corybantic* include *rational, level-headed, sober, self-possessed, sedate* (word 9 of Level 3), *subdued,* and *staid.*

Word 36: AUBADE (oh-BAHD)

A song, an instrumental composition, or a poem greeting or announcing the dawn, or a love song sung in the early morning.

In *Tales of a Wayside Inn,* published in 1863, the American poet Henry Wadsworth Longfellow writes, "There he lingered till the crowing cock . . . / Sang his aubade with lusty voice and clear."

The noun *aubade* comes through French from a Portuguese word meaning a song about the parting of two lovers at dawn, and is related ultimately to the Latin *albus,* white. Coincidentally, perhaps the most famous aubade of modern times is of Portuguese provenance (word 25 of Level 5). "Manhã de Carnaval" (Morning of Carnival), composed by Luiz Bonfá with lyrics by Antônio Maria, is the theme song of the 1959 movie *Orfeu Negro* (*Black Orpheus*) by the French director Marcel Camus, which is credited with bringing the South American samba and the related musical style called bossa nova to the attention of the world.

Aubade, a song announcing the morning, is the companion word for *serenade,* a musical performance given at night, especially a love song.

Word 37: LYCANTHROPY (ly-KAN-thruh-pee)
The delusion that one is a wolf, or the transformation of a human being into a wolf.

The noun *lycanthropy* comes from the Greek *lykos,* a wolf, and *ánthrōpos,* a man, human being. The word dates back to the late 16th century, but the delusion has been noted since ancient times. In 1621, in *The Anatomy of Melancholy,* the British clergyman and scholar Robert Burton (1577–1640) wrote, "Lycanthropia . . . or Woolfe madnesse, when men runne howling about graves and fields in the night, and will not be persuaded but that they are Wolves, or some such beasts." A *lycanthrope* (LY-kun-throhp) is a person affected with lycanthropy—in other words, either a weirdo or an actual werewolf.

English has numerous words for the delusion that one is a particular kind of animal. All combine the Greek word for the animal in question with the suffix *-anthropy,* from *ánthrōpos,* a man, human being. To begin with, *zoanthropy* (zoh-AN-thruh-pee), from the Greek *zôion,* an animal, is the delusion that you're some kind of animal. *Cynanthropy* (si-NAN-thruh-pee), from the Greek *kynos,* a dog, is the delusion that one is a dog. *Galeanthropy* (GAL-ee-**AN**-thruh-pee), from a Greek word that was applied to various animals, is the delusion that one is a cat. And *boanthropy* (boh-AN-thruh-pee), from the Greek *bous,* an ox, is the delusion that one is an ox.

Word 38: NULLIPARA (nuh-LIP-ur-uh)
A woman who has never borne a child.

Nullipara is chiefly a medical term, formed from the Latin *nullus,* none, not any, and the combining form *-parous,* bearing, producing, which comes from the Latin *parere,* to give birth, bring forth. In medicine, a nullipara is a woman (or rarely, a female animal) who has never given birth to a child. A *primipara* (pry-MIP-uh-ruh), from the Latin *prīmus,* first, is a woman who has borne one child or who is giving birth to a first child. And a *multipara* (muhl-TIP-uh-ruh), beginning with *multi-,* many, is a woman who has borne more than one child. The plurals of these nouns follow the Latin: *nulliparae, primiparae,* and *multiparae,* in which the final syllable is properly pronounced -ree. The adjectives are *nulliparous, primiparous,* and *multiparous.*

Word 39: WELTSCHMERZ   (VELT-shmairts)
Sentimental sadness; world-weary melancholy.

Webster's New World College Dictionary defines *weltschmerz* as "sentimental pessimism or melancholy over the state of the world." And the *American Heritage Dictionary* defines it as "sadness over the evils of the world, especially as an expression of romantic pessimism." Why is the world part of these definitions? Because *weltschmerz,* which English borrowed from German in the mid-1800s, means literally world-pain, for it is a combination of the German *Welt,* world, and *Schmerz,* pain.

Merriam-Webster's *Encyclopedia of Literature* explains that *weltschmerz* is "a feeling of melancholy and pessimism or of vague yearning and discontent caused by comparison of the actual state of the world with an ideal state. The term has been used in reference to individuals as well as to the prevailing mood of a whole generation or specific group of people. It is particularly associated with the poets of the romantic era who refused or were unable to adjust to those realities of the world that they saw as destructive of their right to personal freedom."

When I think of weltschmerz I'm reminded of one of the funniest but also most melancholy of Mark Twain's many epigrams: "Man was made at the end of the week's work, when God was tired."

Weltschmerz is still often printed in the customary German way, with a capital *W,* and it still sometimes appears in italics to indicate that it is foreign. But the word has been English for 150 years, enough time for it to be treated like a normal English noun and printed in lowercase roman type.

Word 40: NOETIC (noh-ET-ik)
Of, pertaining to, originating in, or apprehended by the mind or the intellect.

Synonyms of *noetic* include *intellectual, rational,* and *cognitive.*

The adjective *noetic* comes from the Greek *noētikós,* intellectual, which comes in turn from *noein,* to think, and *nous,* the mind. The noun is *noesis* (noh-EE-sis), which in ancient Greek philosophy meant the exercise of reason and which in modern psychology means intellectual function, cognition.

The human faculty of reason is noetic, as is the human imagination. Reading is a noetic activity. And when a great idea comes to you seemingly out of nowhere, that's noetic inspiration.

Review Quiz for Keywords 31–40

In this quiz the review word is followed by three words or phrases, and you must decide which comes nearest the meaning of the review word. **Answers appear on page 487**.

1. *Morganatic* means marrying a social equal, marrying a social inferior, marrying a social superior.

2. *Paraleipsis* is a way of suggesting much by saying little, a way of insulting someone with a veiled compliment, a way of saying no by saying yes.

3. A *mumpsimus* is a person who refuses to listen, a person who refuses to agree, a person who refuses to change.

4. *Bibliophagic* means book-loving, book-devouring, book-destroying.

5. *Corybantic* means even-tempered, unswervingly loyal, frenzied.

6. An *aubade* is a song or poem greeting the dawn, an ode to nature, a victory dance.

7. *Lycanthropy* is the transformation of lead into gold, the delusion that one is a wolf, the fulfillment of a wish.

8. A *nullipara* is a woman who has never given birth, a woman who has given birth to one child, a woman who has borne many children.

9. *Weltschmerz* is world-weary melancholy, personal freedom, a love of wordplay.

10. *Noetic* means moral, physical, intellectual.

Once Upon a Word: German Loanwords

Mark Twain, America's greatest humorist, was no fan of German. Twain traveled in Germany and lived there for a time, and the language never ceased to cause him trouble and consternation. This he assuaged (uh-SWAYJD) in his usual manner: by poking fun at it. He wrote satirical essays with titles like "The Awful German Language" and "The Horrors of the German Language," and he littered his books with withering gibes (JYBZ) about its confounding (word 34 of Level 2) grammar, tortured syntax, and ridiculously bloated words. (A *gibe* is a taunting or derisive remark or joke.) "Whenever the literary German dives into a sentence," he wrote in *A Connecticut Yankee in King Arthur's Court,* "that is the last you are going to see of him till he emerges on the other side of his Atlantic with his verb in his mouth."

Perhaps my favorite of Twain's many assaults on German is this quip from his notebook: "July 1—In the hospital yesterday, a word of thirteen syllables was successfully removed from a patient, a North-German from Hamburg."

It's true that German words can be impressively long, not to mention tricky to pronounce, but the voracious (word 7 of Level 1) English language has proved hospitable to many German borrowings. You've already met several of them: *zeitgeist* is word 16 of Level 7; *schadenfreude* is word 19 of Level 8; *doppelgänger* is word 43 of Level 8; *Treppenwitz* is discussed in *esprit de l'escalier,* word 9 of this level; and you just got acquainted with *weltschmerz,* word 39 of this level. And now, quicker than you can say *gesundheit* (guh-ZUUNT-hyt), literally health, to a person who has just sneezed, here are some other interesting and useful words that English has borrowed from German.

Schmaltz (SHMAHLTZ), which is both German and Yiddish,

means literally melted poultry fat; hence, by extension, schmaltz is excessive sentimentality, maudlin (word 13 of Level 4) emotion, especially in music or writing.

Verboten (vur-BOHT'n), which entered English about 1912, means forbidden, prohibited, as *a verboten subject.*

Sturm und Drang (SHTURM uunt **DRAHNG**), which means literally storm and stress, was the name of a German romantic literary movement of the late 18th century but is more commonly used today to mean turmoil, upheaval, or struggle: "Exhausted from yet another bitter confrontation with her husband, Elena wasn't sure how much longer she could endure the Sturm und Drang of their marriage."

Gemütlich (guh-MOOT-li<u>kh</u> or -lik), a most agreeable word, entered English in the 1850s and means agreeably pleasant or friendly, warm and congenial: "Josie and Carl's dinner parties always featured good food, stimulating conversation, and a gemütlich atmosphere."

Bildungsroman (BIL-duungz-roh-mahn) is a literary term for "a type of novel concerned with the education, development, and maturing of a young protagonist" (*Random House*); in short, a coming-of-age story.

Weltanschauung (**VEL**-tahn-SHOW-uung), which may be printed with a lowercase *w,* comes from *Welt,* world, and *Anschauung,* view, and means literally a worldview, specifically a comprehensive concept of humanity's function in the universe.

Sprachgefühl (SHPRAH<u>KH</u>-guh-fuul) comes from the German *Sprache,* speech, language. In English *sprachgefühl* means a sensitivity to language, specifically an intuitive understanding of what is idiomatic or linguistically appropriate.

The marvelously ponderous (word 41 of Level 2) *Schlimmbesserung* (shlim-BES-uh-ruung) is still not in dictionaries, but I think you'll agree that English sorely needs it. A *Schlimmbesserung* is a so-called improvement that makes things worse. "Is It Progress, or Just *Schlimmbesserung*?" asked the headline for an article in the *Los Angeles Times Magazine* published April 26, 1987, whose subhead proceeded to define this unusual word: "Many Purported Improvements Seem to Diminish the Quality of Modern Life."

And finally, we have one of my all-time favorites: *witzelsucht* (VITS-<u>ul</u>-suukt or VIT-sel-zuu<u>kht</u>) a feeble attempt at humor, from *witzeln,* to affect wit, and *sucht,* mania. Specifically, says *Stedman's Medical Dictionary, witzelsucht* denotes "a morbid tendency to pun, make poor jokes, and tell pointless stories, while being oneself inordinately entertained thereby." Your language maven pleads guilty on all counts.

Now, here are the final ten keyword discussions in *Word Workout:*

Word 41: QUIDDITY (KWID-i-tee)
The essential nature or essence of a person or thing.

The noun *quiddity,* which dates back to the 14th century, comes from the Middle Latin *quidditās,* whatness, so by derivation *quiddity* is that which makes a thing what it is. The word is associated historically with the Christian theologian-philosophers of the Middle Ages, beginning with St. Anselm in the 11th century, who developed a system of thought known as scholasticism, which strove to reconcile faith and reason. "For the greatest of the scholastics," says the *Columbia Encyclopedia,* "this meant the use of reason to deepen the understanding of what is believed on faith and ultimately to give a rational content to faith." The scholastics continually sought rational answers to the questions "What is the quiddity of faith?" and "What is the quiddity of God?"

Since the 17th century *quiddity* has been used less philosophically and more generally to mean the essential nature or essence of a person or thing, as in this 1828 citation from Thomas De Quincey in *Blackwood's Edinburgh Magazine:* "The quiddity . . . of poetry as distinguished from prose"; and this citation from George Blake's 1935 novel *The Shipbuilders:* "His lips and tongue were trembling to frame a sentence that would embody the quiddity of the spectacle." The quiddity of life is what makes life what it is—and if you know what *that* is, you know more about life than I do.

Quiddity has also been used to mean a subtle distinction or quibble in an argument, or a witty remark or quip, particularly in the phrases *quibbles and quiddities, quirks and quiddities,* and *quips and quiddities.* "How now, how now, mad wag? What, in thy quips and thy quiddities?" wrote Shakespeare in *Henry IV, Part I.* And here's a citation from 1998 in *The Washington Post:* "The book is not your usual pussyfooting exercise in quibbles and quiddities."

Word 42: RESISTENTIALISM (RES-i-STEN-shuh-liz'm)
Hostile or malicious behavior manifested by inanimate objects.

Resistentialism is a humorous blend of the verb *resist* and the noun *existentialism,* the modern philosophy that explores the individual's relationship to the universe, the problem of free will, and the responsibility for one's actions that it entails. The word also puns on the Latin word *rēs,* a thing, familiar in the phrase *in medias res* (in MED-ee-ahs **RAYS**), in the middle of things or in the thick of it.

The British humorist Paul Jennings coined *resistentialism* in 1948 in a parodic essay in *The Spectator.* In the philosophy of resistentialism, Jennings tells us, there is "a grand vision of the Universe as One Thing—the Ultimate Thing. . . . And it is against us." In the great scheme of things (think about that!), says Jennings, we are no-Thing and Things always win. Earlier writers knew this, of course. In his 1846 poem "Inscribed to W. H. Channing," Ralph Waldo Emerson observed that "Things are in the saddle, / And ride mankind."

In my book *There's a Word for It* I cited but a few examples of the innumerable resistentialist acts committed every day by hostile inanimate objects: screen doors that snap back at you and smash your nose; rugs that quietly curl up so they can snag your toe; doorknobs that hook your jacket pocket; glasses that sidle into just the right position so you will knock them over; and microwave ovens that sabotage your food so that the first bite is lukewarm and the next one scalds your tongue. And let's not forget plastic wrap, the most resistentialist thing on the planet!

Word 43: NULLIBIQUITOUS (NUHL-i-**BIK**-wi-tus)
Not in existence anywhere.

The adjective *nullibiquitous,* which entered English about 1820, and the noun *nullibiety* (NUHL-i-**BY**-i-tee), which dates back to the 1660s, come from the Late Latin *nullibi,* nowhere. To be nullibiquitous is to exist nowhere, and nullibiety is the state or condition of not existing anywhere, nonexistence.

If you think about it for a moment, those definitions are oxymoronic. (*Oxymoron* is word 24 of Level 5.) How can something exist if it is nowhere? With apologies to Shakespeare's Hamlet, the question is not to be or not to be, but how can you be if you don't exist? For the answer to that you'll need not just a word workout but an ontological (AHN-tuh-**LAH**-ji-kul) workout. (*Ontology* is the branch of philosophy that studies the nature of being or the essence of existence.)

I had the pleasure of bringing the rare word *nullibiquitous* out of obscurity—or perhaps nonexistence—back in 1999, when I wrote a guest On Language column for *The New York Times Magazine* about being a word detective, or "grandiloquent gumshoe," whose job it is to "track down that missing piece in your verbal picture of the world, wherever it may be lurking—in the demimonde of dialect and slang, in the cobwebbed corners of cyberspace, in the benthic darkness of an unabridged dictionary." (*Demimonde* is word 13 of this level, and *benthic,* pronounced BEN-thik, means pertaining to or occurring at the bottom of a lake or ocean.) I wrote: "When clients ask me for a locution [word 22 of Level 6] I suspect is nullibiquitous (not in existence anywhere), I hate to let them down, so I make something up."

As you may have surmised, the adjective *ubiquitous,* existing or seeming to exist everywhere at the same time, is the antonym of *nullibiquitous,* not in existence anywhere.

Word 44: FLOCCULENT (FLAHK-yuh-lint)
Woolly; resembling tufts or clumps of wool, or consisting of loose fluffy masses. Also, covered with a soft, short woolly substance; downy.

The adjective *flocculent* comes from the Latin *floccus,* a tuft or flock of wool, a word that English borrowed from Latin to mean a small tuft of woolly hairs or the downy plumage of unfledged birds.

So you've heard of a flock of sheep, but what's a flock of wool? From the same Latin *floccus,* this *flock* is a tuft or lock of wool or cotton; used in the plural, *flocks,* or sometimes *flocking,* it is wool or cotton refuse, or shearings of cloth, coarsely torn by machinery and used to stuff cushions, mattresses, furniture, and the like.

A *floccule* (FLAHK-yool) is anything resembling a small tuft or flock of wool, and the verb to *flocculate* (FLAHK-yuh-layt) means to form flocculent, or woolly, masses. In chemistry, *flocculent* is used to mean containing or consisting of floccules, loose particles or soft flakes, as when a substance separates from a solution or suspension. In zoology (zoh-AHL-uh-jee, not zoo-), *flocculent* is used to mean covered with a soft, waxy substance resembling wool.

Word 45: BOUSTROPHEDON (BOOS-truh-**FEED**-'n)
An ancient method of writing in which the lines are written alternately from right to left and from left to right.

Boustrophedon comes directly from the Greek *boustrophēdon,* turning like oxen in plowing, which comes in turn from *bous,* an ox, and *strephein,* to turn, the source also of the *-strophe* in *catastrophe,* which means literally a down-turning. Thus, by derivation boustrophedon is writing that resembles the furrows made in plowing a field, with the plow passing alternately one way and then back the other way.

"In such writing, each letter on the alternate lines was written as in a mirror image or rotated 180 degrees," writes Anu Garg at his website A.Word.A.Day. "We still do many things boustrophedonically [BOO-struh-fee-**DAHN**-ik-lee], such as mowing the lawn, vacuuming the floor, etc. In many computer printers, such as dot-matrix and inkjet, the print head usually moves in the boustrophedon mode (though thankfully it doesn't print letters mirrored or rotated)."

When I paint with a brush or wipe a counter or mop a floor, I do so in a boustrophedonic pattern. Can you think of any tasks that you do, or that things do, boustrophedonically?

Word 46: CLINQUANT (KLING-kint)
Glittering or shimmering with gold, silver, or tinsel.

Familiar synonyms of *clinquant* include *sparkling, glimmering, twinkling, glistening, dazzling, brilliant, radiant, resplendent,* and *spangled,* which means covered or adorned with *spangles,* small, thin pieces or circles of glittering metal or plastic. "The Star-Spangled Banner," the national anthem of the United States, which was originally a poem composed by Francis Scott Key in 1814, takes its name from the notion of the stars on the American flag glittering in the night like spangles.

Unusual synonyms of *clinquant* include *scintillating* (**SIN**-ti-LAY-ting), which by derivation means throwing off sparks; *coruscating* (**KOR**-uh-SKAY-ting), giving off flashes of light; and *refulgent* (ri-FUHL-jint), shining or gleaming brightly. Interesting antonyms of *clinquant* include *tenebrous* (word 42 of Level 9); *umbrageous* (uhm-BRAY-jus), from the Latin *umbra,* shade, which means shady or shadowy; *stygian* (STIJ-ee-in or STIJ-in), pertaining to the mythological river Styx, over which the souls of the dead crossed to reach the underworld, called Hades (HAY-deez)—hence dark and gloomy, or infernal, hellish; *Cimmerian* (si-MEER-ee-in), which by derivation means living in perpetual darkness, hence very dark or gloomy; and *caliginous* (kuh-LIJ-i-nus), dark and misty, from the Latin *cālīgĭnis,* which meant fog, mist, vapor, or darkness.

Clinquant, which entered English in the early 1600s, comes directly from the Middle French *clinquant,* clinking or tinkling, and is probably related, through the Dutch *klinken,* to the English verb to *clink.* Originally *clinquant* was used of that which glittered with real gold or silver; later the word was applied to things decorated with imitation gold leaf or tinsel. *Clinquant* may be used as an adjective to mean glittering with gold, silver, or tinsel, or as a noun denoting the real or fake gold leaf or tinsel itself. The word may also be used figuratively either as an adjective to mean having a glittering superficial quality, tinselly, as *the poet's pretty, clinquant verses,* or as a noun to mean false glitter, literary or artistic tinsel, as when the English essayist and poet Joseph Addison wrote in 1711, "One verse in Virgil is worth all the clinquant or tinsel of Tasso."

Word 47: CASTELLATED (KAS-tuh-lay-tid)
Built like a castle or resembling a castle.

The adjective *castellated* comes from the Medieval Latin *castellātus,* fortified like a castle, and is related to the common English word *castle.* The castle, as we think of it today—an integrated group of buildings designed as a massive, high-walled fortress—was an outgrowth of feudalism, the political system of the Middle Ages in which the lord, who occupied the castle, granted his tenants, called vassals, use of his land in return for their sworn loyalty and military service.

The building of great castles flourished in Europe in the 13th century. Although they differed in style and layout, most of them shared certain typical architectural elements. There was often a moat—a deep, wide trench around the castle, usually filled with water—and a drawbridge, a bridge over the moat that could be lowered for crossing it or raised to keep out intruders. There was a portcullis (port-KUHL-is), a grated iron door at the main entrance of the castle that could be raised or lowered when the drawbridge was down. And there was a barbican (BAHR-bi-kun) or gatehouse, a tower protecting the main gate or drawbridge.

There were turrets and smaller overhanging turrets called bartizans (BAHR-ti-zunz) projecting from the walls and towers of the castle, usually at the corners, which were used as lookouts. The tops of the walls had battlements consisting of alternating solid parts, called merlons (MUR-lunz), and open spaces, called crenels (KREN-ulz), as well as loopholes or machicolations (muh-CHIK-uh-**LAY**-shunz), narrow openings or slits in the wall or floor through which an enemy could be observed, weapons could be discharged, or boiling liquids could be dropped.

Then there was the keep or donjon (pronounced like *dungeon*), the great tower and strongest part of the castle, located in the innermost court, which had "walls of immense thickness, suited to form the last retreat of the garrison," says *The Century Dictionary.* And finally there was the oubliette (oo–blee–ET), a word that comes from a Middle French verb meaning to forget and that is related to the English word *oblivion,* a forgetting or the state of being forgotten. The oubliette was what we now call a dungeon, a secret pit in the floor of the donjon or main tower with only a small opening in the ceiling through which prisoners were dropped and then left to perish.

Our keyword, *castellated,* may mean furnished with battlements and turrets like a castle, or resembling a castle: "Walter despised the opulent gated communities of the suburbs, with their castellated mansions." The noun *castellation* means "the act of fortifying a house and rendering it a castle, or of giving it the appearance of a castle" (*The Century Dictionary*).

Word 48: ULTRACREPIDARIAN (UHL–truh–KREP–i–**DAIR**–ee–in) Going beyond one's sphere of knowledge or influence in offering an opinion or advice; giving an opinion on something outside your area of expertise.

Ultracrepidarian comes from the Latin phrase *ne supra crepidam sutor judicaret,* "Let not the cobbler overstep his last," a maxim pertaining to a story about a cobbler and the ancient Greek painter Apelles (uh–PEL–eez). The cobbler noticed a defect in a shoe Apelles had painted and remarked on it. Apelles was grateful for the advice, and the cobbler, emboldened by this, presumed to give his opinion about other elements in the painting. Annoyed by the cobbler's arrogance, the painter scolded, "Cobbler, stick to your last."

The earliest known use of *ultracrepidarian* is in a letter written by the English essayist William Hazlitt,* who may have coined

---

* Pronounced HAYZ-lit, not HAZ-lit, as many dictionaries mistakenly render it; for more, see my *Big Book of Beastly Mispronunciations.*

the word. Hazlitt used it aptly of literary critics, who are infamous for giving opinions on matters beyond their knowledge. *Ultracrepidarian* may also serve as a noun denoting a person who presumptuously offers an opinion on something beyond his or her scope of knowledge. *Ultracrepidarianism* is the act of giving an opinion on something you know little or nothing about.

Word 49: THERSITICAL (thur-SIT-i-kul)
Verbally abusive, foul-mouthed.

Synonyms of *thersitical* include *obscene, profane, slanderous, derogatory,* and *contumelious* (KAHN-t[y]oo-**MEE**-lee-us). But probably the closest synonym of *thersitical* is *scurrilous* (SKUR- or SKUH-ri-lus), using or expressed in language that is coarse, vulgar, and abusive.

The adjective *thersitical* is eponymous; it comes from the name *Thersites* (thur-SY-teez), who, in ancient Greek legend, was a member of the Greek army in the Trojan War and a minor character in Homer's epic poem the *Iliad.* Thersites, says *Webster 2,* was "the ugliest and most scurrilous of the Greeks." He reviled everyone (*revile* is word 43 of Level 4), but he reserved his most slanderous invective for the Greek heroes Ulysses and Achilles—which was not very smart, because when Thersites mocked Achilles for mourning the brave Amazon queen Penthesilea (PEN-thuh-si-**LEE**-uh), Achilles killed him.

In modern usage *thersitical* suggests the kind of gross verbal abuse or slander that could get you fired, sued, punched, evicted from the premises, kicked out of the family, or, depending on whom you are slandering, *whacked,* as the Mafia wiseguys like to say. When the reviling and traducing are especially scurrilous and scathing, use *thersitical.*

Word 50: PERENDINATE (puh-REN-di-nayt)
To put off until the day after tomorrow or to postpone indefinitely.

The familiar verb to *procrastinate* means by derivation to put off until tomorrow, for it comes from the Latin *crastĭnus,* of tomorrow.

The verb to *perendinate* takes *procrastinate* one step further, for it comes from the Latin *perendĭnus,* relating to the day after tomorrow. Mark Twain once said, "Do not put off till tomorrow what can be put off till day-after-tomorrow just as well." Was the great American humorist thinking that it's better to perendinate than to procrastinate?

Perendinate is such a rare word that the *OED* has but one citation for it, from 1656, in the sense defined here, and only two later citations for another sense: to stay at a college as a guest for an extended amount of time. As a writer who specializes in the earnest and dreary labor of putting things off until the day after tomorrow or indefinitely, I can't help hoping that you and others of your word-loving ilk will see fit to give *perendinate* a new lease on life. (*Ilk,* which rhymes with *milk,* means kind, sort, or type.)

So please, don't *delay, postpone, procrastinate, defer,* or *prorogue* (proh-ROHG). Find an excuse to use *perendinate* today!

Review Quiz for Keywords 41–50

In each statement below, a keyword (in *italics*) is followed by three definitions. Two of the three definitions are correct; one is unrelated in meaning. Decide which definition doesn't fit the keyword. **Answers appear on page 487**.

1. *Quiddity* means the reality of something, the whatness of something, the essential nature of something.

2. *Resistentialism* is rebellion, hostility, unusual behavior.

3. *Nullibiquitous* means not responding, not existing, being nowhere.

4. *Flocculent* means waxy, downy, woolly.

5. *Boustrophedon* is writing that forms a design, writing from right to left and left to right, writing that resembles the furrows made in plowing a field.

6. *Clinquant* means shimmering like tinsel, flickering like fire, glittering with gold.

7. *Castellated* means built like a castle, resembling a fortress, built like a prison.

8. *Ultracrepidarian* means being a know-it-all, being a nosy person, talking about things you know nothing about.

9. *Thersitical* means foulmouthed, furious, verbally abusive.

10. To *perendinate* means to put off until the day after tomorrow, to delay indefinitely, to postpone briefly.

Some Final Words on Learning New Words

If I've taught you anything in *Word Workout,* I hope it's that learning new words should be a lifelong activity, a commitment to your long-term verbal health. Here are seven tips to help you continue pumping up your word power after you close this book:

1. *Read, read, read.* Reading is the most effective—and enjoyable—way to build vocabulary. Yet an astonishing number of people who *can* read *don't* read. In a 2001 survey of literate Americans age 25 and over conducted by the U.S. Department of Education, 29 percent of the women and 43 percent of the men had not read a book in the preceding six months. "The average American adult reads one book a year, and reads it with the skills and comprehension of a seventh grader," writes Edward Humes in *School of Dreams.* "The average American child spends 78 minutes a week reading, 102 minutes a week on homework and study, and 12 *hours* a week watching television."

If you're not reading for your own pleasure and intellectual development, it's time to start doing that for at least twenty minutes a day. Make reading newspapers and magazines, print or online, a part of your diurnal routine. Visit the public library—often. Join a book club or literary salon. Listen to audiobooks while you commute, and always listen for words you don't know (see tip number five below).

2. *Expand your horizons.* To build a strong vocabulary, you need to read widely. Venture beyond the familiar and the easy. Seek out writers who don't write down to the reader and look for writing that aspires to eloquence. Try something new. Take risks.

3. *Make it fun.* You won't learn anything when you're frustrated or bored. Challenge yourself, but don't force yourself to read something you don't like. Read what interests you: let your curiosity be your guide. Talk about what you're reading with others, and solicit recommendations from others on good books to read.

4. Don't "read around" words you don't know. This is extremely important. You should never skip over words you don't know or that you *think* you can figure out from context. Bypassing a word you think you know because you've seen it once or twice before, or because you can figure out what the sentence means, is a bad habit—one that in the long run can be detrimental to your verbal health. Unfortunately, I have met many people who are proud that they can understand a passage without knowing the precise meanings of the words it contains. That is a delusion.

Reading around words is not a sign of intelligence; it is a sign of laziness. Furthermore, the consequences of guessing what a word means can be serious. Because the context can be ambiguous and the margin for error is great, more often than not you will guess wrong. You know what you're doing then? Building a vocabulary filled with incorrect definitions! That can only lead straight to bad usage and embarrassment.

The point is, don't ever cheat yourself out of the opportunity to increase your understanding of the language. Every word you learn is another dollar in the bank, another arrow in your quiver, another window on the world.

5. Always look for words you don't know. As a vocabulary builder, your job is to be on the lookout for unfamiliar words. Try to find at least one new word every time you read. And don't forget to take note of any new words you hear when you converse with others, listen to the radio, or watch TV. Seek, and you shall find. And be honest with yourself—do you really know that word or just *think* you know it?

6. Use a dictionary. Whenever you see an unfamiliar word, it's essential that you look it up. Not doing so is tantamount (TAN-tuh-mownt, equivalent) to reading around the word. Keep a print dictionary handy or an online dictionary open while you read so you can look up words right away. Or you can highlight words or jot them down (with the page number or URL so you can find them again) and look them up later.

7. *Review it or lose it*. Review is the key to retention. With today's technology it's easy to create a file or list of the words you've learned. If you can, record not only the word and definition but also the pronunciation, etymology, and context in which you found the word. Try to organize your words in their order of difficulty for you, and review the list often—a few times a week at least.

And now we've come to the end of *Word Workout*. I've enjoyed being your personal trainer in the gymnasium of language, putting you through your verbal paces and coaching you toward a more precise and powerful command of words. Now it's time for you to take the knowledge you have gained and run with it.

If you have a comment about *Word Workout* or a question about language, you're welcome to contact me through my website: www.charlesharringtonelster.com.

Good luck and good words to you!

Answers to Review Quizzes for Level 10
KEYWORDS 1–10

1. No. *Chiaroscuro* refers to the contrast of *light* and shade in a pictorial work.

2. Yes. To *contemn* means to treat or regard with contempt.

3. Yes. An *apologia* is a defense or justification of one's beliefs, actions, or ideas.

4. No. When you *gorgonize,* you stupefy, paralyze, or petrify.

5. Yes. *Scholia* are explanatory notes or comments, which can appear in footnotes, endnotes, or marginalia.

6. No. To *cathect* is to invest emotional or mental energy in someone or something.

7. Yes. *Sortilege* may mean sorcery, magic, or the casting of lots to predict the future, a form of divination.

8. No. Dancing, not singing, is a *terpsichorean* art form.

9. No. A crushing retort thought of *later* is *esprit de l'escalier.*

10. Yes. *Popinjay,* a vain, pretentious person, is related to the Italian and Spanish words for a parrot.

KEYWORDS 11–20

1. False. A *catachresis* is a misuse of one word for another, or using the wrong word for the context.

2. False. *Etiology* is the study of causes or origins, specifically of disease.

3. True. *Demimonde* may denote any group that operates on the fringes of society or that seems to inhabit its own world, often a morally questionable one.

4. False. A *numinous* experience is magical, mysterious, inspiring awe and reverence.

5. True. A lexiphanic person, or lexiphanes, is a showoff with words.

6. False. When you *brachiate* you swing gracefully from branch to branch, like an ape or monkey.

7. False. A *misanthrope* is a hater of humankind. A *quidnunc* is a nosy, inquisitive person, a busybody.

8. False. A *catechumen* is a person being taught the basics of a subject.

9. True. The word *sybarite* comes from Sybaris, an ancient Greek city in southern Italy whose inhabitants were devoted to luxury and pleasure.

10. False. A *quisling* is a traitor, someone who aids and abets the enemy.

KEYWORDS 21–30

1. Synonyms. A *catholicon* is a panacea, cure-all, universal remedy.

2. Synonyms. *Discalced* means barefoot, unshod.

3. Antonyms. *Incondite* means badly constructed, unpolished, unrefined.

4. Synonyms. *Afflatus* is inspiration, especially poetic or divine inspiration.

5. Synonyms. A *flaneur* is a loafer, idler, sluggard.

6. Antonyms. To *philanthropize* is to practice philanthropy, charitable giving. To *quomodocunquize* is to try to make money in any possible way.

7. Antonyms. A *eulogy* is a lofty public expression of praise, usually on some formal occasion. A *pasquinade* is an abusive, publicly posted satire of a person.

8. Synonyms. A *Xanthippe* is an ill-tempered, scolding, browbeating woman; a shrew.

9. Antonyms. *Pococurante* means careless, indifferent, nonchalant, apathetic, or a careless, indifferent, nonchalant person, a trifler.

10. Antonyms. A *behemoth* (word 37 of Level 3) is a massive and mighty creature or thing. A *homunculus* is a little man or human being.

KEYWORDS 31–40

1. *Morganatic* means marrying a social inferior.

2. *Paraleipsis* is a way of suggesting much by saying little.

3. A *mumpsimus* is a person who refuses to change, who obstinately clings to an error, bad habit, or prejudice.

4. *Bibliophagic* means book-devouring.

5. *Corybantic* means frenzied, wild.

6. An *aubade* is a song or poem greeting the dawn, or a love song sung at dawn.

7. *Lycanthropy* is the delusion that one is a wolf, or the transformation of a human being into a wolf.

8. A *nullipara* is a woman who has never given birth.

9. *Weltschmerz* is world-weary melancholy, sentimental pessimism.

10. *Noetic* means intellectual, pertaining to the mind or the intellect.

KEYWORDS 41–50

1. *The reality of something* doesn't fit. *Quiddity* is the essential nature or being of something, its whatness.

2. *Unusual behavior* doesn't fit. *Resistentialism* is hostility manifested by things, the rebellion of inanimate objects.

3. *Not responding* doesn't fit. *Nullibiquitous* means not in existence anywhere.

4. *Waxy* doesn't fit. *Flocculent* means woolly, downy, fluffy.

5. *Writing that forms a design* doesn't fit. *Boustrophedon* is writing in which the lines are written alternately from right to left and from left to right, like the furrows made in plowing a field.

6. *Flickering like fire* doesn't fit. *Clinquant* means glittering or shimmering with gold, silver, or tinsel.

7. *Built like a prison* doesn't fit. *Castellated* means built like a castle or fortress.

8. *Being a nosy person* doesn't fit. *Ultracrepidarian* means giving an opinion on something outside your area of expertise.

9. *Furious* doesn't fit. *Thersitical* means verbally abusive, foulmouthed.

10. *To postpone briefly* doesn't fit. To *perendinate* means to put off until the day after tomorrow or indefinitely.

WORD WORKOUT
SELECTED BIBLIOGRAPHY

The American Heritage Dictionary of the English Language. 4th ed. Boston: Houghton Mifflin Company, 2000.

Ayres, Alfred. *The Orthoëpist.* New York: D. Appleton and Company, 1894.

Barnett, Lincoln. *The Treasure of Our Tongue.* New York: Alfred A. Knopf, 1964.

Bernstein, Theodore M. *The Careful Writer.* New York: Atheneum, 1983.

Black's Law Dictionary. 8th ed. St. Paul, MN: Thomson West, 2004.

Bryson, Bill. *Bryson's Dictionary of Troublesome Words.* New York: Broadway Books, 2002.

———. *The Mother Tongue: English and How It Got That Way.* New York: William Morrow and Company, 1990.

Burchfield, R. W. *The New Fowler's Modern English Usage.* 3rd ed. Oxford: Clarendon Press, 1996.

The Century Dictionary. New York: Century Company, 1914. Accessible online at http://www.global-language.com/CENTURY/.

Cerf, Bennett. *Bennett Cerf's Book of Riddles.* New York: Random House Beginner Books, 1960.

The Chicago Manual of Style. 15th ed. Chicago and London: University of Chicago Press, 2003.

Clark, Roy Peter. *The Glamour of Grammar.* New York: Little, Brown and Company, 2010.

The Columbia Encyclopedia. 3rd ed. New York and London: Columbia University Press, 1963.

Cooper, Samuel. *Dictionary of Literary Terms*. Toronto: Key Book Publishing House, 1970.

Crabb, George. *Crabb's English Synonymes*. New York: Grosset & Dunlap, 1917.

D'Aulaire, Ingri, and Edgar Parin D'Aulaire. *D'Aulaires' Book of Greek Myths*. New York: Bantam Doubleday Dell Publishing Group, 1962.

Davidson, Mark. *Right, Wrong, and Risky*. New York: W. W. Norton & Company, 2006.

Ehrlich, Eugene. *Amo, Amas, Amat and More: How to Use Latin to Your Own Advantage and to the Astonishment of Others*. New York: Harper & Row, 1985.

Elster, Charles Harrington. *The Accidents of Style: Good Advice on How Not to Write Badly*. New York: St. Martin's Griffin, 2010.

————. *The Big Book of Beastly Mispronunciations: The Complete Opinionated Guide for the Careful Speaker*. Boston, New York: Houghton Mifflin Company, 2006.

————. *Test of Time: A Novel Approach to the SAT and ACT*. New York and San Diego: Harcourt, 2004.

————. *There's a Word for It: A Grandiloquent Guide to Life*. New York: Pocket Books, 1996, 2005.

————. *Verbal Advantage: 10 Easy Steps to a Powerful Vocabulary*. New York: Random House, 2000.

————. *What in the Word? Wordplay, Word Lore, and Answers to Your Peskiest Questions About Language*. New York: Harcourt, 2005.

Evans, Bergen, and Cornelia Evans. *A Dictionary of Contemporary American Usage*. New York: Random House, 1957.

Garg, Anu. A.Word.A.Day. www.wordsmith.org.

Garner, Bryan A. *Garner's Modern American Usage*. 3rd ed. New York: Oxford University Press, 2009.

Hale, Constance. *Sin and Syntax*. New York: Broadway Books, 1999.

Hendrickson, Robert. *The Dictionary of Eponyms: Names That Became Words*. New York: Dorset Press, 1972.

————. *The Facts on File Encyclopedia of Word and Phrase Origins*. 3rd ed. New York: Checkmark Books, 2004.

Holder, R. W. *How Not to Say What You Mean: A Dictionary of Euphemisms.* New York: Oxford University Press, 1995, 2002.

Humes, Edward. *School of Dreams.* Orlando, FL: Harcourt, 2003.

Hunsberger, I. Moyer. *The Quintessential Dictionary.* New York: Hart Publishing Company, 1978.

Kohl, Herbert. *From Archetype to Zeitgeist: Powerful Ideas for Powerful Thinking.* Boston: Little, Brown and Company, 1992.

Lanham, Richard A. *A Handlist of Rhetorical Terms.* Berkeley and Los Angeles: University of California Press, 1969.

Lederer, Richard. *Crazy English.* New York: Pocket Books, 1989, 1998.

————. *The Miracle of Language.* New York: Pocket Books, 1991.

————. *The Word Circus.* Springfield, MA: Merriam–Webster, 1998.

Lipton, James. *An Exaltation of Larks.* New York: Penguin Books, 1968, 1977.

McQuain, Jeffrey, and Stanley Malless. *Coined by Shakespeare: Words and Meanings First Penned by the Bard.* Springfield, MA: Merriam–Webster, 1998.

Mencken, H. L. *The American Language.* 4th ed. New York: Alfred A. Knopf, 1937.

Merriam-Webster's Collegiate Dictionary. 11th ed. Springfield. MA: Merriam–Webster, 2003.

Merriam-Webster's Encyclopedia of Literature. Springfield, MA: Merriam–Webster, 1995.

Morris, William, and Mary Morris. *The Harper Dictionary of Contemporary Usage.* 2nd ed. New York: Harper & Row, 1985.

————. *Morris Dictionary of Word and Phrase Origins.* 2nd ed. New York: HarperCollins Publishers, 1977, 1988.

The New Oxford American Dictionary. New York: Oxford University Press, 2001.

The Oxford Companion to the English Language. Tom McArthur, ed. New York: Oxford University Press, 1992.

The Oxford English Dictionary. Online edition, accessed multiple times over several years through the San Diego Public Library website.

Quinn, Arthur. *Figures of Speech: 60 Ways to Turn a Phrase.* Salt Lake City: Gibbs M. Smith, 1982.

The Random House Dictionary of the English Language, 2nd ed., Unabridged. New York: Random House, 1987.

Rawson, Hugh. *Devious Derivations.* New York: Crown Trade Paperbacks, 1994.

Rheingold, Howard. *They Have a Word for It.* Los Angeles: Jeremy P. Tarcher, 1988.

Rosten, Leo. *The Joys of Yinglish.* New York: Plume, 1989.

Safire, William. *Coming to Terms.* New York: Doubleday, 1991.

————. *Let a Simile Be Your Umbrella.* New York: Crown Publishers, 2001.

Shipley, Joseph T. *Dictionary of Word Origins.* New York: The Philosophical Library, 1945.

Siegal, Allan M., and William G. Connolly. *The New York Times Manual of Style and Usage.* New York: Times Books, 1999.

A Standard Dictionary of the English Language. New York, London, and Toronto: Funk & Wagnalls Company, 1897.

Stedman's Medical Dictionary. 22nd ed. Baltimore: The Williams & Wilkins Company, 1972.

Strand, Mark, and Eavan Boland. *The Making of a Poem.* New York and London: W. W. Norton & Company, 2000.

Webster's New International Dictionary. 2nd ed. Springfield, MA: G. & C. Merriam, 1941.

Webster's New World College Dictionary. 3rd ed. New York: Macmillan, 1997.